BIBLICAL
THEOLOGY

The Library of Biblical Theology

Leo Perdue
General Editor and Old Testament Editor

James D. G. Dunn
New Testament Editor

Michael Welker
Systematic Theology Editor

LIBRARY OF BIBLICAL THEOLOGY

BIBLICAL THEOLOGY

INTRODUCING THE CONVERSATION

LEO G. PERDUE
ROBERT MORGAN
BENJAMIN D. SOMMER

Abingdon Press
Nashville

BIBLICAL THEOLOGY
INTRODUCING THE CONVERSATION

Library of Congress Cataloging-in-Publication Data

Perdue, Leo G.
    Biblical theology : introducing the conversationn / Leo G. Perdue, Robert Morgan, Bejamin D. Sommer.
        p. cm.
    Includes bibliographical references and indexes.
    ISBN 978-0-687-34100-9 (pbk. : alk. paper)
    1. Bible—Theology. 2. Bible—Criticism, interpretation, etc. I. Morgan, Robert, 1940– II. Sommer, Benjamin D., 1964– III. Title.
    BS543 .P445 2009
    230'.041—dc22

                                                                                    2009010386

Ancient language fonts were developed in the public domain for scholars who comprise the Society of Biblical Literature, including SPTiberian for Hebrew, SPIonic for Greek, and SPAtlantis for transliteration.

AT indicates the author's translation of scripture.

09 10 11 12 13 14 15 16 17 18—10 9 8 7 6 5 4 3 2 1
MANUFACTURED IN THE UNITED STATES OF AMERICA

CONTENTS

PREFACE

Theologians know that the Bible is the core source document for theological construction and hence that they must be in conversation with the best in critical study of Scripture. For many biblical scholars, the point of what they do is to help the biblical text speak to today's church and world, and realize they would do well to be in conversation with contemporary theology. Yet too often the biblical scholars and contemporary theologians fail to engage one another's work in significant and productive ways. The purpose of the Library of Biblical Theology is to bring the worlds of biblical scholarship and constructive theology together into an interpretative relationship. This series approaches biblical theology as a discipline that describes the faith of the biblical periods on the one hand, and on the other hand articulates how the theology of the Bible contributes to important understandings of modern faith and practice. Thus, the volumes in the series will move from setting forth major theological themes found in the biblical text to making a theological judgment based on one's own contemporary worldview, forged within a community of faith. These themes include God, salvation and eschatology, community, and ethics and law.

Until the 1970s, biblical study had been primarily, although not exclusively, placed in historical categories that included both method (historical criticism) and themes (especially salvation history). Not only had this historical approach sought to circumvent the authoritarian control of doctrinal interpretation set forth by the Church (see the famous address of Gabler in 1787), but also was in line with the major philosophical epistemologies of the Enlightenment (reason and experience). In recent years, biblical theology has begun to move in new directions with a vitality and force that are no longer held captive by a positivist understanding of history and the view of facts derived from reason and experience. More recent approaches now include foci on creation, canon, liberation, feminism, narrative, imagination, postmodernism, and postcolonialism. These approaches make use not only of historical methodologies and the history of religions but also of modern and postmodern understandings of literary analysis, epistemologies, and imagination. In addition, Jewish theology that is concerned with the theology of the Tanak increasingly has taken its place in the conversation. Biblical and contemporary theologies are not limited to events and ideas of history but seek also to move into current horizons of human understanding.

In introducing the theological conversation that includes the Bible, this volume surveys some of the major trends and studies that have appeared since the publication of Karl Barth's *Epistle to the Romans* in 1919. The four essays in this initial volume indicate that biblical theology in the past century has not only been a purely historical approach to Scripture that fails to engage the Bible's contemporary message and meaning. Rather, even prior to the present age, biblical theology had often taken seriously both the interpretation of Scripture in its particular historical context, and the importance of addressing that message to questions that confront contemporary human life and faith. However, in the present age of biblical study, the increasing emphasis placed on the role of the reader in the interpretation of texts has led modern scholars and students to recognize that their questions, important to the contexts in which they are active, are to be addressed to the texts of the Bible. And they continue to realize that the historical context and understandings of scriptural texts cannot be ignored in seeking to listen to voices from the past that have helped shape theological understandings through the centuries.

CHAPTER ONE

DIALOGICAL BIBLICAL THEOLOGY

A Jewish Approach to Reading Scripture Theologically

Benjamin D. Sommer

*"Any disagreement that is for the sake
of heaven is destined to endure."*

m.'Abot 5.19

INTRODUCTION

Strictly speaking, there can be no such thing as Jewish biblical theology. While many definitions of the term "biblical theology" exist, they all accord some privileged place to the Bible. All forms of Jewish theology, however, must base themselves on Judaism's rich post-biblical tradition at least as much as on scripture, and hence a Jewish theology cannot be chiefly biblical. (By Judaism's rich postbiblical tradition, I mean first of all rabbinic literature found in the Talmuds and midrashic collections, which stem from the first through eighth centuries C.E., and also postrabbinic Jewish commentaries, legal litera-ture, mysticism, and philosophy from the eighth century through the present.) Conversely, any theology that focuses especially on scripture is by definition Protestant and not Jewish, for the notion of *sola scriptura* has no place in Judaism[1]—even as an unrealizable ideal.[2] Nevertheless, there can be such a thing as a Jewish theology that attends to scripture along with tradition, or perhaps to scripture as one part of tradition.[3] Such a theology would recover or renew biblical voices that are often lost in Jewish thought, while placing them in the larger context of Jewish tradition. It is in the interaction or dialogue between biblical and postbiblical Jewish thinkers, then, that something we might loosely call a Jewish biblical theology can arise. The model I propose here might also be termed "dialogical biblical theology." This model works well for modern Judaism's attempt to think theologically with its scripture, but it can be adapted for other religious communities. While it is especially appropriate for those forms of Christianity that emphasize tradition, such as Catholic and Orthodox Christianities, it may be useful, we shall see, for Protestant Christianity as well.

In the following, I intend to accomplish several tasks. I will explore the question of whether a field such as biblical theology can really exist; I will articulate a program for what I call dialogical biblical theology, a program that involves a method of reading or a hermeneutic more than a particular theological viewpoint; I will discuss several scholars, Jewish and Christian, who have implied this program in their work without actually articulating it (and, in some cases, without relating it to the field of biblical theology); and I will provide several examples of how a dialogical biblical theology in a Jewish context might work, thus putting to work the hermeneutic I propose. Before doing any of this, however, it behooves me to discuss a claim frequently heard in academic discussions of this field: to wit, that Jews are not interested in biblical theology. Discussing this claim will reveal much about the field of biblical theology as it was practiced in the twentieth century.

ARE JEWS INTERESTED IN BIBLICAL THEOLOGY?

In 1987 Jon Levenson published an essay with the provocative title "Why Jews Aren't Interested in Biblical Theology."[4] He contended that Jews had paid scant attention to that field, and he attempted to explain why this was the case. Moshe Goshen-Gottstein had made similar points about Jews' lack of participation in this field several years earlier.[5]

I hope to show that Jewish interest in this field had in fact been vigorous even before the publication of Levenson's article. Nevertheless, Levenson's essay remains important and instructive. Levenson succeeded in showing that the dominant model of biblical theology as practiced in the past two centuries was uninteresting, indeed deeply problematic and often offensive, for Jews. As a result he implicitly suggested how Jews should *not* do Jewish biblical theology—and how Christians interested in engaging in dialogue with Jews ought not to do Christian biblical theology either.

Jewish Work on Biblical Theology before and after Levenson

As a number of people have pointed out since Levenson's stimulating essay was published, many Jewish scholars have engaged in theological and even systematic expositions of biblical texts.[6] These Jewish scholars did not use the term "biblical theology" in their titles, however, and the structure of their works differed considerably from those of most Protestant biblical theologians. (To Levenson's credit, we should note that nobody found Jewish biblical theology until Levenson prompted his fellow biblicists to go looking for it.) Shimon Gesundheit, for example, recently pointed out numerous examples, such as Leo Adler's *Der Mensch in der Sicht der Bibel*, which was published in 1965.[7] We might readily add Abraham Joshua Heschel's book *The Prophets* (first published in 1962) or numerous works by Martin Buber.[8] It will be noticed that none of these authors are biblical scholars. Adler was the rabbi of the Jewish community of Basel, and he also published on modern analytic philosophy. While Heschel and Buber defy easy categorization, the label "biblicist" does not quite fit either one especially well.[9] On the other hand, all these authors devote considerable space to explicating biblical passages for theological purposes, and they attend to modern biblical scholarship when doing so.

Jewish scholars whose training was primarily in biblical studies and whose academic appointments were in departments of Bible also produced works that can be seen as belonging to the field of biblical theology. I think first and foremost of the most influential Jewish biblical scholar of the modern era, Yehezkel Kaufmann, and his four-volume magnum opus *Toledot Ha-Emunah Ha-Yisraelit*. The title of this work is usually translated into English as *The History of Israelite Religion*, but it might be more accurately rendered *The History of Israelite Belief* or even *The Generations of Israelite Faith*.[10] This magisterial work is an outstanding—and foundational—example of Jewish biblical theology.[11] One might object to my characterization by pointing out that Kaufmann's study is historical in nature and thus presumably not theological. I will return in the next section to the unfounded presumption that a historical work cannot also belong to the field of biblical theology; for my present purpose, it will suffice for me to show that on closer inspection, one finds *Toledot* to share essential features with many works of biblical theology. By investigating one central biblical idea (Israel's monotheism and concomitant rejection of mythology), its growth, and its permutations, Kaufmann wrote a text comparable to some of the most famous works of biblical theology.[12] Many biblical theologians have focused their work on some central idea or process. To name only a few prominent examples: Walther Eichrodt structures his theological analysis of the Old Testament around the idea of covenant;[13] for Gerhard von Rad, the idea of salvation history and the process of transmission and transformations of biblical material work together to form the pivotal concern of the canon and its theological interpreter;[14] Samuel Terrien finds the pivotal theme in Christian scripture in the interplay between divine manifestation and absence;[15] Walter Brueggemann sets out in his theology of Hebrew Scriptures to explicate the process of conflict and disputation through which Israel arrived at complex truth-claims about Yhwh;[16] Yochanan Muffs identifies the genius of biblical religion in its insistence on the personhood of God.[17] We might note further that von Rad's *Theology* is explicitly diachronic or historical in at least one of its dominant concerns: von Rad describes a diachronic process of transmission and transformation, just as Kaufmann describes how the monotheistic idea works itself out so that mythology is rejected ever more clearly over the course of the biblical period.

All these works attempt—in my opinion, successfully—to find unity amid the diversity of material, genre, and period in the Hebrew Scriptures. Although many subsequent critics derided these searches for a *Mitte* (a central idea in scripture), these and other scholars did find unifying factors in scripture. The problem with the attempts was not that no *Mitte* exists. Rather, it is the presumption of many of these scholars that a single *Mitte* exists or that one particular *Mitte* could objectively be labeled most important or most compelling. Further, some scholars failed to acknowledge that their candidates for *Mitte* were absent in parts of scripture. Several unifying themes run through scripture, though no one theme encompasses every single book. Expounding one such theme is a perfectly valid activity for a biblical theologian. Criticisms of the search for *the* center are well-taken, but this does not mean that search for *a* focal point is illegitimate. Scripture might be compared not to a circle with one central point but to an ellipse, with more than one focal point.[18] Scripture is not, as some critics of the *Mitte* hypotheses seem to hold, a random form or a shifting shape without boundaries.

Biblical theologians such as Eichrodt, von Rad, Terrien, Brueggemann, and Muffs uncover unity whose nature is theological: it involves some relatively consistent statement about God or about God's relationship with Israel or humanity. In each case, the unifying element is relevant for a contemporary religious community, and the scholar's focus on that particular element results from the preexisting concerns of that community. (Eichrodt's stress on covenant, while hardly lacking legitimacy in the biblical texts themselves,[19] clearly emerges from and gives succor to Reformed theology. Brueggemann emphasizes the value of theological disputes within scripture, and he insists on the positive religious role played by the doubt, despair, and anger that those disputes evince. Brueggemann's emphasis fits quite well with trends among liberal Protestants in the last quarter of the twentieth century. Muffs explicitly notes the connection between the Bible's anthropopathic view of YHWH and the portrayal of God in midrash and in the Zohar.) Precisely the same point can be made about Kaufmann. The idea he identifies as pivotal in the Bible reflects clearly identifiable tendencies in modern Jewish thought, even as his work implicitly provides scriptural support for those tendencies. Kaufmann asserts that monotheism's emergence in premonarchical Israel represented a revolutionary change from its cultural environment, but he also describes an evolution within Israelite monotheism from early priestly texts found in the Pentateuch to later prophetic ones. Earlier texts do not fully develop the implications of monotheism, but classical prophets such as Isaiah and Jeremiah espouse ideas that necessarily follow from the Bible's radical monotheism. These include the primacy of morality over cult and the eventual recognition of the one God by all humanity. In arguing for the centrality of a monotheism that was above all ethical and universal in its implications, Kaufmann recalls late nineteenth-century and early twentieth-century German-Jewish thinkers such as Herman Cohen.[20] In this sense Kaufmann's work is as deeply connected to a particular religious movement as the work of

Eichrodt or Brueggemann.[21] In short, if Eichrodt, von Rad, Terrien, Brueggemann, and Muffs can be called biblical theologians, so can Kaufmann.[22]

Kaufmann is not the only Jewish biblicist whose work can be understood as belonging to the field of biblical theology. Even before Levenson wrote his 1987 essay, scholars including Moshe Greenberg, Yochanan Muffs, and Jacob Milgrom wrote essays (though not monographs) treating crucial issues of biblical theology in a specifically Jewish manner. In the years that followed the publication of Levenson's provocative essay, more contributions to the burgeoning field of Jewish biblical theology appeared. Many of these have been surveyed ably, and I need not review them here.[23] In addition to the usual suspects (Levenson himself; Marvin Sweeney; Stephen Geller; Marc Brettler; Joel Kaminsky, to name but a few), we should note several books that are markedly theological but are usually not mentioned as examples of Jewish biblical theology: works by Richard Elliot Friedman, James Kugel, Israel Knohl, and Mordecai Breuer.

Friedman's book *The Disappearance of God: A Divine Mystery*[24] represents a Jewish biblical theology for three reasons. First, the book is about how humans perceive and relate to God. Friedman argues that the Hebrew Bible portrays God as becoming ever more distant from humanity through time, and humans as becoming ever more independent as a result. In short, this book is a study of divine-human interaction in the Bible, and thus it is a theology in the most basic sense of the term. Second, it is biblical: its starting point is the tripartite biblical canon as preserved in Jewish tradition. Its thesis is that God slowly disappears as one moves through the Jewish canon from Torah to Prophets to Writings.[25] Third, it is Jewish: not only does he use the Jewish order of the canon as the basis for his argument (his thesis is considerably less striking if one reads through the Old Testament canon as ordered in Christian Bibles), but he moves on to compare the canonical Bible's disappearing God to the God of classical Jewish mysticism. Further, the upshot of his study of God leads most of all to a view of humanity and its responsibilities, and this feature of his work typifies Jewish thinking about God generally.[26] A similar point can be made about Kugel's *The God of Old: Inside the Lost World of the Bible*.[27] As an explication of how the divine manifests itself to humans in early biblical texts as opposed to later biblical and postbiblical thought, this work is also a biblical theology in the most straightforward meaning of the term.

Knohl's *The Divine Symphony: The Bible's Many Voices*[28] differs from the works by Friedman and Kugel in that it does not focus specifically on biblical views of God. In a manner reminiscent of more familiar biblical theologies, it attempts to summarize crucial aspects of biblical thought that recur throughout the Bible. Further, it explicitly links particular strands of biblical thought with postbiblical literature. Knohl shows that the Priestly Torah in the Pentateuch and the book of Job point toward an abstract deity and depict worship as a human responsibility wholly disconnected from any hope of benefit. These austere views, he claims, link up with the Essenes and with rabbinism's somewhat peripheral Shammaitic school. The Pentateuch's Holiness School and Deuteronomy depict a more approachable God and emphasize religious ethics. This more popular religiosity links up with Pharisaism and with rabbinic Judaism's mainstream Hillelite tradition. Oddly, Knohl does not pause to discuss another connection that is, I suspect, the main engine for his comparison: when the Priestly Torah avoids attributing actions or emotions to God (other than the act of commanding), it shows itself to be a predecessor for the leading philosopher of Jewish tradition, Moses Maimonides. In light of Knohl's work, it becomes clear that Maimonides represents the apogee of a long trajectory that goes back to certain parts of the Pentateuch—and that Maimonides' method of reading scripture in the first third of his *Guide of the Perplexed* is more deeply rooted in scripture than scholars have recognized. (Knohl's decision not to articulate this crucial implication of his own work is surprising.[29])

Finally, in the work of Mordecai Breuer, we find an extraordinarily bold attempt to synthesize findings of modern biblical scholarship and Orthodox Judaism.[30] Breuer accepts the division of the Torah into four underlying documents, but, in a strikingly deft combination of source criticism and midrash, Breuer maintains that it was God who composed the four documents, redacted them together, and then used the resulting document as the blueprint for creating the world. (Breuer's work represents the ultimate early dating of P: for him, P—along with the other three sources—is not merely preexilic but precosmic.) Each of the four sources, he insists, reveals a particular aspect of the Deity. Contradictions among the documents result not from differing versions of the events the sources narrate (that is, not from the fragility of human memory), but from the failure of reality to conform to the underlying truth each document embodies. The documents appear to contradict one another only because of the limitations of our physical world, which conforms imperfectly to the four documents that came together to serve as the world's blueprint.[31]

In different ways, all these works can rightly be termed examples of Jewish biblical theology. All draw upon modern biblical scholarship and also on later Jewish thought (more explicitly in some cases and less explicitly in others) to create comprehensive syntheses of biblical texts that deal with a particular set of issues. In all four cases the syntheses focus not on the nature of God in the abstract but on God's connection with humanity; in this regard, they fit the model of most Jewish theology. We need, then, to confront the question: is there any sense in which Levenson's assertion that Jews are not interested in biblical theology remains true?[32] As we shall see, his assertion remains both instructive and relevant.

Jews and the Dominant Models for Biblical Theology in the Twentieth Century

Levenson correctly pointed out that Jews were not interested in biblical theology as practiced by Protestant biblical scholars[33]—which is to say, works that had the terms "biblical theology" or "Old Testament theology" on the cover. He laid out the reasons that Jews were not interested in those works and thus highlighted the aspects of Protestant Old Testament theology that were uninteresting or offensive to Jews. In doing so, he implied ways to create Jewish biblical theologies—and how to create Christian biblical theologies less problematic for Jews. It is worth briefly reviewing a few of the reasons for the Jewish aversion to Protestant biblical theology.

Levenson devotes considerable space to describing the anti-Semitism (better: anti-Judaism) of many classics of Old Testament theology.[34] When Eichrodt describes rabbinic legalism as dead and stultifying, he does not merely offend Jews. More troublingly, he jettisons any pretensions of scholarship, since his description of rabbinic religiosity is based neither on textual analyses of rabbinic literature nor sociological investigations of living rabbinic communities. Rather, his description is founded on preconceptions found in Pauline and later Christian literature. When von Rad speaks of the New Testament as the only possible continuation of Israel's heritage without even acknowledging the existence of another tradition that stems from that heritage, he commits a greater offense. Eichrodt merely misrepresents Judaism, but in this particular assertion, von Rad fails to acknowledge that Judaism exists. Levenson's attack on Eichrodt and von Rad has been critiqued. James Barr is right to maintain that the term "intense anti-Semitism" is not the right one to apply to the works of von Rad and Eichrodt; after all, Levenson does not show that either one of them hated actual Jewish people.[35] For this reason I prefer using the term "anti-Judaism." (In fact, Levenson uses this term more typically as well.) The fact remains that Eichrodt's tendentious misrepresentations of Judaism, which stem from a long tradition within Christian thought, are offenses to both academic integrity and religious ethics.[36]

These features of older scholarship remain worth noting, even in today's different academic climate, for two reasons. First, these anti-Jewish traits appear, paradoxically, in the work of biblical theologians whose overall perspective is perhaps closest to that of many modern Jewish interpreters. Eichrodt's stress on covenant could fit a Jewish reading of scripture quite well, especially if one ignores Eichrodt's curious attempt to empty from the notion of covenant the legal content so essential to it. Von Rad's emphasis on the process of tradition as it is received and reworked can suit Jewish perceptions of the parallel between midrash on the Bible and midrash in the Bible perfectly.

More important, the legacy of this sort of anti-Judaism does not disappear the moment a scholar decides to repudiate it. Leo Perdue points out that contemporary Protestant scholars reject the sort of anti-Jewish attitudes that motivated Wellhausen, Eichrodt, and others.[37] Yet contemporary biblical scholarship remains deeply influenced by those attitudes. I shall give one brief and one longer example to flesh out my claim.

Alexander Rofé has pointed out how Bernhard Duhm's judgment in 1892 that Deutero-Isaiah's corpus must close specifically at the end of Isaiah 55 is largely the product of Pauline and Lutheran anti-Pharisaism *cum* antirabbinism.[38] Few contemporary scholars would admit to sharing the same prejudices that motivated Duhm. Yet the baroque distinctions of authorship Paul Hanson draws within Isaiah 56–66 make little sense without reference to Duhm's sort of reasoning—though I very much doubt that Hanson would admit to any such reasoning on a conscious level.[39]

Similarly, Bernard Levinson and Douglas Dance have provided a fascinating discussion of von Rad's judgment that law is secondary in Deuteronomy, not only chronologically but in terms of the book's essential message.[40] For von Rad, Deuteronomy is first and foremost gospel, not law; its main concern involves the grace the believer receives, not the works the Israelite must perform. Now, the book of Deuteronomy consists almost entirely of two types of documents: a long law code in chapters 12–26, and a series of sermons exhorting the audience to obey the law code. To say that law is not essential to such a book is rather like saying that coffee is not an important ingredient in cappuccino. Consequently, von Rad's approach to the place of law in Deuteronomy calls out for explanation. Levinson and Dance show that von Rad's bizarre assertion stems from his need to defend the Old Testament against neo-Marcionism of the pro-Nazi church of Germany in the 1930s and 1940s. Von Rad attempted to rescue Deuteronomy by arguing that the law— that is, the unhappily Jewish element of the work in question—really was not crucial after all.

Very few contemporary critics would want to associate themselves with such an approach to biblical theology, at either a religious or a method-ological level. Yet many contemporary critics do continue to approach Deuteronomy from the point of view of the dichotomy between law and gospel, which von Rad insisted was a key to understanding (or rather: sal-vaging) this book. Hermann Spieckermann, for example, not implausibly identifies the love between God and Israel as the central idea in Deuteronomy.[41] Oddly, however, Spieckermann claims that the concept of love between God and Israel is not embodied in Deuteronomy's law code in chapters 12–26; it is present rather in the introductory material that precedes the law code, especially in chapters 6–7. In order to main-tain this position, Spieckermann must dismiss the evidence of love of God in Deut 13:4; 19:9; and 23:6 by claiming that these are later addi-tions to the law code under the influence of chapter 6.[42] One wonders why he cannot admit that law and love can be on the same page from the very beginning—all the more so, given Spieckermann's recognition that the introductory material stressing love between God and Israel was com-posed specifically as a preface to the older law code.[43] The present form of Deuteronomy suggests that God's love for Israel manifests itself in (among other boons) the law God gives Israel,[44] and that Israel's love for God manifests itself in loyalty to that law. Spieckermann's presumption that a wedge must be driven between what the biblical text presents as two sides of a single coin may well derive in part from the legacy of von Rad or scholarship similar to his.[45]

The example I chose is not alone. Discussions of Deuteronomy since von Rad have repeatedly come back to the mistaken and artificial dichotomy of law *versus* gospel. This is the case even in the work of some scholars who attempt to move beyond what they recognize as a problematic dichotomy. Georg Braulik, for example, wants to demonstrate that the dichotomy between law and gospel does not exist in Deuteronomy because, he claims, in Deuteronomy law is presented as gospel.[46] One might see in this pronouncement a point of view similar to that of the classical rabbis, who see the law as an example of grace, a generous gift of the God who wants to provide Israel a means of achieving merit.[47] Braulik goes on to argue, however, that Deuteronomy can be classified as gospel because it ultimately denies or severely limits the efficacy of works even as it connects salvation with grace. Braulik claims this message is clear in Deut 9:1-8. According to his reading, the point of this passage is that no causal connection obtains between the people's hold on the land and their works. These verses, Braulik maintains, constitute an argument against those who would attempt to establish their own righteousness through the law rather than accepting the salvation that comes freely from God; in other words, these verses imply a thesis identical to Paul's in Rom 10:3.[48] Alas, Braulik's desire to read Paul into Deuteronomy clouds his exegesis. To be sure, Deut 9:1-8 does assert that the people's claim on the land results from divine grace, in particular from God's promise to the patriarchs. But other passages (e.g., 6:1-3, 10-19; 11:13-21; 28:1-68) make abundantly and repeatedly clear that the people's continued presence in the land depends on their observance of the main points of the law. Deuteronomy's view (stated pithily in 8:1) is two-part yet perfectly self-consistent: (1) the people's right to enter the land results from God's gracious promise to the patriarchs; (2) the people's right to abide there results from their works. By highlighting the former point and overlooking the latter, Braulik achieves his goal, which is to render a text openly obsessed with law into a text that can be described as gospel. In the end, Braulik eliminates the dichotomy between these two by arguing that law really is gospel after all—a hermeneutic move nearly identical to von Rad's, and just as problematic. A more popular example of similar reasoning is evident in the work of Raymond Brown (a Baptist scholar in England, who should not be confused with the famous Johannine scholar Raymond E. Brown, S.S.S.). Brown somehow finds in Deuteronomy an attack on the value of works and an affirmation of the potency of faith alone.[49]

The legacy of von Rad in this matter does not confine itself to theologically oriented works. Form-critical and historical works are affected as well. Henning Graf Reventlow's discussion of the Ten Commandments typifies much post–von Rad work when he maintains that elements of law and sermon in the Ten Commandments stem from two distinct circles in ancient Israel; he does not even consider the possibility that they may constitute both an ideological and a literary unity.[50] In Reventlow's reading, the current version of the Ten Commandments is a sermon that takes its starting point from an older apodictic law. Thus for Reventlow this legal text serves mainly as an anchor for preaching. Old Testament legal texts, then, are really sermons, not law. It follows that Old Testament legal texts relate to actual legal practices in ancient Israel as the New Testament relates to Old: the new uses the old, whose legal content is no longer what matters. This viewpoint is thoroughly indebted to von Rad's work on Deuteronomy.

Von Rad's attitude toward Deuteronomy, to be sure, has not been accepted by all Christian scholars. Some, to their credit, expend considerable effort arguing that law is in fact central to Deuteronomy and that law is a crucial expression of God's grace; this is especially evident in the work of S. Dean McBride, Brevard Childs, and Dennis Olson.[51] Their decision to invest effort demonstrating the importance of law in Deuteronomy might seem odd to someone who reads Deuteronomy itself, but not to someone who reads von Rad on Deuteronomy.

In short: the results of anti-Judaism do not magically disappear from scholarly or religious discourse the moment one commits oneself to oppose anti-Semitism, any more than racist attitudes are lacking among white Americans who want to oppose racism and genuinely believe themselves to do so. For this reason, Levenson's observations concerning theological anti-Judaism remain vital for contemporary biblical theologians. Findings based on problematic reasoning are no less problematic when the motivation behind the findings is no longer recognized as being present.

Two additional aspects of the Jewish avoidance of Protestant biblical theology noted by Jon Levenson are relevant to what follows. First, Levenson points out that Jews tend to see a different sort of value in historical scholarship in comparison with many (though certainly not all) Protestant scholars.[52] The Jewish community, after all, is not only a religious one; Jews comprise a people, an ethnicity, and a political body at least as much as they are a community united by belief or practice. As a result, historical analysis of biblical texts speaks directly to questions of Jews' identity as Jews. For Christians, historical questions about ancient Israel may not resonate at the same existential level. (This is so even for

Jewish biblicists in the Diaspora, most of whom have a religious connection to Judaism of one sort or another; it is even more prominently the case for Jewish scholars in the State of Israel, many of whom are secular Jews without any commitment to Judaism as a religion.) Second, Jewish approaches to the Bible for the past two millennia have centered on a tradition of commentary that consists largely of debate between various interpreters.[53] Midrashic texts from the first millennium of the common era contain differing opinions listed one after another: Rabbi Akiva understands the verse to mean X, but Rabbi Yishmael argues that the verse means Y. Medieval rabbinic commentary continues this format of discussion and debate: on a page of a classical Jewish Bible with commentaries, one finds the varied opinions of several authorities, many of whom disagree with one another, using language that people of a certain gentility find surprisingly strong. The norm for classical Jewish biblical exegesis involves multiplicity and dispute. As a result, Jews tend to be less interested in interpretations that strive for unity or harmony. They are often quite pleased to find discord within scripture, which, after all, nicely matches the exegetical discord that surrounds scripture in the pages of a rabbinic edition of the Bible. On the other hand, many Protestant biblical theologies, especially those published prior to Levenson's essay, tend to be centripetal rather than centrifugal. One sees this tendency both in the search for the *Mitte* that concerned so many earlier biblical theologians and also in the work of biblical theologians influenced by Brevard Childs's canonical approach. To be sure, especially in recent years Protestant biblical theologians have endorsed a model that valorizes multiplicity of meaning.[54] The theologies of Walter Brueggemann[55] and Erhard Gerstenberger[56] come to mind in this regard, for example. Consequently, it is hardly surprising that one can notice much more interest in biblical theology among Jewish scholars today than when Levenson first published his essay.

One might ask in light of Levenson's critiques: what sort of biblical theology *would* interest Jews? Such a theology would accept the multivocality of the biblical text and would eschew attempts to privilege any particular biblical voice, such as that of the redactor or the canonizer.[57] (Examples might include Brueggemann's *Theology.*) Since neither the redactors nor the canonizers would be given the last word on what the Bible means, it follows that a theology of a part of scripture would be as important a contribution to the field as a theology of the whole. Such a theology would not feel compelled to address the entirety of the Hebrew

Scriptures in the totalizing manner of the classics of biblical theology. Rather, it would feel content to examine a particular issue as it appears in various parts of scripture. Examples of such an issue include the complex and mutually supportive interplay in biblical texts between a covenant of law and a covenant of grace, or the relationship between biblical understandings of creation and theodicy. (Works that address these issues have in fact been written by Levenson himself.[58]) Other issues include the relationship between revealed truths and truths the Bible regards as discernible from God's creation, or the doctrine of divine retribution in scripture. (Work on the former has been published by James Barr and John Collins, on the latter by Yochanan Muffs, Meir Weiss, and Joel Kaminsky.[59]) Of course, a close examination of biblical perceptions of divine nature would be a crucial topic. (In addition to the book by Kugel discussed above, work by Stephen Geller is especially noteworthy.[60]) Alternatively, one might write on the theology of a particular book. (Examples abound; outstanding examples include works by Sara Japhet, Ronald Clements, and Hans-Joachim Kraus.[61]) The examples I give here show that books exploring the sort of theology that might interest Jews already exist, and they are not written only by Jews. Two decades after the publication of Levenson's essay, it is safe to say that Jews are interested in biblical theology.

ARTIFACT OR SCRIPTURE?

Before moving on to flesh out how a Jewish biblical theologian might read scripture, it will be useful to introduce two terms into our discussion. A reader may approach the anthology that is the Hebrew Bible with two different sets of expectations. On the one hand, one may be interested in the Hebrew Bible as an *artifact*—that is, as a collection of Northwest Semitic texts from the Iron Age. This collection sheds interesting light on a particular culture that existed near the eastern edge of the Mediterranean over the course of several centuries. It is interesting for the same reason that any cultural expression produced by human beings may be interesting. On the other hand, Jews or Christians may approach the Hebrew Bible as a form of *scripture*—that is, as a document that relates to their own life or to the life of their community at an existential level. This does not mean that the Hebrew Bible must be authoritative for them or that it must be viewed as correct, much less binding. It does mean that its teachings are, in some way, compelling and that they demand a response. One of the hallmarks of biblical theology in its manifold forms is its insistence on approaching the Bible as scripture. Doing so may mean that one refuses to see it as an artifact; or it may mean that one integrates its artifactual nature into one's view of it as scripture. In the former case, one may produce a biblical theology that eschews the methods and findings of modern biblical criticism; in the (rather more common) latter case, one attempts to integrate those findings into one's biblical theology and perhaps also to go beyond them. It is important to note that one need not be a religious believer or practitioner to approach the Bible as scripture. Many secular Jews who do not believe in God and do live in accordance with Jewish law may still approach the Bible as scripture for national, political, or cultural reasons.[62]

BIBLICAL THEOLOGY VS. HISTORY OF ISRAELITE RELIGION[63]

While some (not all!) Christians may see historical approaches to the text as inimical or at least challenging to an attempt to read the Old Testament as scripture, Jews who approach the Bible as scripture may have a significant investment in historical analysis. As members of a community that is as much ethnic and national in nature as religious, many modern Jews have strong motives to view historical method as a suitable tool—perhaps even the most suitable tool—for appropriating the Bible as scripture.[64] Consequently, Jews may regard the dividing line between biblical theology and the study of the history of Israelite religion as amorphous. It will be useful, then, to review attempts that have been made to describe the relationship between these fields. These attempts, in my view, have mostly resulted in a muddle.

If biblical theology is an explicitly constructive and evaluative field, then a clear difference between the history of Israelite religion and biblical theology should exist: the former is a descriptive undertaking, while the latter is constructive. Otto Eissfeldt attempted to draw this sort of sharp line between biblical theology and biblical criticism. He asserted that for any theological understanding of the Bible,

> the perception of the true essence of Old Testament religion merely by application of the otherwise typical methods of historical investigation

is impossible. Rather, it [viz., theological understanding of the Bible] discloses itself only to faith, and this is something different from [the] empathetic reliving [practiced by the historian].[65]

As a result, Eissfeldt argues that biblical criticism and biblical theology cannot have anything to do with each other, for blending them can only be harmful. In this case, biblical theology is a religious pursuit, not an academic one, and an academic field of biblical theology cannot exist.

In this respect Eissfeldt is atypical of biblical scholars. Very few scholars have insisted that biblical theology must be explicitly evaluative and that the field's task is part of the work of the church. Those few would simply read biblical theology outside biblical criticism and indeed outside the academy. Most biblical theologians themselves agree that if biblical theology were a normative, faith-based initiative (that is, if it told members of a religious community what or how they should believe about God, humanity, religious community, and their relationships), then it would not be part of the academic discipline of biblical studies at all. In fact, the hallmark of biblical theology as distinct from doctrinal theology has almost always been its descriptive rather than normative nature. Johann Gabler, often considered the father of the field, maintained that "biblical theology . . . deals only with those things which holy men [who composed the Bible] perceived about matters pertinent to religion, and is not made to accommodate our point of view," in contrast to dogmatic theology, which is varied, subtle, and reflects the evaluation of later thinkers.[66] For Gabler, biblical theologians should describe the religious ideas in the Bible; questions regarding the value of those ideas, their relation to Christian doctrine, and their use today lie outside the realm of biblical theology.[67]

If, as Gabler insists, biblical theology should be descriptive, then it seems in large part to belong to the larger field that has come to be known as the history of Israelite religion.[68] Most biblical theologians, however, would like to insist that biblical theology and the history of Israelite religion are separate pursuits.[69] How, then, can one safeguard the independence (or even existence) of biblical theology? I would like to examine answers that have been given to this question. None of these answers, we shall see, work.

One might argue that biblical theology and the history of Israelite religion are both descriptive but that they describe different things. Walter Eichrodt, for example, proposes that one of the factors distinguishing the one from the other works along roughly these lines:

> If the history of Israelite-Jewish religion is a matter of the genetic under-
> standing of Old Testament religion in the interplay of historical forces,
> then Old Testament theology has to do . . . with the systematic task of
> a cross section through the developed whole, which should illumine the
> entire dynamic content of the religion according to its internal struc-
> ture, and which should perceive its uniqueness over against the religious
> environment—that is, over against the typology of the history of reli-
> gion generally.[70]

Eichrodt argues that by making this cross section, biblical theology will
lay bare the essence of Old Testament religion. Thus the biblical theologian's task differs from that of a historian, who is concerned with a multitude of particulars.[71] According to this line of reasoning, the biblical
theologian emphasizes the whole, whereas the historian of Israelite religion emphasizes stages of development. The former integrates data, the
latter isolates. A somewhat analogous distinction is suggested by Moshe
Goshen-Gottstein, who suggests the term "structural phenomenology of
biblical religion" as a synonym or replacement for the term "biblical theology." Goshen-Gottstein explains that such a structural phenomenology
would differ from biblical criticism's more "comparative approaches
[with] their evolutionary and teleological aspects."[72] Such a structural
phenomenology would be descriptive, but its mode of description would
differ from the historian's: the historian focuses on development and
parts, whereas the structural phenomenologist or biblical theologian
attends to patterns and wholes. It seems to me that such a distinction is
empty of real content. In fact there are historians of religion who com-
pose synthetic portraits of their subject. To take a recent example: Jean
Bottéro's *Religion in Ancient Mesopotamia*[73] does not focus on the development and growth of Mesopotamian ritual practices or ideas of the
sacred; it is not organized chronologically. Rather, it makes a crosscut of
Sumerian and Akkadian literature to illuminate the whole religion as
manifested in several areas: religious sentiment, cult, prayer, the realm of
the gods, mythology. Yet it would be silly to insist that Bottéro's work
does not belong to the field of history of religions and that it must be
termed a Mesopotamian theology. The mere fact of a book's integrative
rather than genetic orientation, or of its systematic rather than chronological presentation of material, does not suffice to indicate that it
belongs to a field other than history of religions.

Similarly, in attempting to answer the question *How does a Gablerian,
descriptive biblical theology differ from a history of Israelite religion?* one might

argue that the emphasis on the essence of a whole literature rather than on particulars differentiates the descriptive task of biblical theology from that of a history of religion. Again, this is a distinction without a difference. Some historians of ideas may well attend to the essence of a culture or a literature—for example, a historian in thrall to Hegel's conception of history. Perhaps you will insist that Hegelian historians are bad historians—but they are historians nonetheless, not theologians. Surely our goal is not to define biblical theology as a descriptive task performed poorly. Nor is there much practical value in Eichrodt's assertion that biblical theology clarifies those areas in which Israelite religion is unique over against its religious environment; any historical-comparative work will accomplish that goal to some degree, and many historians of Israelite religion have in fact emphasized just that theme (one thinks especially of the works of Yehezkel Kaufmann and William Foxwell Albright).[74]

One might suggest yet another way of distinguishing between these two areas of study: the history of Israelite religion attends to Israelite religiosity in all its diverse forms, including Israelite polytheism (which the Bible itself condemns as heterodox). Biblical theology, on the other hand, limits itself to that form of Israelite religion endorsed by biblical authors. For example, let us assume, for the sake of argument, that the Kuntillet 'Ajrud inscription attests to Israelite belief in a goddess Asherah who was the consort of the god YHWH.[75] In that case, the inscription provides material that must be described by the historian but not by the biblical theologian (or it provides material relevant to the biblical theologian's description only for purposes of contrast). But this suggestion does not present any real difference between two academic fields; rather, one field is a subfield of the other. One can write a description of the beliefs and practices of the monotheistic or monolatrous party whose literature is preserved in the Bible, just as one could write a synthetic description of, say, the cult of Inanna in Mesopotamia. There is no reason to deny that these limited descriptions belong to the field of history of religions.

Another nonanswer involves the unity-oriented perspective of biblical theology. The notion of the search for an overarching unity in biblical theology no longer commands the assent it did in, say, Eichrodt's day. If concentrating on the multiplicity of ideas rather than on a *Mitte* lies outside the concern of biblical theology and can belong only to the field of history of Israelite religion, then we would have to exclude from the field of biblical theology a number of works that almost everyone would agree ought to belong to such a field, if such a field is to exist at all. These include Brueggemann's *Theology of the Old Testament*, which emphasizes not a unified set of theological statements but the complex and often tense interactions of Israel's core testimonies, countertestimonies, and unsolicited testimonies (for example, YHWH as constant; YHWH as hidden; YHWH as partner). Another example would be Gerstenberger's *Theologies of the Old Testament*, with its emphasis on various religions of many social groupings in ancient Israel. To be sure, one could argue that Gerstenberger's work really is closer to a history than a theology, since it is less concerned with the witness of the biblical texts than with the social realities that stood behind the biblical texts and are at times hidden by the biblical texts. If we decide to classify it as a history rather than a theology, it would clearly be a history with a pronounced and explicit theological agenda—indeed, a constructive theological agenda, since it has its starting point and its *telos* in liberal Christian theology. Even if categorized as a history, then, this work still makes clear the arbitrary nature of the distinction between the two fields. Similarly, a person who insists that biblical theology and the history of Israelite religion are two distinct fields might argue that Kaufmann's *Toledot* belongs to biblical theology rather than to the history of religions, since Kaufmann focuses his entire work around the centrality and distinct nature of monotheism. Of course, one can define the two fields in such a way, if one so chooses; but a definition that sees a *Theology* as history and a *History* as theology would in fact make the point that I am trying to make: to wit, that the attempt to distinguish between these fields on the basis of a polarity between analyzing particulars and describing wholes or a dichotomy between attempts to examine variations and efforts to uncover unity leads only to incoherence.

Alternatively, one might argue that what distinguishes a biblical theology from a history of religion has to do with attitude: the former is passionately involved with its subject matter.[76] I think that this suggestion moves in a sensible direction, insofar as it intimates the categories of artifact and scripture. On its own, however, it is not yet a sufficient distinction. The mere fact that a historian of ideas maintains some commitment toward the material under discussion does not mean that the work in question is something other than history. Bertrand Russell's *History of Western Philosophy*[77] is a highly partisan work: through-out this book Lord Russell endorses one stream in Western philosophy and attacks another.

But there is no reason to deny that the book is a history of ideas; it is simply a history that makes no pretense to objectivity.

If in the end biblical theology must be described as mediating a dichotomy between the descriptive and the normative or between different species of description, then I think we face a fundamental question. And that question is not simply where along the continuum biblical theology should lie; nor is it whether people who claim to be working according to one model are not in fact working according to the other. Rather, it is whether there really can be such an animal as biblical theology at all if *either* polarity is stressed. Did, say, Eichrodt ever really *do* biblical theology—or was he rather doing a particular type of integrative intellectual history most of the time and Christian apologetics the rest? In short, I am asking whether there really is (to borrow James Barr's phrase) a *concept* of biblical theology. The answer to this question, at least for most of this century, has probably been no.[78] The statement "I am interested in biblical theology" or "I am writing an Old Testament theology" just does not communicate anything about our intentions or methods in the way that other statements do, such as, "I am interested in source criticism of the Pentateuch" or "I am working on anthropological approaches to the Hebrew Bible."[79]

And yet many of us, both Christian and Jewish, sense within both the academy and the church or synagogue the need for a more theological approach to studying the Bible—more specifically, for an approach that allows us to read it as scripture while integrating what we know about it as artifact. After all, to pretend we have not learned a great deal about it as artifact would not so much represent secondary naïveté as bad faith. On the other hand, for the preacher, the religious educator, and the faithful individual, the tools of academic biblical scholarship (which relate to the Bible as artifact) are not adequate. Modern religious people who reject willful naïveté clearly require an approach to scripture that is at once academically critical and religiously engaged, and that approach might well be called biblical theology.[80] The question is how to go about constructing it.

DIALOGICAL BIBLICAL THEOLOGY

I would like to suggest that we move beyond the contrast between descriptive and normative models of biblical theology, a contrast that has proved itself to be at best sterile. It is misleading; it causes confusion; and it can lead scholars pursuing a particular topic to believe that they are not permitted to discuss some aspects and that they must focus on others, when in fact such a boundary is entirely artificial.

A more helpful model for a field that builds upon biblical criticism yet also contributes to theology might be termed "*dialogical* biblical theology." Dialogical biblical theology would attempt to construct a discussion between biblical texts and a particular postbiblical theological tradition. Such a theology would bring biblical texts to bear on postbiblical theological concerns—specifically, on modern Jewish or Protestant or Catholic or Orthodox or post-Christian theological concerns. A work in this field would belong to the fields of both biblical scholarship and either Jewish thought or constructive Christian theology; indeed, it ought to draw on and contribute to all these fields. Let us imagine for a moment two projects of a dialogical biblical theology. One project might compare the place of the land of Israel in the Hebrew Bible and in the work of Rav Avraham Isaac Kook, the early twentieth-century religious Zionist thinker. Such a study might be very interesting to a Jew, especially to a Jew who affiliates with the tradition founded by Rav Kook. But a Christian might also learn much not only about Judaism but about the Old Testament from such a study, which would force him to confront a central aspect of his own scripture to which he had paid little attention before. Another study might examine the notion of grace as it appears in the J document, in Judges, in Paul, and in Luther. A Jew might learn much about the fountainhead of her own tradition from this study. In both these works, it is the interchange between a biblical and a postbiblical set of ideas that makes the study in question relevant to biblical criticism, to Christian theology, and to Jewish thought. The interchange focuses our attention on aspects of biblical thought that we might have missed otherwise. What I am calling dialogical biblical theology can show that the Bible is not as distant from postbiblical traditions as one might think.

Scholarship has not focused on this model, but some scholars already exemplify it. I would like to spend some time describing several works that already fit into the nascent field of dialogical biblical theology. Krister Stendahl, Manfred Oeming, and Rainer Albertz briefly describe a program similar to the one I outline, while studies already published by James Barr, Moshe Greenberg, and Zachary Braiterman exemplify it.

FOREBEARS:
THEORETICAL DISCUSSIONS

Krister Stendahl's essay on biblical theology in *The Interpreter's Dictionary of the Bible*[81] adumbrates something like the dialogical approach, at least if we are willing to modify his proposal slightly. Stendahl famously distinguishes between what the Bible meant and what the Bible means.[82] Biblical theologians, he tells us, attend to what the Bible meant: they describe biblical views of certain issues (one example, not treated by Stendahl there but a concern of his elsewhere, would be the ordination of women).[83] Other scholars, apparently (Stendahl does not identify them), can attend to what the Bible means, or how it can function in our world, and this second process is based on the descriptive work performed by the biblical theologian. (In asserting that biblical theologians describe and that other scholars make use of this description for current concerns, Stendahl's programmatic essay recalls Johann Gabler's seminal call in 1787 for a biblical theology distinct from dogmatic theology.) I suggest that it would be helpful to modify Stendahl's two-part scheme in two ways. First, the crucial distinction is more accurately captured if we speak not of "what it meant" and "what it means" but rather "what it meant" and "how modern religious people can appropriate or reject or accept what it meant in light of the way our respective traditions, in reading scripture, have long appropriated, rejected, or accepted what the Bible meant." Second, Stendahl refers to the first part of this process as "biblical theology," and in doing so he follows the paradigm introduced long ago by Gabler. However, as James Barr rightly points out, the second part of the process also belongs under that rubric.[84] Indeed, the first part need not be called biblical theology at all; as I have already stressed, any attempt to figure out what it meant—whether "it" is the Bible or Sumerian literature or Homer or Dante or Joyce—is a matter of intellectual history. The theological aspect of the project enters only in the second phase, as we attempt to relate what the Bible meant to two other complexes: our own religious traditions, and our own beliefs, intuitions, and settings. What I call "dialogical biblical theology" begins with intellectual history and, if one so desires, with a structural phenomenology (to use Moshe Goshen-Gottstein's phrase), which is to say, a synchronic ordering of material into some readily graspable form. But, unlike Gabler or Goshen-Gottstein or Stendahl, the dialogical biblical theologian does not stop with these various forms of description. That theologian moves forward from there. This term does not appear in Stendahl, but I believe it fits what he implied as he outlined these two stages of appropriating biblical teachings.[85]

A notion resembling what I call dialogical biblical theology also appears in Manfred Oeming's proposal for "biblical theology as exegesis that refers to or connects with value" (*biblische Theologie als wertbeziehender Exegese*).[86] Oeming argues that biblical theology should not attend to fanciful constructions such as the meaning of the Old Testament as a whole or the inherent continuity between the Old and the New Testaments. Rather, it should pursue exegeses of specific passages according to some measure of value taken from outside the Old Testament. For Christians, this measure of value will come from the New Testament and from later Christian theology.[87] Oeming readily acknowledges that this particular measure is not the only possible one. Thus he leaves open the possibility of a Jewish biblical theology that rests on the same premise as a Christian biblical theology: it would find a measure of value in later Jewish literature rather than the New Testament. Such a Jewish biblical theology would have precisely the same claim to validity that Christian biblical theologies have.[88] It is worth comparing Oeming's approach with earlier Christian ones. Von Rad insists that a work can qualify as biblical theology *only if* it makes the link between the Testaments clear; in so doing, of course, von Rad forecloses the possibility of a Jewish biblical theology.[89] For Oeming, a work qualifies as biblical theology if—but not only if—it makes that link clear. Further, for von Rad that link is inherent to the Old Testament and cannot be missed by the careful critic. Oeming insists, on the other hand, that the measure of value applied to the biblical texts must come from outside the Old Testament itself (it is precisely the attempt to bring in a measure from outside the Bible that makes the undertaking theological). As a result, we might describe the application of any such measure of value as *synthetic* in the Kantian sense, rather than (as von Rad would have it) *analytic*: the measure is not necessarily organic to the Hebrew Bible; rather than being derived from the Hebrew Bible, the measure is imposed on it. For Oeming this imposition is perfectly acceptable so long as the exegete or biblical theologian openly acknowledges what I am calling the synthetic nature of the project.[90] Thus Oeming at once allows biblical theology to be denominational and opens it to a wide range of readers; he cuts the Gordian knot that tied Old Testament theology to an exclusivist Christian model and hence to an inevitably anti-Jewish stance.

Oeming does not call merely for judging the Old Testament by some later Christian standard; he insists that the evaluation must be two-way, so that later Christian thought is measured against and enriched by the Old Testament.[91] Both biblical studies and systematic theology, then, will be challenged and enriched by biblical theology.[92] At times, Oeming notes, Old Testament texts will seem of lesser value than later Christian texts, and the former texts will serve as an ongoing goad to Christian thought, which must constantly legitimate the later position. (For this reason alone, Christianity would be poorer for the loss of the Old Testament, he asserts.[93]) In other cases, the two Testaments are of similar value, but they articulate ideas differently, and as biblical theology focuses attention on the earthier, more vivid presentations in the Old, it enlivens Christian thought.[94] Finally, Oeming asserts, the Old Testament gives voice to many ideas and religious feelings concerning which the New Testament remains silent. In these areas, the biblical theologian can make a crucial contribution to Christian theology.[95] I think it especially significant that Oeming emphasizes the dynamic, back-and forth discussion between biblical texts and later theology (*das "wertbeziehende Ineinander historischer Kritik und systematischer Reflexion"*).[96] Contemporary religious involvement with biblical texts easily devolves into the slavish application of norms derived from the religiously correct orthodoxy of our day: one accepts that which suits contemporary orthodoxy, one rejects what is disagreeable, and one simply ignores the many biblical texts that do not present themselves as being spiritually useful or politically relevant. In such a situation, studying the Bible contributes nothing to the formation of faith, community, or outlook; it is merely a matter of gaining a few proof texts for what we already value. Oeming insists, on the contrary, that the Old Testament can teach the Christian, can challenge her, can expand his imaginative range. Oeming's proposal can be readily configured to work for Jewish biblical theology. Indeed, in his method and sensibility, he closely resembles Jewish biblical scholars, with whom he shares much: a focus on individual texts and issues rather than on the whole of the canon or one privileged *Mitte* that holds the canon together; an openness to—indeed, a love of—the Bible's (pro-torabbinic) multivocality; and an awareness of what I have called the synthetic rather than analytic nature of Christian measures of value applied to biblical texts. It is striking that none of the reasons Levenson gives for Jews' lack of interest in biblical theology would apply to a Christian biblical theology that follows Oeming's proposal.

A comparable understanding of the task of biblical theology comes from, of all places, Rainer Albertz's history of Israelite religion.[97] Albertz maintains that a historical approach to summarizing Israelite religion remains desirable not only for the historian but for the theologian as well. Such an approach, he points out,

> describes a dialogical process of struggle for theological clarification, demarcation, and consensus-forming [in biblical Israel] which clearly corresponds to the present-day synodical or conciliar ecumenical learning process of the churches and Christian-Jewish dialogue.[98]

A history of Israelite religion, according to Albertz, not only examines the settings of various biblical ideas,

> but also . . . brings them into dialogue with one another. Its task is to restore the "frozen dialogue" of the Old Testament tradition to a living theological discussion between different groups and parties. . . . The history of Israelite religion is then an ongoing discussion between various Israelite groupings about the way in which particular historical developments are to be interpreted in the light of God and what is to be done, according to God's will, in the face of these challenges.[99]

The concern of Albertz's study, then, turns out to be similar on the one hand to historical work on tradition history and inner-biblical exegesis by scholars such as Martin Noth,[100] Gerhard von Rad,[101] and Michael Fishbane.[102] But it just as readily resembles the work of biblical theologians who focus on the multivocality of biblical texts, such as Paul Hanson,[103] Brueggemann, or, again, von Rad. Moreover, Albertz anticipates a theological use for his historical/descriptive work, even though he does not himself pursue it:

> An important place could come to be occupied by a theological view which took on the task, starting from the burning problems of the present and the controversies in theology and the church about how a Christian solution can be achieved, of making thematic cross-sections through the history of the religion of Israel and early Christianity in order to describe what insights or patterns of behaviour found there in connection with analogous problems and controversies can be important, helpful, and even normative for the church today. However, this would be a different kind of "Old Testament theology" from what has been customary so far.[104]

It would, however, be quite similar to the dialogical biblical theology that I am proposing.[105]

FOREBEARS: CONCRETE EXAMPLES

Not only theoretical or programmatic essays have moved in the direction of a dialogical biblical theology. This model is also suggested, I think, by several studies already published. One of the clearest cases is James Barr's work on natural theology and the Bible.[106] There Barr argues that many biblical texts express or are based on a type of natural theology. His discussion yields insights into both the Bible and natural theology that we might not have made had we not put two seemingly remote sets of texts next to each other. Thus his book is a work at once on the Bible and on Christian theology. Barr's work argues, if only implicitly, for frank and honest interaction between biblical studies and doctrinal theology.[107] Barr presents himself as a theologian, not only as a biblicist, when he argues that natural theology has a place within the Bible—and, moreover, when he maintains that biblical studies have a place in natural theology. The book in question is as much about Karl Barth as it is about the Bible, and this is entirely appropriate for an avowedly theological undertaking.[108] This book does not claim to eschew concerns of Christian theology; it does not limit itself to describing ancient ideas but addresses modern philosophical issues; it unabashedly treats texts from the New Testament along with those from the Old. In all this, it is a harbinger of dialogical biblical theology. It seems to me that for Barr, biblical theology cannot be limited to descriptive concerns; it must be constructive, and hence it very well may come from a specifically Christian, or Jewish, or other religious perspective. It is in part the unembarrassed honesty with which Barr (in contrast to von Rad and Eichrodt) addresses this point that has made his work so refreshing and exciting to Jewish readers. This book, with its explicitly Christian concerns and its treatment of the New Testament alongside the Tanakh, is a rare biblical theology that is not in some way offensive to Jewish readers. Further, its insights into ancient Hebrew texts are just as promising for the construction of modern Jewish thought as they are for Christian theology.[109]

Another example of what I would call a dialogical biblical theologian is Moshe Greenberg. Greenberg is not usually identified as a biblical theologian, but when we define biblical theology dialogically, it becomes

clear that he is, along with Kaufmann, one of the most important Jewish
biblical theologians of the twentieth century—especially in his various
collections of essays.[110] Greenberg's work on biblical texts is not only
deeply informed by rabbinic concerns but I dare say in part motivated by
them in much the same way that Barr's study of natural theology is motivated by a movement in Christian thought. A typical case is his classic
essay on capital punishment in biblical and Mesopotamian law.[111] That
study reveals central values of biblical thinking that were developed more
fully in rabbinic literature. Biblical texts regard human life as sacred and
therefore incommensurable. Hence legal corpora in the Bible insist that
murder must be punished in every case by the execution of the murderer;
fines, substitutions, and other sanctions permitted by Mesopotamian law
in certain cases of murder are rejected by the Bible's law codes. Of course,
the punishment that results from the notion of the sanctity of human life
is rather paradoxical, since it compels human courts to destroy precisely
what it exalts. Much later, the rabbis would institute laws of evidence and
narrow definitions of capital crimes that severely limited—indeed, came
close to abolishing—the application of the death penalty. In so doing, the
rabbis were not so much overturning the biblical legal system as taking its
logic quite seriously, in a sense more seriously than did the biblical law
codes themselves. Although Greenberg's study barely refers to rabbinic
texts,[112] it is nonetheless a deeply Jewish one. At the same time it contributes to our understanding of biblical and Mesopotamian law and thus
is rewarding to any students of the ancient Near East, whether they are
interested in Jewish thought or not. It is at once, then, a study of ancient
Near Eastern legal history and, in a subtle and not fully explicit manner,
an attempt to note the basis in biblical law for a later development in rabbinic law. Greenberg's essay suggests that this later development, on the
surface, seems to go against the grain of particular laws (to wit, the man-
dates for capital punishment), but that it also allows an overarching element of biblical law to express itself more fully (to wit, the sacredness of
human life).[113] In this essay, Greenberg foreshadows Oeming's later program by encouraging readers to contemplate the relations between biblical texts and postbiblical values.

Similarly, Greenberg in effect creates a discussion (at times, an argument) involving various biblical, rabbinic, and medieval voices in several
other essays. Particularly fine examples of this tendency are the essays
"Using Rabbinic Exegesis as an Educational Resource When Teaching the
Book of Joshua" and "How Should One Interpret the Torah Today?"[114]

In the former, Greenberg delineates how rabbinic voices temper and even overturn biblical teachings regarding the Canaanites.[115] His attention to exegetical technique heightens our ability to sense multiple voices on the issues at hand in the biblical texts themselves. In the latter, Greenberg notes biblical and rabbinic attempts at articulating the central value-concepts that should guide Jewish reading of the Bible. It is striking that an explicit rabbinic discussion regarding the fundamental principle in the Torah (*kĕlāl gādôl battôrâ*) (e.g., in *Sipra* Lev 18:19; *b. Mak.* 23b–24a) seems to have made the modern biblical critic more aware of an analogous, albeit implicit, discussion in the Bible itself (e.g., in Ezek 18). Greenberg's work, like Barr's, involves not merely correcting the Bible in light of later values but reading the Bible more closely in light of later texts. Greenberg has for several decades now provided an example of what I would call a dialogical model of biblical theology, or a Jewish analogue to Oeming's model of biblical theology as exegesis that refers to questions of value.

It is important to note that for Jewish biblical theology as exemplified by Greenberg, the main dialogue partner is not dogmatic theology but rabbinic exegesis. Granted, one can imagine certain philosophical texts (e.g., Saadia Gaon, Maimonides, Hermann Cohen, Franz Rosenzweig) or mystical texts being put into discussion with biblical texts, but never at the expense of classical and medieval rabbinic exegesis. I shall end this section by citing an outstanding example of contemporary work that focuses on philosophical texts while attending very carefully to biblical and rabbinic texts: Zachary Braiterman's *(God) After Auschwitz: Tradition and Change in Post-Holocaust Jewish Thought.*[116] Braiterman's book is noteworthy in its serious and respectful treatment of biblical and rabbinic materials. In comparing their attitudes toward innocent suffering, Braiterman does a wonderful job of exploring the variety of positions in both literatures. Eschewing the oversimplifications that are so common when nonspecialists survey literature outside their own field, he shows how both pious (naive?) and daring voices appear in both sets of texts. Further, he demonstrates, in both literatures, how some voices manage to be devout and doubting at once.[117] Finally, he rightly reminds us that in the Bible and rabbinic literature, as opposed to post-Holocaust Jewish theology, daring or doubting voices are located toward the margins. Consequently, the similarities in content between some ancient and post-Holocaust Jewish thinkers must be seen alongside very significant differences of context and form. In short, Braiterman manages to demonstrate that biblical and rabbinic texts can be interesting to modern thinkers, but also that it would be an act of bad faith for moderns to exaggerate the extent to which they have forebears within the tradition.

CONCRETE EXAMPLES

The essays and books just discussed can serve as indicators of how a dialogical biblical theology might work in Christian and Jewish contexts respectively. It is crucial to note how much Jews can learn about their own scripture from the former and Christians from the latter. In some ways, Barr is even more enlightening for Jews and Greenberg for Christians, since each begins with powerfully revealing questions that members of the other faith community might not have asked. In what follows, I would like to provide two lengthier examples of a Jewish dialogical biblical theology.[118] In accordance with Oeming's model, each example will focus on a particular issue and also on a particular text. As in the works by Barr, Greenberg, and Braiterman, each example will take its impetus from a question suggested by a particular religious tradition, and each one pursues its question with the goal of contributing to that tradition—indeed, with the goal of becoming part of that tradition. Precisely for that reason, each promises to be especially enlightening for people outside that tradition.

The Primary Religious Value according to the Psalter and Later Judaism[119]

The first example involves a hierarchy of religious values. Two attitudes toward religious experience play especially prominent roles in rabbinic Judaism. One of these attitudes emphasizes Torah study and intellectualization over prayer and spontaneous joy; the other adopts the opposite hierarchy of religious values. Before turning to biblical texts, it will be useful to summarize relevant material concerning these attitudes from rabbinic and some postrabbinic literature.

The tension between these two attitudes is well-known already in classical rabbinic literature, which, with important reservations and exceptions, tends to regard Torah study as the highest religious value. A few passages will suffice to illustrate the relationship between these types of religious experience in rabbinic texts.

In the central work of rabbinic Judaism, the Babylonian Talmud (specifically, *b. Meg.* 26b–27a), both attitudes are suggested, but one is ultimately endorsed over the other. The discussion in this passage presumes a principle stated at the beginning of the fourth chapter of this Talmudic tractate (25b–26a): to wit, it is permissible to use the proceeds from the sale of a sacred item to purchase an item of greater sanctity, but it is forbidden to use these proceeds to purchase an item of lesser sanctity. In other words, one can always convert an object (or the proceeds of its sale) upward in holiness but not downward.[120] With this principle in mind, the Talmud records the following debate and its resolution:

> Rav Pappi said in the name of Rava, "[It is] permissible [to convert] a house of prayer into a house of study, but [it is] forbidden [to convert] a house of study into a house of prayer." But Rav Pappa taught the opposite in the name of Rava. Rav Aḥa held that the method of Rav Pappi was more likely, since Rabbi Joshua ben Levi had earlier said, "It is lawful to convert a house of prayer into a house of study." The implication is clear.

Pappi, in short, holds that a house of study is of greater sanctity than a house of prayer; Pappa holds the opposite; and the tradition accepts the former, not the latter, view. This viewpoint is not unique to this passage. The same chapter of the Talmud teaches that a prayer hall ought not be used for certain secular purposes, including funerals (see *b. Meg.* 28a–b). However, an exception is made for "funerals of many" or a "public funeral," which, the Talmudic discussion goes on to explain, means the funeral of a scholar or a member of his family.[121] Thus the sanctity of a scholar (or even of a member of his family) overrides the sanctity of a prayer hall.

A few Talmudic texts evince a more ambivalent stance. *Y. Ber.* 1:5 (3b)[122] discusses whether it is permissible to interrupt study in order to pray:

> Rabbi Yoḥanan said in the name of Rabbi Shimon Bar Yoḥai, "People like us, who are involved in the study of Torah [constantly], do not interrupt [Torah study] even for the recitation of the Shema prayer [the recitation of which at a set time is required by biblical law, and all the more so not for the recitation of other prayers, whose timing is not required by biblical law,[123] such as the Standing Prayer]." Rabbi Yoḥanan said in his own name, "People like us, who are not [constantly] involved in the study of Torah, do interrupt [Torah study] even for the

recitation of the Standing Prayer [and all the more so for the Shema prayer]. Each one's ruling is in accordance with his opinions [expressed on other occasions]. For Rabbi Yoḥanan said, "If only one could pray all day long! Why? Because prayer never wanes." Rabbi Shimon bar Yoḥai said, "If I had stood at Mount Sinai when the Torah was given to Israel, I would have requested that the Merciful One make two mouths for human beings, one with which to study the Torah, and one with which to take care of all other concerns."

Each scholar expresses an unrealizable ideal. The highest activity of humanity, which in the best of all worlds would never be interrupted, is either prayer (Yoḥanan) or study (Shimon), and the law takes both views into account. Yoḥanan's legal ruling, which reflects a higher regard for prayer, applies only in cases where exigencies prevent a scholar from studying all the time; whereas Shimon's ruling, which valorizes study over prayer, is applicable only for the purest of scholars. The rabbis cherished both prayer and study, and passages such as these show that their relative ranking was a matter of concern among rabbis in both the Tannaitic and Amoraic periods in Israel and Babylon. But where a clear preference is stated, the classical rabbis inclined to give study the highest place of honor.[124]

The relative weighting of these two religious values remained a question in later Jewish thought as well. The tension between them played a central role in the conflict between two groups of eastern European Jews in the eighteenth century, the Hasidim and Mitnagdim, and these attitudes play a role in the relationship between these groups throughout the Jewish world even today. The Mitnagdim (centered before the Holocaust in the great academies or *yeshivot* of Lithuania and today in their successor institutions in Israel, the United States, and elsewhere) represent the apogee of the viewpoint expressed in the Talmud by Shimon bar Yoḥai, Joshua ben Levi, and Pappi: they esteem study over prayer. A central element of early Hasidism, on the other hand, was its emphasis on prayer over study.[125] (Indeed, Mordecai Wilensky has argued that the Hasidic devaluation of study was the main reason for the opposition of the great Lithuanian rabbis to nascent Hasidism.[126]) Consequently, we might use the terms "Hasidic" and "Mitnagdic" to identify two temperaments within Judaism throughout the ages. For the purpose of this article, *Hasidic* will refer to a form of Judaism that emphasizes prayer and spontaneous joy as the highest way of coming to know God, while *Mitnagdic* will refer to a form of Judaism that focuses on study and intellectualization as the preeminent path toward the Deity.

An additional issue that separated (and separates) historical Hasidim and Mitnagdim will also turn out to be relevant to our discussion: to wit, the style of leadership each group endorses. Many strains of Hasidism emphasize a royal or at times even a messianic model of leadership.[127] The *rebbe* or *tzaddik* who leads the group is treated as a monarch. Thus it is quite appropriate that he is succeeded by his son or some other member of his family. Mitnagdim, on the other hand, look to the scholar as the most important authority for their communities—especially the scholar who holds no official position or holds a decidedly modest one.[128] (While dynasties of scholars exist among the Mitnagdim, most prominent rabbis within that world achieve their positions through intellectual achievement rather than genetic succession.) For our purposes, then, the adjective *Hasidic* will betoken not only an emphasis on prayer but an inclination toward royal or messianic models of leadership. The adjective *Mitnagdic* will suggest an elitist view of learning and a strong emphasis on the honor due to those devoted to it—an elitism with paradoxically democratic implications, since any person,[129] regardless of birth, can aspire to learning.

It will be useful to examine the book of Psalms in light of the tension between Mitnagdic and Hasidic perspectives. Which sort of religious experience does the book of Psalms reflect and encourage? Is the Psalter fundamentally a Hasidic or a Mitnagdic book?

At first blush, the answer seems obvious. The Psalter is, after all, a book of prayers. The exuberant hymns, with their cries of "Praise Yah!" (e.g., Pss 29; 33; 95; 114; 117); the songs of thanksgiving, which disclose the strong connection between the person or persons praying and the God who answered their cries for help (e.g., 18; 30; 32; 116; 118); the personal laments, which are rooted in the worshiper's intimate sense of connection with God (e.g., 3; 4; 5; 71; 77); the communal laments, whose aggrieved tone reflects the very presumption of closeness between community and deity (e.g., 44; 60; 74; 90; 123)—all these genres, which together account for the vast majority of texts in the Psalter, represent a religiosity of feeling, not a religiosity rooted in the intellect. Each genre encourages an individual or a community to address a personal God with intense emotion. Furthermore, the adjective *Hasidic* as I intend it here hints at the central role a royal figure plays in maintaining the connection between God and nation. Consequently, the royal psalms (e.g., 2;

18; 45; 72; 110) also establish the appropriateness of the adjective *Hasidic* in characterizing the Psalter. The Zion psalms (e.g., 46; 48; 76) similarly underscore the importance of the royal family whose palace is on Mount Zion and who sponsor the temple located there. To be sure, some psalms are not really prayers and have no connection to royalty—to wit, the wisdom psalms (e.g., 37; 49; 112). This category, however, represents a small fraction of the texts found in this book.[130] If the contents of any biblical book deserve to be called *Hasidic*, surely that book is the Psalter.

This portrayal applies well to the vast majority of psalms. Yet the canonical *book* of Psalms as we have it in the Hebrew Bible may be more than the sum of its parts. As a result, the question of how the Psalter is presented must be raised as its own question, distinct from a discussion of the individual texts this anthology contains. One can ask the same question about psalms and Psalms and receive different answers for each, since the way psalms are organized into Psalms may spin the psalms in a surprising way. The most prominent way to give any collection of material a particular identity that one might not have discerned from its contents alone is in the way it is either introduced or summed up.[131] I would like to argue that Ps 1 presents, or re-represents, the Psalter in an original and rather surprising way: as a Mitnagdic book.

The poem that opens the Psalter is an odd psalm; indeed, it is not really a psalm at all.[132] It is not addressed to God (as the laments and thanksgiving psalms are), nor does it speak of the Deity in the third person (as is the case with many psalms of praise). Its topic is not God, at least not directly. Rather, its topic is God's *tôrâ*, which may mean God's instruction generally or may refer to a specific document that contains such instruction, such as the Pentateuch. In fact, it probably means both; while the term *tôrâ* may include something general, the phrasing of the psalm presumes that *tôrâ* is found in a particular text. This becomes evident in the psalm's second verse, according to which the happy person is one who takes delight in God's *tôrâ*, reading (*yehĕgeh*) it day and night. The verb *yehĕgeh* at the end of that verse is often translated with the English verb "meditate upon," which may suggest to the English reader an exclusively mental activity (and hence one that need not be connected to a particular text). Nevertheless, nearly all attestations of the verb *hāgâ* in the Hebrew Bible refer to a physical act that involves one's mouth and one's vocal cords; the verb does not refer to pure ratiocination. Certainly the pigeon and lion who are subjects of this verb in Isa 38:18 and Isa 31:4 are making a soft, low sound, not merely cogitating (they are cooing and growling respectively). The physicality of the act is clear in most of its occurrences, with human beings as its subject: see, for example, Ps 115:7, where the throat is mentioned as its organ, just as hands are the organ of touching and legs of walking; Ps 71:24, where it is the tongue that performs the act in question; and Josh 1:8, where it is the presence of the Book of the Torah in Joshua's mouth that allows him to *hōgeh* it. Three texts do identify the mind (*lēb*) as the organ of this activity, yet they also put the verb *hāgâ* alongside words indicating verbal expression, such as the verb *dibber* (speak) or *hibbîa'* (utter) or nouns referring to parts of the mouth such as *peh* (mouth) and *śāpâ* (lips) (Isa 33:18-19; Prov 15:28; 24:2). The meditation described by the verb *hāgâ*, then, is not the silent act that the word *meditation* may conjure up for many contemporary speakers of English, an act that is thought to be deeply spiritual or rational. Rather, it is something done aloud, perhaps very softly but nonetheless physically. Its connection with the mind (*lēb*) shows that this physical act can involve contemplation or learning as well.[133] This being the case, the *tôrâ* to which Ps 1:2b refers consists not only of abstract ideas but of specific words that can be enunciated; in other words, it is a text. It is impossible to decide whether the text of which the author of Ps 1 speaks is more or less identical to our Pentateuch (like the *tôrâ* to which the books of Ezra–Nehemîah and Chronicles refer) or consists of some predecessor text, such as the book of Deuteronomy or some early edition thereof (to which the book of Kings refers when it uses the term "Moses' *tôrâ* ");[134] further, it is possible that the author of the psalm meant the term in one way, while the editor who put the psalm at the head of the Psalter (if that editor was not also the author of the psalm) meant it in some other way. What remains clear, however, is that as the introduction to the Psalter, our psalm refers us to another text; the book of Psalms begins by putting itself in relation to a book called Torah, whatever that Torah may be.

That editorial act has two implications. First, as many scholars including Meir Weiss, Claus Westerman, Joseph Reindl, and Gerald Wilson have noted, the editor who placed this paean to Torah-study at the head of the Psalter suggests a radically new vision of that anthology and its setting. While individual psalms are prayers, which one uses in cultic settings (including, but not limited to, the Jerusalem temple), the Psalter that begins with Ps 1 is a textbook, to which one turns for guidance and instruction. One recites or sings a psalm; one reads or studies the book of Psalms.[135] In short, Ps 1 attempts to convert the book of Psalms into another form of Torah. It suggests that one ought to learn this text, just as one learns the Pentateuch. By intimating that one can receive teaching from the Psalter, Ps 1 also makes the somewhat surprising move of transforming prayers into instruction. What one might have regarded as a human's words to the Deity become a form of divine revelation to humanity.[136] (One might object to the suggestion that Ps 1 transforms prayer into learning, arguing that the phrase *yehĕgeh bĕtôrātô* in verse 2 might refer to prayerful recitation of the Torah. In that case, Ps 1 would attempt to make the Torah into a prayer book rather than the Psalter into a study book. However, the verb *hāgâ* is almost never used to refer to an utterance made in prayer. In the few cases where it does, it means to articulate a particular idea in the context of a prayer, not to sing or chant.[137] Similarly, one might refer in English to a person "uttering God's praises," but this does not mean that the word *utter* by itself suggests a liturgical context. Further, the object of the verb in Ps 1:2 is "T/torah," which definitively places the phrase *yehĕgeh bĕtôrātô* in a context of study, because *tôrâ* means "instruction, that which is studied.")

The second implication following from the placement of Ps 1 at the head of the Psalter involves the shape of the canon. What does it mean to begin the book of Psalms—and hence the Writings (the third section of the Jewish biblical canon) as a whole—by praising the Torah and recommending its study? The answer to this question becomes sharper when we realize that the phrasing found in Ps 1:2 also appears in the very first chapter of the Prophets (the second section of the Jewish canon).[138]

> This book of Torah (*hattôrâ*) should never leave your mouth; learn it through recitation day and night (*wĕhāgîtâ bô yômām wālaylâ*) so that you will carefully observe everything written in it. Then your way will succeed, and you will achieve understanding. (Josh 1:8)

> [The righteous individual] takes delight in Yhwh's Torah (*bĕtôrat yhwh*), learning His Torah through recitation night and day (*ûbĕtôrātô yehĕgeh yômām wālaylâ*). (Ps 1:2)

Especially when viewed alongside each other, these verses have a clear message. The former asserts the subservience of the text that begins with Josh 1, which is to say, the whole of the Prophets to the Pentateuch. The latter proclaims the subordination of the Psalms, and with them all the Writings to the Pentateuch.[139] The two verses work together to shape the canon, dividing it into the unequal parts known from later Jewish tradition.

Within scripture, Torah is what really matters; the remaining material is worthwhile insofar as it can serve as an adjunct or spur to studying and observing the Torah.[140]

In short, Ps 1 fosters a particular sort of piety, which I have called Mitnagdic, and it fosters a particular view of scripture, which we might simply call Jewish. It attempts to put the book of Psalms and by extension the phenomenon of prayer in their place. That place, to be sure, is important; the Psalter remains a part of scripture, and prayer remains part of the religious experience of the ideal Jew. But that place is also secondary: Psalms is less important than the Pentateuch, and prayer is less important than study. The phrasing in Ps 1:2 is especially important for understanding how appropriate the term "Mitnagdic" is for this psalm. The ideal person never moves away from Torah study according to that verse, since the Torah that is his delight and desire is on his mind and in his mouth all the time.[141] This is precisely the sort of study that Shimon bar Yoḥai presents as a sadly unrealizable ideal in the Talmudic passage cited above (y. *Ber.* 1:5 [3b]), and that contemporary Mitnagdim, especially those living in the State of Israel, have come strikingly close to realizing after all.[142]

Of course, the viewpoint reflected in the editorial placement of Ps 1 as the introduction to the Psalter is not the only one possible. Other scriptural attempts to characterize that anthology seem to have been suggested in ancient times as well. I will briefly review a few of them.

Just as an introduction sums up a work, so too does a conclusion. In this light, the contrast between the first and last poems in the Psalter could hardly be more striking.[143] Psalm 150 focuses on prayer; and within the realm of prayer, it focuses on praise. (The rather tendentious name by which the Psalter is known in Hebrew, *těhillim* ["Songs of Praise"], picks up on the same characterization of the anthology, which is of course by no means limited to songs of praise.) The final chapter of the Psalter is not concerned with Torah study, recitation, or meditation. Indeed, it is not concerned with words at all. Rather, Ps 150 calls on all living creatures to praise God through music. Although the psalm specifies the types of music with which to praise God, conspicuous in its absence is singing. The whole world should praise God with trumpets and harps, with drums and cymbals—but not, apparently, with the voice. The logocentrism of Ps 1 is challenged by the nonverbal music of Ps 150. This summation, then, posits a Hasidic view of the book that is in tension with its Mitnagdic introduction. Further, the two psalms mention different religious institutions, thus deepening the contrast between them. Psalm 150 opens with a reference to God's holy place, which either means the Jerusalem temple or at least hints at it. The only locus of religious meaning mentioned in Ps 1, on the other hand, is the text of the Torah. Here again we find a contrasting set of religious values. One psalm emphasizes the importance of sacred place, and perhaps implies the importance of royalty who sponsor that place; the other psalm regards the holy as a function of the sacred word, open to any who are willing to study it.[144]

Another attempt to characterize the Psalter may appear in Ps 2. Like Ps 1, Ps 2 seems to play an introductory role; Pss 1 and 2 stand apart from all the other poems found in the first of the five divisions of the Psalter in that neither has a Davidic superscription.[145] It is possible that Ps 2 can be taken as an introduction to the first division of the Psalter, just as Ps 1 is an introduction to the Psalter as a whole.[146] Alternatively, Ps 2 may once have been the introduction to the Psalter, to which Ps 1 was subsequently added as another, rather different, introduction.[147] (Some support for this speculative suggestion may come from the ancient tradition, known from some manuscripts of the MT and the New Testament, which numbers what we call Ps 2 as Ps 1, leaving what we call Ps 1 without a number.[148]) If one can imagine, at least for purposes of argument, a Psalter that began with Ps 2, one finds a very different conceptualization of the anthology. Psalm 2 is a royal psalm. As an introduction it emphasizes David's connection to the Psalter. The first introduction to the book looks toward Moses and the mode of religiosity he represents as the best guide for one who will read the Psalms. The second introduction insists that readers should think of David as they sing his songs.[149]

We have seen, then, that ancient editors suggested two different views of the Psalter. In so doing, they created an unresolved debate within the canon. Is David the epitome of a Jew's connection to God, or does Moses take first place even in a Davidic collection? Is the highest way to the Deity to be found in song or in study? It is significant that voices on behalf of both viewpoints appear; while Ps 1 may be said to have superseded Ps 2 as the primary introduction, Ps 150 still gives the Hasidic stance the last word—at least for someone who has followed the Mitnagdic advice of Ps 1 and studied the whole Psalter as a textbook.

Precisely the same debate appears in the classical rabbinic commentary on Ps 1 found in *Midr. Tehillim.*[150] Indeed, only in light of this debate among various editors of the Psalter are the opening sections of the midrash or rabbinic commentary to Ps 1 comprehensible. That midrash begins by linking the happy man described in Ps 1:1 with David and goes on to point out that David instituted the working arrangements of priests and Levites who worked in the temple built by his son Solomon (*Midr. Tehillim* 1§1). The midrash bases this teaching on 1 Chr 24, whose connection to Ps 1:1 seems baffling: what has the long bureaucratic list in 1 Chr 24 to do with the wisdom saying in Ps 1:1? The answer becomes clear if we keep in mind what we might call the debate implied by the juxtaposition of Pss 1 and 2 as introductions, or by the juxtaposition of Pss 1 and 150 as introduction and conclusion. *Midr. Tehillim* 1§1 addresses David's relationship to Moses. One might have regarded the priestly and Levitical offices as inherently Mosaic in nature, not only because Moses was a Levite and his brother the ancestor of the priests but also because Moses established both offices and wrote down the laws concerning their responsibilities (see, e.g., Lev 8 and Num 18). *Midr. Tehillim* begins, however, by reminding us that it was David who instituted the priestly and Levitical offices as they functioned in the First and Second Temples. In other words, the initial section of *Midr. Tehillim* comes to answer an implied question, which is the same question suggested by the editorial juxtaposition of Ps 1 and Ps 2: who is more important, Moses or David?[151] We should pause to note the irony of the answers provided by the Psalter and the *Midr. Tehillim* respectively. The final form of David's Psalter puts Moses (more precisely, Torah) first; but the midrash, composed by sages who regarded themselves as inheritors of Moses' mantle, puts David first. Thus the sages' first comment on Ps 1 attempts to overturn the viewpoint of that psalm. The rabbis created a Hasidic homily on a Mitnagdic text—which in turn attempted to displace the most natural understanding of the Psalter as Hasidic!

Immediately thereafter, the midrash presents a debate concerning who is permitted to sit in the presence of God (*Midr. Tehillim* 1§2). Citing 2 Sam 7:18, Rabbi Ḥiyya teaches that no one other than a Davidic king may sit in the temple courtyard (i.e., in God's presence). The midrash points out that even in heaven the angels must stand in God's presence, which makes the exception granted to Davidic kings even more remarkable. Rabbi Ammi enters the discussion to deny that Davidic kings were permitted to sit in God's presence, explaining that 2 Sam 7:18 ("And David came and sat [*wayyēšeb*] in God's presence" AT) should be understood to mean merely that David leaned against a wall while standing, or perhaps that David set his mind (*yiššēb*) toward intense and focused prayer. The midrash then asserts that it was not the king but the high priest who was permitted to sit in the temple courtyard, as evidenced by 1 Sam 1:9: "And Eli the priest was sitting upon his chair at the doorpost of God's Temple" (AT).[152]

At first glance, this discussion seems tenuously connected to Ps 1:1, on which it purports to comment. The teaching that only Davidic kings may sit in the temple court is based on 2 Sam 7:18 and need not mention Ps 1. This teaching appears many times in other rabbinic texts, and in most of these attestations Ps 1 is not cited.[153] But the teaching's relevance to our psalm becomes clear in light of the debate among the editors of the Psalter discussed above. *Midr. Tehillim* 1§2 is unique among the many rabbinic attestations of the teaching in question, because it is the only passage that uses this teaching to set up a comparison between King David and the high priest Eli. The significance of this comparison becomes clear when we recall that Eli is a member of Moses' family. In the standard rabbinic view, he is descended from Moses' brother, Aaron.[154] Thus the comparison made in *Midr. Tehillim* picks up on the antithesis between Ps 1 and Ps 2—that is, between a sapiential outlook and a royalist one. The comparison implies the question: who is of the highest status, David and the kings descended from him or Moses and the priesthood related to him? As is the case in the canonical Psalter, the competition between these polarities is not resolved in the midrash; two answers to the question are presented without either one being rejected. The citation of a rabbinic teaching concerning 2 Sam 7:18 in a midrash on Ps 1:1 might have seemed a non sequitur, but the application of this teaching here turns out to be deeply connected to the debate sparked by the editorial role of Ps 1. Put differently: the first unit in *Midr. Tehillim* 1§2 comments not on Ps 1:1 but on the implication of Ps 1 as introduction and hence on the Psalter's relationship to the Torah.

The issues raised by the editorial placement of Ps 1 recur as the midrash progresses. The last part of *Midr. Tehillim* 1§2 compares David and Moses, beginning with a citation from 2 Samuel:

> "For this is the Torah of man" (2 Sam 7:18). What man? The greatest of the prophets, or the greatest of kings? The greatest of the prophets was Moses . . . and the greatest of kings was David. You find that whatever Moses did, David did. Moses brought the Israelites out of Egypt, and David brought the Israelites out of subjugation to foreign kingdoms.[155] Moses fought a war against Sichon and Og, and David fought a war against all around him. . . . Moses reigned over Israel and

Judah . . . , and David reigned over Israel and Judah. Moses split the sea
for Israel, and David split the rivers for Israel. . . . Moses built an altar,
and David built an altar. This one officiated at a sacrifice, and the other
one officiated at a sacrifice. Moses gave the five books of the Torah to
Israel, and David gave the five books of Psalms to Israel. . . . Moses
blessed Israel, saying "Happy are you!" (Deut 33:29), and David blessed
Israel, saying "Happy is the man" (Ps 1:1).

The connection of this teaching to Ps 1:1 is not in question, since the
passage ends with a reference to this verse. At the same time, its placement near the beginning of *Midr. Tehillim* is telling. Like the two teachings it follows, its subject, this time explicitly, is a comparison of Moses
and David. Here again we find the midrash grappling not with the
wording of Ps 1:1 but with the issue raised by the editors of the Psalter.
Whereas the first teaching in the midrash (1§1) exalts David over
Moses and the second (beginning of 1§2) presents two opinions, one
exalting Davidic kings over all other created beings and the other exalting a Mosaic priest over all other beings, this tradition equates David
and Moses. In a rabbinic context, such a teaching is perhaps surprising,
the more so in an interpretation attached to our Mitnagdic or Mosaic
psalm.

The midrash to Ps 1 moves on to other themes in subsequent sections,
but it occasionally comes back to our debate. To cite but two examples:
A comparison between the Psalter and the Torah occurs in *Midr. Tehillim*
1§8. There we are told that David expressed the hope that his book would
not be read like the books of Homer. He wishes, rather, that people will
read it and meditate on it. By doing so, they will merit reward as though
they had studied two tractates from the Mishnah (the earliest compendium of rabbinic law and the foundational document of the curricu-
lum in a rabbinic academy), specifically, the tractates concerning leprosy
and impurity resulting from the presence of a dead body in a dwelling.
These two tractates are among the most difficult and technical parts of
the Mishnah. The locus of value assumed by this comment is Mosaic law;
David's own book can only aspire to match its value. On the other hand,
this comment suggests that one might be able to gain the sort of merit
associated with Torah study through recitation of psalms, which puts the
Psalter on the same level as Torah—at least if the Psalter is studied as a
Mitnagdic text.

The midrash addresses the relation between prayer and study directly
in 1§16, which comments on Ps 1:2 ("But he takes delight in Yhwh's

Torah, studying His Torah day and night" AT). Rabbi Eliezer asserts there that Israel wanted to study Torah all the time (to the exclusion of all other activities), but they did not have the opportunity to do so. God reassured Israel by referring to *tefillin* or prayer-phylacteries that Jews wear each day as they recite the morning prayers. By observing the commandment to wear tefillin, the children of Israel bring upon themselves merit equal to that gained by constant study. Rabbi Joshua suggests another response by God. According to Joshua, the recitation of the Shema prayer in the morning and in the evening can be the functional substitute for constant Torah study.[156] In spite of their differences, Eliezer and Joshua share a basic perspective: some form of prayer (whether nonverbal prayer through the donning of tefillin or verbal prayer through the recitation of the Shema) can be the moral equivalent of Torah study. A scholar named Bar Qappara, however, has a very different suggestion: a person who recites two chapters from scripture each morning and two each evening has, for all practical purposes, fulfilled the ideal of constant Torah study. Rabbi Ḥiyya explains that Bar Qappara meant not only that a person should recite the two chapters but should engage in their elucidation; the requirement, then, involves not only two chapters of scripture itself but two *halachot* or legal teachings from rabbinic tradition as well. This section moves on to other matters, ending with a statement of Rabbi Naḥman in the name of Rabbi Mani: a person who praises God seven times a day (in accordance with Ps 119:164) has performed the equivalent of constant Torah study. *Midrash Tehillim* 1§16 gives voice to rabbis who assert the Hasidic viewpoint (Eliezer, Joshua, Naḥman, and Mani) as well as ones who uphold the Mitnagdic view (Bar Qappara, Ḥiyya). While the last word comes from one of the former, no definitive resolution is reached.

Midrash Tehillim, in short, begins by addressing precisely the same question implied by the redactional setting of Ps 1: is the Psalter fundamentally a Hasidic or Mitnagdic book? The midrash directs our attention to two aspects of this polarity: the dichotomy between king and priest or sage, and the dichotomy between prayer and study. It provides a range of answers to the implied question. Insofar as it includes voices that value David over Moses or at least put them on an equal footing, it undermines Ps 1's attempt to transform the Psalter into a Mitnagdic anthology. At the same time, it allows for a variety of rabbinic opinions to be expressed on the issue. Thus the midrash to Ps 1 reenacts the juxtaposition evident in the final form of the Psalter, which begins with a Mitnagdic voice in

Ps 1, moves directly to a Hasidic voice in Ps 2, and ends with another Hasidic voice in Ps 150.

In the foregoing, I have attempted to draw a comparison between the explicit discussions of the rabbis in *Midr. Tehillim* 1 and the implied discussions of the redactors who placed Pss 1, 2, and 150 in their canonical locations. This sort of comparison provides a clear example of what I have called a dialogical biblical theology. Some models for biblical theology emphasize the work of the final redactors; these would attempt either to harmonize the tension between Ps 1 and Pss 2 and 150[157] or to privilege the voice of what we think is the final redactor.[158] A dialogical biblical theology, however, puts no particular emphasis on the redactor.[159] The message of the redactor who made Ps 1 the abstract for the Psalter is not definitive for a Jewish exegete. But the questions implied by the redactional placement of Ps 1 emerge as Jewishly interesting for two reasons. The first of these is the fact that rabbinic exegetes picked up on those questions, even as they sometimes answered it in ways differing from the proposal of Ps 1 itself. The second is the fact that the questions with which the redactors and *Midr. Tehillim* concern themselves are addressed not only in the midrash to Ps 1 but in many other parts of rabbinic and postrabbinic Jewish literature, usually in formulations that do not refer to Ps 1 itself (for example, in the Talmudic passages quoted above). In other words, it is not merely the work of the redactors but postbiblical Jewish tradition that must guide an attempt to generate a Jewish biblical theology, and in this case, Jewish tradition clearly used the ancient debate among the psalms' redactors as a starting point for continuing the redactors' discourse. In the particular case under discussion, the various rabbinic answers largely follow in the path of the biblical answers, since the rabbinic answers, like the redactors' answers, can be readily classified as either Hasidic or Mitnagdic. It is also possible, however, that postbiblical thinkers will continue to address the biblical questions while providing new sorts of answers. In questions of theodicy, for example, the rabbinic doctrine that human beings are rewarded and punished after death is just barely adumbrated in biblical texts.

A description of this cross-generational discussion is representative of a Jewish theology that turns toward scripture without eclipsing tradition. In the end, neither the Psalter nor *Midr. Tehillim* provides a definitive answer to the questions at hand. Both contain Hasidic as well as Mitnagdic voices, and any reading of the Psalter's final form or of the midrash that privileges one perspective over another is a reflection of the reader, not of the texts themselves. One could, for example, claim that the first psalm is the most important and hence that the Psalter is ultimately Mitnagdic; but one could just as easily argue that the last psalm is conclusive, and therefore the Psalter is Hasidic. Similarly, Jewish tradition in its widest senses never fully resolves the debate concerning prayer and study or the controversy regarding the most ideal model of leadership. While the Talmuds clearly lean in one direction, many alternative voices are preserved in their pages, and even more appear in haggadic rabbinic literature outside the Talmuds. Further, we have seen that later forms of Judaism continue the debate. It is significant that Hasidism, which began in the eighteenth century by emphasizing one of these sets of values, moved within a few generations to a sort of rapprochement with the other, even as the Mitnagdim produced thinkers who valued direct contact with God and messianism. The biblical redactors, then, did not so much provide an *answer* as an *agenda* concerning what issues are to be pondered. Consequently, a Jewish biblical theology need not—in fact, should not—set for itself the goal of definitively stating what the Bible says; rather, it should look for what the Bible invites us to attend to, and it should examine how rabbinic and later Jewish literatures pick up that invitation. It is by attending to the same issues, and by turning them over and turning them over again, that Jewish biblical theology can become part of the all-encompassing discussion that is Torah.

Kingship and Messianism[160]

My second example of a Jewish hermeneutic for reading the Bible theologically and dialogically focuses on attitudes toward kingship in biblical, rabbinic, and contemporary Jewish thought. Scholars have often noted the range of attitudes toward human kingship in the Hebrew Bible. It is particularly noteworthy that even within a single book two distinct attitudes may be present. This is quite evident in both the book of Isaiah and the book of Samuel.

In the first section of the book of Isaiah (chaps. 1–39) we find the work of an author or authors deeply committed to the Davidic monarchy. (If only for convenience, I will refer to this author or authors as "Isaiah.") Following the covenant of grant (known to us from texts such as Ps 89 and 2 Sam 7), Isaiah trusts that there will be an eternal royal line descended from David. Unlike his older contemporary Hosea (see Hos 5:1; 7:3-4; 8:4), he never condemns the institution of monarchy itself, even if he sometimes is frustrated by a particular king. He reacts with horror at the prospect of the Davidic monarch being replaced with someone from another family in chapters 7–8; when King Ahaz rejects the prophet's counsel by disdaining YHWH's protection, Isaiah predicts that Judah will be invaded, but he does not foresee the overthrow of the monarchy or the surrender of David's city. Indeed, the notion of Zion's inviolability is central to Isaiah's work (viz. to Isa 1–39).[161] The prophet's hope for the future is bound up with the Davidic monarchy: the era of universal peace and recognition of YHWH that Isaiah famously predicts will be ushered in by a member of the royal family, an ideal king who will also be a prophet. This king's ability to judge perfectly (not on the basis of mere empirical evidence but on the basis of his prophetic spirit; see 11:2-3) will result not only in justice for his own subjects but in peace for the world. In 2:2-4, we learn that in this ideal future, nations in conflict will submit to arbitration at Mount Zion. The temple will become the headquarters of a divine Security Council with a membership of One and unsurpassed ability to ensure compliance. The divine ruling (*tôrâ*) that nations receive in 2:3 will come through the mediation of the Davidic prophet-king described in Isa 11:1-10. In short, the first part of the book of Isaiah evinces a matrix of closely related ideas: the perpetual right of the David monarchy to rule over Judah; the eternally protected status of that dynasty's capital city; the belief that a Davidic king ruling in that city will lead the way to humanity's happy submission to the world's sole Being worthy of exaltation. Whether this matrix of ideas is the product of the eighth-century Isaiah himself or a later redactor is not important to the point I wish to make here; what matters for my purposes is the presence and consistency of the ideology of David and Zion in chapters 1–39.[162]

When we move past chapter 39, however, we find a completely different set of ideas. (I shall refer to the author or authors of Isa 40–66 as Deutero-Isaiah, since these chapters present a single consistent point of view in regard to the issues at hand.) Writing during and after the Babylonian exile, Deutero-Isaiah had no loyalty to the (now unemployed) Davidic dynasty and did not look forward to its renewal. To be sure, the royal family still existed in this prophet's day, as the end of 2 Kings reminds us. Nevertheless, Deutero-Isaiah does not hope for the renewal of its rule. This aspect of the prophet's thought becomes evident in the many allusions found in Isa 40–66. When Deutero-Isaiah borrows phrasing and ideas from older biblical texts that valorize the Davidic monarchy, this prophet of restoration pointedly omits any reference to the king and nationalizes whatever motif was associated with him. For example, in 60:17–61:1, Deutero-Isaiah borrows multiple terms and motifs from Isa 11: the terms *nēṣer* ("sprout," 11:1 // 60:21); *rûaḥ* ("spirit," 11:2 // 61:1); the root *ṣdq* expressing "just rule" (11:3-5 // 60:17); *ʾereṣ* ("land," 11:4 // 60:21); and the theme of peace within the city (11:6-9 // 60:18). Further, the idea of nations coming to Zion appears in 11:11 and in 60:5-10. Both passages look forward to an ideal era of justice and its inevitable consequence, peace. But Deutero-Isaiah does not mention a king who will usher in this new era by ruling equitably. Vocabulary that described the king's role in Isaiah is now applied to the people as a whole. The "sprout" in 11:1 referred to the new or future Davidic monarch, but in 60:21 the "sprout" planted by YHWH is the nation Israel. In 11:4-5, the king governs in justice and wears justice as a garment, but in 60:21 we are told, "Your whole people are the just ones" (AT). When reshaping the earlier prophecy, Deutero-Isaiah transfers royal prerogatives to the nation even as he refrains from predicting that a new king will arise.[163]

The same pattern occurs in other Deutero-Isaianic allusions as well. Three passages, Isa 44:28–45:8; 49:7-23; and 60:1-21, borrow vocabulary and motifs from the royal poem in Ps 72. When reworking material from this psalm, the prophet consistently removes any reference to the Davidic dynasty. What happened to the king in the psalm provides the pattern for what happens to the people as a whole in the Deutero-Isaianic texts. For example, in the psalm, foreign rulers bowed down before the king, but in Deutero-Isaiah they pay obeisance either to the city of Jerusalem or to the people dwelling there. The transference of royal motifs to the whole nation Israel is perhaps most evident in Isa 55:3.[164] There we read:

> Incline your ears, all of you, and come to Me;
> Listen, so you will live,
> So that I will make with you an eternal covenant,
> The steadfast allegiance belonging to David. (AT)

These lines reassign the Davidic covenant to the whole nation; the allegiance God swore to David's family in texts such as 2 Sam 7 and Ps 89 is now understood to refer to his family in the broadest sense—including all Israelites, not just direct descendants of Jesse, David, or Solomon.

(The second-person plural forms of address in the Hebrew of these lines are significant, since they make clear that God is speaking to a group here, not to one would-be king.) A different sort of transfer occurs in Isa 44:24–45:8. There Deutero-Isaiah borrows vocabulary from Ps 2, in which God expressed a special favor for David and his descendants. Deutero-Isaiah applies the crucial terminology not to a member of the Davidic family but to the Persian emperor Cyrus.[165]

Deutero-Isaiah's repeated refusal to apply Davidic language to an actual Davidic king is striking—especially since other exilic and early postexilic texts do express hope for the monarchy's renewal (Jer 33:14-16; Ezek 37; Zech 3:8; 4:6-10; 6:12; and Hag 1:12-15; 2:21-23). That Deutero-Isaiah nowhere refers to a king in the renewed commonwealth intimates that he did not look forward to a restoration of the monarchy. Deutero-Isaiah's allusions to Davidic promises nullify the special status of the royal family, since the whole nation Israel (and also a foreign ruler) share in what had been the Davidides' unique relationship with YHWH.

A different, and more complex, duality of attitude is found in the carefully coordinated unit that is the books of Judges and Samuel. Second Samuel 7 represents the apogee of the pro-Davidic viewpoint as it promises David that his descendants will never be removed from the throne, thus presenting God as an advocate of the Davidic monarchy. On the other hand, texts like 1 Sam 8 regard the monarchy as an unfortunate if unavoidable concession to human frailty, while 2 Sam 11–24 paint a devastating portrait of God's favorite and his family. More important, some texts that are clearly promonarchy turn out, when reread in light of what comes later, to intimate a more ambivalent posture. The book of Judges concludes with a description of the sexual misconduct, violence, and civil war that capped off the era of the chieftains (chaps. 17–21). This section, with its repeated line, "In those days there was no king in Israel" (17:6; 18:1; 21:25), clearly looks forward to the rise of kingship as the solution to the chaos that results from the absence of central authority. More specifically, it looks forward to Davidic kingship rather than Saulide kingship.[166] All the villains in the horrific story of the concubine at Gibeah in Judg 19–21 connect in one way or another to Saul as depicted in 1 Samuel. For example, the rapists in Judg 19 are, like Saul, Benjaminites from Gibeah; the cruel husband cuts his concubine's body into twelve pieces that he sends to all the tribes, just as Saul cuts a pair of oxen into twelve pieces that he sends to all the tribes. The concubine is the only character for whom the readers feel sympathy, and she hails from David's hometown, Bethlehem. Thus the story not only describes kingship as the solution to chaos and lawlessness but recommends David's monarchy over Saul's. On the other hand, the end of the narrative of David's reign in 2 Samuel describes a nation in which the king's family is responsible for sexual misconduct (David's adultery with Bathsheba in 2 Sam 11; Amnon's incestuous rape of Tamar in 2 Sam 13), violence (Absalom's murder of Amnon in chapter 13), and civil war (Absalom's followers vs. David's in chapters 15–18). It is no coincidence that the historians who shaped the books of Judges and Samuel describe precisely the same problems at the end of Judges and Samuel. Read in light of the last part of 2 Samuel, the pro-Davidic text in Judg 19–21 turns out to contain a hidden polemic against David: the solution to the three problems described at the end of Judges re-created just those three problems at the end of Samuel.[167]

Another pro-Davidic text appears in Hannah's song in 1 Sam 2, and this text too contains a hidden polemic against David. This poem proclaims that God gives triumph to his anointed king (v. 10). This and other examples of royal language (e.g., the glorious throne in v. 8) make clear that in the wider context of the book of Samuel, the poem concerns not just the newborn baby Samuel but the monarchy that the elderly Samuel will one day establish. Moreover, when one reads further into 1 Samuel, one realizes that the poem, with its repeated references to the surprising elevation of a humble person to great prestige, hints forward to the humble shepherd, the youngest brother from an insignificant clan, who becomes King David. Yet the disastrous end of David's career makes clear that the language of this poem cuts both ways. Seen from the perspective of the beginning of his career, David is the poor man whom God lifts up to sit on the throne of glory (1 Sam 2:8). But from the perspective of his later career, he is the wicked man who is silenced in the darkness, having realized that it is not by means of power that a person prevails (1 Sam 2:9). "God casts down, but He also lifts up high," Hannah tells us in 1 Sam 2:7—which means that while God lifts up high, God also casts down (AT).[168]

It would be simplistic to find a pro-Davidic source and an anti-Davidic source in Judges and Samuel, since some passages—indeed, some verses and even phrases—are both pro and anti. Rather, these books form a literary unity that evinces an extraordinarily intricate understanding of an extraordinarily enigmatic character. Even at its most negative, the book of Samuel does not quite repudiate the monarchy. It endorses monarchy, while reminding us how dangerous the monarchy will be.

These tensions within the Bible on the question of kingship foreshadow a debate in later Judaism. It is at this point that the tensions become relevant to a dialogical biblical theology, for the recognition that biblical documents engage in a discussion similar to that found in postbiblical Judaism at once legitimizes the postbiblical debate and sets parameters for it.

For most of the late Persian and the early Hellenistic periods, we find no indications that Jews hoped for the renewal of the Davidic monarchy: Deutero-Isaiah's viewpoint prevailed over those of Haggai and Zechariah. But at some point during the Hellenistic period, this hope suddenly reemerged, leading to the various forms of messianism so well known from late Second Temple period Judaism.[169] Belief in a Davidic messiah had become a Jewish standard belief by the time rabbinic Judaism began to emerge in the first and second centuries C.E. The Talmudic rabbis pay considerable attention to the messiah, speculating on the timing of his arrival, debating whether it is even advisable to predict this timing, and discussing ways Jews can hasten it (see especially *b. San.* 93b–94a, 96b–99a; *Midr. Tehillim* 2). Some rabbinic statements glorify the messiah to an extraordinary degree, attributing magical or godlike powers to him (e.g., *Midr. Tehillim* 2:3; the opinion of R. Yoḥanan in *b. Sanhedrin* 98b). Nevertheless, as Reuven Kimelman shows, the *Amidah* prayer (the so-called "Eighteen Benedictions"), recited thrice daily in rabbinic Judaism, downplays messianism.[170] This is highly significant, since the *Amidah* is the single summary of central beliefs the rabbinic movement produced; as Daniel Leifer pointed out to me, the *Amidah* functions as the rabbinic credo.[171] Consequently, it is of great import that the daily *Amidah* never use the word *messiah* and never refer to the future Davidic ruler as a king. It does, however, pointedly include the phrase "May You [God] rule over us as our king" in its eleventh blessing, which articulates the hope for the restoration of Jewish political sovereignty without even alluding to the Davidic monarchy. True, the future Davidic ruler is mentioned (without the term "messiah") in the first, fourteenth, and fifteenth blessings. But Kimelman astutely notes that the Davidic king's appearances in these three blessings are even more revealing, for they never make him the subject of an active verb. In the *Amidah* the Davidic monarch's role is entirely passive: he is brought by God and placed on the throne so that he can be seen by the people as a symbol of the new era. This central rabbinic document, then, reduces the messiah as much as possible without actually jettisoning the concept altogether. Rabbinic Judaism, then, includes voices that emphasize the Davidic monarch's role in the eschatological future and voices that minimize his role.

This same tension reemerges more strongly in modern Judaism. While Orthodox forms of Judaism continue to hope for a personal Davidic messiah, Reform Judaism has for well over a century renounced belief in this man. This difference is made clear in the liturgies of the various Jewish movements. Orthodox and most Conservative liturgies continue to use the classical rabbinic *Amidah*, which, we have seen, refers to God as bringing a redeemer to the Jewish people, even though it never makes that redeemer the subject of an active verb and assigns him no specific redemptive role. The *Amidah* prayers of Reform and (more recently) Reconstructionist prayer books go even further in the direction the classical rabbinic prayer began. In the first blessing of these versions, God brings *redemption* (*gĕʾûlâ*), not a *redeemer* (*gôʾēl*). The modern dispute between the liberal and traditional versions of the *Amidah*, like the tension involving rabbinic texts that mention the messiah, is not a new one. It closely resembles the conflicts we found in scripture: Orthodox Jewish thinkers affirm a role for the Davidic monarchy (like First Isaiah) while Reform thinkers pointedly ignore any such role (like Deutero-Isaiah). When we examine the liturgy of the former, the text of the *Amidah* might be seen as pro-messianic (it at least mentions the idea) or more neutral (since its messianic language is so reserved); thus, as was the case with Judges–Samuel, our understanding of their liturgy depends on the context in which we examine it.

Parallels of this sort may prove to be of interest to not only the historian of ideas but to the theologian as well, and to the biblical theologian in both roles. What might seem like a radical revision made by Reform Jews in the nineteenth and twentieth centuries turns out to be in some sense conservative or even reactionary. By emphasizing divine kingship at the expense of human kingship, Reform Jews are simply reviving a line of theologizing that goes back to one part of scripture, rather than subscribing to another. A self-styled traditionalist who would condemn Reform theology on this point should pause to realize that the object of her polemic encompasses not only modern innovators in Berlin and Cincinnati but much older and indubitably venerable figures as well. At the same time, the biblical precedent in some ways might challenge a Reform thinker. The final form of the book of Isaiah, after all, includes both the pro- and antiroyalist positions, and the Deuteronomistic History mixes these positions together in Judges and Samuel. The practice of the rather pluralistic anthologizers who created scripture might be contrasted with the anthologizers who produce contemporary Reform prayer books such as *The Gates of Prayer*.[172] This prayer book contains multiple versions of the *Amidah* prayer, but all of them reflect the nonroyalist point of view. Given their innovative decision to present worshipers with several different versions of a prayer from which to choose, it seems somewhat unscriptural not to follow the lead of the book of Isaiah by providing both royalist and nonroyalist options. One recent Conservative prayer book moves in this direction: it includes two versions of the first paragraph of the *Amidah*, one with the word *redeemer* and one with *redemption*.[173] No Orthodox prayer book presents any choices of this sort.

As was the case with my previous example, an investigation into attitudes toward monarchy (and perhaps more broadly, political power) typifies dialogical biblical theology. The Bible does not present a doctrine so much as it endorses an agenda. Postbiblical literature does not find a harmonizing spot on the continuum between polarities that affects a compromise but insists on maintaining the polarity itself.

CONCLUSION

The foregoing examples have shown that dialogical biblical theology is not totalizing, comprehensive, and grand in the style of the classic biblical theologies of the twentieth century. It does not limit itself to large, hard-cover two-volume works! It attends to discrete texts or to particular issues as they appear throughout the Bible or in one section of the Bible. Rather than attempting a crosscut of the whole of scripture, dialogical biblical theology remains content with a close reading of particular selections.[174] This is because a dialogical biblical theologian realizes that a theology of *part* of the Bible can be as major a contribution to biblical theology as an attempt to deal with the whole. If dialogue between biblical and postbiblical figures is the most productive model for biblical theology, then the participants on the biblical side need not be limited to the canonizers or the redactors. On the contrary: the goal of this venture is to foster discussion among ancient, medieval, and modern voices, and for this reason too much attention to the voice of the redactor or canonizer would squelch other voices who deserve a place at the table. It is not only the final form of, say, the Torah or the book of Samuel that is relevant to this project; the discrete entities within those collections may be just as interesting conversation partners. P, or J, or Dtr$_1$ have just as much right to participate in this conversation as do the redactors or canonizers. In stressing the need to examine discrete texts underlying our biblical books, I am not necessarily proposing to undo the work of the redactors. After all, in a great many cases these redactors knowingly put together documents full of tension without doing much to dampen our perceptions of those tensions. They might very well be pleased to know that contemporary scholars revel in the dialect they devised. On the other hand, exegetes who attempt to bring that dialectic to closure or to find unity within a canonical form of a text may often work against the biblical redactors.

I shall conclude with a reflection on the method of dialogical biblical theology. Stendahl and Oeming maintain that the biblical theologian does not just describe but may at times evaluate. Neither scholar, however, addresses the question: how, precisely, does the modern religious scholar measure biblical and postbiblical texts against each other? The examples above (not only my own concrete examples but the work by Greenberg and Braiterman I summarize) suggest that if biblical theology genuinely intends to participate in contemporary Jewish or Christian religious thought, then scholars must seek answers to these questions within each tradition's own history of exegesis. For example, Jewish biblical theologians would think about appropriating, accepting, or rejecting biblical teachings in light of the ways rabbinic traditions have appropriated, accepted, and rejected the Bible over the past two millennia. The process of grappling with scripture is by no means new, even if we are more conscious that we are engaging in it than our forebears tended to be. A Jewish scholar, in short, will set up a three-way discussion among the ancient Near Eastern anthology that is the Hebrew Bible, rabbinic literatures, and modern Jewish communities of readers. A Christian scholar would create a discussion among the Testaments, Christian theology in its richly differing manifestations, and contemporary Christians.[175] It follows, then, that dialogical biblical theology is an unambiguously confessional enterprise, since the measures of value that are used to evaluate biblical texts and that are themselves measured by biblical texts come from confessional traditions. It is important to note, nevertheless, that (contra John Collins's supposition) a confessional enterprise is not exempt from the demands of argumentation that characterize academic study of the

Bible.[176] A confessional enterprise rooted in a tradition of interpretation involves exegetical argumentation rather than baldly asserted faith-claims. Thus this model also moves away from the model proposed by Brueggemann, for whom "there is no court of appeal beyond the [biblical] text itself."[177] Here we arrive at an essential feature of dialogical biblical theology: for religious Jews and Christians (at least those willing to jettison the concept of *sola scriptura*),[178] there is indeed an appropriate discussion partner for scripture: to wit, tradition, which grew up alongside scripture and continues to evolve today.[179]

The respective Jewish and Christian discussions among voices from scripture and from tradition will prove useful, and not only for members of each confessional group.[180] These discussions will focus our attention on aspects of biblical thought that we might have missed otherwise, and thus will aid even the historian of ideas for whom the confessional enterprise of the dialogical biblical theologian is uninteresting. They show that certain modern religious concerns are not solely modern but were concerns of ancient authors as well. The dialogical biblical theologian will find surprising points of contact between later religious readings and overlooked aspects of the biblical texts recovered by modern critical methods.[181]

Moreover, the interpretations offered by the dialogical biblical theologian reveal limits on the process of appropriation and rejection. Jewish texts from Psalms on engage in a debate concerning what form of religious experience is the most important, study or prayer, but they consistently recognize the importance of each. This suggests something important about attempts to jettison one or the other form of religious experience. These attempts might include a purely academic or intellectual Judaic experience without a liturgical component, or a spiritual consciousness based on Jewish mystical practice without an anchor in the traditional study of classical Jewish texts. An intellectual or spiritual trend of either sort moves outside the bounds of the flexible and varied stream of Jewish tradition. Similarly, one cannot overlook the fact that both Isaiahs remain confident, in the face of increasingly enormous amounts of evidence they witnessed in their own lifetimes, that God would ultimately bring salvation, even though they disagreed regarding the role a particular family would play in that event. Judaism's eschatologies are diverse, but a Judaism without an eschatology is not possible.

By uncovering these connections within a tradition, by shedding light on neglected parts of a tradition, and by establishing parameters of the tradition's discourse, the hermeneutic described here will allow biblical criticism to become a constructive part of theological discourse. It will thus renew the Hebrew Bible's status as a Jewish book and as a Christian book, making clear to both communities what they have in common and where, for the sake of heaven, they agree to differ.

OLD TESTAMENT THEOLOGY SINCE BARTH'S *EPISTLE TO THE ROMANS*

Leo G. Perdue

THE DEVELOPMENT OF BIBLICAL THEOLOGY

The Birth of Modern Biblical Theology[1]

It is appropriate to note at the beginning of this section that the agenda for biblical theology set out in J. P. Gabler's famous inaugural address at the University of Altdorf in 1787, while important for differentiating the dogmatic theology of the church from the historical theology of the Bible, has not been carried out as it was formulated by those doing biblical theology during the past two centuries.[2] This is in part due to the fact that the dichotomy he proposed was too precisely made and not at all capable of being so adroitly articulated in a biblical theology. According to Gabler, an important differentiation should be made between dogmatic (systematic) theology and biblical theology. Prior to Gabler, biblical theology was the handmaiden of dogmatics. This meant that the Bible set forth the divine, universal, eternal truths that dogmatic theology was to arrange in systematic order. In opposing this view, Gabler argued that biblical theology was a historical enterprise that sought to portray the theology of the biblical authors. The appropriate method to follow was historical criticism. Gabler makes the distinction between true biblical theology that is the limited, conditional theology of the biblical writers (historicism), and pure biblical theology that seeks to discover the eternal theological truths of divine revelation (idealism). Dogmatic or systematic theology was concerned to shape a coherent theology that applied the theological truths of pure biblical theology to the contemporary world. Thus, Gabler tried to mediate between biblical theology as a historical exercise to reconstruct the history of Israelite religious ideas and biblical theology as a tool of systematic theology that was to incorporate the salient, universal ideas of the Bible into a systematic form addressing current situations.[3] Gabler's agenda is somewhat flawed and incomplete, since he leaves out the issues of context, the questions of truth and the possibility of its attainment, and diversity, and lacks a more nuanced epistemology in which the interpreter participates in determining meaning. Heuristically, however, Gabler's dichotomy might be embraced as an operating procedure that allows for the differentiation between ancient belief and modern faith.

The Concept of Biblical Theology

An important place to begin this concluding section of more recent trends is the definition of biblical theology. One of the major problems confronting contemporary scholarship has been that of clearly defining this discipline and its purposes, methods, and objectives. In his recent volume, *The Concept of Biblical Theology*, James Barr has dealt in detail with the issue of definition, although the approaches he is willing to concede have value as biblical theology are limited to those that came to the fore prior to the 1980s. In my judgment, this is a serious shortcoming, for it limits theological discourse to historicism. Yet his study is a place to start in seeking to obtain necessary clarity about the concept of biblical theology. According to Barr, there have been several key ways of defining and understanding biblical theology. This concept has been seen as:

1. "something that is done by biblical scholars, whether of Old or New Testament."

2. "something new, in the sense that it is searching for something that is not already known." It is not "something already laid down in a past or ancient tradition." Rather, it *is something that has still to be discovered.*"

3. something "possessing an *ecumenical* potential," even though the "actual theologies that have emerged have been very different."

4. something that should be asked "whether (it) is really theology in the proper sense at all." This means that biblical theology must have "features and aspects that are *analogous* to the working of theology in the proper sense."

5. something "having clarity only when it is understood to mean theology as it existed or was thought or believed within the time, languages and cultures of the Bible itself." This implies that the concerns of biblical theology have often come from people of the modern period seeking answers to their questions from the texts of the Bible. Yet these modern questions must pay close attention to the views of the cultures that expressed their faiths in the content of scriptural texts.

For Barr, biblical theology is at its essence a "*contrastive* notion." This "notion" assumes a different shape, depending on its contrast with each of the following:

1. Doctrinal (systematic, dogmatic, or constructive) theology. Normally, biblical theology has been understood as a descriptive, historical discipline in contrast to dogmatic theology (viewed as the articulation of what is to be believed by Christians) in the variety of Christian communities.

2. Nontheological study of the Bible. Historical criticism largely has concerned itself with textual philology, historical background, older literary criticism, form criticism, and tradition history and not, as is the case with biblical theology, with the "message" of the Bible, its theological themes, and its underlying convictions for the communities of faith.

3. History of religions and corresponding approaches. The approach of historians of religions tends to speak of the biblical writers' borrowing from earlier and concurrent ancient Near Eastern and Greco-Roman religions. At times the biblical understanding wrongly was thought to have evolved in order to reach a "higher plane." In

addition, the biblical references to other cultures and their religions are often obscure. Nevertheless, the study of these religions tends to fill in the gaps in the historian's knowledge to understand the distinctive features of Old Testament religious thought. These distinguishing characteristics of the Hebrew biblical texts and the religion of Israel have been viewed at times as expressive of true faith in contrast to the false views of so-called pagan religions. Of course, this latter argument largely has been rejected.

4. Philosophical theology and natural theology. Many modern scholars (e.g., Karl Barth and Krister Stendahl) have argued that biblical thought contrasts with modern philosophical approaches, including natural reason. This view contends that revelation through biblical writers and their texts contrasts with understandings of God and the sacred that may derive from human reason and the understanding of the world.

5. The interpretation of *parts* of the Bible as distinct from the larger complexes taken as *wholes*. This view presents the understanding that individual texts and traditions have their own unique theologies and not a common theology running throughout. To write a comprehensive biblical theology is thought to be impossible.

Barr's articulation is especially clear, but it operates on the basis of a rather dated set of assumptions that include a positivistic understanding of history and language, a rather inflexible rationalism, and a traditional set of theological approaches that do not take into consideration the significant developments in theological thinking of the past two decades. His criticism of postmodernism, for example, provides some insight into his reluctance to regard this method as one of biblical theology. But it would be helpful to know his reasons for omitting contemporary understandings of biblical theology, which, in addition to postmodernism, include feminism, ethnicity, narratology, imagination, sexual orientation, and postcolonialism. He also ignores many of the pressing hermeneutical issues and contemporary reconfigurations required of theological reflection in writing an Old Testament theology that addresses modern concerns. His book, while incisive and trenchant in the analysis of older methods, was apt for the 1980s and older historical-critical approaches but is sorely devoid of contemporary theological readings.

Barr professes that he sees biblical theology, on the one hand, as a discipline that describes the faith of the biblical periods and, on the other hand, as normative for articulating modern faith and practice. This distinction is significant to maintain in the study of biblical theology, and yet it is the second part of his agenda that, in my judgment, falls short in his book. I also do not think that hermeneutical judgments should be bracketed, for there are contemporary biblical theologians who build bridges between biblical text and contemporary implications that are much more substantial and compelling than his remarks suggest. One is also disappointed in discovering that he is never clear about contemporary hermeneutical methods for understanding the contribution of biblical theology to modern discourse. The question for me is whether the biblical scholar is competent to move from a biblical text through the traditions of the church over the centuries into the present and thus to present his or her own articulation of the faith. This may be done, but only with hard work and a self-imposed demand to attempt to make biblical theology address the present.[4]

KARL BARTH AND DIALECTICAL THEOLOGY

Karl Barth (1886–1968), who became the most significant theologian of the twentieth century, broke the strong grip of the history of religions approach on biblical studies with the appearance of his commentary *Der Römerbrief* in 1919, only a year following the end of the Great War.[5] While Swiss, Barth was teaching at Bonn when Hitler became the Führer of Germany. Barth was expelled from Germany when he refused to take the oath of loyalty to Hitler and later participated in the Confessing Church against the Nazi tyranny. He returned to his native Switzerland and joined the faculty of Basel, where he served as professor of theology. He largely shaped the Barmen Declaration.

Barth emphasized that the theological key to the interpretation of the Bible resided in the word of God that was located in both scripture and the believing community and not in human religious experience or in the social and cultural life of human beings.[6] He insisted theology must be relevant to the life of the contemporary church, while the Bible was to serve as the foundation for that theology. The unifying feature of his biblical interpretation expressed frequently in his *Church Dogmatics* is the affirmation that the Bible serves as a witness to the word of God. He interpreted scripture as the canon, rather than as a text reconstructed by historical criticism. Scripture contains the word of God, most fully realized in Jesus Christ, and speaks in human words that comprise proclamation as encounter. Even so, the word of God is not to be confused with human words, for God is not comprehended by anyone. The Word of God is the Divine Spirit located in and empowering Scripture. It is possible for the church to know the Word of God only through this text and yet, at the same time, this knowledge allows for the proper interpretation of the text. This Word of God is not an element of the thought worlds of human beings or their cultures but rather is the divine Christ, who, as the Word, addresses them and demands a yes or a no answer. This means for Barth that the word of God is a dialectic, not in the sense of Hegel but rather in the understanding that this divine word addresses human beings and requires a response. As a confessing Christian, Barth stressed that all biblical texts were to be understood in their relationship to Jesus Christ. Thus, Barth gives a christocentric interpretation to the Old Testament, and not only to the New. Jesus Christ is not only the one to whom biblical texts testify but also the one who is the active subject of the salvific narratives that comprise the Christian story. Barth's interpretation of scripture centers on the themes that may be shaped into dogmatic tenets and on the narratives of the Bible that comprise the gospel's story for the community of faith. Barth's influence, while not pervasive in Protestant discourse, did lead to a rekindling of interest in the writing of biblical theology. We need, argues Barth, a new Old Testament theology that cannot be brought about simply by reconstructing its history of religion. This is due to the belief that Christian faith for modern humanity is not primarily historical.[7] The major disappointment for Old Testament scholars is that, while Barth knew of historical criticism as practiced in his day and used it to achieve and support some of his theological positions, he still reverted at times to a more literal interpretation of the Bible, thus avoiding historical issues of complexity regarding its diversity, chronological lapses, factual errors, and limited viewpoints.

The Epistle to the Romans[8]

As Bultmann noted, Barth's commentary on the *Epistle to the Romans* may be summarized by one sentence: "The book attempts to prove *the independence and the absolute nature of religion*."[9] It makes a radical distinction, as does the Epistle, between faith and works. Barth seeks to oppose forcibly the psychologizing and ethicizing concept of religion dominant in the Liberalism of Ritschl and Harnack. He rejects any effort to understand religion as issuing forth from the sociocultural context of historical life.

For Barth, faith has to do with the unspeakable reality of the divine encounter with the transcendent God. In this understanding, Barth repudiates both historicism that equates faith with human experiences in the world of events and psychologism that identifies feelings, emotions, desires, piety, and mysticism with religious belief. Grace that allows the encounter leading to belief is beyond human grasping. Faith comes only by the divine encounter, initiated by the God who is wholly other.

Barth rejects any affirmation of nature as the revelation of God. Natural religion limits God to a worldly form, which negates his total otherness and transcendence and supposes that faith is nothing other than human perception of the world to come to a knowledge of and thus faith in God. God is neither a psychological impulse nor one who stimulates it, and God is not a natural power whose character may be derived and perceived by human observation. Thus, there is not an inherent dualism avowed by Barth in which God and the world are opposites, but rather a dialectic, that is, a contrast between God and the world that must be transcended. The announcement of the Divine Word that encounters humans is the means by which faith that transcends the bounds of space and time is created as a vital entity of human engagement with the Other. Barth also rejects mysticism, or a flight from the world, as well as asceticism and martyrdom as paths to God. Faith negates any human effort to come to a knowledge of God. What Barth affirms, then, is a Pauline radicalism concerning faith and grace. Even so, within the confines of this No is the Yes, for denial of the world is the necessary precondition of faith. This No issues from the awareness of crisis into which we find ourselves as human beings. We stand in our nakedness reaching toward the Yes of redemption. Only from redemption can one grasp the fact that one is unredeemed, only from righteousness that one is a sinner, only from life that one is not justified, redeemed, saved. The No that confronts us is God's No. The condition of faith becomes possible only by subjecting oneself to the No of God.

Faith as a Miracle

The world is conditioned by sin: this includes history, nature, and humanity. All people stand under the judgment of God. The world is one of relativity and death. Thus, as believers we say no to the world. We are ultimately and totally dependent on God for redemption. Thus, the first no to the world is spoken by God. Its foundation is the negation of all worldly wisdom, when there is a complete and total giving up of self to God. This submission is neither resignation nor despair. It is only a miracle that produces faith. Faith is the breaking into history and the human encounter of God himself in the incarnate Word. God is always beyond human reach. Faith is always a new creation in which there is a no to self and a yes to God.

Barth influenced, to a degree, the formation of Old Testament theology, beginning with Eichrodt and continuing through von Rad into the present. Indeed, one may trace several Barthian features of dialectical theology that permeated the efforts to revive the biblical discipline. These included von Rad's rejection of creation as a theological doctrine due to its easy identification with natural theology.

Barth also faulted cultic religion as an involvement in myth and liturgical practice that had the tendency to lead to elements of symbolism of natural features and produced mystical experiences. Thus, this rejection of myth and strong criticism of cultic religion, which von Rad discovered in the authentic religion of the prophets, were connected to Barth's dialectic theology. In addition, von Rad saw worship as the context for confessing the salvific acts of God but not as the renewal of creation, at least in the early, more authentic expression of Israelite faith. This was also true of George Ernest Wright, who saw in proclamation the announcing of God's acts in history on Israel's behalf.[10]

Most important in determining Barth's influence on biblical theology is his strong emphasis on covenant, which found expression in Eichrodt and later biblical theologians, including Patrick Miller and Bernhard W. Anderson. However, the stronger influence on these Reformed theologians was federal theology, which took shape after the Reformation and has continued in various streams of theological hermeneutics.[11] Most central to federal theology was the emphasis placed on covenant as the unifying factor for biblical theology. Although presented in a variety of expressions, federal theology included covenants of biblical and systematic theological expression: the covenant of redemption (in more recent biblical theology, the salvation history of the chosen), the covenant of works (including especially ethics, ritual, and legal requirements expressed by the divine will for humanity but impossible to follow in their totality), and the covenant of grace (faith in Christ becomes the means by which salvation is freely granted to the believer by God). In the

Old Testament, the covenant of grace moves through a succession of covenants with Noah, Abraham, Moses, and David. These culminate in the final expression of the supreme covenant of Jesus Christ. These features find their place in the covenantal theologies that will be discussed below.

OLD TESTAMENT THEOLOGY AND THE HISTORY OF RELIGIONS

Since the late nineteenth century, the history of religions and biblical theology often are considered to be different disciplines with different methods, objectives, and orientations. This does not imply that the history of religions has not been used by numerous biblical theologians in understanding Old Testament faith and practice. Even so, the demarcation between the methods and their objectives has often been noted. One of the clearest differentiations between the two disciplines was made in an early, formative essay by Otto Eissfeldt in 1926.[12] According to Eissfeldt, the problem of the polarities of absolute/relative and transcendence/immanence was to be addressed in doing Old Testament theology. The *crux interpretatum* for the Old Testament, raised by the history of religions approach, is whether Israelite religion is one religion among many or is in some way the "true one" as is asserted in Old Testament theology, that is, it consists in some fashion as the revelation of God. According to Eissfeldt, "the religion of the Old Testament [must] be investigated by the same means with which historical scholarship otherwise works: linguistic and historical-critical mastery of the sources, and analysis of their content on the basis of an empathetic personal reliving."[13] Eissfeldt noted that Old Testament theology required that the biblical text move beyond the methods of historical criticism to insist that its message may be accessed only by faith. Arguing from the location of the interpreter standing within the church, Eissfeldt asserted that the importance of the contents of the Old Testament is to be decided on the basis of what is significant for and corresponds to the Christian faith, with Jesus Christ becoming the apex of Christian theology. Thus the relationship between the two Testaments became important for Eissfeldt in his effort to carry out the aims of biblical theology. In spite of their differences, Eissfeldt argued that the two methods are a unity and that they both strive to know the same truth "by which faith is grasped."[14] This correlation of the two disciplines is important, since it offers a corrective to Barthian neo-orthodoxy and its less-than-convincing dichotomy drawn between faith and religion. This Barthian polarity has resurfaced in a variety of Old Testament theologies, perhaps best demonstrated in the theology of Brevard Childs, to be examined shortly, a fact that, in my judgment, diminishes the compelling character and even the value of his presentations.

CLASSICAL APPROACHES TO THE HISTORY OF RELIGIONS[15]

While incorporating numerous and diverse theoretical foundations ranging from comparative religions to cultural-anthropological to social-scientific methods, the history of religions is a compilation of approaches that have in common the effort to set forth the formal expressions of religious practices and ideas emanating from many different cultures.[16] This does not mean that this approach does not on occasion focus attention on one particular religion, but in doing so the efforts to identify the nuances of that religious formulation take explicit shape by comparison and contrast with other religions, in particular those that existed contemporaneously and interacted. Practitioners of this approach seek to explain the development and change of religious themes and practices and their social institutions and roles even within the same culture.

The influences, comparisons, and contrasts are noted in the material culture that includes architecture, art, tools and utensils, cultic paraphernalia, and pottery; and, more important, in the literature (e.g., myths, laws, narratives, legends, royal chronicles, wisdom texts, psalms, and literary metaphors), religious rituals, and social institutions (priesthood, temple, sages, and kingship) of different but geographically and temporarily approximate locations. Proposed similarities and comparisons, while some have been dubious, may be explained in a variety of ways, including cross-cultural borrowing and the sharing of a common cultural context. Yet, others may be due to the participation of different cultures in analogous social, economic, and anthropological locations and processes that are unrelated. Of course, some appear to be only tangential to Israelite religion. In addition, even when Israel appropriated a particular element, it may have been transformed into an understanding or practice that made it acceptable to its new religion. However, a conservative trend, represented by the Albright school, has argued ideologically that Israel transformed mythic traditions and other aspects of ancient Near Eastern religions into forms compatible with and expressive of their own beliefs and views. This seems to be an obvious way of attempting to hold on doggedly to the presumed uniqueness and thus the superiority of Israelite religion.[17] This use of the methodology of the history of religions should be negated in favor of one that is more open in identifying parallels and influences that may be identified in the material cultures of different nations.

The formulation of a particular history of religion inevitably involves to some degree the subjectivity of the scholar.[18] Each historian approaches his or her discipline not only with a particular philosophy of history (e.g., positivism, idealism, neo-Marxism, and others) but also from a particular social location that has shaped his or her particular view of history. Furthermore, each scholar functions with a particular ideology that cannot be completely eliminated in interpreting events. Even so, the tools of the history of religion used in defining its own distinctive place within historical-critical research are to be used in the writing of any credible history.[19] To dismiss the historical approach as essentially ideologically driven borders on naïveté intermingled with incredulity. While the historian cannot determine necessarily what is normative for modern culture, the theologian who uses this approach does not have to remove himself or herself from the making of value judgments. Among important historians of religion in ancient Israel, several have shaped the history of the discipline, and a number of more recent ones have carried on this tradition in recent and contemporary scholarship, including some biblical theologians.

Julius Wellhausen (1844–1918)[20]

Wellhausen wrote the first important, scientific history of Israel, the major features of which continue to shape a good deal of our understanding of First Temple Israel and Second Temple Judaism. He was influenced in particular by Heinrich Ewald,[21] his teacher, but they later parted company for political and methodological reasons. Wellhausen also came under the sway of other major Old Testament historians of religion, including de Wette,[22] Vatke,[23] Reuss,[24] Graf,[25] Smend,[26] and Kuenen.[27] Perhaps the most important element in his view of the history of Israel was the historical place of the Torah that he argued first emerged as significant in Deuteronomy in the late seventh century and then became formative in shaping Judaism in the Second Temple period. He is best known for his clear formulation of the documentary hypothesis, which allowed him to relate the literary documents of the Pentateuch to the history of Israel. Like many Old Testament scholars, Wellhausen combined two features to write his history. The first was the methodology of the history of religion, and the second was the theological polarity of Yahweh, the God of Israel, and Israel, the people of Yahweh. This affirmation was the basis for Israel's national consciousness. The sages and scribes, according to Wellhausen, reorganized the universal character of wisdom that was possessed not only by Jews but also by the nations witnessed by their compositions. This contrasted with the conservative party, whose work culminated in the efforts of Ezra and Nehemiah in seeking to prevent the loss of Jewish identity by the incursion of foreign elements into Jewish identity shaped largely by the Torah. In Wellhausen's view, there was a strong degree of legalism that characterized constituents of this more conservative party in the Second Temple period.

The History of Religions School

The early history of religions school included such notable scholars as Hermann Gunkel,[28] Albert Eichhorn,[29] William Wrede,[30] Wilhelm Bousset,[31] Sigmund Mowinckel, Hugo Gressmann,[32] and, as already noted, Rudolf Smend. Due to their formative work, the major tools of research, which were phenomenological, historical, archeological, and comparative, were shaped and applied rigorously and scientifically.

Hermann Gunkel (1862–1932)

Gunkel was the first scholar of the Hebrew Bible to make systematic use of the textual discoveries of the ancient Near East, in particular, Mesopotamia, in composing his history of Israelite religion. In his most important work in the field of the history of Israelite religion, *Schöpfung und Chaos*, he insisted that the Babylonian creation myth, *Enūma Elish*, strongly influenced the Israelite suppositions and articulation of creation. However, by the time of the completion of the Priestly Document, so he concluded, Babylonian polytheism had been excised and the particular Israelite convictions were fully integrated into the Old Testament's expression of monotheism. The chronology of Babylonian influence was broken down into three sections: the original Babylonian myth of Marduk's creation, the Hebrew poetic formulation of the creation myth, and the priestly narrative's almost total excision of mythology. Gunkel advanced two general views. One was that significant religious ideas in human history were articulated by great personalities only after a period of lengthy struggle. The second was that revelation is not opposed to history and does not exist outside history but rather occurs within the history of the human spirit. This suggests that he did not separate theology from the history of religions.

Karl Albert August Ludwig Eichhorn (1856–1926)[33]

Eichhorn studied under several leading scholars, including Emil Schürer,[34] Wilhelm Baudissin,[35] and Paul de Lagarde.[36] As Rollmann has noted, this New Testament historian of religions emphasized three important dimensions that characterize his study of biblical religions: the study of ideas and practices in their sociohistorical context in contrast to the evaluation of texts set forth by literary source critics; the traditio-historical approach that notes the changes due to the evolution of the Israelite and Jewish communities; and the significance of Mandaean writings for understanding the Gospel of John. This last dimension, when extended more broadly, has continued in scholarly assessments of the types and examples of influence of the cultures of the ancient Near East and the Greco-Roman world on Israelite, Jewish, and early Christian religions.[37]

Sigmund Mowinckel (1884–1985)

Mowinckel, a leading figure of the Scandinavian school of the history of religions, was a prodigious writer whose works proved revolutionary in shaping the discourse and direction of the history of Israelite religion. The most influential of his writings were his six volumes on the Psalter, *Psalmenstudien*,[38] in which he developed his seminal thesis of sacral kingship in Israel and the ancient Near East. In his analysis, the Psalms were written for the national festivals that included mythical-sacramental dramas. The most important was the New Year's festival in which the king and queen played key roles in representing the community's reexperiencing of the generative powers of creation and their salvation from sin and destruction. In the combat myth that was dramatically performed during the New Year's festival, the king assumed the role of the creator in defeating chaos, ascending the throne as ruler of heaven and earth, re-creating the world, and participating with his consort in a *hieros gamos* that revitalized the forces of fertility of the earth and its inhabitants, thereby providing blessing and well-being for the coming year. This festival also celebrated the enthronement of Yahweh as ruler of the cosmos and the reign of his representative, the Israelite king (e.g., Pss 47; 93; 95–100). Most likely, argued Mowinckel, this New Year's myth was borrowed from the Babylonians. For Mowinckel, this festival provided the context for the development of Israelite eschatology in which salvation and creation were repeated consistently each year on the "Day of Yahweh."[39]

Hugo Gressman (1877–1927)

A prodigious writer, Gressmann appropriated various kinds of material culture discovered in the ancient Near East for his efforts to understand the Bible. He joined Gunkel in being instrumental in the fashioning of the major features of form-critical methodology and moved on to set out the distinctive parameters of the traditions of the history of religions. His expertise in ancient Near Eastern literature and culture led to his producing what became a major standard work in German, *Altorientalische Texte und Bilder zum Alten Testament.*[40]

The British Myth and Ritual School

While not held in the same esteem it had enjoyed prior to the emergence and thriving of dialectical theology due to the prodigious theological work of Karl Barth, the approach of the history of religions in Germany continued to produce important studies up to the present period. In addition, two groups of other scholars, the British Myth and Ritual school and the Scandinavian school, worked independently, although they both concentrated on the relationship between myth and ritual in the ancient Near East, including ancient Israel, and arrived at similar conclusions. Especially important were their emphasis and understanding of the New Year's festival, the mythology of creation, and the mythic and ritual role of kingship.

The so-called British Myth and Ritual school continued after the initial German phase of research to articulate the major features of the history of Israelite religion, although many who did Old Testament theology until the more recent period did not hold this approach in high regard, due to the commanding influence of Karl Barth. The stimulus for the myth and ritual scholars came from the anthropologist James G. Frazer.[41] In 1933 and again two years later in 1935, S. H. Hooke edited the papers of two symposia (*Myth and Ritual*,[42] and *The Laybrinth*[43]). Among the important scholars who participated were W. O. E. Oesterley,[44] Theodore H. Robinson,[45] and E. O. James.[46] These first two collections were followed a quarter of a century later in 1958 when Hooke produced a third collection, *Myth, Ritual, and Kingship*.[47] Among the influential scholars of this later group were A. R. Johnson[48] and H.-J. Kraus. While often differing on specific issues, the scholars who wrote for this collection generally held that there was a common myth and ritual pattern that existed in the ancient Near East. This mythic pattern involved two major elements: a New Year's festival and sacral kingship. This mythic and ritual pattern found its most significant expression in an annual New Year's festival that led to the well-being of the community for the coming year. For example, the Babylonian *akitu* (or New Year's) festival consisted of several recurring features, including a dramatic reenactment of the death and resurrection of the god, a reading of the myth that empowered the event, a ritual combat between the god of creation and the powers of chaos, the *hieros gamos* or sacred marriage, and the culminating enthronement of the victorious god, who then re-created the world and renewed its vitality for the coming year. The king, who was chosen by God to rule as his "son," played the role of the immanent god and performed a significant, cultic role in Israelite religion. The king possessed a sacral character and was even considered to be divine by at least some Israelites (cf. Ps 45:7). This school's work rejected what was then the prevalent view of the moral monotheism of a spiritual religion articulated by the prophets, who were essentially anticultic and were opposed to ancient Near Eastern mythology. Instead, Israel was said to have a dynamic mythic religion that included an important role for cult and ritual.

The Scandinavian School

The myth and ritual approach had its greatest influence through the scholarship of Scandinavian scholars who continued to develop the features of the history of Israelite religion. Among the more influential Scandinavian scholars were Ivan Engnell,[49] Helmer Ringgren,[50] Alfred Haldar,[51] Sigmund Mowinckel,[52] Johannes Pedersen,[53] and Aage Bentzen.[54] The same emphases mentioned above in the work of S. H. Hooke and his group drove the research and publications of these influential interpreters. Engnell even argued that the Israelite king was divine, since he was the embodiment of Yahweh, while Haldar contended that at least some of the prophets, for example, Amos, were cultic officials, thus suggesting their books may have been liturgies uttered during ritual worship.

Summary of the Early Stages of the History of Religions

Not surprisingly, these studies in the nineteenth and twentieth centuries made use of early cultural- and social-anthropological, as well as social-scientific studies that, with more recent theoretical studies, strongly impacted later Old Testament scholarship.[55] The anthropological investigation of the religion of Israel has become one of the most important areas of study for at least thirty years, and it has gained enormous attention as interest in the area of Old Testament theology began to wane once again in the late 1960s. Beginning in the 1960s, scholarly focus, particularly in North America, began to shift away from biblical theology to social-scientific and literary methods. The history of religions began once again to obtain an ascendancy over biblical theology, especially due to its easy adaptability to social-scientific methods. However, the earlier tendency of some Continental scholars to view late Judaism based on the Torah as legalism is discarded and replaced with the community's joy in receiving a divine gift that enables its righteous members to live lives of moral responsibility and obligation to God. Perhaps the most prominent historian of religion in recent years has been Rainer Albertz, whose studies of Israelite history have advanced the major emphases of earlier history of religions methodology and correlated them with Old Testament theology.

Rainer Albertz

In his early work,[56] Albertz pointed to several features to which he would return in his later writings. These included the pluralism of Israelite religion and the popular piety that rivaled official religion throughout the successive periods of Israelite history. This popular religion was revealed partly in the personal names of Israelites and partly in the material culture itself. According to the typology Albertz has constructed, there was another type of religion, that of the village, that existed alongside family and state religions. Methodologically, he also compared Israelite and Babylonian religions, noting the many similarities and important contrasts between the two.

In the introduction to his religion of ancient Israel, Albertz articulates his methodological assumptions and positions in a clear and concise fashion.[57] He recognizes that all scholars, including those engaging in the discipline of the history of religion, cannot be totally objective.[58] However, there must be common controls established that keep the investigation from being completely subjective. Data must be brought into view and evaluated in as objective a manner as possible to set forth the fundamental tenets and practices of Israelite religion.

Albertz's study of Israelite religion consists of the following major diachronic and synchronic (i.e., thematic) sections: Israelite religion prior to state formation (small family groups, a liberated larger group, the religion of the pre-state alliance, and family piety), Israelite religion during the monarchy (the formation of a monarchical territorial state, the dispute over the religious legitimation of kingship, the main state cult in the South, the main state cult in the North, the dispute over official syncretism in the ninth century, the theological controversies in the social and political crisis of the eighth century, family piety under the late monarchy, the Deuteronomic reform movement, and the political and theological controversies after the death of Josiah), Israelite religion in the exilic period (sociological developments during the exile, the struggle over a theological interpretation of political catastrophe, the support for Yahweh religion from family piety, and the move to a new beginning), and the history of Israelite religion in the Second Temple (political and sociological developments in the Persian period, the key experience of the failed restoration, the struggle over the identity of the community, the social and religious split in the community, the convergence of the religious strata and the dichotomy between official and personal pieties, the rise of the Samaritan community, and a prospectus on the history of religion in the Hellenistic period). In terms of the late Hellenistic period, he traces the sociological developments, the scribal ideal of a theocracy (Chronicles), Torah piety, and the late prophetic and apocalyptic theology of resistance. While chronological, this treatment of Israel's religion is also synchronic (thematic) in noting the contrasts between personal piety and the changing official religion through the generations.[59]

This reconstruction, like any critical history, has received both favorable and unfavorable responses. In essence, my own reaction is quite favorable, although I am not convinced that the differentiation he makes between national religion and private piety is a compelling argument. I would prefer to understand the simultaneity of these two areas, since state religion and its relationship to political events was a public display of participation in the national life undergirded by religious affirmations, while private piety found expression in familial and clan worship that centered on its individual deity, religious duties and responsibilities to the clan deity and the larger kinship group, and the continuing presence of the ancestors, even following death. Nevertheless, Albertz has provided a historical matrix into which the constituent elements of Israelite religion could be placed and understood. Particularly important, in my judgment, is his recognition of the diversity of Israelite and Judahite religion, not only diachronically but also synchronically, which is consistently present throughout the materials we have for reconstruction. Finally, he might have been more adroit in his explications in two significant areas. First, his use of material culture, especially in reconstructing national and popular religion, could have been substantially enlarged; and second, he could have considered in greater detail the additional cultural religious expressions found in both Canaanite and Aramaic literature and especially in the Hellenistic period Egyptian and Greek sources. After all, these assist in understanding the material and ideological contexts in which Israelite religion developed and continued to change through the centuries.

Albertz also continues down the well-worn path traveled by earlier historians of religion that have preceded him. For example, he is heavily influenced by Scandinavian scholarship when he considers royal ideology in ancient Israel to have been quite close to ancient Near Eastern sacral, even divine, kingship. This dependence on Scandinavian scholarship may also be noted in his characterization of royal religion in Jerusalem.

Receiving considerable debate have been his efforts to include Old Testament theology within the matrix of Israelite religion, thus attempting to bring together these two disparate disciplines. In my view, he is correct in affirming that the bifurcation of these two into different disciplines has led to the diminishment of both. He helps to provide a necessary correlation between the two fields of study and the two areas that are entwined in Israelite religion.

Erhard Gerstenberger

In his important volume outlining the theologies of the Hebrew Bible, Erhard Gerstenberger also is heavily oriented to the history of religions as the matrix and method for understanding the beliefs of ancient Israel expressed in both the Old Testament and the material culture of Israel and later Judaism.[60] Beginning with the family and clan, Gerstenberger notes that this type of personal piety or familial religion involved the social world of the household,[61] which harkened back to the shadowy mists of the early beginnings of Israel and its forebears and yet continued to be the setting for the local, popular form of Israelite and early Jewish religion as late as the rise of rabbinic Judaism.[62] While in practice everyone shared the household's possessions, the father was the *pater familias* who owned the property and ruled over everything in the family household, from animals to members socially defined by kinship, gender, and hierarchical features. The household usually survived on a subsistence existence primarily supported through farming and the pasturing of small cattle, sheep, and goats. In the religious expressions of the family, household members recognized that the earth, the sun, and the rain gave life and nourishment to flocks, produce, and people. Subsequently, deities responsible for the fertility of fields and vineyards, flocks, and human beings became those who were honored and worshiped by the family in order to receive their powers of fecundity that were necessary to survive. By contrast, demonic powers that threatened the household and brought sterility to the family, flocks, and soil were to be repelled through magical means as well as by means of the powers of the household gods. Sacrifices were offered to communicate with the family gods, to assuage them, and to provide for their needs. It is particularly in the religion of the ancestors that the family deity became a companion who dwelt with the household, blessed it with life, and commanded its allegiance (cf. Gen 28:20f.; see the "Mighty One of Jacob," the "Fear of Isaac," and the "Shield of Abraham").[63] These household gods were depicted in the form of images (*těrāphîm*, Gen 31:19, 30-35) and were provided a shrine in a special location in the house. Even when one deity was considered the god of the clan, this worship occurred in the context of a polytheistic world in which there were many divine beings.

Female images were frequently found in Israel as figurines or seal images. In the second millennium these were generally depicted as naked with sexual powers portrayed in erotic and fecundated forms that were at times highly exaggerated. Later images were depicted with twigs, plants, trees, and animals to demonstrate symbolically the fertility of the goddesses and their dominion over the world of creatures. One frequent example of a male figure is Bes, originally an Egyptian guardian of birth and child-care who also repelled demons. Amulets of Bes were found throughout ancient Israel in the periods of the monarchy and exile, pointing to his widespread worship and to Egyptian religious influence. The household cult in Israel also included Baal and Asherah (cf. Deut 18:10f.), although this fertility religion eventually received strong condemnation by the Deuteronomists.

The second sociohistorical stage of Israelite religion and its theology examined by Gerstenberger focuses on deities and socioreligious practices of the village (small-town) community.[64] The ethos of the village was based on the principle of family solidarity, while the families largely related by blood and marriage together worked common fields and herds. Their religious beliefs and practices were based on these shared tasks. Presumably these villages worshiped storm and fertility gods and goddesses in open-air sanctuaries, with standing stones (*maṣṣēbot*) representing the male deities, and trees and wooden pillars portraying female deities (*'ăšērôt*). These deities also blessed the villages with fertility through the sending of rain and the fructification of soil and productive herds and families. These gods, similar to Baal and Anat of Canaanite mythology, were also warriors who protected the villages from their enemies. The theology of the villages was based, then, on the everyday struggles for survival and on the required solidarity in work, defense against enemies, and legal decisions. The deity of the village was not only its leader but also the originator and judge of laws and important customs that undergirded its social life. Thus the village god was the deity of fertility, war, and law.

Gerstenberger then addresses the god and goddess in the tribal alliance.[65] He begins by rejecting Gottwald's thesis of the origins of liberated Israel resulting from a successful peasant revolt in Canaan, which was stimulated and aided by slaves who gained their freedom from Egypt and worshiped Yahweh as the one who gave them freedom.[66] Gerstenberger opts instead for a group of tribes who were independent and on occasion formed alliances for military and legal reasons. It appears that pre-state Israel already had begun to worship Yahweh, possibly at a shrine where the tribes expressed their worship that celebrated military victories against common enemies. Yahweh religion more than likely originated from outside the tribes, and possibly was borrowed from migratory, wilderness peoples such as the Kenites or Midianites. This deity would have been a storm and warrior deity, much like Baal (Ps 29), Adad,[67] Chemosh, and Resheph.[68] As a god of war, Yahweh[69] led the combined militias of various tribal groups into battle against a threatening enemy (see Judg 5; Hab 3:5-7).

Kingdom religions, according to Gerstenberger, are the next development in ancient Israel and Judah.[70] The monarchic state was a centralized and bureaucratic system ruled by the king, who presided over a royal entourage of officials. In Judah, the divine promise of a Davidic descendant was embodied in the oracle of Nathan (2 Sam 7; Ps 89). Yahweh is the one who chose David and his descendants to rule over the kingdom and selected Zion as his divine dwelling place in a location adjacent to the palace (Pss 46; 48). Key to the royal ideology is the kingship of God, who chose the human ruler on the day of his enthronement to be his son (Ps 2:7), who was understood by some to be divine (cf. Ps 45:7). The religion of the state focused on the kingship of Yahweh, the election of the House of David, and the divine dwelling on Mount Zion in the temple. The coronation of the human ruler (2 Sam 5:1-5; 1 Kgs 1:32-40; and 2 Kgs 11:4-12) included the presence of Yahweh, who adopts the newly enthroned ruler as his "son," the anointment of the new ruler, his riding of the royal mule, and his drinking from the sacred spring of Gihon (see the royal psalms, 2; 45; 89; 110; and 132).[71] Ruling on behalf of Yahweh, the king was the one who brought fertility to the land, established and maintained justice, and was the leader of the army.

Gerstenberger then examines the community of Israel following the exile. Now the commandments and the salvific narratives are written down and eventually become the basis for a scribal religion. In addition, monotheism develops in its full form, allowing Israel to worship Yahweh in a foreign land and to negate the existence of other deities (cf. the wisdom texts, including Wis 13–15). With the exiles in Babylon, the Jews began to encounter mythologies that influenced their religion, including those that had to do with creation. Especially important was the Babylonian god Marduk's defeat of Tiamat, the personification of chaos. Following the death of Tiamat, Marduk creates the world, a mythological narrative that is reflected in the Bible (*těhôm*; Gen 1:2, Pss 18; 77; 104; 114; and Isa 52:7f.). Yahweh, the Supreme Deity, created both the cosmos and humanity (Job 38:4-11; Ps 8). Images of the defeat of chaos are found in the Yahweh speeches in Job 38:1–42:6. This use of ancient near Eastern creation imagery in Job points, among other sapiential texts, to the international character of wisdom theology. By the fifth century B.C.E., the Torah was shaped into its final form, followed by the canonization of the Prophets approximately at the beginning of the second century.

Thus, from Gerstenberger's theologies, one discovers the major understandings of Yahweh that arose within the context of the changing social
settings of ancient Israel and early Judah. Paradigmatically, he too
emphasizes the diversity that existed among the Israelites and their successors in many areas, providing a guide to assist us in tracing not only
chronologically but also synchronically the diversity of Israelite religion
and its developing theology.

Summary

With the work of Albertz and Gerstenberger, we are able to interpret
the history of Israelite religion that provides a concrete picture of religious themes and their related theology within the cultural and social life
of ancient Israel and early Judaism. This approach allows us to recognize
more clearly the diversity of Israelite religion and its theological expressions within changing, historical contexts. There are an important number of other affirmations inherent in the methodology of the history of
religion that should be mentioned. First of all are the theoretical adapta-
tions of the studies of history, the philosophy of history, sociology and
social history, anthropology, the scientific fields that are used in the areas
of archaeology, and the specialties of classical studies, Northwest Semitic
cultures, Egyptology, Assyriology, Akkadian texts and society, Hellenism,
and Roman rule and civilization. Second, there is focus placed on the
sociocultural life of ancient Israel and early Judaism. Ideas are not transcendent but rather are generated by communities, which in turn are
influenced by them. Consequently, idealism is replaced by a more socially
construed understanding of human thought, faith, and practice.

Third, the history of religion as a discipline is descriptive and does not
make normative evaluations in and of itself. This does not mean that historians of religion are uninformed about the ideologies that shape the
composition of texts and their own subjectivity that may reside behind
their interpretations. But the effort is made to make historical judgments
on the basis of theories of historiography (especially positivism and more
recently neo-Marxism) and empirical evidence. These have been taken
by some biblical theologians and used to inform their own reconstruction
of the faith and practice of ancient Israel. It is at this point that on
occasion value judgments are rendered. Efforts to move away from
rational and empirical assessments and interpretations for historical
reconstruction, in my judgment, are largely failures, which, if followed to

their logical consequences, lead to the deconstruction of knowledge and social systems.

Fourth, histories of Israelite religion approach the biblical text as a human document to be critically evaluated through the methods of historical criticism in the same way that all religions and their sacred literatures are assessed. Fifth, histories of Israelite religion examine all relevant data of material culture in Israel and the ancient Near East with the objective of presenting both the official and popular expressions of religious life in ancient Israel. They are attuned to the realization that orthodoxy and heterodoxy often reflect the political and social ideologies of the composers and redactors of text. Popular religion (e.g., that of Elephantine or the worship of the fertility goddess Asherah throughout the Israelite Iron Age culture) points to the views and practices of many men and women in ancient Israel and early Judaism. Thus, historians have come to recognize that most, if not all, of the Hebrew Bible is written by the elite and their subservient groups who articulate theological and religious expressions of an ideology supporting their own interests and not by social inferiors and the marginalized of ancient Israel and early Judaism.[72] Diversity, not orthodoxy, is the significant recognition advanced by historians of religion, and we see this not only in the biblical and deuterocanonical texts but also in noncanonical literature and the communities and groups that composed them. Finally, through the combination of a synchronic and diachronic approach, historians of religion offer us important information for writing a biblical theology that takes socioreligious and cultural data seriously and seeks to avoid biased presentations based primarily on the ideological interests of the interpreters.

OLD TESTAMENT THEOLOGY AND SALVATION HISTORY

Gerhard von Rad

During a tumultuous period of German and European history, Gerhard von Rad taught at Erlangen as a tutor (1929), Leipzig as a Privatdozent (1930), and Jena as a professor (1934–1944). In spite of suffering from a heart condition, he was drafted into the German Luftwaffe as a truck driver in the summer of 1944, eventually taken prisoner, and placed in an

American prisoner of war camp for a quarter of a year.[73] Following the end of World War II and his release, he accepted appointment toward the end of 1945 at Göttingen, where he served as a professor (1945–1949). His last appointment was as a professor of Old Testament at Heidelberg, where he taught during the years of 1949 to the time of his death in 1971. One of the most seminal biblical scholars of the twentieth century, he shaped the field of Old Testament theology for much of the second half of the twentieth century, and many of his penetrating insights continue to be influential today.

Best known for his two-volume Old Testament theology (*Theologie des Alten Testaments*, 1957–1960), von Rad asked two decisive questions in the initial volume that continued to reside at the center of his theological work. First, should we accept the history that is articulated by the biblical writers themselves or the one that is reconstructed by scholars? Second, if the Old Testament has to do with the disclosure of God in redemptive acts, then where does this revelation reside: in the history written by scholars or in the numerous pictures of God that are present in the variety of literature contained in the Old Testament? Of course, von Rad used historical criticism, in particular traditions history, in reconstructing his own history of Israel. When he wrote his theology, he made use of critical exegesis as understood in the mid-twentieth century in articulating the acts of salvation rendered by God on Israel's behalf. And he valued the scholarly reconstructions of Israelite and Jewish history to which he himself made important contributions. Revelation, for von Rad, resided within the traditions of faith that were expansions of Israel's creedal beliefs about God. Thus, von Rad contended that Old Testament theology is to focus on Israel's multiple testimonies of faith that proclaim God's activities of redemption in history and on divine revelation. The traditions of Israelite faith become the source for identifying the constituent elements of Old Testament witnesses to God.

In shaping his own theology, von Rad rejected the systematic form given unity by a central concept like covenant, and yet he still found a type of organizing principle in the redemptive acts of God on Israel's behalf, first articulated and confessed in an ancient creedal form.[74] For von Rad, then, the substance of Old Testament theology was not to be expressed by placing the concepts of the Hebrew Bible into the systematic categories derived from the dogmatic theology of the church but rather in what Israel itself has said about God. Thus, in essence Old Testament theology consisted of Israel's own testimonies of faith found in tradition (narratives and poems) and the new articulations of later generations of believers in the process of retelling. Von Rad wrote, then, not a history of Israelite religion but rather a history of religious traditions, especially those understood as redemptive for the nation, which it understood as divinely revealed. These theological traditions develop their own history by continuing to be interpreted and reinterpreted by the successive communities of Israel. Each generation did not simply rehearse the traditions of the past but rather faced the necessity and the challenge to determine for itself what it meant to be Israel. This they did in the formulation and reformulation of traditions. Indeed, the earliest proclamation in Deut 26:5-9 eventually was expanded during the monarchial period to include the Zion tradition (the dynasty of David and the presence of Yahweh in the temple), and in the Second Temple to encompass the new traditions of creation and the Sinai revelation (covenant and law). Speaking from the context of the church, von Rad used typology to describe the relationship between the two Testaments.[75] The typological formulation of the traditions of faith foreshadows the final salvation history to which the New Testament gives witness. Thus, when von Rad argued that "the Old Testament is a history book,"[76] he was speaking, not of historical events that may be reconstructed, but rather of the kerygmatic proclamation of the developing traditions of Israel's faith and worship. A better translation of this misunderstood sentence is "the Old Testament is a storybook" or "book of traditions." This led him to concentrate his theology, not on concrete events, but rather on the history of tradition, or, simply put, the word. According to von Rad, "History becomes word, and word becomes history."[77] This history of tradition, for von Rad, eventually broke forth into what became, when added to other theological areas of authoritative understanding, including culture and experience, normative theology for the church, a connection that begins in its early formation as typologically moving from the acts of salvation in the Old Testament to those in the New.[78]

As the most influential Old Testament theologian of the twentieth century, Gerhard von Rad placed his indelible stamp on Old Testament theology that continues today to provide a major interpretation and to serve as a starting point for many important theological contributions that have followed. He began to set forth his theological views in a provocative essay published in 1936, where he subordinated creation theology to saving history.[79] He argued: "The Yahwistic faith of the Old Testament is a faith based on the notion of election, and therefore is primarily concerned with redemption."[80] At this period of his life and indeed until he began to offer some new understandings at the end of his life, von Rad considered creation to be but a prelude to the history of salvation. Subsequently, von Rad viewed Israel's God as the one who acted redemptively in history on its behalf, from election, to statehood, to eschatology. At the same time, he attributed the conceptions of covenant and law to the later development of the originally pristine historical faith during the Second Temple. He argued that the Sinai tradition, which comprises a significant portion of Exodus, Leviticus, and Numbers and is reconfigured in the book of Deuteronomy, comes into formation in the exile and the Second Temple.

Viewing the events of salvation as articles of a confession of faith, von Rad considered the earliest ancient credo to be found in Deut 26:5-9, dating prior to the monarchy. He noted that the latest two traditions, creation and Sinai, were not incorporated into the creedal faith until Neh 9 in the fifth century B.C.E. But, if salvation history was the content of early Israelite faith that is developed into narrative and poetic forms, what are we to do with texts that make no mention of these acts? Von Rad's only recourse, at least until the end of his life, was to consider them as later developments, implying that they possessed less theological value.

In addition to rejecting Eichrodt's systematic formulation, von Rad also opposed natural theology, which, cast in a demonic form, was abused by Nazi theologians and sympathizers. In 1934 and even after the war, von Rad opposed a theology that identified nationalism and the nation as one of the orders of creation, combined with the distorted Romantic emphasis on "blood and soil."[81] Indeed, this was likely one reason he gave creation an insignificant place in Old Testament theology.

The omission of covenant and Sinai in the earliest creeds led von Rad to conclude that this tradition was absent until the formation of the pre-Deuteronomic materials of law that were transformed into hortatory addresses or sermons by the Levites. Deuteronomy itself was grace, not law, and subsequently did not contain legal materials of its own creation. Rather, Deut 12–26 was pre-Deuteronomic. As Benjamin Levinson has argued, von Rad sought to preserve the Old Testament from the efforts of its exclusion from the church and National Socialism by the German Christians during the Nazi period.[82] In so doing, he focused much of his attention on authentic Deuteronomy as a text of grace in which salvation was grounded in the divine acts of redemption. For Levinson, this was an attempt to rescue the Old Testament from its rejection by the anti-

Semitic German Christians. As early as his dissertation *Das Gottesvolk im Deuteronomium*, published in 1929, von Rad does not discuss the law contained in this book but rather argues that this book had no concept of legal formulations and teachings.[83] Even the prophet was interpreted as not being subject to the law. Rather, what stood at the core of this text was the promise of grace. Indeed, the introduction of priesthood, ritual laws, and festivals led to the "disintegration" of this text. This ignoring of the legal materials in chapters 12–26 continues to be discussed in "The Form-Critical Problem of the Hexateuch," which appeared in 1938. He chose, rather, to emphasize the public reading of the text in a covenant renewal ceremony. Furthermore, Deuteronomy was a "Christian book" in its form (*Gattung*). By this he means that this book, as well as Chronicles, derives from Levitical preaching, enabling it as paraenesis or homily to be acceptable to the German church of his day.[84] Thus, Deuteronomy consisted of sermons of wandering Levites, and not a written text that had become a dead letter of the law. In this way, von Rad attempted to rescue at least elements of the book from what he considered to be Jewish legalism. Of course, this view of Jewish legalism, identified with the Second Temple, builds on the common Protestant assumption since Luther that Judaism was a religion of acts of obedience and not redemptive faith. This view has been rejected increasingly by many Old Testament theologians during the past two generations.

Von Rad did not address the legal aspects of Deuteronomy until his work on *Deuteronomium-Studien* appeared in 1947, two years after the war, when he was a professor of Old Testament at Göttingen.[85] He included in this study of the form of the Levitical sermon the legal materials of the book (chaps. 12–26). These are now said to be the expansion of the kernels of the legal material that the Levitical preachers transformed into hortatory sermons designed to address individual consciences. Yet these legal texts, both the early laws and their interpretation, are notably devalued as "pre-Deuteronomic." Deuteronomy *per se* came into being only after the Levitical preachers had transformed the laws into homilies. Even the legal materials existed prior to the Levitical preachers! Deuteronomy itself did not produce or contain legal materials. However, von Rad did allow that post-Deuteronomic materials included some laws. Thus what was truly Deuteronomy was gospel that took precedence over Torah. This dichotomy never disappeared from his writing. Subsequently, even the Torah (or the Sinai) did not enter into the creedal confession until

Neh 9, written during the high-water mark of the legalism during the period of the Second Temple. This devaluation of Torah, of course, fit well a Christian interpretation based on Luther's reading of Paul and the contrast between salvation by faith and redemption by righteous deeds based on the law. It would be ironic, of course, that the Deuteronomic scribes, who had a high regard for the law and its interpretation, would place this ancient creed in a prominent location in the very book they themselves fashioned and thereby demote its significance.

In volume 1 of his *Old Testament Theology*, von Rad treated Deuteronomy as the most central theological document in the Hebrew Bible.[86] In its view of the revelation of Sinai, it broke through to the fundamental understanding that the "laws, statutes, and judgments" formed a fundamental theological unity by which, in the making known of Yahweh's will, this divine revelation outgrew the cultic sphere. The earliest form of the book originated at the covenant renewal festival at Shechem. At Sinai Israel received the Ten Commandments, but being incapable of hearing Yahweh's voice again, the "whole law" was imparted to Moses. Moses taught this law to Israel in the plains of Moab, prior to his death and the entrance into Canaan.

Deuteronomy is the result of the preaching activity of the Levites and consists of a kaleidoscope of their sermons that were paraenetic in form. In its final form, the structure of the book moves from the introductory sermon, to the commandments, to the pledging of obedience to the covenant, to the blessings and curses. These sermons originated in the later period of the monarchy and point to Israel's standing between its election to its fulfillment of the promises made during the entrance to the land. Because Yahweh has elected and loved Israel, the chosen are to reciprocate by loving him. Even the laws are taken from their original cultic location and given a homiletic formulation, meaning they are commandments that are the subject of preaching. The oneness of Yahweh is demonstrated by the single cultic center in which the divine name dwells, the singularity of the revelation in the Torah, and the one inheritance, that is, the land given Israel. Election precedes obedience, indicating that this divine choosing of a lowly and insignificant people is an act of sheer grace.

For the Priestly source, cultic materials are presented with little theological explication. It essentially sets forth the periods of the growth of the cultic institutions and laws. Yet with its presentation of creation in Gen 1:1–2:4a, it seeks to indicate that the election of Israel becomes the goal of the evolution of the world. At Sinai, P emphasizes that it was here Yahweh founded Israel's cult.

Von Rad noted also that the large Sinai tradition in Exod 19:1–Num 10:10 consists of many strands of materials that are related to one single event, the revelation at Sinai.[87] He concluded that its absence in the ancient creeds meant that this expansive tradition was inserted secondarily into the tradition of the wanderings in the wilderness. The JE narrative of Sinai (Exod 19–24; 32–34) is dwarfed by the huge block of materials in P (Exod 25–31; Num 10:10). The earlier narrative is likely a "festival legend" belonging to the old festival of covenant renewal. This earlier narrative contains preparations for the theophany, Yahweh's descent to the mountain, the proclamation of the Ten Commandments, and the people's engagement in the cultic festival. This tradition has no place for a cultic understanding of the Ten Commandments. The revelation is for people to engage in everyday life. In this older festival legend, the commandments are for laity to conduct their daily lives and are never considered to be law. This revelation became a saving event that effectuated the gift of life by establishing a relationship with Yahweh, who selected Israel to be his chosen people. To this narrative, P adds the mass of cultic regulations, instructions for the building of the tabernacle, the priesthood, Yahweh's glory descending upon the tent, and the ordination of Levites to secondary service in the cult. The revelation is that of a sacral order to establish communion with God. The revelation of Sinai as a saving event did not cease by becoming an absolute law in the Second Temple. However, the law was transformed into an unconditional entity requiring strict unwavering adherence, letter by letter and word by word. This understanding became the basis for a strict legalism that stripped the Torah of its character as a saving event and eventually even transcended the cult. Deuteronomy became the last stand against this legalism, even though it eventually failed.

Von Rad noted the later developments in the theology of Judah, beginning with the monarchy and continuing into the exile and the Second Temple. Deutero-Isaiah represents the most important reflection in the Hebrew Bible on creation faith, while election is understood in terms of the divine creation of Israel (see the verbs *create* and *redeem* that are associated in Isa 43:1; 44:21, 24; 46:3; and 54:5). Von Rad's soteriological understanding of creation beginning with this prophet of the exile now becomes an important feature of the theology of redemptive history. The only Second Temple texts in von Rad's view that do not find themselves aligned with this basic understanding are Pss 19 and 104:8 and Job 38–41. They instead witness to the power of God in the making of reality, and thus they speak of creation standing alone as a theological tradition.[88] However, von Rad argued these two psalms are on the periphery of Old Testament theology, precisely because they do not speak of the soteriological function of creation. The same lack of soteriology in the tradition of creation is true for Job 38–41. He even thought that they likely derived from a foreign origin. Wisdom literature, which includes the theology of creation, is troublesome for him, and he oddly enough places these texts under Israel's response to Yahweh, the same classification used for the Psalter.

As a biblical scholar, von Rad was deeply concerned with recovering the history of Israel. Indeed, as noted earlier, he enthusiastically proclaimed, "The Old Testament is a history book."[89] However, in contrast to Wright's understanding that history should be based on recoverable concrete events in space and time, von Rad contended history was a recounting of saving history (*Heilsgeschichte*, i.e., traditions of history) that witnessed to God's continuing redemptive actions for Israel and the world. The recounting of Israel's faith takes a variety of forms, including confessions, psalms, and narratives. Thus, while Wright sought to discover the grounding of Israel's "Mighty Acts of God" in the context of space and time through the combination of the historical-critical method and archaeology, von Rad understood "history" in a very different way. For him, Old Testament history was in essence story or narrative, meaning that it referred to the origins and developments of major traditions of Israelite faith and not to "events" central to formative faith traditions that actually occurred. Thus, while Wright stripped away the "accretions" to the traditions in order to discover the concrete history of the "Mighty Acts of God," von Rad retained these oral and written interpretations and took them to be the substance of the core beliefs of Israelite faith. Thus, when doing theology, von Rad was not concerned with the historicity of the events around which interpretations developed. His approach avoids the pitfalls of Wright and his followers, who, confronted with the sparseness of historical data, historical inaccuracies in the biblical texts, and multiple contemporary explanations of even core events, found themselves in a protean box. Thus, von Rad was concerned to trace the social and historical development of Israel's theological traditions, for it was in these that Israel's changing faith was embodied in all its variety. Who developed these traditions, their major themes, the social groups who transmitted them, and their redaction were the primary concerns of the method of traditions history (*Überlieferungsgeschichte*). Thus, the opening section of von Rad's initial volume traced the development of Israelite religion and its major religious and social institutions from their origins in pre-Mosaic times to the beginnings of scribal religion in the postexilic period.[90] It was within this diachronic context that von Rad traced Israel's developing faith.[91]

Von Rad was opposed to theologizing, which approached its work by the articulation of bloodless, abstract concepts such as covenant, faith, and righteousness. This approach, based on systematic categories in Continental biblical theology, and on word studies in England and North America, was part of the strategy used by the biblical theology movement that assumed meaning was located in and derived either from the careful articulation of theological themes or from individual words.[92] These ideas tended to be articulated by means of generalization and abstraction and not located in the social matrix of Israel and the church. Von Rad understood the historical task of the biblical theologian to be that of uncovering the witness of social communities to divine action within the context of tradition history and its development in changing social locations. Themes were an intrinsic part of the growth and expansion of tradition complexes, not so much in a progressive, evolutionary fashion, but rather like a flowing river moving sometimes backward but more often forward while forming new channels and tributaries. Subsequently, to use and extrapolate on an apt expression from von Rad, each generation of Israel was responsible for determining what it meant to be the people of God in their own time by encountering tradition and reshaping it in view of their particular context and experience.

The Little Creed (Das Kleine Credo)

The linchpin of von Rad's theology was the isolation of what he considered to be confessions of faith that were embedded within larger literary texts. He argued that Israel's earliest faith was expressed in what he assumed to be an ancient, historical creed found in Deut 26:5b-9, going back, so he proposed, to a liturgy of thanksgiving in which this "confession" was uttered during a festival of firstfruits at a local sanctuary (cf. Deut 6:20-24; Josh 24:2b-13). Von Rad argued that this creed, taking the form of either a confession by or a hortatory address to the congregation within a liturgical setting, is a succinct expression of the redemptive acts of God and contains the earliest faith of Israel.[93] These redemptive acts include the promise to the fathers, the exodus from Egypt, the wanderings in the wilderness, and the gift of the promised land. As noted earlier, Sinai was not included until the Second Temple.

Since the earliest credos in Deut 6 and 26 and Josh 24 ended with the conquest or entrance into the land, von Rad ignored the canonical shape of the Torah consisting of five books (Genesis through Deuteronomy) by adding a sixth: the book of Joshua. Thus, von Rad spoke of the Hexateuch (adding Joshua) as embodying these early traditions that continued to be reformulated, and not the Pentateuch. The Hexateuch (Genesis through Joshua) contains for von Rad two large tradition complexes that developed over several centuries. The exodus-settlement tradition, very early in its history, incorporated the promises to the ancestors and celebrated God's guidance and redemptive activity of the patriarchs, the slaves in Egypt, and their descendants who entered into the land of promise, while the Sinai tradition portrayed theophanic vision, the coming of God to his people, and the entrance into a covenant relationship that included the law. It is not difficult to see that von Rad is differentiating between what he considers to be "law" (Sinai) and "gospel" (exodus-settlement). Originally, the cultic setting for the exodus-settlement tradition was the offering of firstfruits during the Feast of Weeks. Thus, the creed was the earliest part of the religious narrative of this important pilgrimage festival at a time when ownership of the land was a live issue. This would have been shortly after the entrance into the land but before the emergence of the monarchy of David some two centuries later. Von Rad concluded that the sanctuary where this religious narrative originated was Gilgal, near Jericho. Here the territorial boundaries of the tribes were ritually recognized.

In terms of origin, the Sinai tradition, in von Rad's view, is perhaps the latest stage in the development of the Hexateuch. It developed as the religious narrative of the sanctuary of Shechem, the chief northern Israelite temple from the time of the tribal federation during the formative period of the judges. The two dominant features, the coming of God and the entering into covenant, presuppose a pilgrimage festival, most probably the Feast of Booths, celebrated during Israel's autumnal New Year. Even the structure of the book of Deuteronomy, which presents the reformulation of historic faith and covenant, reflects the major features of a cultic ceremony: historical presentation of the events at Sinai, the reading of the law, the sealing of the covenant, and blessings and curses.

Deuteronomy derives from the formal pattern of this liturgy. And its characteristic mentioning of "today" emphasizes that the saving events, which provided the basis for covenant and law, were the objects of response by the assembled community. In saying yes to God's redemption, formalized within the renewal of the covenant, salvation is reactualized liturgically in the community's present experience. In the ceremony of covenant renewal, the lordship of God over Israel is reaffirmed.

Von Rad then proceeded to trace the development of these two major hexateuchal traditions, indicating how they were eventually included in the major literary sources of J, E, D, and P. Von Rad's treatment of J is illustrative of this development. For von Rad, central for J was the exodus-settlement tradition, although this writer did include an early form of the wilderness complex. But it was a considerable period of time before the combination of these two traditions was generally accepted. J was responsible for the first blending of the "two fundamental propositions of the whole message of the Bible: Law and Gospel."[94] In addition, the Yahwist was responsible for the inclusion of the creation tradition, also late in being accepted by the community of faith as a redemptive activity of God. It was more of a prolegomenon to the historical faith of Israel than an independent tradition of belief itself. With this inclusion of creation, however, the Yahwist indicated that the purpose of Israel's redemption was to reconcile all humanity to God. In a view that reflects his Protestant orientation to religious understanding, von Rad argues that this secularization of redemptive history and covenant by the Yahwist led to the development of a spiritualized faith in which the cultus was tolerated but not seen as fundamentally important. Indeed, the theological problem of the Yahwist was that the sacral sphere no longer guaranteed the truth of the creeds. Now it is the theological emphasis on the providential direction of history that is developed. This understanding enabled new traditions to appear, grounded in Israel's continuing history.

New traditions came to include the promise of an eternal dynasty to David (2 Sam 7; Ps 89) and the election of Zion (Jerusalem) as the dwelling place of God (Pss 46; 48; 76). God was not limited either to the past or to the sacred sphere but continued to act in history to effectuate redemption through new agents and events. In addition, even creation came to be understood as a theological tradition, especially in the Wisdom literature, but it never achieved a commanding status as a tradition of faith. Von Rad argued that creation for most of the Old Testament canon was understood only as the prolegomenon to salvation history, until the time of Ezra, whose "creed" also included creation as one of the salvific acts (Neh 9:6f.). Seen for many centuries as ancillary to redemption for all but the sages, creation theology was held in suspicion because of its possible association with fertility religion and natural revelation. While Israel undoubtedly knew the major creation myths of its neighbors and understood its central place in the religions of the ancient Near East, it was not appropriated by their faith until much later. According to von Rad, decisive for this appropriation was the prophet of the exile, Second Isaiah, who spoke of creative redemption. However, this prophet, he contended, still gave primacy to revelation and redemption in history, certainly a questionable view when noting the important role of creation in this prophetic text of the exile.

It is important to remember that for von Rad the two major traditions in the Hexateuch, exodus-settlement and Sinai, originated and developed over the years within different liturgical celebrations. These two traditions represented, not the attempt to write history in the modern sense, but rather the efforts of successive generations to articulate and celebrate their faith within worship. Nevertheless, the ancient faith could be taken by the shapers of theological tradition, such as the Yahwist and the prophets, and given a narrative character that validated the authenticity of belief outside worship. The sacred and the secular continued to be the two spheres, at times in tension, that expressed the vital faith of the chosen people.

The Traditioning Process

The major thematic traditions isolated by von Rad were quite similar to those of Wright: the promise to the fathers, the exodus, the Red Sea victory, the wilderness wanderings, the land of Canaan, and the later additions of Sinai covenant and law, the David-Zion complex, and creation. Unlike Wright, however, the emphasis was placed not on the nucleus of demonstrable events but rather on their interpretations that continued to develop and change over the years. Wright saw his task to be the reconstruction of Israelite history, out of which one could then begin to do Old Testament theology. His scholarly reconstruction of history differed at times rather dramatically from Israel's own accounting. The contrast between Israel's own accounting of her story and the history of Israel reconstructed by scholars posed a serious problem for von Rad, one which he never fully resolved. Even so, he took much more seriously

Israel's own rendering of her history than did Wright when it came to doing biblical theology. Indeed, what Israel says about God's action is primary for Old Testament theology.[95] Thus, the proper mode of engaging and actualizing the faith of Israel, for von Rad, is "re-telling." And what Israel says is not dependent for its legitimacy upon the actual occurrence of salvific events or the ability of the historian to "prove" these events took place. While von Rad does not appear to doubt that some sort of historical experience lay behind the redemptive acts, the real significance of the traditions resided within the development of the content of the faith expressed in words. In von Rad's formulation of the task of biblical theology, one is by necessity forced to take seriously what Israel *says* about its own salvation history. For von Rad, Israel's faith is not grounded in history but rather in a *theology* of history.[96] This is the fundamental difference from Wright. Indeed, for von Rad, Israel's theology, and therefore our own, is the critical engagement and response of each generation to the proclamation of the preceding generations. The role of the believer became active in creating and reformulating tradition. In the context of worship, the people Israel reactualized, that is, made living and new, the faith for their own contemporary existence as a community. In and through ritual, the community made the past present, and thereby participated in the sacred stream of redemptive history. Von Rad concluded that the same process is at work in believing communities, especially in liturgical settings.

As for the New Testament's testimony to God, von Rad argued that Old Testament traditions continued into the early church, where they received new formulations. Thus the relationship between the Testaments was not radical discontinuity but rather durative.[97] Yet it is rather strange that he then develops a typological method in associating the two Testaments, instead of continuing to press for a history-of-traditions understanding of biblical theology.

In von Rad's thinking about the Old Testament in the New, history has three hermeneutical features: typology, promise-fulfillment, and reactualization. Redemptive acts as historical events were unrepeatable, once-for-all occurrences. However, in presenting his own view of an ancient, early Christian theological category, "typology," von Rad concluded that the events of Old Testament salvation history became the prototypes for the New Testament's corresponding antitypes.[98] This means that salvific events in the Old Testament pointed beyond themselves to acts in the future, especially the Christ-event. In von Rad's words, "The primeval event is a type of the final event." Levenson draws the undeniable conclusion that this leaves Jews out of von Rad's theological equation.[99]

Von Rad took the promise-fulfillment scheme and argued that each event points beyond itself to ever greater and more significant fulfillment, until the Christ-event provided the ultimate culmination of history.[100] This allows the Christian to read the Old Testament as a "book of ever increasing anticipation."[101] Inherent within the formulation of each redemptive tradition was the feature of divine promise pointing toward new and even greater fulfillment in the future. Each development in the tradition allowed for God to enter into it once again, leading to both different interpretations and similar, though new, events. Especially for the prophets (and this is the point of origin for von Rad's understanding of promise-fulfillment), there was to be a new exodus, a new covenant, a new Jerusalem, and a new David. Indeed, even creation, which von Rad saw as a redemptive "act," was to become new. Von Rad regarded this hermeneutic as intrinsic to the Old Testament itself, for Israel's theologians understood that there were ever-new fulfillments and that the community always lived between the now and the not yet, in anticipation of later, even grander fulfillments that resided still in the future. God continued to be active by bringing about new acts of salvation for the chosen.

Von Rad gives important status to the hermeneutical character of Psalms, the Prophets, and Deuteronomy. These texts demonstrate the receptivity of new acts of salvation where God intrudes to engage in new beginnings. There is the fulfillment of the Old in the New, yet this too opens itself to new possibilities. While von Rad attributed a "once-for-all" character to God's ultimate and final act in Jesus Christ, the traditions of faith opened themselves ever again to new and creative possibilities, revitalized understandings, offered fresh hope, and presented an anticipated final climax in the eschaton. Von Rad contrasted this view of typology, which was rooted in history, to ahistorical allegory that did not take lasting root in Christian theology.

Like the changing theology he sought to describe throughout his life, von Rad also continued to reshape his own views. In the last volume he was to write, he even regards creation as a theology that is either parallel or perhaps even an alternative to saving history. *Wisdom in Israel* points to the importance of creation (including the theology of providence in revitalizing the cosmos) in wisdom theology (see especially Prov 8–9;

Job 38–41; cf. 9:2f., and Sir 24). Faith in the Creator came to be seen as the framework and foundation for talk about God, the world, Israel, and the individual. Creation became revelatory to those who trust in it. Creation may be trusted because it was viewed as very good (Gen 1:31). In contrast to the cult and the various canonical views of salvation history, wisdom's soteriology is based on the life-giving blessings inherent in creation itself. Practical wisdom was stimulated not by divine actions in history but rather by the basic questions of humankind for existing in the world. How was one to live both actively and passively within the environment of the world so as to be successful? Later, wisdom's view of the world called to humanity to listen. And what humans are to hear is the offer of salvation, that is, life in abundance, but not the liberation of salvation history. Humans are to learn to trust the creation, its orders, and the Creator who brought them into existence and through them provided the gift of abundant life.[102]

CREATION THEOLOGY

In spite of an increasing interest in various forms of literary criticism, ranging from rhetorical criticism to postmodernism and deconstruction, history has continued to dominate both the content and the method (in particular, positivism) of Old Testament theology. Most scholars have reconstructed theological themes and often plied a center that provides the unifying factor for expressing the faith of ancient Israel.[103] However, there are numerous texts and traditions in the Old Testament canon and deuterocanonical texts that do not focus on Israel's redemptive history. This includes, among others, the books of wisdom prior to the work of Ben Sira in the early century B.C.E. In addition, limiting hermeneutics for current theological meaning to history has been a consistent problem. How is it possible to move beyond the suggestion that God continues to operate in history through providence by simply focusing on Israel's earlier faith in redemptive history, in either events or the traditions of interpretations of those events? Law conceived as commandment, not as narrative story, also deals with history, but only in the foundation of the institutions of state, society, and cultus in which the legal codes and dictates are located. Indeed, when entering the middle of the Second Temple, some in the Jewish community began to extricate Torah from a historical grounding in redemptive events and their explanations. Torah becomes another way of celebrating life and living as the elect apart from emphasizing its validity on expectations of future redemptive acts. This is not to suggest that history (redemptive events and their interpretation) is not an important way of expressing Old Testament theology, but it is to say that redemptive history cannot, in and of itself, circumscribe within its boundaries all the Old Testament literature.

Creation as the Dominant Theme in Old Testament Theology

While not as prominent as redemptive history has been in describing and interpreting the centrality of Old Testament theology, creation has been the major focus of numerous scholars, including among the more impressive studies those of especially Hans-Heinrich Schmid, B. W. Anderson, Jon Levenson, and Rolf Knierim. The tendency to lessen the theological importance of creation has been due to the strong criticism of natural theology in the writings of Barth and many other neo-orthodox theologians, the incorrect view that natural religions, including those in the world of ancient Israel, were a more primitive theological expression, and the related affirmation of the primacy of redeeming word found in the Old Testament's interpretation of salvation history over the world of mythic origins and gods of fertility. The resources and methodologies used in the identification and thick description of creation as the thematic center of Old Testament theology have been found in the important studies in contemporary theology, especially those delving into ecotheology and the social-scientific understandings of myth present in the history of religions in general and the ancient Near East in particular.

Ecotheology has been a major theological focus in contemporary theology since the end of the 1960s. This theology concentrates on the interrelationships of religion and nature, with a view to environmental concerns. More recently, the scientific and theological communities have addressed the growing crisis of global warming. Ecotheology argues that an intimate bond exists between human religious/spiritual worldviews and the contrast of the support or degradation of nature. It explores the interaction between ecological values, such as the enduring sustainability of nature, and the human violation and pillaging of the environment and other forms of life, based on an arrogant and misconstrued anthropology of human domination of the natural world. This tendency toward dominance is found in the closely related exploitation of both the earth and the poor.[104]

Myth and Ritual in Europe

In addition to contemporary theology, the history of religions, social anthropology, and social-scientific studies of religion also have stimulated important work in Old Testament creation theology.[105] To understand creation, its intrinsic relationship to myth has led many to understand the social-scientific and history-of-religions formulations of myth.[106] Earlier, two circles of Old Testament scholars, the so-called British Myth and Ritual school of S. H. Hooke and the Scandinavian school, used the insights drawn from their respective cultures' examinations of cultural anthropology along with ancient Near Eastern myth to develop the notion of a common mythic and ritual pattern present throughout the ancient Near East, including Israel.[107] While this idea of a common pattern has largely disappeared, its quest was one of the motivating factors in studies of myth and ritual in the first half of the twentieth century. From these investigations, scholars began to use the views in important ways to capture creation theology in the Hebrew Bible.

Basing his theory on a diffusionist model (made popular by the British anthropologist Sir James George Frazer) in his now classic study of comparative folklore, magic, and religion, *The Golden Bough* (1922), Hooke did not simply argue that myths from Babylonia spread throughout the Fertile Crescent and eventually made their way into the literature of the Bible. Rather, he argued there was a common ancient Near Eastern religious pattern of myths and associated rituals that are reflected in Hebrew religion. Furthermore, myth and ritual were inextricably linked together. According to Hooke and his circle, the Babylonian New Year's festival dramatically presented the death and resurrection of the god Marduk, recited the myth of creation, portrayed the ritual combat in which Marduk defeated the dragon, consummated the sacred marriage between Marduk and his consort, and concluded with the triumphal procession climaxing in his enthronement. Through the power of ritual performance and mythic word, the world was re-created and destinies fixed. This diffusionist model is found throughout the cultures of the eastern Mediterranean world.

Hooke and his colleagues succeed in shaping an imaginative reconstruction of a myth and ritual pattern that was, in their estimation, useful in understanding Israelite religion, influenced studies of biblical theology's conceptions of time and space, and even supported such major tenets of classical Liberalism as universalism. While serious questions have been raised about both the theoretical base and the conclusions of this approach (the rejection of the diffusionist theory of religious models, the separation of myth from its connection to ritual, and the attempt to force a wide variety of data from culturally distinct areas into a common pattern), the Scandinavian school continued to advance this distinctive synthesis.[108]

Myth in American Old Testament Circles

Due to the impact of neo-orthodoxy on the biblical theology movement in America, very little theological interest in myth and ritual developed in this country during the period following WWII until the middle of the 1960s. Yahweh was the "Lord of History," as George Ernest Wright proclaimed, not a nature deity in cosmogonic and world maintenance myths.[109] Myth was placed in opposition to history, historical thinking, and thus salvation history. This distinctive place given to history in religion and theology meant that the Hebrew theology's teachings of a God of History was considered superior to ancient Near Eastern fertility gods and their cosmogonic myths involving the annual renewal of the earth along a seasonal pattern. This supercessionist theology has fallen into a great deal of disfavor in current theological reflection, but it was quite powerful and convincing at the time it was proclaimed.

One of the theoretical bases for the biblical theology movement of the 1950s was the writing of Henri and H. A. Frankfort, John A. Wilson, and Thorkild Jacobsen, *The Intellectual Adventure of Ancient Man* (*Before Philosophy*).[110] These ancient Near Eastern scholars, following the theories of the French anthropologists Cassirer and Levy-Bruhl, argued that primitive human thought, represented in the high cultures of the ancient Near East, was mythopoeic, that is, addressed the world and its objects as a "Thou" not an "It," and perceived things in their parts rather than in their wholes.[111] Mythic literature tended to be poetic in its formal composition rather than narrative in style. These scholars contended the relationship between ancient Israel and God occurred in the framework of history and thus contrasted to the relationship of the Canaanites and other ancient Near Eastern nations with their gods, which supposedly occurred primarily within the seasons of the renewal of nature. In contrast to the gods of the ancient Near East, Yahweh was a transcendent deity who at times became immanent in history, not nature.[112]

The Albright school adopted this approach, especially Frank Moore Cross Jr., who argued that Israel mythologized historical events by using mythological images as a poetic way of describing historical events believed to be redemptive.[113] Mythic language was borrowed from Canaan and elsewhere to enable Israel to speak of the actions of Israel's God. Cross contended Yahweh was both a creator deity and a divine warrior who fought on Israel's behalf.

Myth and Creation

Significant presentations of creation theology in the Old Testament have appeared in recent years that draw on contemporary theology, history of religions, and social-science analyses of myth. These include the work of four scholars who approach history and creation in distinctive ways: H. H. Schmid, B. W. Anderson, Rolf Knierim, and Jon Levenson.

The Common Horizon of Old Testament Theology: H. H. Schmid

In 1972 H. H. Schmid,[114] using a history of religions approach, stated his concern that creation had largely been overlooked in past theologies of the Hebrew Bible. Salvation history had come to dominate the theological description, making it the primary belief in the faith of ancient Israel. Creation, by contrast, was either relegated to secondary status or denied a theological status, making it preliminary to the salvific faith of ancient Israel. The continuing suspicion that creation was an element of natural religion, a view held by neo-orthodox theologians, had negated the theological validity of creation. Creation was also devalued by scholars who considered it to be a late development in ancient Israel, entering into Israelite worship and confession only in the Second Temple. Thus, one sees the theological importance of the theme for the first time in the redemptive creation of Second Isaiah (Isa 40–55) who spoke of a new exodus in terms of a pristine creation and in the Priestly Document, especially in Gen 1:1–2:4a, in which the belief was given a liturgical setting within the celebration of the Sabbath on the seventh day of divine rest.

Schmid especially took on the views of creation expressed by von Rad and argued that creation and the order of righteousness that permeated the world was the "common horizon of Old Testament theology." Schmid even situated creation as the primary doctrine of the faith of ancient Israel, regarding it as the primal context in which redemptive history could transpire. Instead of relegating creation to a secondary status, Schmid emphasizes that it is the context for and fulfillment of human history.[115] Working from the perspectives of an historian of ancient Near Eastern religion and a theologian of ancient Israel, Schmid emphasized there is not a single culture in the ancient Near East that does not speak about creation in a variety of literary forms, ranging from myth, to psalms, to wisdom. However, myth is the primary form in which creation in the ancient Near East is expressed. In his own views of myth, Schmid includes in particular the understanding that creation involves two primary functions: first, to demonstrate and give potency to the divine, continuing revitalization of nature on a daily, seasonal, and annual basis; and second, to provide for the founding and legitimizing empowerment of the state. The state, through its legal and royal institutions, is to reflect the just order of creation in order to guide and enable to flourish human society. Creation, thus, is the essential and fundamental theme of Old Testament theology.

From Origins to Eschatology:
B. W. Anderson

We have already mentioned Anderson's most recent Old Testament theology, which focused on covenant as the central theme in understanding the faith of ancient Israel. In spite of this later emphasis, Anderson has written numerous compositions on creation in ancient Israel, situated within the context of the religions of the ancient Near East. Anderson is especially known for his synthesis of American and Continental (especially German) theologians and historians. Evaluated from this point of view, the entirety of his work has been unusually successful in drawing understandings of theological and religious topics from a wide variety of sources. This is true in his studies of creation theology, which bring together Old Testament theology, the history of religions in Israel and the ancient Near East, and social-scientific understandings of myth from a variety of theoretical perspectives. His editing of a collection of essays on creation in the Old Testament demonstrates the breadth of his command of secondary scholarship.[116] In his collection of seminal articles, he composes an introductory essay that delineates clearly the major views and treatments of this theme, since Hermann Gunkel and the impact of Babylonian studies on understanding Israel and the Hebrew Bible, and concludes with an essay written in 1978 by George Landes on creation and liberation. Ten years later he published a collection of his previous essays on creation in the Overture Series, which offers a rich interpretation of creation and carves out for it a major place in Old Testament theology.[117] In all these studies, Anderson never succeeds in breaking from the fundamental view that redemptive history is not only the center of Israelite faith but also provides the meaning given to creation.

Over the years Anderson's views of creation have been solidly rooted in a keen interpretation of the witness of Scripture. Among the more significant views in his writings is the affirmation that creation faith points to the important belief that God is the author of the meaning that resides behind human history and the world of nature, indicating, then, that history and nature do not demonstrate or contain their own intrinsic meaning.[118] Picking up Barth's point, Anderson stresses that the Divine Word is the interpretative force that provides meaning to all of creation. Yet Anderson still adheres to von Rad's contention that election theology, which leads to Israel's redemption, is that which defines the importance and meaning of creation. Thus, one needs to read the call of Abraham and the story of election and redemption of Israel backward to creation to derive the latter's true meaning. Anderson also continues to emphasize throughout his writings on the subject that Israel understood creation was totally dependent on the power and providence of God. Without the power of God, creation would return to chaos.[119]

Also important for Anderson is the affirmation in the priestly creation account that humanity is made in the image of God (Gen 1:26-28).[120] This theological anthropology points to humanity, male and female, as the apex of divine creation, that humanity is the "thou" addressed by God, that humankind's purpose is to join with all creation in a liturgy of praise of the creation, and that the role of humans on the earth is to express the sovereignty of God over all that is created.[121]

Finally, Anderson also directs us to the importance of the new creation announced in the Prophets and in apocalyptic literature.[122] The Prophets are more attuned to the corruption of creation by a sinful humanity. God's original shaping of a "good" creation that exists to engage in the glorification of the Creator is polluted by human sin arising from hubris.

This sinfulness has led to the perversion of both Israel's election and human history and to the distortion of God's creation, including both the world of nature and of human creatures. Among the Prophets, Second Isaiah combines history, soteriology, and creation into an eschatological vision of the future in celebrating Israel's deliverance from Babylonian captivity and return home. For him, God is both the Creator and the Redeemer who is engaging in a new creation in the redemption of Israel. Later in Trito-Isaiah, the prophet speaks of a "new heaven and new earth." This theme is especially pronounced in early Jewish and primitive Christian apocalyptic. The current world, filled with sinful distortions, will lead to a transformation that results in the dawning of a new creation in which the wicked are eliminated, while peace and blessing remain the eternal constants of existence under the reign of God.

Finally, Anderson points to the variety of theological understandings at work in different texts and tradition complexes. The exodus-covenant tradition presents Yahweh as the divine warrior who in the defeat of Israel's enemies also overwhelms the power of chaos, is enthroned as sovereign, and is hailed as King over creation (cf. Exod 15:1-18). The other major tradition complex is that of David and Zion, in which the kingship and dynasty of David and the dwelling of God in the sacred temple become the institutions by which divine blessing is mediated.

The Subordination of History to Creation: Rolf Knierim[123]

Rolf Knierim has set forth a provocative number of insights into the theology of creation, although he has not composed a comprehensive study. One of these is his "prolegomenon" to an Old Testament theology, in which he reaches back through the generations dominated by redemptive history and calls for a return to a systematic presentation. He is quick to recognize that this approach is constructive theology that replaces the so-called descriptive approach of an earlier generation of scholars. What is particularly important in this composition is his subordination of history, including salvation history, to creation.

For Knierim, God's universal domain is not history but rather creation. God's continuing reign precedes, transcends, and follows the conclusion of history. Subsequently, this means that the sovereignty of God is not dependent on human beings, thus denying the validity of an anthropologically centered reality. In addition, this God is understood monotheistically, a unity that enables the theologian to achieve a systematic rendering of the multiple creation traditions present in the Hebrew Bible. Recognizing the plurality of Old Testament theologies in the text, Knierim seeks a monotheistic structure that relates and systematizes these features into a systematic whole. In speaking of monotheism, Knierim indicates that the theological structure that it constructs is the "the universal dominion of Yahweh in justice and righteousness." God is not spoken of individually but only in relationship to a reality that consists of cosmos, nature, history, society, and the individual. Old Testament theology is to flesh out these relationships that are shaped by the key features of divine rule: "justice" and "righteousness."

Furthermore, Knierim contends that universal history and Israel's own election achieve their true significance only when they witness to and act out God's universal dominion.[124] History becomes the realm in which the struggle for the meaning of creation is to be actualized. Israel's redemption from the oppression of the empires underlines and witnesses to God's universal redemption of the world of order from being engulfed by chaos. It is in this common redemption from chaos and oppression that the meanings of creation and salvation history are achieved. In addition, the rest (*mĕnûhâ*), which God gives to Israel in order to settle the land, approximates the Sabbath rest of creation, which is the justice Israel is to establish and continue in its social life to become the righteous community that reflects the order of creation and the divine rule of the cosmos.

Space and time, according to Knierim, comprise the two major areas of creation. "Heaven and earth" is the oft-repeated expression that points to the order of space and indicates two realms, the first being the location of divine creation and the second the world of human habitation. The temple points to the residence of Yahweh on the earth, although it is the mirror of the heavenly dwelling. This polarity cannot be overcome, lest the world return to chaos.[125] Knierim suggests that the world is not self-sustaining but rather continues due only to the just power of God. Only God is the "ground and guarantor of the unity and the wholeness of the world." This is the "ultimate theodicy."

Knierim points also to the polarity of time: cosmic (cyclical) and historical (linear). Once more it is the righteous power of God that sustains the cycle of both types of reality. They find their unity only in the singleness of divine reign. Even so, cosmic time takes precedence over epochal history, since the cosmos precedes and will continue well beyond the temporal existence of humankind.

Creation and Theodicy: Jon Levenson

Writing in response to the Holocaust and its implications for the problem of evil, Jon Levenson's creative composition *Creation and the Persistence of Evil* examines the ever present problem of theodicy raised by the attribution of creation and providence to Israel's God.[126] The theological conundrum is especially how to affirm two essential attributes of God: sovereignty with the implication of divine rule and power over the cosmos, and compassion for human beings and the larger world of nature. The Holocaust makes the confession of these two essential characteristics of God especially acute for a modern audience shocked and grief-stricken by the murder of the six million. Placed within the swirling vortex of unbelievable inhumanity, Levenson questions how it is possible to reconcile the sovereignty of God with divine compassion and justice.

Levenson slowly builds a careful theological response to this persistent and torturous question. He begins by rejecting the later Greek-influenced notion found in early Christianity of *creatio ex nihilo*. Not only does the Hebrew Bible, he contends, view creation as a divine act of transformation of material chaos into form, without eliminating all vestiges of disorder, but it also negates "a false finality or definitiveness" to creation. The comos continues to exist in all its fragility by means of divine power.

Levenson's most significant insight resides in his treatment of creation within the context of liturgy. He situates the priestly creation story, which is one of the dominant portrayals in the Hebrew Bible, in cultic liturgy. In doing so, Levenson builds on the recognition of scholars of myth and ritual that ritual in word and deed issues forth a divine means of sustaining the cosmos. The Sabbath rest and the worship of God on the day firmly grounded in the structure of creation enables, first of all, creation and history to gain a respite from the devastating forces of chaos. At the same time, cosmic and historical space meet in the symbolism of the temple. For Levenson, the temple serves as a microcosm of the world as it should be, orderly, harmonious, and restrictive of chaos. In the reconstruction and rededication of the temple, priests and congregants participate once more in the divine ordering of the world. Within the contexts of sacred space and time, Israel proleptically participates in the ultimate defeat of chaos and the extinction of its disruptive powers.

Finally, Levenson seeks to shape a relationship between cosmos and history, both in understanding the sovereignty and domains of divine presence and action and in constructing a dialectic consisting of humanity's submission to divine suzerainty and God's dependence on humanity. While not discounting the destructive power of chaos in creation, Levenson suggests that it is especially active within Israel's historical experience. While Israel attempted to maintain its faithfulness to divine sovereignty, the struggle between Yahweh and the chaos monster continued, leading to the projection of its defeat in the eschaton (cf. Isa 24–27). This victory will forever lead to the end of the disruptions of chaos in Israel's history and the life-giving beneficence of creation. Nevertheless, this faith is expressed before, not after, the final victory, leading to a theology of hope.

Levenson takes up the dialectic of cosmos and history expressed in the two theological expressions of creation and covenant. Israel's belief in the ultimate defeat of chaos and its refusal to give even this fearsome power divine status is expressive of a strong monotheism and the rule over the divine council. This monotheism calls for uncompromising allegiance to God, given formal expression in the concept and language of covenant. It is only when other gods, promising Israel greater blessings, are worshiped that steadfastness to the covenant and God's sovereignty are compromised. Indeed, for Levenson, God's sovereignty is dependent, at least in part, on Israel's continual affirmation of its monotheistic faith in worship. God's rule over history required the repetition of the covenant in ritual celebration and loyal, freely given obedience to its requirements. The potency of divine power rests, to some extent, on Israel's continuing affirmation of the oneness of God within the context of cultic liturgy that includes covenant renewal and testimony. Yet Levenson stresses that Israel, like all of humanity, must be free to recognize and then submit to divine rule, a belief that leads to the continuing tension between autonomy and heteronomy, that is, human freedom and submission to divine sovereignty. To express this tensive quality, Levenson draws on ancient Near Eastern suzerainty treaties in which a vassal freely enters into covenant with the suzerain, all the while recognizing his lordship. To avoid the breakdown of this treaty, not only is the vassal required to follow the dictates circumscribed, but also the sovereign is to fulfill the responsibilities of the suzerain in the treatment of the underling. Thus, while Israel is chosen for service, it must choose to serve.[127] The autonomy of humanity allows people to argue with and to question God and even win, but the force of heteronomy brings them back into submission. Argument and worship are both acts of faithful spirituality.[128]

These are four of the more provocative treatments of creation theology in the past half century. Each has its insights and its weaknesses. But it is especially clear that the day is long past when Old Testament theology could be legitimately understood within the rubrics of history and redemptive history, either as events or interpretations of tradition. The present world cannot rest content with the severe restraints that history imposes on theological expression.

OLD TESTAMENT THEOLOGY AS THE DIALECTIC OF SALVATION HISTORY AND CREATION

Claus Westermann

The significant Old Testament theologies during the last half of the twentieth century focused their attention on the singular importance of redemptive history or creation, with one taking priority over the others. Another approach that is more comprehensive and, in my view, better able to handle the diverse texts and traditions assembled in the canon of the Hebrew Bible, is the dialectic between history and creation. The best modern example of this theological dialectic is found in the theological writings of Claus Westermann,[129] also a former professor at Heidelberg, who uses primarily the categories of form criticism and the history of religion to articulate the theology of the Old Testament.[130]

Westermann's own experiences as a Lutheran pastor, soldier in the Wehrmacht fighting on the Russian front, and internment in a Russian prisoner of war camp shaped his understanding of the theological richness of the Hebrew Bible and gave him the ability to penetrate beyond the words of a text to the existential strivings of the human soul in search of God.[131] Born in Berlin to a former German missionary to Africa who then taught African languages and ethnology, Westermann received his university education in the areas of philosophy and religion, finishing in 1933. He then entered a practical seminary for a year of study but left with twelve other students due to the influence of the Nazis and the Deutsche Christen. They then came together as a practical seminary headed by Max Niemoller, a leading pastor in the Confessing Church who opposed Nazism. Upon graduation, Westermann entered into a Lutheran parish church but was drafted into the army and served as a translator at the Russian front. Following his release from the Russian prisoner of war camp, he became a pastor of a German church in Berlin. In 1948, he was invited by Walther Zimmerli to study Old Testament with him at Zurich in the doctoral program. He completed his dissertation in 1949. He then returned to Berlin to reassume his pastoral duties and taught at the city's Kirchliche Hochschule. He eventually joined the Heidelberg faculty in 1958, where he taught until his retirement in 1978.

Drawing upon his experiences as pastor and captured soldier trapped in the horrors of war, he approached the study of Old Testament theology as an interchange between and integration of divine blessing and saving history that, together, comprises the faith and practice of ancient Israel and moves beyond the chosen to include the entire world. He always taught, lectured, and wrote for the larger world of the church, while not relinquishing his role as a scholar. While these two thematic areas are separate, he concludes the two themes cannot be clearly divided. He notes that the Hebrew Bible continues to "break through the dividing line between these two realms."[132] For example, when God comes to save, the realm of nature responds, including the quaking of the earth or the crossing of the Red Sea (Exod 15). Likewise, Westermann rejected the systematic formulation of timeless theological abstractions that were found in church dogmatics. Thus, it was not surprising that he spurned Eichrodt's conceptualizing in favor of the embodiment of theology in historical events and processes of nature.[133]

The Saving God of History

Westermann could not say that the faith of the Old Testament was simply a confession of the acts of God on behalf of Israel. At the same time, he repudiated historicism and the naive understanding of history as a compiling and arranging of data. Instead, he chose to speak of a process that involved growth, multification, and preservation of life in history and creation. For Westermann, the spoken word shaped the theological traditions of the theology of the Old Testament. In a manner similar to von Rad's, Westermann understands that the Old Testament speaks of the redeeming God of history in the form of a narrative or "story," and that its theology focused on the interpretation of divine events and not the formulation of concepts.[134] Abstract themes like covenant and revelation are based on nouns, while Old Testament theology tells of divine actions of redemption performed by God. The God of the Hebrew Bible encounters the chosen in events as a merciful deity and then engages in dialogue with them in order to become their God. Their destiny is shaped by this God of election and redemption. With the exception of Wisdom, all other sections of the Hebrew canon relate a sacred memory of the saving God in acts of redemption.

While recognizing the importance of the acts of redemption, Westermann does not limit his interest to these alone. Particularly useful is his noting of a particular sequence of acts of God: Israel's need, the summons of the people in this situation, the address of their plight, and their salvation conditioned their response to God. Two other features of redemption history are important: Israel's election leads to the confession and proclamation of the divine acts of salvation God has performed on the people's behalf (Deut 7:6-8), and the covenant (*bĕrît*) that articulates the relationship between God and the chosen. Even so, it is the body of divine actions of God's originating in saving grace, not covenant, which is determinative for the faith of Israel. These divine actions are not limited to the ones of Israel's past origins but continue to occur throughout its history. As the response to divine redemption, Israel offers to God its praise (see the hymns of national redemption in the Psalms).

The understanding of covenant derives from Deuteronomic tradition, which emphasized Israel's relationship with God as static, not active. Westermann contends that the historical creed in Deut 26:5-9 speaks of the whole of God's continuing acts of salvation, not merely individual acts that are simply pieced together. It was Deuteronomic theology that spoke of the divine revelation at Mount Sinai and the giving of the Torah, which transformed this saving event into "a condition, i.e., the continuing covenantal relationship."[135]

For Westermann, God is a universal deity who is active in human history, and not simply with Israel. Once again deliverance stands at the center of this redemptive history. While Yahweh has acted on Israel's behalf, this gives its people the responsibility to serve as the avenue through which universal salvation is to be accomplished. This saving encounter of God with humanity begins in the primeval history following creation and will continue until the end time.

The Blessing God and Creation

Westermann lamented that the theology of creation had become a neglected theological tradition, largely due to the Enlightenment and the development of modern science.[136] Unlike his Heidelberg colleague (von Rad), Westermann provided creation a place of theological importance in Old Testament theology, comparable to that given redemptive history. One of the major expressions in Westermann's compositions about creation is blessing, a divine power that gives life and well-being to the world of human habitation and humanity itself. While blessing is not a well-construed theological dogma that is to be confessed, it remains an important theme for theological understanding.[137] The related terms "creator" and "creation" likewise are not only affirmations of faith but also serve as important expressions in Israel's theology. Westermann agreed with von Rad that creation is a preliminary activity of God that precedes faith and was unwitnessed by human observers. Yet narratives, poems, and psalms encompass its thematic features and point to its importance in the Hebrew Bible. Contrasting with acts of redemption that occur in particular times and places, creation is a durative process that originates, sustains, and revitalizes.[138] In the remembered stories and poems of creation, humans enter into the whole of reality and experience their own vitality and continuation. As is the case with other theological themes, multiple attestations to creation and a variety of statements and understandings are present in the Hebrew Bible. These are found in Gen 1–2, creation psalms, several Prophets, especially Second Isaiah, and the wisdom texts. Thus, creation is present in each of the three parts of the Hebrew canon. Furthermore, one of the arguments peculiar to Westermann is the view that there are two major creation traditions in the Hebrew Bible: the creation of humanity, which is the older; and the creation of the world, which, though later, speaks of origins and providence guiding the cosmos, nature, humanity, and the chosen people.[139] Israel came to understand God was responsible for what happens from the beginning to the end of time and in every sphere of life, including that of Israel and the nations, and is active providentially in the blessing that gives life and vitality to all that exists.

Eschatology also enters into this equation, for the "new heaven and new earth" of apocalyptic corresponds to the creation of heaven and earth in the beginning and during the time of the existence of the present world. In this way, creation moves from world origins to providence to the eschaton.[140] Creation taught Israel to understand both God and its own purpose for existence beyond the boundaries of particularity. God was the Lord of both universal history and the cosmos, while Israel was the chosen people from among the nations who remained under the dominion and blessing of God.[141]

Blessing as the Vital Force of Salvation and Creation

Originally, God shaped creation with blessing that served as the vital power that gave life and vitality to existence. The connection of blessing with creation and with redemptive history transformed this power into a force that enhanced the well-being of the nations. It was through Israel that divine blessing was channeled, leading to the understanding that it was at work in both creation and history. Blessing is present in other elements, including maturation of life, multiplication, and the bearing of fruit. Thus blessing merges with and is present in redemptive actions to shape the character of Old Testament theology.[142] Blessing especially finds one of its more complementary expressions in the notions of "peace" and divine "presence."

In Westermann's interpretation of the Hebrew Bible, living creatures and plants were endowed with blessing during the actions of primal creation. Blessing continues to sustain life into the future. Unlike redemptive history performed for the chosen, God's blessing was universal and served to preserve the well-being of all life. Divine blessing is delineated into a variety of components: the empowering of the movement of the human generations through time and space in the continuing cycles of life, the power of procreation that sustains life, the ability to defeat one's enemies, and the experience of well-being in living. This blessing sustains Israel's existence in the present and into the future. Westermann demarcates three major transitions of blessing in the history of Israel. The first was the transition from the wilderness to the land of promise that is fertile and teeming with life. The second was the transition from the tribes to kingship, where the monarch is chosen to mediate divine blessing to Israel. The third was the collapse of the state that leads to new, future salvation (Deutero-Isaiah and apocalyptic). Socially, the family, the cult, and kingship served as the spheres of the divine blessing of humanity. Included as major features of the Old Testament's understanding of blessing is the establishment of a relationship to God, the commandment to engage in work, and the human ability to produce the arts of culture, intellectual activity, and reflection. The human response to divine creation and actions in nature and history is praise, as demonstrated by many of the hymns of the Psalter. Finally, the importance of creation for Old Testament theology results in including the canonical Wisdom literature, since its theology in the canon is based on creation and not redemptive history.

God's Judgment and Compassion[143]

In addition to salvation history and the process of the vitality of the forces of nature, there are also divine commandments that are a part of history and creation. Human transgression, beginning in the primeval garden, disobedient acts of Israel against God and the world, and sinful actions among the human community occurred throughout history. Westermann replaces the concepts of "sin" and "the fall of humanity" with the acts of disobedience and transgression. Disobedience is a rejection of the divine teachings that direct human behavior and enable dialogue with God and the establishment of communal relationships with others. Transgression is a feature of both human nature and activity. Transgression is not only violation of the relationship with God but also activity that harms others. Those who transgress against others and God's commandments receive punishment in a variety of forms: illness, destruction by enemies, and the harm of their community. The relationships with people and God are disrupted and spoiled.

The other side of judgment is divine compassion, which may lead to the forgiveness of the guilty who confess and repent. The penitential response may restore the relationship of the transgressor with God and with others. God's compassion, grounded in the divine goodness, experiences no limit in forgiveness and restoration. Even prophetic judgment proclaimed in oracles of disaster may be followed by promises of salvation that are based on compassion and forgiveness. Finally, in the visions of apocalyptic, transgressors and their destructive powers are ultimately eliminated.

The Human Response[144]

For Westermann, Old Testament theology regards praise, prayer, and offering to comprise the human response to God. This is especially true of the Psalms. Hymns of praise declare the divine works of God in history and creation, while lamentations are an appeal to God to deliver from suffering when confession and repentance are offered. God promises for-giveness and restoration through the prophetic word and the priestly announcement. The human response to God's acts of blessing includes not only human devotion but also meditation on divine acts of blessing and teachings directed to humans. Meditation leads to the recognition of the goodness and compassion of God, who acts to forgive and deliver, and to the understanding of the limits of human behavior and mortality. Humans come to understand they cannot live complete lives apart from their relationship to God, whose image they bear. God is known, not through abstract teaching, but rather by means of a relationship with the worshiper.

The Old Testament, Hermeneutics, and Jesus Christ[145]

Since Westermann has the objective of addressing Old Testament theology to the church, he describes the relevancy in historical terms. His understanding of hermeneutics draws on historical criticism applied to the critical reconstruction of the history that moves into the period and texts of the early church and its canon.[146] While the current histor-ical interpretation is relative, since it depends on what is known in the present, Israel's history and religion nevertheless should be recon-structed according to the history of religion and the theological faith of its people. Thus, Westermann reconstructs the faith of the Hebrew Bible as a theological understanding of history. This understanding is shaped by the Word of God that becomes incarnate in Jesus Christ. The incarnation is the culmination of the events and movement of history in the life of Israel and the beginning of primitive Christianity. The Christ-event, which contains the promise of salvation, brings history to its fruition. In contrast to neo-orthodoxy, Word and history reach a symbiosis in the incarnation.

Following his approach of developmental history, Westermann regards the New Testament as following the three sections of the canon of the Hebrew Bible: the Law, the Prophets, and the Writings. Thus, Westermann's association of the two Testaments is based on the concept of a sequential development of canonical literature. Yahweh's deliver-ance of Israel from Egyptian slavery in the exodus is comparable to the redemption of Christ, the Savior. The same God delivered Israel and brings about redemption in Jesus Christ. Furthermore, common to both

Testaments is the theology of creation in which God is the Creator and sustainer of both the world and humanity. Thus, the First Canon's depiction of God as Creator and Redeemer continues in the New Testament's proclamation. Finally, both Testaments present the theology of the blessing God who shaped the two peoples who developed a common faith and worship.

Yet there are also important theological differences between the two Testaments. While God acts to establish Israel as a nation possessing political and military power, he forms a community of believers in Christ that does not possess features of a state. Other differences include material gifts in the Hebrew Bible, while the New Testament focuses on spiritual gifts, including especially eternal life following, although this contrast is largely perfunctory. According to Westermann, far more significant is the Hebrew Bible's setting forth of the history of a nation of people, while the New Testament speaks of the early stages of a community of believers who form a common bond based on spiritual relationships.

Westermann's theology succeeds in bringing together the theology of creation and redemptive history and in pointing to one way the church may understand and then appropriate the relationship of the two Testaments. However, he should have emphasized and expanded more than he did the universal character of both creation and history and, at the same time, demonstrated how history, including a triumphalist version of the history of salvation, could stand in opposition to creation and lead to its decimation.[147]

OLD TESTAMENT THEOLOGY AND CANON

Brevard S. Childs

A student of Walther Eichrodt and Walther Baumgartner at Basel, where he completed his ThD, Brevard Childs attended the lectures of Karl Barth and was profoundly influenced by neo-orthodoxy. In the 1970s, following the composition of several distinguished works as a historical critic, Childs's interests shifted to biblical theology, where he began to develop what he considered to be an authentic way of appropriating the faith found in the biblical books. This new approach, in his view, was not simply another method but more of a hermeneutical understanding of the formation of the canon and the reception of its faith as divine revelation. The fundamental assertion made repeatedly by Childs is that Scripture is the theological context in which authentic, theological affirmations of the church are made.[148]

Childs's numerous works on biblical theology make use of his canonical approach, which he has described in detail in his many writings.[149] He begins with regarding the historical-critical method as theologically bankrupt. This does not mean he discards traditional methods of exegesis, but he feels these methods, taken together, not only face major difficulties in the attempt to produce a consensus of views about many specific issues but also are unable to construct a biblical theology for communities of faith, both past and present. It is the "Word" contained within the canonical text for Childs that is revelatory, not the particularities of the historical and social circumstances that may have influenced those authors, tradents, and editors of social communities who produced and preserved the tradition over many years of historical events reconstructed by scholars. The focus of the theologian is the final form of the text that entered into the canon, and not earlier traditions and sources that existed prior to the completion of a canonical book.

Historical criticism, in Childs's view, has failed theologically because of three significant omissions. First, it has ignored the canonical form of the text that bears the authority and normative value of scripture given it by the community of faith. Second, historical criticism has failed to understand the "canonical process" at work within the generations of faith communities that eventually construed the final shape of Old Testament books. And third, historical criticism has not taken seriously the creative dynamic operating between canonical books and the communities that not only produced them but also came to honor them as normative and authoritative. Due to these omissions, historical criticism has failed to lead to both authoritative biblical theology and contemporary hermeneutics for the confessing church. The only way to approach biblical theology, for Childs, is to recognize that the canonical books of the two Testaments are both intrinsically theological and authoritative for believing communities.

Childs describes this canonical process as in essence a hermeneutical one: bearers of tradition and their communities of faith transmitted the traditions that came to make up the Hebrew Bible and the New Testament. He proceeds upon the basis of two primary assumptions. First, the canon is the proper context for interpretation. This means that the interpretation of a text occurs within the entire canon. Second, the Old Testament is a normative, authoritative collection of texts. Texts were intentionally shaped by communities of faith to address the divine word to future generations.

Childs insists that communities of faith that shaped and handed down their traditions possessed a "canon consciousness." Thus when they transmitted their traditions of faith, they were aware that they were shaping them for present and future communities. This canon consciousness is theological and is not the result of sociopolitical forces that influenced the communities. Theological meaning is located, neither in the mind of the author nor in how the original audience may have understood what was written or said, but rather in the boundaries of the text itself. Childs points to several biblical texts that indicate a canonical process is at work in the shaping of the canonical books and the final canon. For instance, the book of Deuteronomy, written in the last years of the monarchy, provided the canonical interpretation of the law of the Pentateuch.

Childs reiterates the view of von Rad that Israel's earliest faith was redemptive theology that began with the exodus from Egypt. For Childs, historically speaking, creation was a secondary element that developed later as an element of Israelite faith. Yet this is not the case canonically, for the shaping of the corpus of books in the Old Testament still begins with creation. Childs notes that the beginning of history (Gen 1–11) does not start with Israel (Gen 12–50) but rather with "the preparation of the stage for world history."[150] While noting the difficulties entailed by efforts to set forth the relationship between the Yahwist and Priestly sources, Childs argues that the development of the creation is not due simply to the ancient Near Eastern sources. The concern of the Old Testament theologian should be to uncover the various forms of the tradition of creation in the Hebrew Bible.

The priestly account of creation (Gen 1:1–2:4a) makes use of the verb *bārā'* (בָּרָא) in order to describe creation as unique to divine activity. While the priestly account of creation mentions divine rest on the seventh day, there is no reference to the Sabbath. Rather, this connection between the seventh day of creation and the Sabbath is made in the priestly rendition of the Decalogue in Exod 20. This connection of Sabbath and creation stresses to Israel the importance of honoring the sacred day that allows them to participate in the divine power of creation. The priestly account of creation does not contain any reference to covenant. However, Exod 31:12ff. points to the Sabbath as the sign of the "perpetual covenant" between the Creator and his people. In keeping the Sabbath, Israel remembers the creation of the heavens and earth in six days and the hallowing of the seventh day by divine rest. Finally, the structure of the six days of creation parallels the building of the sanctuary (Exod 24:15-18). It is only in the events of the Sinai that the mystery of God is revealed to Israel, his people, and in their dwelling in the land where God assumes his divine residence.[151]

For Childs, the Yahwist account of creation (Gen 2:4b-25), which sets forth a contrast between creation and reality existing before time and space existed, is a part of the narrative that includes human disobedience in chapter 3. Thus, the creation story serves as an introduction to the alienation between Yahweh and humanity. The editing of the various J narratives in Gen 1–11 transforms this material into an account of the history of the world, followed by the history of Israel's ancestors.[152] Elsewhere in the Old Testament, according to Childs, the theological theme of creation is frequently used to express Yahweh's lordship over the earth, the nations, and Israel. In the Psalter, God is the Creator of the world (Pss 8 and 104) and Israel (Ps 100). Psalm 136 praises God as the Creator of the cosmos and the redeemer of his people, Israel. Psalm 104 points to God's creation of the world and makes use of some of the battle imagery against the sea (vv. 6-9). The royal psalms use creation theology to underscore divine power, the covenant with David, and the establishment of Zion, which was understood to be the place chosen for divine dwelling (Pss 74 and 89). Psalms 47; 91; and 93–99 point to the kingship and Israel in Zion as the vertical axis located between the celestial and mundane realms.

The Prophets, in particular Deutero-Isaiah, make significant use of the creation tradition in the shaping of their messages to the peoples of Israel and Judah. The prophet of Babylon praises God as the Creator of the "ends of the earth" (40:28) and as the one who has "stretched out the heavens" (44:24). He is the divine judge who "make[s] weal and create[s] woe" (45:7). In 51:9ff., Yahweh is the one who defeats Rahab, the dragon who personifies chaos. Consequently, this prophet integrates creation, the exodus, and the return to Jerusalem through the wilderness into a grand theological synthesis. Later in the book there is a prophetic emphasis on the creation of new heavens and a new earth (65:17ff.; 66:22f.). Taken as a whole, in this prophet there is a full movement from creation to redemption at the end time.[153] However, in spite of his emphasis on the canon as the context for Israelite faith, Childs does not use his canonical method to examine the sapiential texts in order to state their theological understanding. This represents the greatest weakness of his work, for he tends simply to restate von Rad's major positions articulated in his *Wisdom in Israel.*

In regard to his articulation of the faith of Israel, Childs rejects Bultmann's view that the New Testament replaces the failed theology of the Old Testament and argues instead that the First Testament speaks to the contemporary church as scripture. The authority and theological witness of the Old Testament are not simply found in the New Testament's use of Old Testament theological themes and texts but rather the Old Testament has its own integrity and should continue to address the church in the present.[154] While the Old Testament can reflect only one witness to Christian theology, it is still a part of Christian Scriptures. What binds the testaments indissolubly together is their witness to the selfsame divine reality and to the subject matter, that undergirds both collections and cannot be contained within the domesticating categories of "religion." Scripture is also not self-referential but points beyond itself to the reality of God.

Childs is not simply concerned to write an Old Testament theology but seeks to set forth the faith of the entire Christian canon (Protestant, not Roman Catholic), Old and New Testaments, combined. Thus, the task of biblical theology is to reflect on both the Old and the New Testaments. While Childs gives the New Testament theological priority over the Old Testament for the formation of the faith of the church, he contends that both Testaments ultimately witness to divine redemption, which culminates in its most significant expression in the incarnation.[156] Childs contends that biblical theology is both an inner-scriptural dialectic between the Old and New Testaments, and an interactive dialogue between the Christian community and a canon that has two Testaments. The dialogical move of biblical theological reflection is from the partial grasp of fragmentary reality found in both Testaments to the full reality the Christian church confesses to have found in Jesus Christ. Systematic theologians have the responsibility for incorporating the faith of the Bible into their own works. The Old Testament is also the canonical Bible for Judaism and is appropriately interpreted within this community.

Finally, in the view of Judaism and Christianity, the Old Testament is scripture and not only contains the religious ideas of historical communities but also, and more important, witnesses to the word of God in ways that must be taken seriously by ongoing communities of faith. Childs does not deny to Judaism the authenticity of the First Testament or the Jewish Bible. Nor does he insist that various kinds of Christians must have the same canon in order to come to a theological presentation of the Bible. But he does insist, in following Barth, that theology is confessional and is not simply a collection of themes within the history of Israelite religion. The Bible is not a collection of ancient records, studied by contemporary historians to assist in their historical reconstructions, but rather a sacred canon that is normative and authoritative for the faith and practice of living religious communities.

Childs's theology comes under heavy criticism from many circles for his confusing definition of canon, canonical approach, and believing community and for his failure to include Judaism and history in his theological work.[156] These are critically important for any successful presentation of theology. Furthermore, he is not successful, in my judgment, in trying to adjudicate between the three major canons of Catholicism, Judaism, and Protestantism, which hold differences in the collection of books and in the order of their arrangement. These variations seriously diminish the validity of his efforts to give primary importance to canon as a theological category of divine revelation. Finally, Childs's dismissal of social and historical categories in the shaping of Scripture and its revelation removes the Bible from the context of human experience and participation and fails to explain the enormous variety that exists among the canon's various and often contradictory expressions of faith.

Canonical Theology and Rolf Rendtorff

Rolf Rendtorff also centers his attention on the canon in approaching Old Testament theology, although, unlike Childs, he does not attempt to write a comprehensive biblical theology.[157] His analysis of the order and themes of the three sections of the canon and the interactions of the texts within each is insightful and provides a variation from Childs's efforts to write both an Old Testament theology by considering the entire canon and a biblical theology that takes into consideration the authenticity of the multiple voices of the canon. For Rendtorff, each of these three sections has its own distinct understanding of the nature and activity of God and includes as well other theological themes. For example, he emphasizes that the primary importance of the Torah is on the actions of God, while the Prophets stress more the divine word that Yahweh speaks. By contrast, the Writings draw attention to humans who speak. While these are general variations, they do add a richness to the canon's variety of theological expressions. Rendtorff asserts that each section of the tripartite canon presents its own distinctive understanding of God and the world, the foundation for life and thinking, human self-understanding, the rituals and practices of worship, and the communal life. It is only when these three sections are brought together into a dialogical relationship that one discovers the theology of the Hebrew Bible. This set of views about the tripartite canon provides the foundation for Old Testament theology traced in the first volume.

In his second volume, Rendtorff takes up the major traditions of the Old Testament (creation, covenant and election, the patriarchs, the promised land, the first and second exodus), the Torah, life before God in the cult, Moses, David and the dynasty, Zion (temple and city), the major names of God, and the presence of strife in the framing of the issue of monotheism, justice and righteousness, and the need of Israel to repent. He then examines the theological dimensions of prophecy, worship and prayer, and wisdom (he calls them the three spheres of life). Interpretations of three other traditions follow: Israel's relationship to the nations and their gods, the question of Israel's perceptions of history, and then Israel's portrayal of future.

In the last section of volume 2, Rendtorff examines Old Testament hermeneutics, in which he examines the implications of the canon for hermeneutics. Other issues involve the importance of including both diachronic and synchronic interpretation in understanding Old Testament theology; the importance of the period in which the canon was shaped; the use of the Hebrew Bible for both Jewish and Christian theology; the Christian theology of the Old Testament; and biblical theology, which, for Christians, includes the New Testament. Unlike Childs, he notes the importance of the social context for shaping the theologies of the different books and sections of the canon. He thus gives history an important role in the process of doing theology. He notes that the Old Testament has a dual role, that is, as the Bible of Judaism and the First Testament of the Christian community. Even though the church and synagogue provide different settings for interpretation, the essential theology of the Hebrew Bible should not be affected. Even in the Christian community with its two Testaments, the Hebrew Bible does not lose its theological importance and dignity as a text, for it is to be honored for its own distinctive witness and considered an important part of the larger Christian Bible. The tension between the two should not be eliminated, any more than the tensions among the voices of each of the three sections of the Hebrew Bible. Rather, this tension should be appropriated in the larger Christian theological enterprise. While he recognizes its necessary development, Rendtorff stops his theological work with interpreting the Old Testament itself.

One example may suffice to demonstrate how this theology works: the relationship of creation and history.[158] In his Heidelberg lectures in 1985–1986, he noted that the last previous reference to creation in the summaries of Old Testament theology was in the 1873 volume by G. F. Oehler.[159] Rendtorff notes that Hermann Schultz, while taking a historical approach to the development of Israel's religion, does in his final section deal with "God and the World" and "Creation and Providence." Schultz had concluded that the idea of creation was a part of Israelite religion from the beginning, and he argued that this was an important part of early Semitic religion.[160] Rendtorff then refers to the approach of Bernhard Stade, who argued that it was the syncretism of Manasseh and his successors in the seventh century B.C.E., when Israel developed a view of the creation of the cosmos. According to Stade, this understanding resulted from the influence of Assyrian and Babylonian religions.[161]

In addition, Rendtorff notes that many Old Testament scholars have argued that the creation traditions developed separately from those about the patriarchs, the exodus, the giving of the law, the wanderings through the wilderness, and the entrance into the land of Canaan.[162] The most frequently encountered scholarly position is that the traditions of creation developed at a time later than those involving the exodus. The dating for creation traditions ranges from the beginnings of the monarchy and the influence of Canaanite religion to the imperial period of Assyria and Babylonia.

Rendtorff asks the question: "How far is the idea of Yahweh as Creator a relevant and immediate conception, over against his redemptive function?"[163] He seeks to answer this question in his subsequent work. In addition, he also determines the relationship between creation and covenant in the Old Testament.[164] Similar to the canonical approach of Brevard Childs, Rendtorff argues that the first two books of the Bible comprise the way an Old Testament theology should begin.[165] For Rendtorff, the Noachian covenant is central. The primeval history in Gen 1–11 and the Sinai story in Exod 19–34 show a parallel structure. The use of the term "covenant" (*běrît*, בְּרִית), which is more important theologically than creation in the Old Testament, is key in the reestablishment of the foundations of existence for human life. Israel's obedience to the divine commandments of these covenants with the ancestors (Abraham, Jacob), humanity and the earth (Noah), and Israel (Moses) makes it possible for creation (cosmos and humanity) and the nation to exist. For Rendtorff, covenant is a divine gift that enables human life and Israel to exist. The covenant of Noah indicates that God will never again destroy the earth as long as the seasons and day and night continue. The world is no longer "very good" (Gen 1:31), but it will continue to exist due to the guarantee of God expressed in his covenant. Thus, humans may trust the orders of creation, due to this divine pledge. Creation will continue, and it becomes a pattern for divine salvation on Israel's behalf. God's covenant with Israel at the same time reflects the covenant with Noah. The latter covenant continues as the guarantee of creation in the prophets, in particular Deutero-Isaiah (Isa 54:7-10, the "covenant of peace") and Ezekiel (the "covenant of peace," in 34:25-31). In Deutero-Isaiah, the "covenant of peace" points to the restoration of Israel from the chaos of the Babylonian conquest and exile, while in Ezekiel this covenant follows the exile and includes all of nature (cf. Jer 5:21-25 and 14:19-22). For Rendtorff, the binding of creation and covenant makes possible the existence of Israel.

In following his canonical approach to Old Testament theology, Rendtorff stresses that the design of Israel's historical understanding of creation is placed at the beginning, prior to the ancestral narratives. Thus, one sees in Gen 1:1, "in the beginning" (*bĕrēšît*, בְּרֵאשִׁית), the first of God's acts. This understanding is repeated elsewhere: Ps 90:2; Deut 4:32 ("the day that God created human beings on the earth"); and Prov 8:22-31. The later sapiential reference, according to Rendtorff, speaks of the creation of wisdom as the first of the divine acts of origins ("at the beginning," *rē'šît*, רֵאשִׁית). Thus, in the Hebrew Bible, when the creation of the earth and humanity is mentioned, God is the one at the beginning who originated them.[166]

Rendtorff goes on to note that the major weapon used by God in the defeat of chaos, prior to world and human origins, is the "word" (Gen 1 and Ps 104). This is true of Job when Yahweh states that he has "shut in the sea with doors" when, by means of his divine commandment, he erected barriers to keep its chaotic waves from inundating the earth (Job 38:7-11). The Joban poet, when he refers to chaos as the reality prior to creation, agrees with Ps 104:9 that chaos is not eliminated but continues as a part of reality even after the acts of divine ordering (cf. Jer 52). Also in Gen 1 God "separates" (*habdîl*, הַבְדִּיל) between the waters above and those below the earth by means of the establishment of the firmament, allowing the dry land to appear (Gen 1:6-10). However, these floods are loosed in Gen 6–8. This takes on mythical proportions in being described as a battle with chaos in Isa 27:1; 51:9f.; and Job 26:12f. However, in the Prophets and the Psalms God is called upon to save Israel or the individual offering a lament, based on the soteriological understanding of creation demonstrated in the defeat of chaos.[167]

Finally, Rendtorff argues that there are references to the Creator without a special explanation. He suggests this is due to the ready recognition that God is the Creator. One finds this in Gen 14:19f. and 18:25, as well as in Qohelet (12:1), which admonishes the reader to think on divine creation and all that the Creator has made (3:11).[168]

Oddly enough, Rendtorff's second volume on Old Testament theology omits wisdom's view of creation theology.[169] Instead, this literature is misinterpreted as ethical guidance for human life, grounded in a theory of retribution.[170] Wisdom attempts to structure the relationships of individuals to their social environments. Even the "fear of the LORD" (Prov 1:7; 9:10; and 15:33) has to do only with human experiences that lead to a life of well-being. Rendtorff thus suppresses the theological richness of this literature and its key affirmation of the "fear of God."

POSTMODERNISM AND LITERARY INTERPRETATION

Introduction[171]

The past thirty years have witnessed the emergence of new literary paradigms for interpreting biblical texts and approaching Old Testament theology. One of the more influential is postmodernism. Among the most prominent postmodernists who write on the theory of literature and language are Jacques Derrida,[172] Jean-François Lyotard,[173] Michel Foucault,[174] and Roland Barthes.[175] Postmodernism resists facile definitions, since it is inherently diverse, complex, and inclusive of many manifestations. However, a modest definition follows. As a literary theory, postmodernism affirms the diversity of meanings inherent in texts, embraces their profound complication, points to inherent contradictions within texts and their variety of levels of meaning, and underscores the linkage of multiple levels of understanding. In the history of thought, postmodernism represents a reaction against modernism's epistemological claims ("post" in the sense of "against" and not temporally "after"), organizing principles, grand metanarratives that define science and culture, consistency of meaning, objectivity, and linear thought.

For Derrida, postmodernism (or his preferred term, "poststructuralism") understands literature by means of "indeterminancy," that is, the view that texts lack one definitive understanding. This view is based on what he termed "deconstruction," that is, aspects of the text and internal complications subvert the consistency of a single meaning and thus the assumptions from which it operates. This is not to be confused with deconstructionist readings of interpreters who reject one reading of a text as the single or true reading. Texts thus have multiple, even contrastive meanings, residing on the same and different levels. Texts are freed both from their origins in time and space and from the controlling influence of their authors.[176] Likewise, the readers or speakers of texts are denied any authoritative interpretation. Rather, the readers or speakers are shaped by the conventions of language inherent in their individual cultures. Taken together, these elements dismiss the notion that there exists one meaning of each text. Derrida rejects the argument that poststructuralism is nihilistic. Instead, deconstruction poses questions about the essence of the text and the multiple, inherently contradictory meanings it sets forth.

Lyotard argues against modernity's efforts to create "metanarratives" through literature in order to provide a sweeping interpretation of what is real and valued.[177] Instead, there are "little narratives" that arise within cultural complexes that continue endlessly in the efforts to gain some semblance of meaning and signification. Grand narratives, shaped by cultures, have no authenticity outside their own boundaries. This means that any of the metanarratives cannot be applied to cultures outside the realm of literary creation. This would be true of the notions of salvation history, covenant, and canon in biblical theology.

Foucault argued that understandings of human beings are created by both discourse and action. Texts have multiple meanings, indicating that a single, true understanding cannot be isolated and supported. The meaning of a text does not reside within the intellectual domain of the author or his or her subgroup, but rather texts point to hierarchies of power, intertextualities, and their multiple contexts. What is to be recognized as false is the ideology of a text that attempts to give authority to political interests of its creators or interpreters. Two features are intrinsic to his literary theory. First, "archaeology" analyzes discourse according to "rules of formation" that exist in a culture and shape and delimit the words of a text. Second, genealogy is diachronic and points to the origins and development of discourse. While there is no single basis that may be identified, there are associations of things existing in relationship. For Foucault, there is no single authoritative meaning or single interpretation of a text, for there is no absolute ground of meaning or authority granted to a particular position. The imposition of these is accomplished only by the tyranny of power.

COMMON FEATURES OF POSTMODERNISM

From the insights of these and other intellectuals, we learn that postmodernism resists acknowledging that the foundations of knowledge are rationalism and empiricism, affirming efforts to reconstruct objectively the linear history of human events and thought, accepting the claims of objectivity by the scholar in the search for abstract truth that is unelaborated and verifiable, and the bestowing of universal veracity to metanarratives produced by self-described, dominant human cultures and civilizations. In its core, postmodernism is a critique of epistemologies and rejects the claims of various theories of knowledge as means for acquiring understanding of what is real. The epistemological assumptions of postmodernism include the view that insight, in its multiple forms, derives from the interaction of the interpreter, his or her multiple locations and networks of identities, and the linguistic-cultural possibilities of the meanings of texts. However, there is no one meaning or understanding that expresses what is accurate and true. There are many narratives with significant differences in content.[178] Postmodernism examines and gives multiple understandings to every aspect of reality, including cosmology, anthropology, epistemology, sociology, psychology, art and architecture, and language. What unites the various interests of postmodernism is its lack of a common center of knowing, for the approach affirms the elusive nature of all that is thought to be known. Graham Ward states this in the following: "Postmodernity promises neither clarification nor the disappearance of perplexity."[179] Nevertheless, postmodernism does deal with cultural translation. Various elements of a culture are delineated, rethought, and converted into the culture's own logic.[180]

In addition, postmodernism seeks to overcome the distance separating the products of culture and both their creators and those who interact with them. This is one of the major reasons that postmodernism removes from consideration the notion of linear time. Indeed, all linear thinking that moves from cause to effect is rejected as unfounded supposition. Even the differentiation between history and fiction tends to blur.[181] Postmodernism also denies that reality and its component features are objective, or that something exists "out there," apart from the human mind, when it comes to the knowing process.

Modernism's limitation of interpretation to the elite of the Western academy results in the underpinning of oppressive imperial and neocolonial states, along with economically exploitative multinational corporations with headquarters located in and controlled by the West. Other modes of interpretation and cultural centers located outside the West and normally under the political and financial control of the G8 are stigmatized as lacking convincing construals of what is real and true and what is inferior in understanding. Non-Western cultures and ways of knowing are marginalized and denied serious consideration. Instead of one grand metanarrative constructed in the West, postmodernism holds to the plurality of meanings that derive from a variety of peoples, cultures, and civilizations. Thus, heterogeneity is preferred over homogeneity. There can be no view or understanding that is universally accepted. Rather there are many.

POSTMODERNISM AND OLD TESTAMENT THEOLOGY: WALTER BRUEGGEMANN[182]

While Brueggemann indicates his theology does possess several of the key principles of postmodernism, a thorough reading indicates he does not use many of its core emphases. These include the affirmation of truth, although it exists before concrete identification, and the use of historical criticism to set forth the literary, social, and historical character of biblical texts. As a theologian who approaches biblical theology within the context of the church, Brueggemann uses arguments fashionable in postmodernism to bring into question "regnant" and "conventional" theologies and epistemologies and their dominant modes of power. This latter point is critical, for a central feature of his work has been a call for justice and an end to the powerful elite's control of resources and oppression of the weak in society. Too often, in his estimation, historical criticism, especially in its positivistic orientation, which has led to a number of important theological approaches, has served as a form of academic and theological legitimation of the West's domination of the two-thirds world and the dominant social group's exploitation of the poor. While historical criticism originally challenged the authoritarianism of the church, it now has been co-opted to endorse the elite's ideological control of political and economic institutions in the globe. Thus, Brueggemann seeks to determine in the present "postcritical" age how the church can respond faithfully to the inhumanity of the West and its system of rampant capitalism. What is now being challenged is the privileged position of Western, white, male colonialists and neocolonialists.

While Brueggemann continues to use historical criticism in shaping his own theology, he does so with an eye to recognizing the need to offset its misuse by means of the church's advocacy for social justice to be extended to the weak. Through his theology, he seeks to hold the church accountable in recognizing and supporting the humanity of every person. Thus, historical exegesis may not be abused by dominant and powerful nations to sustain their own status and self-interest. He also criticizes historical criticism for regarding the Old Testament as "history." For Brueggemann, the canon is not a record of events but rather a product of "imaginative interpretation" at work in the minds of its composers and tradents as well as its contemporary interpreters. This process of interpretation he construes as "imaginative remembering" of poems and narratives from the past and not as sheer fantasy in which the interpreter simply invents understandings of texts.

Brueggemann considers Enlightenment epistemologies, residing at the basis of historical criticism, to be in crisis, since we have come to recognize that values and beliefs are not universal but rather contextual. Ways of knowing in the areas of culture and religion are now regarded to be pluralistic, since values and beliefs are the expressions of localized communities. Thus they are contextual and given assent only by groups who express and affirm them. In addition, objectivity has been unmasked as the ideology of the elitist group who shapes metanarratives that give its members authority, position, and power. Furthermore, while truth exists, there is no final arbiter to render judgment on what is right and what is false. With these considerations in mind, Brueggemann interprets the theology of the Hebrew Bible from the position of "perspectivism," that is, reality is to be seen through the lens of the interpreter. There is not a single, inherently truthful interpretation that may be sustained universally and is valid for all time. However, this is not an affirmation of relativism. Rather, Brueggemann's own avowed hermeneutic recognizes and opposes the elite's position of power and control.

Brueggemann's theological approach is both strongly dialogical and imaginative. When considering dialogue, he asserts that Christian biblical theology is only one view among many in a conversation that is open to many religious traditions. Christians are denied a privileged position in this interpretation. Thus, this recognition allows Christians to engage in authentic dialogue with Jews who claim the same Hebrew Bible. As for imagination, an orientation that he has often used to describe the process of interpretation,[183] he accepts that the text of the Old Testament "does not purport to be 'history' in any modern sense of the term," because it is not "a product of 'events,' but a product of imaginative interpretation."[184] Therefore he reasons that the Old Testament is not a product of sheer fantasy but is rather the result of an interplay of "historical reportage" and "canonical formation," which becomes "the work of tradition," a process of transmission and interpretation that he calls "imaginative remembering."[185] Brueggemann's approach to Old Testament theology is to interpret the text through the metaphor of testimony that is situated in the courtroom. This root metaphor of "courtroom" provides Brueggemann with a heuristic tool for the presentation of his Old Testament theology. He certainly disdains any one thematic center that unifies and systematizes the theological content of the canon. He also seeks to engage the text critically and constructively, not resting content to provide an exposition of the variety of texts in the Hebrew Bible, but seeking to bring each of them under judgment.

For Brueggemann, there are three major types of testimony: theological affirmation that seeks assent in the face of counterassertions; dispute that challenges the authenticity and veracity of the affirmation; and advocacy, which asserts the truth of the claims of reality in the face of opposing evidence and witnesses. In this context there are both core witness and countertestimony that form a continuing, unresolved dialectic. The core witness of theological affirmation is understood as the "grammar" of full sentences organized around an active verb. This action is "transformational" and brings about what is real in old or new forms. Examples are

"God creates," "God commands," and "God leads." In the counter-testimony, the basic witness is probed and questioned both by Israel and communities outside the elect nation. Two other types of witness in the Old Testament courtroom, which are important but less so than the three mentioned above, are (1) unsolicited testimony in which Israel gives additional information, extraneous to its speech about God, which is the only thing the court considers relevant, and (2) embodied testimony present in the Torah, the king, the prophet, worship, and the sage.

Brueggemann's dialectic of testimony and countertestimony involves three thematic contrasts: (1) covenant and exile, (2) hymn and lament, and (3) presence and theodicy. The first dialectic, covenant and exile, contrasts the trustworthiness of God and a community responsive to his requirements with the exile, which deconstructs the promises of covenant. This dialectic continues throughout the Hebrew Bible. In regard to the second dialectic, Brueggemann notes that Israel's hymns of praise speak of God's central characteristics of goodness, faithfulness, and power. However, the lament subverts these claims by speaking of remoteness, mystery, and caprice. This dialectic continues and does not come to resolution. Finally, the third dialectic places in opposition divine presence in the traditions of the ancestors, the exodus, and the temple that effectuates blessing; and redemption is countered by the absence of God and the questioning of divine justice, which one finds in Old Testament books like Habakkuk and Job.

As evidenced by the Hebrew Bible, Israel's understanding of the Holy One is endlessly dialectical, for these oppositions never reach final closure. Even the Christian view of the revelation of God in Christ that seeks closure is rejected. This means that Old Testament theology points to a God through testimony and countertestimony in "acts of imaginative construal that admit of no single reading but that generate many possible futures."[186]

OLD TESTAMENT THEOLOGY AND POSTCOLONIALISM

Understanding Postcolonialism

In her notable essay "Can the Subaltern Speak," Gayatri Chakravorty Spivak[187] argues that consciousness is created by discourse. Thus, economically deprived and politically dominated persons of former colonies exploited by Western empires and their successors need to break the code of silence precipitated by the dominance of Eurocentric intellectuals. Even third-world intellectuals often have articulated a discourse that ignores the cultural diversity that exists among former colonies by stereotyping them as expressing one common view. Cultural homogeneity, espoused by Western intellectuals and their non-Western imitators, subverts the reality of the varieties of cultures among subalterns. When postcolonial writers and thinkers speak of cultural homogeneity, they make non-Western peoples into the very thing that colonialist and neocolonialist propaganda has made them, an undifferentiated mass lacking any distinctiveness. Thus, she criticizes not only Westerners but also subaltern intellectuals who create paradigms of control of subalterns. Since the discourse of the latter can also be male, elitist, intellectual, and privileged, it also requires deconstruction.

Due to postmodernism and postcolonialism, Eurocentric theology, including Western biblical theology, is losing its position of self-assumed superiority and influence and may well be on its way to its demise, at least in many non-Western cultures present in the contemporary world. The audience listening to Western, white, male intellectuals grows smaller each year, even as former colonial empires have disintegrated and have been replaced by nations seeking intellectual, theological, and economic independence. The greatest danger presently to the "two-thirds" world is neocolonialism, in which global corporations and their location in national centers in the West have wrought economic hegemony. But, even now, new voices resistant to this more recent form of exploitation are emerging to give utterance to both their own cultural values and resistance to the assumptions and forces of Western supremacy. If biblical theology has any ambition of addressing social injustice, then it is required to participate in the shaping of a worldview in which the marginalized are supported in their struggles to effectuate global equity and universal well-being.[188]

Colonialism and Imperialism[189]

Postcolonialism refers generally to a perspective emerging in nations whose populations were exploited by European trading companies in England and Holland and later ruled as colonies by European empires until their fragmentation in and following the Second World War. As indigenous expressions of many different national and cultural groups, postcolonialism is not a method of philosophical or theological studies, say, in comparison to liberation philosophy/theology, but more of a perspective that emerges from localized settings and traditions. The impetus of colonialism was economic profit derived from the exploitation of peoples and resources in non-Western countries. The different Western empires used military force to establish political control over other lands and people in order to procure land, natural resources, trade, and cheap labor, including slavery. The British, French, and Spaniards were the most successful in building empires that originated in the sixteenth century. The imperial rule of Great Britain and France continued until the aftermath of World War II. Postcolonialism has now been replaced by self-serving, economic policies of the G8, which by means of their transnational corporations, the International Monetary Fund, the World Bank, trading "partnerships" with poor nations, and political subterfuge successfully controlled the resources of the two-thirds world.

Missionary Religion

Western Christianity, in the form of missionary religion, has been abusive by using its teachings to legitimate the exploitation and dehumanization of poor nations. Indoctrination in the "superior" nation's history, form of government, and culture was carried out by the imposition of Western education and values. Many of these Western schools were established by various expressions of Catholic and denominational Christianity. The internalization of these ways of seeing the world through the images and representations of the colonial power became the major tool in achieving stability throughout the empire's colonized world. The fundamental doctrine of colonial propaganda was that it was a divinely ordained right for the empire's ruling nation to control "barbaric peoples" through education and religion. Cultural genocide became an insidious weapon in the arsenal of the Western empires and continues to be misused, especially by American conservatives and "neocons."[190] This inculturation into the dominant nations' worldview becomes propaganda designed to control poor nations. The colonized and now the cultural and economic marginals who have sought to advance in the neocolonial world were expected to acknowledge Western superiority and participate in the ravages of rampant capitalism. The West repudiated indigenous values and beliefs contrary to its own and rewarded only those who bowed the knee to neocolonial metanarratives.

Postcolonialism and Western Paradigms

Indigenous scholars and biblical theologians speak from very different locations than those in the West. As long as Eurocentric interpretations of biblical theology are nothing more than the legitimation of a seriously misconstrued metanarrative of imperial dominance, then the reclaiming of the biblical text can be accomplished only by the creation of contextual theologies that radically question Western interpretations and their models of understanding, faith, and ethics. Subaltern criticism of Western biblical theology involves three stages: exposure, deconstruction, and the creation of new theoretical knowledge issuing forth in different articulations in the former colonies themselves. Exposure examines the classics of Western literature, in this case the theologies of biblical scholars earlier described in this volume, and understands the self-interest in their depictions of the biblical world and their implied degradations of colonial cultures. Postcolonial thinkers sometimes utilize various models of deconstruction (Derrida, Lyotard, and Foucault) to demonstrate that the metanarratives of Western ideology lack consistency and a unifying theme that is demonstrable and universal. They emphasize that subalterns are not to be homogenized into an indistinguishable mass that obscures particularity and diversity. Postcolonial theology recaptures elements of indigenous traditions and engages in the retelling of history. The subaltern experience cannot be forced into a generalized abstraction devoid of social and cultural context. The replacement of the metanarratives of the imperialist countries requires the return to indigenous traditions and the local retelling of national histories.

Thus, biblical theologies that are systematic or based on a Western understanding of social contexts are strongly censored. New forms of knowledge emerge in postcolonial cultures that are based on indigenous constructs of society, values, beliefs, and understandings.

Postcolonial readings of biblical theology emphasize that literature must be placed within both its own social, cultural, and historical contexts and those of the modern interpreter. Through this engagement of interpreter and text and the social locations of both, meaning is created. And yet, due to the varieties of the interpreter's social contexts and particular culture, it would be erroneous to think that there is only one true and authentic signification. As the social and cultural locations of biblical texts vary, so do those of the interpreters. This leads to interpretative variety. Postcolonial readings of biblical theology also challenge the metanarratives of first-world nations, their transnational corporations, and the economic corruption of unrestrained capitalism. The ultimate goal of postcolonial interpretation is the shaping of a new paradigm of human community to which the Bible, if read through a critical lens, may contribute.

Contextual and Intercultural Interpretation

Postcolonial, biblical interpretation follows an inculturation model of interaction between the Bible and the contemporary readership. Social location becomes critical in this process. Intercultural interpretation is not limited to understanding the text within its own cultural and social history and then applying its insights to the present. Rather, according to John Ukpong, the readership brings a variety of worldviews and social realities to the text and interprets it through these various lenses. This means that the interpreters are not limited to Western exegesis and theology to obtain the proper meaning of the Bible but also use their own experiences to come to an understanding. Thus, meaning results from the reciprocal engagement of the Bible in its context and the cultural and social knowledge of the readership brought to bear on the text.

African feminists have used this approach in enabling women in postcolonial societies to find and then express their voices through their own particular experiences. For example, Mercy Amba Oduyoye, like John Ukpong, also points to the importance of the social settings of the contemporary readers and asserts that biblical hermeneutics and theological meaning derive from both the experiences of women in biblical stories and those of contemporary women.[191] The latter use their own experiences to create their narratives that engage those in the biblical text, providing them with new insights and understandings. Eschewing historical criticism's methods and theological limitations, she asserts that biblical stories are read, not to reconstruct the historical life of ancient Israel and the early church, but rather to demonstrate divine presence in human lives, both in the past as well as in the present. She also seeks to set forth a theology of liberation that enables people to gain freedom from the sociopolitical bondage and victimization of powerful people and to shape a reality in which God is present in the lives of people.

THE MAJOR THEORISTS IN POSTCOLONIALISM

Postcolonialism has numerous important writers and scholars in a variety of disciplines who have shaped postcolonial thinking in recent years. The list includes such important figures as Edward Said, Frantz Fanon, Homi K. Bhabha, Gayatri Chakravorty Spivak, Paul Gilroy, Anne McClintock, Neil Lazarus, and T. Minh-ha Trinkh. Of course, many others could be added to this shortened list. Of these, the views of Franz Fanon, Edward Said, Gayatri Chakravorty Spivak, and Homi K. Bhabha are incisive and hold a good deal of promise for future biblical theologies.

Frantz Fanon[192]

The best known of the earlier postcolonial scholars was Frantz Fanon, a psychiatrist and leading intellectual whose life covered the years 1925 to 1961. Born to a black man and a mother of mixed race on the Island of Martinique, his homeland was a French colony and later a French département (i.e., a French overseas department of the French political and cultural center in Paris that offered the possibility of French citizenship). His premature death, attributed to leukemia, cut short a brilliant career that led to the refinement of several key postcolonial insights into racism, the importance of solidarity with the victims of colonization, cultural analysis that in its broad sweep influenced in revolutionary ways psychiatry and psychoanalysis, sexuality, economics, philosophy, and literature. Having studied medicine and psychiatry in France, he soon left his French practice to move to the then-French colony of Algiers, where he became eventually a leading spokesperson of the Algerine revolution. Indeed, his life as a revolutionary who opposed imperial domination, but not by violence, became the seedbed for two of his most provocative revolutionary manifestos: *Black Skin, White Masks* and *The Wretched of the Earth*.

He wrote his initial book, *Black Skin, White Masks*, while residing in France. The book explores the effect on the black psyche of the white man's view that blacks are inferior. The dominant thrust of the volume reflects Fanon's own experience of existence in the world of whites, where he was regarded as lesser due to the color of his skin. Here he moves away from economic and political factors in examining the results of subjugation, and instead chooses to pinpoint the damaging, psychological effects of colonialism. Blacks, forced to regard themselves as dependent and inadequate, are driven to feelings of alienation, shame, and self-revulsion in the white man's world. This is even more true of blacks seeking upward mobility in this imposed imperial reality. The task of extricating themselves from this world of colonialism is complicated by the fact that in speaking the colonizers' language and adopting the expressions of their literature, science, and popular culture, they support the "weight" of the empire's civilization and its common self-understandings. To break away from this cultural degradation of shame, blacks are to repudiate both the white man's "error" of superiority and the black "mirage" that redemption comes only through emulating the colonial culture. But the shameful taboo exposed by Fanon is his most important insight: the origins of racism toward blacks is not primarily economic gain but rather the sexual attraction of blacks to whites who castrate and lynch blacks in an attempt to extinguish this unspeakable desire. Racism, then, results from "the stare," which refers to sexual desire, in this case, of whites for blacks.

Fanon composed *The Wretched of the Earth* (*Les Damnés de la Terre*) during his participation in the Algerian revolution against French colonialism. Once again, Fanon draws on his education as a brilliant psychiatrist by addressing the effect colonization produces on the psyche of a people subdued by an empire. From this basis, he seeks the decolonization and liberation of colonials. Fanon examines the roles of class, race, culture, and struggle in the quest for freedom from imperial aggression. While the introduction by Jean-Paul Sartre interprets too extremely Fanon as a proponent of violence in the revolutionary efforts to attain liberation by a people's casting off the shackles of colonialism, it is the case that Fanon condemns the violence of colonialism and the effect it has on a subjugated people. This focus derives from the book's opening chapter, "Concerning Violence," which is a caustic indictment of colonialism and its legacy. Indeed, Fanon does speak of violence as the catharsis of a people when revolting against their subjugation. For him, revolution is to be led by peasants living in rural areas and outside the colony's urban centers. These peasants are considered by the colonizers and even colonial sympathizers to be the lowest (hence, the "wretched") of the earth. To accomplish this liberation, it is necessary for rural peasants, independent from the colonizers and not the dependent industrial proletariat, to engage in struggle. At the same time, he issues a warning to the oppressed of the severe problems in moving from colonization, to decolonization, to a neocolonial reality.

Fanon's work traces three epochs of postcolonial literature. The first is the colonized writing of a literature of imitation, using the schematic models of the imperialists. The second moves to a reaction against the colonial literary and ideological models and their replacement with a literature of nostalgia that consists of indigenous traditions. Finally, the third consists of the composition of literature that seeks to subvert colonization and to shape a postcolonial culture that is egalitarian. While these three stages are schematic and reductionistic, they still provide a paradigm for the development of postcolonial literature. Among the aftermath of each stage, there are inherent difficulties, including, for example, the lack of comprehensive inclusion of differences in gender, class, education, and social standing.[193]

Edward Said[194]

Born in Jerusalem, Edward Said (1935–2003) witnessed the end of the British Mandate, the formation of the State of Israel, and the early period of conflict between Arabs and Israelis. He then migrated to the United States for his education and eventually taught at Columbia until his death in 2003.

Like Frantz Fanon, Said penetrated the forces of colonialism to argue that its origins and continuing domination of indigenous groups and nations were not simply due to the drive for economic gain, supported especially by military power, but by a discourse of knowledge, deriving from the colonizers, that was presented as universally true. According to Said, deep within the subconscious of the colonizers was the conventional image of "orientalism," which typecast peoples residing in the Eastern world. Orientalism was the Western fantasy of superiority that projected a mysterious, uncivilized, irrational, and alien facade of otherness that justified the conquest, exploitation, and subversion of residents of the East and their cultures. This erroneous portrayal included misogyny, in that the East was presented as seductive and alluring; and racism, in that its populations of people of color were considered inferior to white-skinned Europeans. Intellectuals, politicians, and theologians in Western society created the myth of superiority in order to legitimate imperialism and other models of domination. In addition, Westerners sought to infuse their values into the cultures of the Eastern world. These attempts at dehumanizing the "others" have even entered into Western universities, media, and literature. By disassembling this fallacious stereotype, Said argued the Western metanarratives of self-understanding, conquest, and continuing political and economic domination would collapse. This rejection of Western metanarratives and their mistaken depictions of non-Westerners could be accomplished by demonstrating the fallacy of Western metanarratives through the creating of a new discourse. Postcolonial discourse not only points out the erroneous claims of Western myths of superiority but also retells the history of the former colonized from their own locations and on the basis of their worldviews. The goals are to wrest colonies and the liberated nations from Western hegemony and to inculcate within the Western mind new cosmologies and understandings of non-Western peoples.

POSTCOLONIAL BIBLICAL THEOLOGY

Itumeleng J. Mosala

Among the more politically radical postcolonial biblical scholars is Itumeleng J. Mosala, a former biblical scholar who now serves in the South African government established following the fall of apartheid. Mosala begins his biblical interpretation with the recognition that the Bible is not simply an innocent text with truths embodied in its words.[195] Using a neo-Marxist approach, Mosala asserts that the ideologies of the Bible are present and are to be recognized, if appropriate meaning of the present is to be obtained.[196] Furthermore, he notes that there is no innocent reading of the text, for each person approaches the Bible from the perspectives of the ideology with which he or she understands the texts. Western scholars are to recognize both their participation in the oppression of marginals by using biblical interpretation to legitimate Western metanarratives that claim the superiority of the imperialists and their position of socioeconomic privilege. This means they are especially required to articulate their own ideologies when engaging in biblical interpretation. While the Bible is not innocent, it does on occasion contain a message of justice and thus becomes a powerful tool in fighting tyranny. It is incumbent upon Western scholars to discover those texts, often neglected, that address the evils of oppression and point to liberation of especially the marginalized.[197]

As a neo-Marxist, Mosala uses social materialism to serve two purposes: first to demystify Western scholarship and second to delegitimate its frequent support of neocolonial domination. Socioeconomic and political factors give rise to culture. This is true of biblical literature and for the wide variety of cultures in the present. Culture develops out of political, social, and economic spheres of human reality. The distortion of this fact occurs when the powerful use present conditions to justify their own domination of others. Imperialists and neocolonialists transform the biblical texts into propaganda to justify their own control and domination. Thus, the working classes use their labor and its products to create the means by which the ruling class is challenged. In addition, class conflict is inevitable, but ultimately it will lead to the workers' obtaining social change that results in egalitarianism. The Hebrew Bible becomes a text that may be understood through the lens of class struggle that culminates in the ultimate liberation of the oppressed.

R. S. Sugirtharajah[198]

R. S. Sugirtharajah, a Sri Lankan who is a professor at the University of Birmingham in the United Kingdom, has not written a complete biblical theology, but his numerous writings on the Bible, especially the New Testament, and postcolonialism have set forth numerous, important elements of this approach to biblical interpretation. He has defined postcolonialism as "signifying a reactive resistance discourse of the colonized who critically interrogate dominant knowledge systems in order to recover the past from Western slander and misinformation of the colonial period, and who also continue to interrogate neo-colonializing tendencies after the declaration of independence."[199] His fundamental thesis is that postcolonialism is a way of reading texts or a type of discourse that seeks to deconstruct the various elements of Eurocentric totalitarianism, which has abused the Bible to legitimate its position of domination.[200] This leads to liberation from dominant, controlling structures imposed on former colonies by the West and from Western values alien to postcolonial cultures.[201] Thus the goal of postcolonial interpretation is to uncover the bond between socioeconomic capitalism, imperial political power, and the self-interest of the powerful and political power and the self-interest of the oppressors.[202] In the place of Western principles and standards, postcolonial interpreters make use of their own cultural values in creating a just world freed from domination by Western powers.

Sugirtharajah asks what better place for this creative effort to reflect on human worth and to shape a new world free of imperialist domination than the margins.[203] Thus, inculturation and contextual interpretation (liberation) are the twin poles of postcolonialist interpretation of the Bible.

However, the postcolonialism of Sugirtharajah is not a one-sided attack on imperialists but rather calls for a discourse in which the experiences and values of both the colonizer and the colonized are engaged. This attempt to read and speak together is part of the larger view that all cultures should speak from their locations and express their views and values in the larger human effort to engage one another openly and constructively.

OLD TESTAMENT THEOLOGY, PLURALISM, AND THE IMAGINATION

We are truly at the end of one dominant age of theological interpretation and at the beginning of another. The threats to the present world order, grounded in what Brueggemann calls "military capitalism," abound in frightening form. In its "Christian" form, this ideology, especially as used by the Religious Right, has undergirded and sought to legitimate the current Promethean world order of the West in general and the United States in particular. Brueggemann seeks to undo this cultural ideology by pointing to Israel's fundamental affirmation of the justice of God.

Perhaps the dominant theological problem is that of pluralism. It would be foolish to suggest that pluralism is only a modern convention. Truth, knowledge, and virtue have ever been the objects of human questing as well as the subjects of continuing disputations even within the same cultures. However, in our contemporary age, perhaps there is a greater awareness of and consternation occasioned by the abiding presence of this epistemological debate. Western cultures are not the first to experience the unease occasioned by the uncertainty of what is true. However, in the West, especially growing out of the Enlightenment and taking root in liberalism in its political, cultural, and religious forms, the conviction developed that truth could be attained through the careful and critical application of reason that gave rise to methods of science, religious interpretation, and philosophy. Biblical interpretation and its handmaiden, Old and New Testament theology, fell under the gaze of reasonable certainty regarding the meaning of ancient texts and, for some scholars, their application to the present. The Great Depression, World War II, and the Cold War brought this false sense of security in "demonstrable" propositions or data advocated by a Western world view to a sure and certain end. The grand and engaging Old Testament theologies of Walther Eichrodt and Gerhard von Rad, which evoked an exciting response and came to hold a commanding presence in Old Testament theology, began to teeter and then largely collapse under the uncertainties of real and potential social, economic, and environmental catastrophes.

Since the 1960s, we have struggled to overcome the problems of pluralism and the challenges to a once-imperialistic way of approaching the meaning of scripture, both for its ancient audiences and its modern communities of faith. This self-assured method was historical criticism. However, the modernist world is under severe criticism by those who regard its epistemological ways of gaining knowledge and perspective as arrogant and limited. The world of postmodernism, while no contemporary phenomenon, as the skeptical tradition in Plato's academy should remind us, is nevertheless the challenge that calls for response. It is the challenge of pluralism in a postmodern world, a pluralism of faith, methods, and interpretative communities.

Brueggemann begins at the outset of his own theology to set forth the dilemma and the challenges posed by pluralism. He notes that the magisterial theological constructions of Walther Eichrodt and Gerhard von Rad, while continuing to be read and admired, no longer dominate contemporary Old Testament theology. A confident theological construal of Israel's ancient faith, whether systematic (Eichrodt) or traditio-historical (von Rad), and issuing from a Eurocentric, largely white male, historical-critical, and Protestant approach, is no longer possible in a postmodern reality replete with competing epistemologies grounded in many different social, cultural, and ethnic realities (e.g., the variety of liberation theologies of the third-world, feminism, and ethnic minorities). Indeed, as Brueggemann notes, one of the ironies of an earlier age of Old Testament theology is that the careful application of historical criticism has revealed the wide-ranging present of pluralism even in affirmations about God in the Hebrew Bible. Thus, pluralism is present not simply in the context of interpretation (whether ancient or modern), or in the variety of methods used to excavate or create meaning, but also in the biblical text itself.

Pluralism is both the dilemma and the opportunity for Brueggemann's imaginative rendering of Old Testament theology. Brueggemann's wrestling with pluralism, as modern exegete and contemporary theologian, provides the axis around which his interpretations, often penetrating and incisive, and never commonplace, revolve.

Brueggemann recognizes, however, that Old Testament theology has not been consigned to the graveyard of modern theological inquiry. Continuing to emerge are new and insightful theologies that are both provocative and capable of construing the Old Testament's complex theologies.

Eschewing a predominantly systematic approach, Brueggemann's root metaphor of "courtroom" provides a heuristic tool to present his Old Testament theology. He certainly disdains any one thematic center, unless one proposes the general theme "God," a theme that does not provide any real assistance in setting forth the theology of the First Testament. Brueggemann also seeks to engage the text through the historical-critical method and constructively with his own theological insights for the contemporary church, not resting content to provide an exposition of the variety of texts in the Hebrew Bible but seeking to bring them under judgment.[205]

CHAPTER THREE

NEW TESTAMENT THEOLOGY IN THE TWENTIETH CENTURY

Robert Morgan

CHALLENGES

New Testament theology is a contested discipline. That was so shortly before the twentieth century began, and it is so shortly after it has ended. In 1897 William Wrede of Breslau (now in Poland), a member of the Göttingen group of junior faculty later called "the history of religions school," published a searching critique of the discipline.[1] His lectures (to a clergy school) were occasioned by the recent appearance of a major New Testament theology textbook by the leading New Testament scholar of the time, Heinrich Julius Holtzmann[2] of Strasbourg. The history of religions school set the agenda for German biblical scholarship throughout the twentieth century and later became influential elsewhere, largely through Rudolf Bultmann, who inherited and developed its radical historical criticism and whose classic mid-century synthesis of New Testament theology was both a continuation and a response to that outstanding generation of liberal protestant scholarship.

Bultmann was impressed by the theological exegesis of Barth's *Epistle to the Romans* (1922) and became part of the new theological movement that followed the First War. He accepted the Reformation emphases of Barth's theology and its openness to philosophy but never shared its postcritical aspects. He set his own creative new interpretations of Paul and the Johannine theology in the context of the critical-historical reconstruction of early Christianity pioneered in the 1830s and 1840s by F. C. Baur, corrected by Weizsäcker (1822–1899) and Holtzmann's generation, and sharpened by Bousset's history of religions and Wrede's history of traditions research.

That radical historical-critical paradigm was maintained by Bultmann and his pupils, and in the 1960s became an influential part of the new flourishing international and ecumenical biblical scholarship. Several of the critical classics were translated into English, but the continental philosophy and kerygmatic theology that Bultmann had combined with his critical scholarship had less appeal outside Germany, and in the 1970s this style of New Testament theology was challenged by a more empirical historical research sometimes enriched by social-scientific perspectives. More literary approaches, advocated with deep theological insight by Amos Wilder, also became popular in North America on a wave of new literary theory, much of it made in France and not theological in any traditional sense. Already the discoveries at Qumran had revitalized the study of Second Temple Judaism at the same time as the full horror of the Holocaust was being assimilated. The study of Judaism by Schürer and Schlatter, Bousset and Billerbeck, Dalman, R. H. Charles, and G. F. Moore, among others, at the start of the century was ripe for revision—and continuation. The radical history of religions school found some surprising allies, and further possibilities for history of religions research were opened up by the discoveries of Gnostic texts at Nag Hammadi. English-speaking scholars have generally found the historicism of Wrede's generation more appealing than the heavy theological interests that dominated mid-century biblical studies. The criticisms of New Testament theology made by Wrede in 1897 can therefore provide a counterweight to the centrality of Bultmann in clarifying the century that followed.

The Wrede effect can be summarized as the emergence of a clearer distinction between New Testament scholarship and that part of it called New Testament theology. In the nineteenth century, biblical theology was distinguished from "critical introduction," which tried to answer literary and historical questions about the texts, but the overall aim of theological faculties was ecclesial and theological. They trained clergy who would understand both the human origins and the theological content of the scriptures from which they would preach. Without intending to leave that theological matrix, but with a liberal protestant theology that could allow historical research its independence, Wrede adopted a stance that would eventually allow New Testament scholarship to develop completely free of church theological interests in these documents.

However, his obituary for New Testament theology proved premature. The German faculties remained strongly theological, and New Testament theology continued to flourish. Elsewhere, modern "Introductions" serve a wider range of educational aims, secular and religious, than New Testament theology textbooks. The latter provide overviews of a discipline that has become increasingly specialized, but their rationale remains primarily theological. Their historical descriptions of the doctrinal content of scripture harnessed modern scholarship to the needs of churches teaching and preaching from scripture and wanting their theology to be in accord with scripture. But by the 1890s even the Ritschlians' liberal protestant combination of faith and historical reason was coming under pressure from a fast-developing critical-historical research. Wrede and Holtzmann could count on general agreement about the historical aims and methods of a New Testament scholarship that culminated in textbooks synthesizing what was there in the texts, but Wrede argued that even Holtzmann was inconsistent. Reflecting the theological character of the earlier New Testament theology textbooks by B. Weiss[3] and more recently W. Beyschlag,[4] he had not only restricted himself to the canonical writings but also described their content largely in doctrinal terms. Wrede insisted that for historical research canonical boundaries are irrelevant, and that what is there in the sources is best described as early Christian religion, not doctrine alone, however important the theological aspect of his religion was for Paul. "New Testament theology makes doctrine out of what in itself is not doctrine, and fails to bring out what it really is."[5] The traditional relationship of the discipline to dogmatics had distorted historical scholarship and must now be abandoned.

Wrede suggested that the phrase "New Testament theology" be replaced by "the history of early Christian religion and theology."[6] That would make clearer both the historical character of the discipline (its task and method) and also what was there to be described. He thought it "self-evident that somehow a historical development of the ideas of the New Testament has to be demonstrated, and also that one must try to present these ideas not in line with a dogmatic scheme which is alien to the biblical writers, but according to their own points of view."[7] The historical program is clear, even though the fragmentary data sets limits to developmental schemes. Wrede did not consider why New Testament theology had used doctrinal language in a heuristic way to describe the biblical material. It not only serves as a shorthand (with the admitted dangers of distortion) but also implies and helps clarify what has usually been taken for granted in New Testament theology: that the New Testament writers are talking about the same subject matter as that which subsequent Christians have also acknowledged.

As a Christian, Wrede agreed with that up to a point, despite the differences between his own and their Christianity, which it was his task as a historian to recognize. He saw a great difference between Jesus and Paul, and found much to object to in John, but probably thought that the religion of Jesus and perhaps even that of Jesus' original followers corresponded in essentials to his own. They all worshiped the same God on the basis of shared traditions. His awareness of historical distance and cultural differences did not make his defense of the integrity of historical scholarship antitheological.

His remark that "the name New Testament theology is wrong in both its terms"[8] was saying only that historical research cannot be bound by the canon, and that the historian must recognize in these texts the religion, not only its theology. He was not denying that he was himself a theologian or that his historical scholarship was a theological discipline, as some of his successors would do. He had little sympathy for dogmatics, which he thought was like practical theology, less *wissenschaftlich* than biblical studies and church history, but he was a liberal theologian describing the origins of his own religion now purified of ancient superstition and dogma. However, the terms in which he insisted on the independence of his specialism would later support those who wanted to take it out of its church theological context. Heikki Räisänen of Helsinki has found Wrede's description of the task appropriate to the secular university where some think the modern world is better served by research on the past than by training clergy. As ecclesial theology, New Testament theology is a proper concern of churches, but it is time for universities to move beyond New Testament theology.[9] A wag might call his excellent account of the historical discipline in the past century *New Testament Theology Finished.*

Christian theology today flourishes in many different contexts and countries, but much of the best New Testament scholarship can now be found in the United States. In his 2004 presidential paper to the international Society for New Testament Studies, Professor Wayne Meeks of Yale University, among the most creative New Testament scholars still writing, declared (admittedly by way of "provocation") that "we should start by erasing from our vocabulary the terms 'biblical theology' and, even more urgently, 'New Testament Theology.' Whatever positive contribution these concepts may have made in the conversation since Gabler, we have come to a time when they can only blinker our understanding."[10]

In the 1960s many became distrustful of "biblical theology" as the postwar theological movement so named was being subjected to some justifiable criticism.[11] Those who are unconvinced by the combinations of Old and New Testament theologies sometimes signified by the phrase since the 1980s will warm to Meeks's remarks. His finding the term "New Testament theology" in even more urgent need of erasure is surprising, however, since this discipline has usually avoided the pitfalls most associated with "biblical theology." New Testament theology interprets texts whose authors aimed to express what we now call Christianity, and this has allowed it to remain more closely in step with the rest of historical critical scholarship than is possible for a "biblical theology" that includes Christian understandings of what Christians call the Old Testament, and relates the two Testaments theologically.

In the mid-twentieth century that phrase had a conservative Anglo-American flavor, whereas Old and New Testament theologies were located primarily in German theological faculties where a highly developed critical biblical scholarship dovetailed with modern "theologies of the Word" as it had previously with idealist philosophy. The old pietist idea that biblical theology could replace philosophy and systematics was a feature of the "biblical theology movement" not shared by German New Testament theology. Bultmann and his pupils did "theology as scriptural interpretation,"[12] and a few substituted hermeneutics for dogmatics, but even the high priest of hermeneutics, Gerhard Ebeling, also a competent New Testament theologian, went on to publish in 1979 a superb systematic theology.

In his lecture Meeks restricts the biblical scholars' task, or at least their authority, to the realms of their historical and exegetical expertise.[13] What he calls a "covert relocation of the warrant" takes place when biblical theology "implicitly claims textual and historical warrants for propositions that in truth arise only out of continuing transactions between text and readers through many times and places."[14] That is rightly criticized: "it invites our complicity as historians in this masking of the source of authority."[15] The claim sometimes made in contemporary debates, that "the Bible clearly teaches," is usually a sign of this happening.

All that needs to be said, especially in churches where the appeal to biblical authority in such disputed matters as homosexuality, the ordination of women, and current Middle Eastern politics has often done more harm than good. Whether New Testament theology as currently practiced colludes with this misunderstanding of biblical scholarship's role in the formation of theological judgments is worth asking. Coming from an outstanding scholar whose innovatory work has proved fruitful for Christian theology, including New Testament theology, and whose hermeneutical reflections have generally been as profound as they are cautious, Meeks's "propositions to be debated"[16] demand to be taken seriously, not least in an essay whose title might have to be "erased."

Any suggestion that biblical scholars, in virtue of their specialist knowledge of texts that are (in some sense) authoritative for the Christian church, have some privileged position from which to make theological judgments, can be quickly disowned. They have important contributions to make, constructive as well as critical, but neither exegesis nor history is systematic theology, and when biblical scholars venture onto that turf (which like anyone else they are free to do), they do not speak *ex cathedra.*

Particularly welcome is Meeks's insistence that "the *formative* uses" of scripture, "in liturgy, hymnody, and contemplative discipline, in the shaping of ethos and formation of conscience, in the making of discourse and of art—are logically and developmentally prior to the normative uses."[17] The relationship of scripture and its interpretation to "right doctrine" is a complex issue, traditionally described as scripture being a "source and norm" of Christian faith and theology. "Source" here comes before "norm." Faith is elicited by witness before it is tested. How scripture can function as a norm has become problematic,[18] and in the view of some who dislike norms anyway, impossible. Using it "to establish right doctrine" covers its use as both source and as norm. Even if only the former is fundamental, a heavy emphasis on the doctrinal use of scripture is not "a curious prejudice inherited mostly from western church polemics",[19] or not merely that. It is no doubt less important for many modern biblical scholars than it was for the Reformers, but the question of "right belief," which includes the relationship of contemporary formulations of Christian belief and practice to scripture, is as much an issue for the Christian church today as it has been throughout its history.

That relationship may well be conceived in new ways and generate new theology, as Meeks hints in his criticisms of "privileging doctrine at the expense of life"[20] and in his hostility to "a cognitivist model of religion."[21] But the structure and consequences of this relationship are secondary to its fundamental importance for the Christian church. This relationship is the underlying issue in New Testament theology, even though it has often been taken for granted rather than been made explicit. The discipline has been an arena in which biblical scholarship and Christian theological reflection have combined, sometimes to the point of symbiosis, even though most biblical theologians are professionally biblical scholars rather than philosophical or systematic theologians. Their combination of strictly scientific methods with strong theological interests carries risks, but a breakdown in that relationship would surely be bad for both. Theology would become less biblical, and presumably less Christian, and (a thought for some) the market for biblical professors would contract.

Meeks is right to insist that "the *uses* of the text ought to be at the forefront of our hermeneutical thinking," while continuing to insist that "it is the job of the exegete to stand as the defender of the text's integrity."[22] It is precisely this double concern, only with "uses" qualified as "theological uses by the Christian church," which has motivated a historically and exegetically responsible New Testament theology. Where its theological interests have interfered with the integrity of the texts, improved performance is needed, not the abolition of the discipline. Its correcting the beliefs and practices of the Christian community carries obvious benefits. A historically controlled and theologically engaged biblical scholarship offers guidance to churches as they seek to preserve Christian identity in a changing social and intellectual climate. It also offers both churches and states some protection against the dangerous irrationality of religion.

The deeper issue in Meeks's remarks and in contemporary biblical studies generally is the loosening of the relationship between scholarship and the churches in the late twentieth century. His title "Why Study the New Testament?" raises questions partly answered in New Testament theology, especially concerning the Christian readership for which most modern, like earlier, biblical scholars have worked. Since the papal encyclical *Divino afflante Spiritu* (1943) and the Second Vatican Council, this has included Roman Catholics without this altering the discipline's typical protestant orientation to preaching. But "the world has changed beneath our feet. That culture of Christendom which, however fragmented and attenuated, could still be taken for granted when our discipline took shape has now faded until hardly as much is left of it as the Cheshire cat's grin."[23]

The "importance of recognizing this 'post-Christian' culture for our hermeneutical task"[24] makes Meeks's analysis chilling, above all for the kind of New Testament theology practiced throughout the twentieth century. This, like the rest of the biblical scholarship that he discusses, has occupied the "middle ground" between "general religious skepticism, on the one hand, and religious fundamentalism, on the other."[25] It has contributed significantly to the "reasoned discourse about matters of religion,"[26] which he sees as now under threat. The "social and cultural bases" that supported modern biblical studies

> have all changed. As a result we find ourselves today approaching a state of complete isolation: within the university, lonely practitioners of a quaintly antiquated craft; in the larger world, distant voices scarcely heard within communities of faith and, in the noisy public realm informed by global corporate media, not noticed at all except when we say something truly outrageous.[27]

Meeks was addressing his particular audience about "our role as teachers of Christian communities," and he is clear that "the primary audience will continue to be the whole unruly assortment of faith communities for whom the documents we are interested in are construed as sacred scripture."[28] But he speaks from within the university, "where any actual religious conviction is likely to be seen as an infection threatening the value-free operating theatre of the mind."[29] His audience was mainly members of faith communities, but when he said, "It is perfectly appropriate that we should speak first of all to believers,"[30] it is not clear how far "we" and the "believers" stand shoulder to shoulder. The personal stance of the scholar is apparently irrelevant to the tasks being performed.

There is much to be said for scholars' not wearing their convictions on their sleeves, but any implied disjunction between scholars and faith communities would cut against the grain of New Testament theology, which has always been, in practice if not always in theory, an ecclesial task. It has been practiced mainly in theological faculties with a strong, usually institutional, relationship to some church or association of churches. Where this relationship has become weak the character of biblical studies is changing. Aims and interests have become more diverse, and those seeking to develop and communicate the Christian tradition are in consequence having to become more explicit about what they are doing. This is leading some New Testament theologians to abandon the New Testament theology typical of twentieth-century biblical scholarship, where the religious commitments of the interpreter remained largely implicit, in favor of a more explicit style of theological interpretation less constrained by historical criteria.[31] Other scholars move in other directions, whether ignoring the older religious associations or seeking to undermine them.

That is the changing climate to which Wayne Meeks has drawn attention. It need not be seen as a cultural war between Christianity and unbelief. More interesting than the element of antireligious polemic that has sometimes been present in biblical criticism are the disputes between different theologies. Meeks does not develop a liberal theological program and his appeal to his "post-liberal" colleague (above, n. 21) gives no more than a hint, but the direction of his thinking recalls the program of the most original theologian from the mid-nineteenth century, Richard Rothe.[32] Meeks's opposition to New Testament theology could be construed as opposition to the kind of ecclesial theologies with which this discipline has been associated, and a new insistence that "Christianity" cannot be simply identified with the church. All that he says about the wider possibilities for a secular biblical scholarship has deep theological as well as cultural resonances.

It also draws attention (by way of opposition) to the strongly traditional and ecclesial character of modern New Testament theology—even when this has been written by Christian theologians as radical as F. C. Baur and Rudolf Bultmann. That is reinforced by Räisänen's history and proposal for the discipline (above, n. 9). Both Meeks and Räisänen adopt Wrede's standpoint as a modern critical historian, and not a theologian in the sense of one articulating or only implying a contemporary form of Christianity. This scholarly history of religions standpoint is different from that occupied by New Testament theology and opens up an alternative path for biblical studies. Its historical scholarship brackets out the religious interests that have contributed to the theological character of most biblical scholarship. It wants the religious aims of the biblical authors to be described historically without allowing the modern interpreters' possible religious standpoints to play any part.

Twentieth-century theology has benefited from that separation of church and state, and the related "secularization" of biblical scholarship.

The removal of doctrinal spectacles has allowed a fresh look at the historical data and has sometimes improved vision. "Secularization," however, meant originally "the alienation of church property," and the effect on both church and society of separating biblical scholarship from religious practice is not necessarily positive. New Testament theology is a bridge between them, allowing modern critical rationality to inform and challenge Christian practice and belief. It has loosened but not disrupted the broad doctrinal framework within which Christians read their scriptures, reinforcing the centrality of the Bible in Christian life at a time when this was threatened by the disintegration of older models of authority and modes of interpretation.

This mediating discipline has often seemed suspect, both to religious conservatives and to radicals, but it is one form that the perennial theological task of articulating a traditional religion in terms responsive to modern thought has taken. New Testament theology introduces the rationality of critical scholarship into religious systems in ways that reinforce rather than destroy those that can withstand rational scrutiny. Even secularists who would prefer them destroyed might concede that if religion is going to persist, the state has an interest in theological faculties that cultivate a critical New Testament theology, as well as in supporting cultural history. Similarly, since the rational study of religion is likely to persist, even conservative believers will see merit in this being pursued within a context that takes religion seriously.

Working in a confessional theological context, but one that made ample room for purely historical disciplines, Wrede wanted to remove from his specialism the kind of theological residue that was distorting it. Such practical theological questions as how Christians should understand their scriptures today could safely be left to dogmatics. Biblical scholars were concerned with origins, and did their historical work best when they kept their own religious interests out of it.

Meeks has wider concerns. He did not need to argue for the integrity of historical scholarship in biblical studies, at least not to the professors he was addressing. When he emphasized the gap between biblical scholarship and theology, he was, like Stendahl, defending the integrity of the latter, not (like Wrede) his own specialty, which by the end of the twentieth century had long disowned theologically motivated distortions. The earlier, still largely Christian biblical scholarship had by then yielded to a new pluralism, and in this wider world the dominant Christian voices are not those of the academy. It was therefore the relevance of the discipline that Meeks addressed, suggesting "we may learn that it is not nec-essarily the case that God wants all the world to be like us."[33]

Granted biblical scholarship's primarily Christian audience, he is embarrassed that "so little of what we say and write is of any immediate use" to it.[34] But even allowing for "a bad conscience for having claimed too much in the past" and "defensiveness against those who want to jet-tison historical criticism altogether,"[35] that is far too modest. Learning "more about what the earliest Christians were probably like"[36] is admit-tedly an interesting luxury rather than necessary unto salvation, but where Christ is accepted in those Christian terms, the scriptural witness to him remains essential, and understanding it responsibly (which includes using whatever methods can help it be heard accurately) remains as important as ever. What needs elucidating is how the witness of scrip-ture to God in Christ can best be understood, and that is the business of New Testament theology (as well as systematic theology) rather than social history, valuable as the contribution of that auxiliary discipline surely is.

Despite the dangers of distortion inherent in the interpreters' interests, this concern for contemporary appropriation of the theological witness of scripture is constitutive of New Testament theology). Räisänen speaks of "contemporizing interpretation,"[37] others of "actualizing interpretation," and Gerd Theissen of "the normative exposition of a religion through an interpretative summary of its canonical texts."[38] Relating historical research and religious appropriation while avoiding the dangers of distor-tion is the challenge of New Testament theology. Wrede could see the distortions in the New Testament theology of his day and set about purg-ing his discipline. But he improved New Testament scholarship at the expense of the hermeneutical dimension of New Testament theology. To improve both it is necessary to distinguish more clearly between them, but a century later New Testament theology is still a contested discipline.

DEFINITIONS

Theology and History

The link between New Testament theology and dogmatics, which Wrede saw as an obstruction to a fully critical-historical study of early Christianity, runs right through the history of the modern discipline and stems from what preceded it. Although the phrase "New Testament theology" was not current until G. L. Bauer published his *Biblische Theologie des Neuen Testaments* (4 vols., 1800–1802), the origin of the modern discipline is rightly dated to the inaugural lecture in 1787 of his colleague at Altdorf, J. P. Gabler.[39] This distinguished between "biblical theology" as a historical discipline, and dogmatic theology, which uses philosophy to craft a credible form of Christianity for its own day.

Gabler's aim was to provide a secure biblical base for dogmatics in an age when the old orthodoxy was crumbling and much of the historically conditioned Bible could not credibly be considered divine revelation. His distinction gave some independence to the historical discipline, but his aim was primarily theological. To link biblical study with dogmatics he proposed a first step of historical description (shortly afterward undertaken by G. L. Bauer), to be followed by a second step of sifting out, from what he later called that "true" descriptive biblical theology, all that was historically conditioned, in order to leave a "pure" distillate of revealed truths. This second step of Gabler's proposed Enlightenment biblical theology became in effect the intelligent layperson's approach to the Bible, but it was theologically unsatisfactory and was never carried through by the professionals. It made reason and morality the criterion of authentic Christianity without necessarily relating these to the hearing of the gospel in faith, and in any case everything in the Bible is historically conditioned. But Gabler's first and Bauer's only step became the Old and New Testament theologies of the next two hundred–odd years.

Gabler's theological aims here were continuous with those of the older "biblical theology." This had provided proof texts for the dogmatics of protestant orthodoxy and also a way into criticism of this by some pietists.[40] But his emphasis on history was new. Gabler in principle and Bauer in practice made modern historical methods foundational in their still-theologically-motivated accounts of the biblical witness. This theological aim and motivation remained strong as the historical study of the Bible made rapid advances in Germany, where most of the textbooks were written. The separation of Old and New Testament studies reflected the new historical orientation, but the main purpose of both disciplines remained clergy education.

The story of New Testament theology in the nineteenth century is less exciting than "the quest of the historical Jesus," and it has not had an Albert Schweitzer to tell it.[41] Yet it is the prerequisite for understanding what happened in the twentieth century, and some map work is necessary. The term "New Testament theology" itself is associated with the textbooks bearing that title, but these are a very small part of the discipline called New Testament theology, a subdivision of modern New Testament scholarship and central to modern theological study. Theoretical discussions of the discipline have usually focused on these textbooks (abbreviated here, New Testament theology) because that is where its character and problems are most visible, but it is the discipline itself that has been important for the twentieth-century church, and the textbooks must be understood in the light of what they epitomize.

Understanding the modern discipline involves seeing not only how the phrase has been used but also what has been presupposed. It was self-evident that as well as accurately representing what the New Testament says, the task of New Testament theology was to present the biblical material in a way that related it to a correct contemporary understanding of Christianity. It was written, lectured on, and studied on the assumption and intention that contemporary protestant theology should be in accord with scripture. Behind the "descriptive-historical" task of "presenting" this material, religious interests influenced *how* it was presented. Language taken from dogmatics was assumed to be appropriate, because the New Testament and Christian dogmatics were thought to be expressing (in different genres and generations) the same Christian truth. Doctrinal language both reflected and reinforced that belief. New Testament theologians were not simply engaging in the history of ideas, even doctrinal ideas, but were talking about their own religion too. They were at least reflecting on this, and so doing Christian theology. "Biblical theology," like other theology, was (and still is) usually the "name of an action," reflecting on and communicating the biblical message (a phrase that implies an endless process of interpretation, abstraction, and synthesis), not merely a collection of conceptual materials, however much that contributes to the task. Biblical theology interprets the scriptures on the assumption that what they intend is of the highest possible contemporary significance.[42]

The phrase "biblical theology" has also been used to describe an "object," the theology (or theologies) contained in scripture. But it is what biblical theologians thought about this object that made the activity of describing it *theology*. They thought they were *doing* theology by interpreting scripture. The older definitions of New Testament theology speak only of describing the biblical material historically (Gabler's first step), but in doing that many scholars have been doing their own theology.

This implicit reference to contemporary Christianity is what makes biblical *theology* a modern theological discipline, not merely a historical task. The historical has been complemented by a hermeneutical interest, and historical and exegetical methods have served modern theological aims, often to the detriment of the historical scholarship, but sometimes deepening historical insight.

From G. L. Bauer (1800) on, definitions of New Testament theology spoke of "presenting in an intellectually respectable way (*wissenschaftliche Darstellung*) the theological ideas contained in the New Testament." There was no need to say that it was important for contemporary Christianity, or that this was why it was being done. What was emphasized were the historical methods used, and it is not hard to see how this passion for historical truth could give New Testament scholarship a life of its own, separate from its concern to inform and correct contemporary Christianity. That did not (with rare exceptions) happen in the nineteenth, or even in most of the twentieth, century because the institutional links of the discipline (in theological faculties) to the churches were so strong. A more "independent" exegesis emerged on a very small scale in France[43] where these links were weaker, but elsewhere most New Testament scholarship was New Testament theology, or its scholarly adjuncts and supports. It was oriented and related to contemporary Christianity, whether or not this was made explicit.

This link with contemporary religious belief and practice is (arguably) what makes New Testament theology "theology" properly so-called, rather than simply a part of the *history* of Christian theology. "Theology" means "talk of God," and it is possible to talk of things that do not exist, or exist only in the imagination of deluded persons. That would seem to many today to be the case with theology, and the noun and even more the adjective are sometimes given that pejorative connotation. But few of those who practice theology would accept that account of their work. Even if they are not themselves participants in a religious community, those who call themselves theologians and "speak of God" think that they are talking of some ultimate reality and that doing so is somehow self-involving, like prayer or preaching, even though essentially critical and reflective, as those primary or first-order religious activities need not be. Whether theology is necessarily a "confessional" activity is debated. Without agreeing that only believers can do it, most accept that in a secular and pluralist culture it is the language of specific religious communities and therefore needs an adjective specifying which tradition of

God-talk is intended. But the close relationship of philosophy and theology in Christianity, and the dominance of Christianity in Western culture, has often led to the qualifying adjective being dropped and the false impression being given that this religious context is not part of what the word *God* means, or essential to its proper use.

There is admittedly some advantage in using both the word *theology* and the phrase "New Testament theology" to refer to any history or analysis of theological ideas and concepts, regardless of the reality of their referents. That allows academic "theology" to be done with no more and no different personal involvement than is required in other disciplines. But even theologians who deny that their discipline is "confessional" mostly work from within a religious tradition that refers to God, who is worshiped. Regardless of their own personal beliefs and practices, they can accept a definition of theology that recognizes this. The adjective *theological*, by contrast, often designates scholarship devoted to this tradition without any reference to the reality of God. Linguistic, textual, and historical work can be done without reference to the truth or value of a tradition. But the noun *theology* and the verb "to theologize" are better reserved for a discourse that is at least interested in the scope of its religious subject matter and is articulated from that standpoint.

Most New Testament theology has been done from an interest in contemporary Christianity. Historians who want to keep the personal existential question of God out of biblical scholarship, even if they are interested in ancient theology, now usually avoid the phrase "New Testament theology," leaving that label for a study of the New Testament oriented to contemporary Christianity. This respects the origins of the phrase and preserves the self-involving aspect of God-talk which may be lost when describing someone else's religion historically or analytically, but which can be retrieved by historical or philosophical theologians' adopting the standpoint of the person whose religion they are describing or analyzing. When they do this they can say that their subject matter is God, not merely someone else's religion (though it is that too). They are then doing theology (speaking of God), in this case historical theology, or New Testament theology. Without a definition of the subject matter that connects their work to contemporary faith and practice, New Testament historians remain historians, prefer not to be called theologians, and generally reject the label New Testament theology for their work.

A possible objection to this account of New Testament theology is that because scholars are under no obligation to reveal their standpoint (much less their personal religious commitments), it is often unclear whether a piece of New Testament interpretation was written as "theology" (the writer thinking the subject matter is God) or as a sympathetic history of religion. But who needs to know? Librarians can classify it as New Testament studies, and any reader can choose whether to read it as New Testament theology or as history of early Christian thought. In a secular and pluralist culture, religious texts will be read in different ways and with different resonances. This is reflected in a biblical interpretation, which can be written and read either as *theology* (where the scholars or their readers identify with what these texts are getting at), or as *history* (where they not only preserve the distance between then and now that both sides acknowledge, but may also decline to accept anything like these texts' account of their subject matter). Far from dissolving the discipline called New Testament theology, this ambiguity allows it to colonize work done under other descriptors and also to be corrected by other historians and exegetes wherever the interests of theologians lead them to misread the texts.

Historical Jesus Research and New Testament Theology

The ecclesial and often conservative religious character of New Testament theology can be observed by contrasting it with the nineteenth-century "quest of the historical Jesus," which was sometimes integrated in New Testament theology and sometimes pursued independently, especially by liberal theologians and independent scholars. New Testament theology does (in new ways) what much Christian study of scripture has aimed to do, to clarify the biblical texts and their authors' witness to the crucified and risen Jesus as the saving revelation of God. It uses modern historical and exegetical insights to help understand and communicate their message. The new historical study of the New Testament had the potential to subvert that witness, but the textbook New Testament theologies do not do that. They present the biblical material in ways that facilitate its appropriation and dissemination by Christian preachers and teachers. The historical perspective of New Testament theology might challenge as well as inform dogmatics, but they coexisted on the new map of theological studies drawn by Schleiermacher.

Historical Jesus research had a more freethinking origin among the English deists, and the classic example of Reimarus showed how dangerous it could be for traditional Christianity. For more than three hundred years that research has always threatened and sometimes tried to undermine this by going *behind* the biblical witness unfolded in New Testament theology and claiming that Jesus was more or less different from what the church and even from what the Bible claimed. A radical historical study of the Gospels and Christian doctrine could tear up Schleiermacher's map, replacing New Testament theology and dogmatics with new perceptions of the human Jesus and some modern religious philosophy. By looking for the truth about Jesus *behind* the texts, and using methods that did not speak of God to describe him, historical Jesus research contributed to a new kind of protestant Christianity, different from that of the Reformers, protestant orthodoxy, or pietism. Those older Protestants all shared more doctrine with Roman Catholicism than with the eighteenth-century deists who pioneered historical Jesus research, or with their radical neo-protestant successors.

By the time these new impulses were becoming culturally significant following Strauss's *Life of Jesus* (1835), protestant theologians were already integrating them into more traditional versions of Christianity. Schleiermacher had lectured on the life of Jesus from 1819 and developed a Christology that tried to combine a historical perception of Jesus with the doctrinal definition of him as truly human, truly God. Baur considered this compromise unsuccessful and Strauss attacked it,[44] but when its weaknesses were corrected, it provided a template for twentieth-century Christologies claiming continuity with classical doctrinal formulations. However, the revolutionary potential of Reimarus's and Strauss's gospel criticism (recognized by Marx) was not extinguished, and it remains a threat to orthodox Christianity. The claim that Jesus was more or less different from what the Bible and the church teach has drawn many to new forms of Christianity based more directly on Jesus' life and teaching, and has led others to repudiate it altogether.

Most New Testament theology, by contrast, interprets the postresurrection witness of these texts, and so points Christianity back to its foundational claim that Jesus was vindicated by God and is the decisive revelation of God. When it engages in historical Jesus research, it looks for continuities between the word and work of the Galilean and the disciples' response to him, confirmed in their Easter experiences. Interpretations of the texts developed in New Testament theology may fail to represent their witness accurately, but they *aim* to correspond to the biblical authors' intentions, as historical Jesus research does not. This seeks to understand its sources, but then draws its own conclusions from them. B. Weiss described the difference by calling biblical theology a "descriptive historical," but not a "critical-historical," discipline.[45]

Modern historians writing about Jesus not only dispute their sources' reliability but will necessarily write a different kind of account of Jesus from that of their gospel sources. Unlike New Testament theology, historical Jesus research does not aim to communicate the message of these texts that Jesus is the Christ, the Son of God. It does not offer life in Jesus' name. New Testament theology is not preaching either, and it makes use of the same historical methods as other biblical scholarship. But while it need not presuppose the truth of the biblical witness, it has usually been sympathetic to the texts it is trying to interpret in a way of which these authors would themselves approve. It works with the grain of their (religious) account of the subject matter. It is more likely to adopt a hermeneutics of consent, open to hearing the witness of the texts, than a hermeneutics of suspicion that is already prejudiced against them.

Historical Jesus research typically subjects its gospel sources to a more radical critical scrutiny, as it tries to determine which parts of the evidence can be accepted. Here understanding the religious witness of the texts can be a step toward sifting or discarding them as to a large extent historically unreliable. This has also provided a way of eliminating material found religiously unhelpful. Historians have taken a similar critical approach to church history, in principle untrammeled by any apologetic interests. This critical history of the early church was pioneered by F. C. Baur in 1831[46] and developed impressively over the next century and more. Like historical Jesus research, it looks *behind* the texts in attempts to reconstruct the real history, but this did not hold a dagger to the heart of Christian belief, as gospel criticism did when it destroyed the old arguments for the divinity of Christ and constructed purely human historical pictures of Jesus. The new critical history shocked many by treating the Bible like any other historical source, but belief in biblical inerrancy was already being eroded, despite rearguard actions.

Baur's historical research uncovered the diversity in early Christianity, and theological diversity within the New Testament posed a problem for Christian use of the Bible as a norm for doctrine. New Testament theology would have to suggest a new way of understanding the unity of scripture if this was to remain a norm as well as a source of faith. Wrede was realistic in thinking that theologians would be likely to understate the difficulties posed for traditional Christianity by historical research.

His hope that New Testament scholarship as a whole would free itself of theological interests was less realistic, but for some of its tasks that is appropriate, and some scholars have legitimately chosen to be historians of religion and not theologians. Others have adopted historical and other rational methods while defining their subject matter theologically, in essential agreement with the biblical authors. That is properly called New Testament theology.

Fluid Boundaries

The two distinctions made so far have in reality been blurred. New Testament theology is a historically and exegetically informed interpretation of the New Testament texts, articulating their Christian witness. It can be distinguished from historical scholarship, which goes *behind* the texts to reconstruct the past (whether or not with a view to developing a more modern form of Christianity). But it is not satisfactory to limit New Testament theology to interpreting the biblical texts, excluding from the discipline any historical research that looks behind them. Both these tasks may be theologically motivated, and when the latter is done with a view to developing Christianity today, as it often has been, it can arguably be called New Testament theology, contrary to that distinction. The discipline could be loosely described as any modern critical New Testament scholarship oriented to a contemporary understanding of Christianity. The ambiguous position of historical Jesus research in New Testament theology reflects the fact that it can be done either as New Testament theology, or without theological interests. If pursued with antitheological intent, it would be odd to call it New Testament theology, but its antiorthodox tendency is not a reason for defining New Testament theology in a way that excludes it. The discipline can embrace the range of theological positions that speak of Jesus and God on a basis of scripture. Historical Jesus research has a place in New Testament theology when it is related positively, but not uncritically, to the witness of the texts, clarifying the relationship of the earthly Jesus to postresurrection faith, as done most recently by Hahn and Wilckens.[47] When it *replaces* that witness, it might still be Christian theology of a sort, but hardly New Testament theology, being at odds with both the theology contained in these texts and their intentions.

Even though the history behind the texts plays a subordinate role in most New Testament theologies, it has usually been presupposed. How biblical scholars interpret a text theologically is sometimes influenced by what they think about its prehistory. These two different tasks cannot be kept apart for long. Christian theology is interested in Jesus and therefore inevitably in the historical study of Jesus and in how this relates to Christian witness to him, contrary to some early reactions against liberal life-of-Jesus research.

A second distinction also emerged in the preceding discussion, that between the Christian theological interests of most interpreters on the one hand, and their scholarly methods on the other. Historical methods naturally serve historical aims and goals, but they may also serve other aims and interests such as political, religious, or other cultural aims, or some combination of these. It is therefore necessary to distinguish between historical and theological aims, while recognizing that this distinction is also blurred because most interpreters of the New Testament combine both these aims in varying degrees. Wrede concluded from the historical method and task of New Testament theology (so-called) that scholarly interpreters could have *only historical aims.* This needs to be corrected by distinguishing New Testament theology, where historical methods serve theological aims, from other legitimate scholarly tasks, including historical reconstruction of early Christianity for its own sake. Though usually combined by biblical scholars, these aims can be distinguished and allow us to define New Testament theology in these terms. Reference to the theological conceptual content of New Testament theology is included in the phrase itself, and the phrase also identifies the religious texts being interpreted, but the aims of the interpreters are also a feature of the discipline, and these have to be made explicit in defining it.

It may not always be obvious whether a work of scholarship is theologically motivated, and the distinction between history and theology is sometimes blurred, but it seems to be decisive for the definition of New Testament theology that it aims to speak of God, who is worshiped today, as it describes early Christian religion or interprets these texts. Historians who think they are (indirectly or implicitly) talking of God in and through their historical work are theologians doing New Testament theology, even when they do not use the word. We may call them "anonymous theologians." They submit their work to the public scrutiny of other historians and exegetes whose methods they share, but they are also interested in its relationship to their own understanding of the gospel.

Both these distinctions help clarify modern New Testament scholarship. Biblical scholars are interested in the texts and in what lies behind them. Most of them have theological as well as historical interests. Interpreting the biblical texts historically and articulating their Christian witness can lead to theological questions about the truth of that witness. Looking behind the texts for information about the person they are interpreting does not answer these questions, but a more accurate historical picture of Jesus and Christian origins may surely contribute to an answer. Christianity involves much more than historical information, but as well as threatening it, this may enhance its credibility.

Probing the biblical witness by rational methods has been considered a poisonous infection by some and soft apologetics by others. The former charge can be answered by emphasizing the religious and theological aims of New Testament theology. Outside that framework, historical criticism can indeed be destructive of any traditional religion. The latter charge of apologetics corrupting research gives reason to welcome the watching brief of an independent historical research. As historical research, New Testament theology is subject to the constraints of that discipline and open to challenge by nonreligious historians. Religious interests may deepen historical understanding or they may distort it, but distortions can always be corrected. There is room (where the evidence is so limited and so suspect) for a range of credible historical reconstructions. Some of these are more congenial to modern religious interests than others, and there is no reason to think the reconstructions (such as those of Reimarus or even Albert Schweitzer) that are most problematic for traditional Christian belief are the most true. But the case for holding one's religious views at a distance (not denying or concealing them) in doing historical work is today widely accepted, and the checks provided by independent historical research are widely welcomed.

Some still see modern rationality as a poisonous infection, but most nineteenth-century university theology embraced it. As historical research accelerated toward the end of the century, biblical theology declined, but after the First World War theologically weighted interpretations of scripture reappeared. The religious and theological interests that have usually motivated New Testament studies were continued by conservative scholars but also reasserted by some liberal and radical theologians and biblical scholars, leading to the rejuvenation of New Testament theology, led by Bultmann. That new convergence of radical critical-historical scholarship and theological interpretations of scripture dominated twentieth-century German New Testament studies. A recent reaction against it among secular protestants has been balanced by the expansion of New Testament theology among Roman Catholics and evangelicals who value their continuity with the New Testament itself.

All history has a contemporary interest, but historians emphasize the distance and otherness of the past. New Testament theology is schooled in history and well aware of the difference between then and now, but by the questions it asks it also forges links between these ancient documents and contemporary Christian belief and practice. Other historians are right to insist on its difference from their own work, despite the very large overlap. The biblical theologian's relationship to scripture is closer to some literary critics' respectful relationship to literature than to the suspicion with which critical historians treat their sources. Literary critics are aware that what a literary text is about may transcend what can be adequately described or paraphrased.

The character of New Testament theology has been obscured by the overwhelmingly historical character of biblical scholarship. The interpretation of ancient texts always involves the study of languages and history, but that does not mean the theologian's reading of these texts can only be that of the historians. On the contrary, theologians benefit from and contribute to the work of historians for their own partly different purposes. New Testament theology aims to read these texts responsibly, with respect to what can be divined of authorial or textual intention, which requires historical and exegetical work, and also in ways that may illuminate and correct contemporary Christianity. The main question about New Testament theology is whether these two concerns are compatible. Most New Testament theology has assumed that they are, though the practice of the discipline has not always confirmed this.

Wrede at the Crossroads

A century after his early death, Wrede is again heard beckoning biblical scholarship into a less-theological future than his successors who continued the enterprise called New Testament theology could accept. His emphasis on historical research at the expense of the (often implicit) hermeneutical aspect of New Testament theology undermined its claim to be *theology* through history and made it simply history. Modern historians do not speak of God. Most biblical scholars, however, work with religious interests. Even when ill-equipped to venture beyond their historical and exegetical specialism, they have held together their scholarship and their religious beliefs. These have usually been silently presupposed, affecting the questions they ask of the texts and sometimes skewing their historical judgment, but usually dovetailing with their scholarship, not just tacked on at the end. As biblical theologians they have assumed that rigorous historical work was at least compatible with, and perhaps a prerequisite of, good theology.

Wrede opened a door to a historical study of the New Testament less oriented to modern Christianity. Within a generation (in the 1920s), Bultmann was half-closing it again by integrating Bousset's history of religions and Wrede's history of traditions research into a new theological synthesis. Only as this lost some of its plausibility some forty years later, in the late 1960s, did the "secularization" inherent in Wrede's program take root and begin to marginalize New Testament theology.

Breaking the link made by New Testament theology between historical study of Christian origins and modern belief is a legitimate scholarly option. So is rethinking this link, as Bultmann later did. Wrede's focus on the historical weaknesses of the then current New Testament theology, weaknesses evidently caused by its religious interests, blinded him to the legitimacy of theological aims in that form of biblical interpretation, and to the possibility of pursuing these without corrupting historical research. He assumed that his critique of current New Testament theology, which failed to measure up to the latest historical research, implied its total demise. Instead, it challenged biblical theologians to integrate this research into a new theology.

Both Wrede's preference for history and Bultmann's new theology offered ways forward for Christianity in the twentieth century. The reason Wrede could part company with the older New Testament theology without trying to replace it with a more satisfactory one was that his own liberal theology did not need a traditional New Testament theology, as it was largely independent of the Pauline and Johannine witness to God in Christ. It needed the Synoptic Gospels as historical sources for Jesus' life and teaching because liberal protestants venerated Jesus as a religious teacher who confirmed their belief in God and morality, but their new form of Christianity did not need the full theological witness of the New Testament writings that New Testament theology interprets.

Wrede's determination to break the link between biblical scholarship and (a rather outmoded) dogmatics went further than Gabler's, who had given biblical theology a relative independence but intended it as a first step toward making modern theological judgments. Like Gabler, Wrede himself remained a theologian, but his argument detached the biblical scholar's historical work more thoroughly from theological interests in order to preserve its integrity:

> So long as New Testament Theology retains a direct link with dogmatics as its goal (*Zweckbeziehung*) and people expect from it material for dogmatics to work on—and that is a common view—it will be natural for biblical theology to have an eye to dogmatics. Biblical theology will be pressed for an answer to dogmatic questions which the biblical documents do not really give, and will endeavor to eliminate results which are troublesome for dogmatics.[48]

"Having an eye to dogmatics" does not necessarily involve pressing the texts for answers to doctrinal (or ethical) questions that these do not intend to give. We may distinguish between squeezing the texts for answers to modern questions, and simply presupposing that they bear witness to the reality with which contemporary Christianity is also concerned. Wrede's protest needs to be heard wherever the Bible is used naively to provide simple answers for contemporary moral or doctrinal questions. That religious use of the Bible usually misreads the texts and also misunderstands how modern Christian theological and ethical judgments are formed, as Stendahl and Meeks insisted. But to accuse New Testament theology of that kind of naïveté misses its true character. Like all Christian interpretation of scripture (but with more historical and critical sense than most), New Testament theology understands these texts to be speaking of God's engagement with the world in Jesus Christ. Its theological interpretations must refer to the faith of Israel as the essential context of this historical figure and of his initial reception. By pitting a rigorous historical criticism against some arguably outdated theological interpretations, Wrede obscured what New Testament theology was doing instead of rethinking it in the light of his own radical historical conclusions, as Bultmann was to do.

The difference between Wrede's critical-historical scholarship and the New Testament theology that preceded and followed him is that the latter presupposed (usually without needing to declare it) a Christian belief about the subject matter of scripture: that it spoke of the revelation of God in Christ. Wrede not only challenged Holtzmann's New Testament theology in the interests of better history of religion but denied that Christian presuppositions should influence historical research. That rejection in principle of religious aims or interests marked the point at which his "New Testament theology" (so-called) was no longer theology but simply history of religion. He defined biblical scholarship in a way that made the scholar's religious interest irrelevant. That is one option, but no longer New Testament theology as understood before and (by some) since.

Wrede's refusal to combine modern religious belief and historical scholarship is clear in his caustic remarks on B. Weiss and W. Beyschlag. Both the critical conclusions and the Christian beliefs of these two authors of New Testament theologies were more conservative than Wrede's, but their beliefs did not exclude critical scholarship, as a belief in biblical inerrancy or a historical argument for miracles would have done. Their disagreement with Wrede about New Testament theology is therefore independent of their scholarly disagreements with him, as it is also independent of their different personal beliefs. The issue is simply whether the latter can be presupposed when doing historical work in New Testament theology.

Beyschlag claimed that biblical theology *presupposes* "the revelation character of the biblical religion,"[49] while denying that a historical treatment of the material depended on accepting this belief. One might paraphrase that as saying that the church's view of the Bible (that it speaks of God, however this is understood) is compatible with studying it with the help of modern historical methods. Wrede's response was that "a simpler way of stating that would be to say that it does *not* comprise the presupposition of the discipline." However, that is not the paraphrase of Beyschlag it claims to be but the assertion of a different view of how biblical scholarship should now proceed. Wrede here distinguishes between a biblical theology (including New Testament theology), which agrees with the biblical authors about God and describes their beliefs historically, and his own New Testament scholarship, in principle independent of modern Christianity, which simply describes the biblical authors' beliefs historically. Since the two might well appear identical, Wrede thought this supposed distinction between theological history (or historical theology) and his own critical history of religion unreal. There is only good history and bad history. B. Weiss is treated with similar contempt for saying that New Testament theology presupposes the normative character of the New Testament writings. Again, if this presupposition does not make any specifiable difference to the history as written, it is in Wrede's view unreal, and only an excuse for bad history. But that is too simple. More attention admittedly needs to be paid to what differences, if any, Christian belief might make to a critical-historical study of Christian origins written from that perspective, but one does not have to agree with Weiss that this belief "has been demonstrated by dogmatics" to assert with him that New Testament theology presupposes it, and therefore understands the subject matter of scripture differently from some historians of religion.

B. Weiss, Beyschlag, and Wrede were all religiously motivated to study the New Testament, and were all agreed that the biblical material must be described using ordinary historical methods, and they all thought the New Testament (or part of it) more or less compatible with their own Christian beliefs. Setting aside their critical conclusions, which differed considerably, the line between them is scarcely visible, and yet it is vital for the definition of New Testament theology. Wrede's account of the discipline is dictated by the methods it uses. For him historical methods imply historical tasks, and these imply historical aims, which must not be interfered with by other (religious) aims. Rather than making himself the slave of these new methods, Beyschlag gives more weight to his own theological aims and presuppositions as an interpreter, while agreeing with Wrede that this must not distort his historical judgment. Wrede thought it did, and in practice always would. But Beyschlag's program is not impossible in principle. Even though the use of historical methods implies a naturalistic worldview that excludes supernaturalism from modern New Testament theology, it is possible to understand the history being described in New Testament theology as compatible with Christian belief in God. This is not demonstrated but *presupposed* in New Testament theology. The kind of difference it makes in practice is comparable to Marxist historians who (at their best) know that they must not force the evidence to support their theory but may read it in that light and raise questions that to other historians might seem unimportant.

Beyschlag's view was in accord with the past and the future of the discipline, whereas by excluding the presupposition of Christian belief Wrede points to the different (but overlapping) task that he was right to call *history* of religion rather than New Testament theology or historical *theology*. But Wrede left room for theology, even if (unlike Gabler) he did not see this as his own task in (wrongly so-called) New Testament theology or "biblical theology." He restricted himself, as does most New Testament theology, to Gabler's first step, and assigned the second step to dogmatics.[50] What is often overlooked, however, is that by defining the first step without reference to the second, and denying that New Testament theology could be done "with an eye to dogmatics,"[51] he was flagging a possible change in the character of some New Testament scholarship, which would dissociate it from any religious interest in Christianity.

This was not his intention. He even offers his own (two-stage) account of the relationship between New Testament theology and belief:

> Biblical theology investigates the New Testament writings first of all without presuppositions to find out the content (*Inhalt*) of the biblical religion. Then afterwards a judgment is made about what is discovered: it is revelation in such and such a sense—i.e. the judgment is demonstrated. For before I can call something revelation I have to know what this "something" is.[52]

But by excluding the Christian "presupposition" of Beyschlag and normal New Testament theology, and not only describing but also seeming to understand the phenomenon of religion in purely human terms, he left no room at this first stage for his own personal belief about the theological content or subject matter (*Sache*) of these texts. If all reflection on God in Christian origins is transferred to dogmatics, New Testament theology is finished.

The superficial reason Wrede prefers this two-stage model is the probability of the believer's religious presupposition corrupting historical judgment. The deeper reason is surely that it is the natural approach to the past in a secular world. In that case, moving the accent in New Testament theology from explication of the *textual* witnesses to historical reconstructions of their religion was a false step, a faux pas, so far as New Testament *theology* is concerned.

It was a natural and legitimate step for biblical *scholarship* to try to reconstruct the history of Israelite, Jewish, and early Christian religion. To anyone holding Baur's idealist metaphysical beliefs it was also theologically attractive. But as these gave way to positivism, it left biblical scholarship stranded, impressive in its own terms but with no route into theology. The problem with Wrede's two-stage model of (1) New Testament scholarship, followed by (2) dogmatics, is simply that theological judgments (stage two) do not follow easily from historical description (stage one). They may even be made more difficult by historians emphasizing the distance between past and present. Theological statements based on the New Testament do not derive from the New

Testament alone. They owe much to the subsequent tradition and to the interpreter's standpoint. Further analysis of this process is needed. Historical descriptions of the origins of the ancient religion are only one part of what may go into understanding these texts as Christian scripture speaking of God today. New Testament theology is primarily a matter of understanding the texts on this presupposition, not reconstructing the religion behind them, however much this important and interesting scholarly task may contribute to that theological enterprise.

Gabler's account of the first (historical) stage of his "biblical theology" was still a matter of understanding the *texts* as Christian scripture, rather than reconstructing the *history* of the religion behind them. That paradigm shift came later. Even Baur presupposed that his sources, early Christian texts, contained a modern theological content, and something of that survived for the post-Hegelian generations of Holtzmann and Harnack. Wrede, Bousset, J. Weiss, and Gunkel were no less pious, but the gulf between their religion and its history on the one hand, and traditional theology on the other had deepened, and interest in a New Testament theology that might hold these together had weakened.

Gabler maintained the Christian presupposition that is definitive of New Testament theology. A century later most of his successors shared it, but they were beginning to define their work in terms that did not require it. Gabler had intended to proceed to stage two. This shows both his Christian theological standpoint and his focus on the theological content of the *texts* rather than the religion behind them, which he pondered only to help him discard some of the texts. Wrede had no such intention to proceed to stage two. That was the dogmatician's task. He would remain a historian of early Christianity, untainted by such modern theological interests, even though he happened to have some.

Gabler's standpoint was preserved in subsequent New Testament theology in the form of a Christian presupposition about the subject matter of scripture (Beyschlag) and an interest in the contemporary religious appropriation of these texts (above, n. 42). New Testament theology describes the biblical texts by the rational methods of historical exegesis helped by historical reconstruction but understands them to be referring (indirectly and inadequately) to transcendent reality. It cannot describe that reality historically, but it can imagine it as the hidden truth to which these texts bear theological witness, a truth once expressed in the religion for which these texts are also sources.

Theological interpreters identify with the witness of the texts, hopefully not stretching the evidence to fit their religious presuppositions, and perhaps even being persuaded by the weight of evidence or by exegetical conclusions to modify these presuppositions, but denying that the two sides are in principle incompatible. They can welcome the controls provided by other historians who do not share their Christian presuppositions, and are happy to learn from them, but they continue to understand the New Testament in a specifically Christian way as speaking of God, and bearing witness to the revelation of God in Christ. New Testament theology reduces the gap between scholarship and ecclesial religious practice by allowing Christian belief a strong though not controlling interest in biblical interpretation.

Both Wrede's and Beyschlag's concepts of revelation were soon overtaken by twentieth-century theologies that recalled the Reformers and associated the Word of God (incarnate, written, and preached) with faith, rather than with religion or the history of religion. But the definition of New Testament theology does not depend (as the character of any particular New Testament theology does) on what concept of revelation is held. The discipline has been practiced by theologians who give quite different accounts of this. It does, however, always presuppose some kind of belief in revelation because it presupposes that the New Testament speaks of God, who is worshiped today, and God is known (Christians assume) only on a basis of God's self-revelation, whether this is understood to include the natural world and "other religions" or is restricted to the biblical witness to Christ.

The modern religious interests that are present in New Testament theology correspond broadly to the intentions of the biblical authors who also had religious aims, and they are true to the texts themselves, which are religious literature. But religion can be described sympathetically or unsympathetically, and with greater or lesser personal identification with what is described. Religious literature can be read with essential agreement (which leaves room for disagreement about details), or with distaste and even the hatred that Albert Schweitzer thought gave Reimarus his critical edge. But interpreters have to find categories that adequately describe the texts and also imply or express their own view of what these are saying. Describing them as doctrine is inaccurate, as Wrede saw, and "privileging doctrine at the expense of life"[53]) is an unattractive interpretative option today. The religion reflected in the New Testament, like Christianity in every age including today, involves spirituality and institutions as well as patterns of behavior and belief.[54] But any *definition* of New Testament theology today will make explicit the aims of the interpreters to relate their unbiased historical and exegetical investigations to their own contemporary understandings of Christianity, because today other aims are also validly pursued by the same historical and exegetical methods.

New Testament theology teaches believers, and anyone else who is interested, how to read the New Testament in accord with the fundamental intentions of the texts themselves and the Christian church. It does this by interpretations that maintain the bridges between these ancient texts and the contemporary Christians appropriating them. These bridges exist wherever Christians read their scriptures, but many of them now seem inadequate to the gulf they have to span, magnified by modern historical perception. New Testament theology uses these new historical insights to strengthen the foundations of these hermeneutical bridges and so makes scripture more likely to inform and challenge contemporary Christianity by fresh accounts of its classical, in some sense normative, witnesses to the saving revelation of God in Jesus. This requires historical spadework, but what is "carried across" these bridges (i.e., "translated") is not merely historical information and insight but material for contemporary Christian proclamation. Biblical language is understood historically in its settings in the worship and life of the early churches, and "translated" into new settings in the lives of worshiping and witnessing communities of faith today.

New Testament theologies organize the biblical material in ways designed to communicate its subject matter. The doctrinal model has been criticized, but thematic approaches will always be needed, and the classical doctrinal topics do roughly correspond to the material they were originally designed to express. But in New Testament theology they are used heuristically and more loosely than in textbooks of dogmatics, to help describe the material in accord with the biblical authors' "own points of view," as Wrede insisted.[55]

The preponderance of historical presentations of New Testament theology reflects not only scholarly preoccupations and enthusiasm for the explanatory power of history but also the long popularity of theological and philosophical theories of God's self-revelation in history. As the latter have faded, canonically shaped New Testament theologies have come to seem more appropriate to the phrase "New Testament theology," but a mixture of historical and canonical factors usually determine the shape of a New Testament theology. Historical insights help understand this collection of texts and reinforce the presumption in favor of New Testament theology's asking about the authors' intentions. New Testament theologies, which resist the grain of the historical and exegetical work out of which they are constructed, will not be persuasive.

Wrede's protest against the phrase "New Testament theology" and the restriction of the discipline to the canonical texts is compelling when the discipline is redefined as the history of early Christian religion and theology. It has some validity even in New Testament theologies properly so-called. Where these locate revelation in the real course of history they cannot plausibly pick out a selection of sources or events, as some "salvation history" theories do. They will need to consider all the evidence and also the prehistory of the biblical traditions. Even where a New Testament theology finds revelation in the texts' witness to the incarnate Word or in contemporary proclamation based on this witness, understanding these ancient texts will require the study of many other texts, especially material illuminating the Hellenistic Jewish context of these writings. A full discussion of this other material would swamp the texts being interpreted, but theological (like literary) interpretation can be informed by all relevant historical information.

When critical-historical research is made constitutive of the modern discipline, it can describe the material as it sees fit, whether as "doctrine" (Baur) or as "religion" (Wrede). But this use of historical methods was originally directed to theological aims, and where that remains the case theologians have resisted the subversion of theology by historicism, continuing to define the subject matter in their own ways, reading the history of early Christian religion and analyses of its language and literature as somehow about the God who is worshiped by Christians today.

If what Christians claim is the subject matter of scripture can be better communicated by reading scripture as religious literature rather than as sources for reconstructing the history of religion, literary approaches will become the ruling paradigm for New Testament theology and Wrede's project becomes an alternative scholarly concern. Which literary theories are then adopted and which are rejected will depend on the purposes for which New Testament theology (or New Testament theologies) are written. All Christian reading of scripture involves a strong element of reader response, but New Testament theology has also insisted on textual determinacy and (where possible) respect for authorial intention, implying a continuing need for historical and exegetical scholarship. That is because it has been associated with the normative use of scripture, which requires stable meanings and some agreement about them. The search for authorial intention provides the best hope of securing a consensus because it can adopt historical and exegetical procedures well-established across different disciplines. However, what Meeks called "formative" uses of scripture do not require this, and Christians have always lived with a plurality of interpretations. Texts are multivalent. Private devotional uses of scripture can delight in the free play of figural interpretations. Even public preaching, which aims at credibility and is usually subject to some ecclesiastical norms, can explore a range of possible interpretations, not all of them verified by historical exegesis.

Reservations about the hegemony of historical research in New Testament theology stem from its using methods and achieving results that do not speak of God. Historians can redescribe and explain the biblical material in non-Christian terms as evidence from the past for a religion to which they themselves may or may not subscribe. Absolute idealism made history bear the weight of revelational claims, but that proved unrealistic, and most New Testament theology has been content to presuppose Christian belief rather than verify it through historical study. But this makes New Testament theology more subjective than its claims to truth seem to require. A few theologians have therefore preferred to contest the modern worldview that gave birth to critical-historical study, and to reject some dominant trends in the interpretation of scripture. They do not mind breaking off what they dismiss as merely a conversation within the academy. That stance may undermine the credibility of the Christian message, but it has been one strand in the story of twentieth-century theology and New Testament theology. The antithesis to Wrede's thesis, leading on to Bultmann's synthesis, will accordingly be found in a conservative theologian and biblical scholar of genius, A. Schlatter (1852–1938).

BULTMANN, BEFORE AND AFTER

Our overview of two hundred years of New Testament theology, from G. L. Bauer (1800–1802) to Ferdinand Hahn (2002), will emphasize what Wrede (and some recent historians of early Christianity) resisted but most practitioners of the discipline take for granted: the relationship of New Testament theology to contemporary faith and theology.

Christian biblical scholarship since Origen has usually operated with a "believing hermeneutic," sharing the faith of the communities that sponsor it. When the sixteenth-century Reformers challenged church authority on appeal to scripture, they could do so only on the basis of a shared assumption that the Bible speaks reliably of God and the saving revelation of God in Christ. When that was challenged in the eighteenth century, the relationship of biblical scholarship to the church began to change.

Wrede's response to Holtzmann in 1897 can now be seen as pivotal—contrary to his own intentions. Wrede's immediate predecessors had seen New Testament theology as the proper goal of New Testament scholarship, the point at which Christian scholars were aiming and where they handed the baton on to dogmatics. Wrede had no objection to systematic theologians' picking up and using his historical conclusions, but he thought that aiming to give them something they could use was corrupting scholarly work. He saw that historical-critical scholarship in his day really was in principle independent but was still in practice done with an eye to dogmatics. He insisted it should be more consistent and do its own historical work in its own terms.

In retrospect, we must say that although Wrede himself identified New Testament theology (wrongly so-called) and historical reconstruction, this stance implied a distinction between biblical theology, which prefaces its biblical scholarship with a Christian presupposition yet is determined to prevent this conviction from corrupting its historical judgment, and a critical biblical scholarship, which accepts no such presupposition. Neither side speaks of God, because both use modern methods and historical descriptions do not speak normatively of God, but what makes New Testament theology *theology* is the standpoint of the interpreters and the questions this standpoint elicits. Whether the resulting scholarship is intended or read as theology (implicitly referring to God), or simply as history of religion or literary criticism, is largely a matter of the intentions and aims of the interpreters and their readers. The distinction is not important for anyone else. Librarians classify it as New Testament studies, not New Testament theology, or history, or literary criticism except where they use the phrase "New Testament theology" improperly to refer to historical, literary, or linguistic studies of theological concepts or texts.

This distinction between New Testament theology, or New Testament studies with a legitimate theological intentionality, and a scholarship that equally legitimately lacks that, has recently acquired sharper focus.

Modern rational methods have long brought independence from traditional doctrinal formulations, but the theological aims and assumptions of most biblical scholars in the twentieth century kept their historically descriptive New Testament theology truly theological. This shared Wrede's concern to preserve the integrity of the discipline's historical *methods* but again combined historical with religious *aims*. Without advocating a "believing hermeneutic," which would require theological interpreters to be believers, it developed interpretations relevant to contemporary faith by presupposing a Christian view of the biblical subject matter. However, a growing number of scholars (including many believers) have declined to write New Testament theology and preferred to pursue their biblical scholarship independently of the traditional religious aims and beliefs associated with New Testament theology. Some have advocated liberal theologies quite remote from the beliefs of the biblical authors; others have kept any religious interests at arm's length. Both can appeal to Wrede. What Wrede's map could not accommodate was those scholars who preferred to carry on writing New Testament theology properly so-called. These continued to do their biblical scholarship under a Christian presupposition about the subject matter of scripture and with traditional Christian aims, looking for some correspondence between the theologies that their scholarship uncovered and contemporary Christianity. The latter has claimed to be authentic by being in some sense biblical.

The alternative between New Testament theology and a nontheological biblical scholarship implicit in Wrede's program was to some extent concealed for most of the twentieth century because most New Testament scholars were still Christians working in Christian theological environments. Most of their work was still governed by a theological intentionality and was broadly New Testament theology or pointing in that direction. Work on the Synoptic Problem, for example, was driven by a theological interest in having reliable historical information about Jesus. The divisions during this period were not, on the whole, between Christian and non-Christian scholarship but between conservative and more radical Christian scholarship. Most of the latter was German, or German-influenced, as it had been since Strauss's *Life of Jesus* (1835, Eng. trans. 1846) and F. C. Baur's *Paul* (1845, Eng. trans. 1875). The divisions were most evident in gospel criticism, with conservatives no longer defending the historicity of the Johannine discourses or the miracle-stories, but insisting on the substantial historicity of the Synoptic Gospels against the skepticism of Wrede's *The Messianic Secret in the Gospels* (1901, Eng. trans. 1971), followed by Bultmann's form criticism.

In New Testament theology, Wrede's program for a "history of early Christian religion and theology" was taken up with liberal theological intent by his colleagues within the history of religions school and its sympathizers, notably in W. Bousset's *Kyrios Christos* (1913, 1921, Eng. trans. 1969) and J. Weiss's posthumous *Primitive Christianity* (1917, Eng. trans. 1937) from the original Göttingen group, and outside it P. Wernle, *The Beginnings of Christianity*, originally "The Beginnings of Our Religion" (1901, Eng. trans. 1903–1904), and H. Weinel's untranslated *Biblische Theologie des Neuen Testaments* (1911), more accurately subtitled *Die Religion Jesu und des Urchristentums*.

These books stand in the tradition of K. H. von Weizsäcker's *Apostolic Age* (1886, Eng. trans. 1894–1895) and O. Pfleiderer's *Primitive Christianity* (1887, Eng. trans. 1906) as much as Holtzmann's textbook New Testament theology, but they were all equally theological in intention, and historical in method. None of these liberal theologians' own versions of Christianity was very close to the first-century theologies they uncovered, but all claimed some continuity with what that tradition represented. It was still "*our* religion" whose beginnings they analyzed, much as a Bousset might disapprove of the "Christ cult" whose history down to Irenaeus he described. This is not *a* New Testament theology but is entirely New Testament theology, revealing its author's own views by its occasionally hostile tone.

Conservative theologians expected far more continuity with their biblical roots, and their New Testament theologies provided that. Following the Chicago Lutheran systematician R. W. Weidner (1891) and E. P. Gould (1900), the first substantial textbook New Testament theology of the twentieth century was by G. B. Stevens, a onetime student of B. Weiss and Pfleiderer in Berlin who became at Yale a moderately conservative New Testament professor and then a moderately liberal systematics professor. This substantial work had a deservedly long life, but its critical judgments and theological standpoint place it with the older (1868, 1903) textbook of Weiss (n. 3 above), well to the right of Holtzmann and Wrede.

The attempts of B. Weiss and G. B. Stevens to serve the church by mediating between conservative and liberal theology and exegesis were continued by Paul Feine.[56] As a supporter of "religion"—but opponent of the history of religions school he emphasized (against Wrede) the continuity between Jesus and Paul, and was sharply criticized by more-radical scholars, especially Bultmann. The future of New Testament theology lay with those who like Bultmann combined Feine's theological aims and interests with a more avant-garde scholarship, but his definition of the task echoes B. Weiss and Beyschlag, insisting that it is a historical task, but adding that "we engage in this research as Christian theologians with the conviction that the content of the NT is unique and normative for us today."[57]

Neither Stevens's nor Feine's widely read books had much influence on the history of the discipline, but both assert the "normal" view of the discipline, that New Testament theology is written from a Christian standpoint. Stevens rejects "the presuppositions on which Holtzmann's construction and estimate of New Testament history and theology rest."[58] His own "assumption which is carried into the present study" is that "Christianity transcends its historical relations and limitations, and can be justly estimated only by recognizing its divine origin and singularity."[59] He goes beyond the parameters of "normal," nonsupernaturalist New Testament theology by adding that this is "equally a conclusion which is established by the study itself."[60]

Even more conservative, and much less influential, was the thematic New Testament theology of T. Zahn some years later.[61] Not even the compact liberal synthesis of the Ritschlian systematician J. Kaftan[62] made much impact. The one theologian between Holtzmann and Bultmann whose New Testament theology has abiding significance despite its uncritical historical judgments is Schlatter.

From *Faith in the New Testament* (1885), itself virtually a New Testament theology, through popular theological commentaries on the whole New Testament (1887–1910), a classic New Testament theology (1909–1910), nine weighty scholarly commentaries (1929–1937), and a stream of New Testament theology for a wider Christian readership best exemplified in his last book, *Do We Know Jesus?* (1937, ET 2005), Schlatter wrote New Testament theology on a monumental scale. He also wrote extensively on Judaica, history of doctrine, systematic theology, ethics, history of philosophy, epistemology, autobiography, and more devotional works. His extremely conservative critical position, including belief in the apostolic authorship of Matthew and John, and his isolation from the scholarly mainstream, makes him hard to read and easy to disregard, but several of his biblical works have been constantly reprinted and some on New Testament theology have recently been translated into

English.[63] By no means a representative figure, he can here represent the conservative strand in New Testament theology that rejects or remains uneasy with the prevailing *concordat* between theology and Enlightenment-inspired historical criticism.

Schlatter's struggle against the liberals' "atheistic method in theology,"[64] seemed to other theologians who were also historians a lost cause. He thought that historical "observation" shows "as an undeniable reality with a power demanding assent from the theologian," how "Jesus lived in God."[65] Believers may well see that in the gospel records, but the essential first step of "observation," or receptivity to the evidence, does not require historians to understand it in the same terms as their sources. Even if we agree with Schlatter about the absurdity of an atheistic dogmatics, and share his belief that when "our students read the New Testament just like they read Homer, and our exegetes explain it like they do Homer with determined elimination of every God-directed idea, then the theological faculties have reached the end of the line,"[66] his protest against an "atheistic" history of religion nevertheless overshoots the target. It is reasonable to reject an immanentist worldview, and so set limits to what modern historical methods can achieve, but to reformulate these to make God a dimension of what is described is to turn history into theology. Schlatter (following Kähler) might respond that recent "life of Jesus research" was worthless. There are also good reasons to doubt whether critical-historical research should determine (rather than contribute to) how Christians write about Jesus, but the methods Schlatter held at arm's length had already proved their value in biblical studies. It was necessary to define their limited scope, not expand this until it embraced theological judgments.

In using modern historical methods that do not speak normatively of God, most biblical theologians hold their own beliefs in suspense. In his brilliant methodological essay "New Testament Theology and Dogmatics" (1909), Schlatter accepts that in historical work "our own convictions which determine our thought and will are held at a distance."[67] He thus accepts Gabler's two-stage model, only (like Wrede) assigning the second stage to dogmatics. But like Gabler, and unlike Wrede, he expects the second step to affect his understanding of the first, arguing that the biblical material confronts scholars with more tasks than can be settled by historical methods: "As historians we can give only a partial answer to the truth issue," and "since we cannot pose the question of truth merely in this limited way, there is always bound to be a further task alongside the historical one. That is the dogmatic task, which goes on to ask questions about the truth of what is said."[68]

But that depends on who "we" are. Most historians are perfectly well able to pose the question of truth in this limited way. It is only theologians who cannot or should not. They hold their convictions at a distance when they do their history, but they cannot deny them, and that requires New Testament theology to be aware of a truth beyond its historical observation. So we may agree with Schlatter that since New Testament theology is done by theologians, "to make New Testament theology independent of dogmatics is an illusory fiction"[69] without today expecting all biblical scholars to be theologians. Both New Testament theology and dogmatics stand "on the boundary of science . . . perhaps even over the boundary" on some definitions of *Wissenschaft*, because agreement about the New Testament requires interpreters to be "united in the basic direction of our thinking and willing," including "our view of nature, the norms of our will, the concept of guilt, the whole content of our God-consciousness."[70]

This theoretical account of New Testament theology corresponds to the normal practice of New Testament theology in which historical and exegetical work is done with a Christian presupposition, and Schlatter gives some account of why this must be so. But history is so important to him and to the church that he cannot hand it over to historians. His criticisms of his contemporaries lay down markers for the rejuvenation of New Testament theology in the century ahead, but his own historical practice ignored too much of what others have found persuasive to play much part in the history of the discipline. Most New Testament theology allows free rein to critical-historical judgments that challenge the biblical and traditional pictures of Jesus and Christian origins, allowing these provisional and speculative proposals undue weight in understanding Jesus. Schlatter by contrast expects his (uncritical) historical scholarship to confirm religious beliefs he thought were well-founded in the history of the Christ. This surely asks more of historical study than it can provide without ceasing to be critical. That objection to some New Testament theology recurs throughout the twentieth century.

Despite its lack of influence,[71] the two volumes of Schlatter's New Testament theology, *The History of the Christ: The Foundation of New Testament Theology* (1909 as *The Word of Jesus*, 1920, Eng. trans. 1997), and *The Theology of the Apostles* (1910 as *The Teaching of the Apostles*; 1922, Eng. trans. 1999), contain insights that still challenge the discipline, and formulations worth hearing afresh. The first volume could be called one suggestive instance of Martin Kähler's "historic, biblical Christ," the kind of composite picture that is a necessity for Christian faith. Whether that need can be credibly met in this way is another question. That the history of Jesus is fundamental for Christianity, and therefore requires a volume rather than a chapter, and that it should be the *history* (or story) rather than the abstracted "teaching of Jesus," is at least arguable.

The second volume of Schlatter's New Testament theology is more a "canonical" than a critical-historical New Testament theology, despite the reference to "development" in its subtitle. That remains one option for structuring New Testament theology. It was less historical than Schlatter thought, but no less valuable, especially in its emphasis on the moral community and the place of beliefs in establishing this.

In view of Schlatter's impossible critical position, it is perhaps surprising to find him the hero (alongside F. C. Baur and the history of religions school) of Bultmann's "history of scholarly New Testament theology," at the end of his New Testament theology.[72] But like many accounts of the state of scholarship, this one is guided by its author's view of the central issue. For Bultmann this was the character of theology as the theological thoughts that stem from faith and explicate the understanding inherent in it, and the relationship of theology to the kerygma, the Christian proclamation which awakens faith.[73] Schlatter is praised for refusing to separate life and thought, anticipating Bultmann's own existential(ist) interpretation of the New Testament. He understands the importance of the human will driving action and so sets the thinking of Jesus and his followers in the context of the history they are making.

Bultmann's textbook New Testament theology did not appear until 1948–1952, but it was the product of more than forty years of writing and university teaching, a career that continued the history of religions school's history of traditions research and broadened its exploration of the possible antecedents of Christianity, especially (and dubiously) Gnosticism. Impressed by the second edition of Barth's *Romans* (1922), Bultmann had joined this "latest theological movement"[74] without abandoning his liberal critical scholarship or imitating Barth's powerful prophetic style of explicit theological interpretation of scripture. His own "theological exegesis"[75] remained on the whole within the constraints set by modern biblical scholarship, like most New Testament theology, and he worked philosophically and theologically to make his critical history and his modern theology coincide. The model he worked out between 1922 and 1927 was later called "existential(ist) interpretation."[76] It depended on the view that both history and theology seek to interpret human existence, and that the kerygma or Christian proclamation challenges and may affect a change in the hearer's self-understanding.

For this "existentialist"[77] theology, only Paul and John in the New Testament are truly theologians because only they write self-consciously about human existence. Paul's theology can (with some squeezing) be presented as theological anthropology, analyzing the concepts in which the apostle explicates human self-understanding before and then "under" faith. Bultmann sketched this out in an encyclopedia article in 1930[78] before presenting it in detail in *Theology of the NT* (vol. 1, 1948). His even more impressive account of the Johannine theology was published in his Meyer Commentary (1941)[79] before being distilled in his *Theology* (1952). Unlike Paul, John does not articulate his theology through anthropological and soteriological concepts, but his dualism of God and the human world, in which Jesus reveals himself as the revealer and elicits the decision of faith, shows how John too speaks of God by speaking of human existence.

These two masterpieces of theological interpretation, more or less within the limits of historical-critical scholarship,[80] are set within the framework of a "history of early Christian religion and theology" as advocated by Wrede. Bultmann also breaks with the tradition of making the historical figure of Jesus or his teaching part of a New Testament theology on the grounds that a New Testament theology is Christian theology, and prior to the cross and resurrection there was no kerygma. He includes a fine sketch of the "proclamation of Jesus" but insists that this "is a presupposition for the theology of the New Testament rather than a part of that theology itself."[81] His earlier book, *Jesus* (1926),[82] shows that he could *do* New Testament theology by reflecting on the earliest traditions about Jesus, who had called his hearers to decision, but he does not include this in his own New Testament theology textbook.

Insofar as he succeeded in making his history and his theology "coincide," Bultmann's New Testament theology represents his own modern theology and makes Gabler's second step redundant.[83] For some of his followers it could almost make systematic theology unnecessary. Even though within Bultmann's "school," Gerhard Ebeling published a magnificent *Dogmatics of Christian Faith* (1979) inspired by Luther and Schleiermacher as well as by Bultmann, a hermeneutically sophisticated

New Testament theology that could fulfill some of the tasks of dogmatics, at least for as long as the synthesis seemed plausible.

For some that was not long, not even an instant. Just as the component parts of Bultmann's New Testament theology were in place by the end of the 1920s, so the critical discussion of his theology had begun several years before the publication of his *Theology of the New Testament*. It began in the 1920s with deep reservations expressed about his *Jesus*,[84] and from 1927 on, about his use of Heidegger,[85] but it was the demythologizing debate unleashed in 1941[86] that placed his theology center stage. This also diverted public attention from the character of his biblical interpretation to the broader issues of liberal *versus* conservative theology, but New Testament scholars continued the narrower specialist arguments that provide the material of New Testament theology. They sometimes even ventured into the wider theological territory that this discipline fertilizes. Most of the reaction to Bultmann's theology came from those who thought him too radical, but just as F. Buri thought he should take his demythologizing further and eliminate the kerygma, so Herbert Braun thought to radicalize his existential interpretation. Whereas Bultmann had presented theology *as* anthropology, Braun wanted to dissolve it *into* anthropology, yielding a Christian humanism that does not depend on the kerygma.[87]

For more than half of the twentieth century, political and economic factors applied a brake to the conversation between English and German New Testament theology, which had been making some progress around 1900. The liberal Protestantism of Harnack, which combined massive historical learning with cautious New Testament scholarship, was more congenial to Ritschlians outside Germany than the radicalism of the history of religions school. Harnack was much translated and widely read. The most important works of Wrede and Bousset were not translated until around 1970, partly on the back of Bultmann's impact and international prestige. Most British biblical scholarship was theologically oriented throughout the period, with the conservatism of Swete and Sanday's generation yielding to the more modern scholarship of A. E. J. Rawlinson (1887–1960) and J. M. Creed (1889–1941), and above all C. H. Dodd (1884–1973), from North Wales, who was as theologically committed as those four Anglicans. The Methodist Vincent Taylor (1887–1968) produced some notable New Testament theology, but textbook New Testament theologies have rarely been written outside Germany.[88] E. C. Hoskyns[89] died young in 1937. In North America B. W. Bacon

(1860–1932) stands out among earlier critical New Testament theologians, and James Moffatt (1870–1944), E. F. Scott (1868–1941),[90] and H. J. Cadbury (1883–1974) a generation later. An older style of biblical theology had been pursued by C. Hodge's successor at Princeton, B. B. Warfield (1851–1921), and J. G. Machen (1881–1937). At the opposite pole, the Chicago school of E. DeWitt Burton (1856–1925), Shailer Matthews (1863–1941), Shirley Jackson Case (1872–1947), and (at some distance) Edgar J. Goodspeed (1871–1962) is celebrated for its social history, but much of its work could be called New Testament theology in the broad sense adopted here, on account of its liberal theological intentions.

Popular New Testament theologies, such as those of F. C. Grant[91] in the United States, Alan Richardson[92] in England, and A. M. Hunter[93] in Scotland, were not where the conceptual theological work of New Testament theology was being done. C. H. Dodd's theory of "realized eschatology"[94] was a serious challenge to the reconstructions of Jesus' proclamation of the kingdom of God by J. Weiss[95] (followed by his pupil Bultmann), and Albert Schweitzer,[96] but it could not be maintained exegetically.[97] The liberal historical Jesus research being continued in America and Britain was about to be eclipsed as a more skeptical form criticism than Dodd's began to take root outside Germany. Jeremias's historical Jesus research provided a bridge across the North Sea,[98] but Jeremias was becoming an isolated figure in post–World War II Germany, as was (more obviously) Ethelbert Stauffer.

Stauffer's New Testament theology (1941, Eng. trans. 1955), organized thematically to present "the christocentric theology of history in the New Testament," was widely read in ecumenical church circles, as was Alan Richardson's, but like F. Büschel[99] before them, these made no significant contribution to New Testament scholarship and therefore remained on the fringe of professional New Testament theology. Not even the more substantial work of M. Albertz[100] made the impact it might have made a little later, when the discipline had become more international. The beginnings of substantial Roman Catholic contributions to the textbook genre can be dated from M. Meinertz (1950)[101] and J. Bonsirven (1951),[102] but the commentaries of M. J. de Lagrange (1855–1938) contained much New Testament theology in their historical exegesis during the dark years for Roman Catholic scholarship that followed the lamentable excommunication of A. Loisy in 1908.

Despite being constructed by one of the leading New Testament scholars of his day, Oscar Cullmann (1902–1998) of Strasbourg and (from

1938) Basel, the most widely discussed alternative conception to Bultmann's New Testament theology, belongs as much to the church-oriented "biblical theology movement" as to academic New Testament theology. The latter operates within the rules and assumptions of modern historical-critical research, which does not speak directly of God or revelation, even though written from that standpoint or silently making that presupposition. Inspired by Barth, the "biblical theology movement" was more explicit about its Christian presuppositions and commitment. Both leave room for these beliefs but, as modern scholarly writing, New Testament theology holds them "at a distance" whereas "biblical theology," in the sense often used pejoratively from the 1960s to the 1990s, blurred the line between normative and descriptive statements in its eagerness to advance the gospel. The boundary is far from clear, because New Testament theology also wants to communicate Christianity today. The dispute between Cullmann and the Bultmannians was not about declaring their theological hand in doing New Testament theology but about the hand they held. Bultmann's main objection was to Cullmann's theory of revelation, identifying it with a select part of the historical process. This was so opposed to the apostle Paul and Luther and the neo-Reformation theology of the 1920s that it was not redeemed by being supposedly held by Luke.

Cullmann did not write a New Testament theology, though both his *Christology of the New Testament Theology* (1957, Eng. trans. 1959) and *Salvation in History* (1964 German *Heil als Geschichte*; Eng. trans. 1967) contain a large part, but most of his writing *is* New Testament theology. *Christ and Time* (1946, revised 1962, Eng. trans. 1951, rev. 1962) contains a historical description of "The Primitive Christian Conception of Time and History" (subtitle). It declares its modern theological aims at the outset, including its polemic against allowing "a philosophical standpoint" to determine what is central to Christianity.[103] The target is Bultmann, even if the shot is wide of the mark. Cullmann argues that "the *specifically Christian element* of the New Testament revelation" is "what it does not have in common with philosophical or religious systems,"[104] but instead of finding this in Christology, he finds it in a theory of time and history (linear rather than cyclical).

That kind of direct transfer of a construction of the biblical evidence into a modern theology was typical of the biblical theology movement's naive hostility to philosophical and systematic theology, but the objections to Cullmann's theory of *Heilsgeschichte* (first badly translated "redemptive history" and later "salvation history," which is not perfect either) lie in the theory itself and its confusion of a theological category with modern historical research. Bultmannians rejected the category because it identifies God with the world, revelation with history.

To some believers in the incarnation, that sounded more orthodox than the minimalism of Bultmann's connection of the kerygma to the history of Jesus. However, this actual history (and the course of the history of Israel and Judaism of which it is a part) cannot be simply identified with the uncertain results of modern historical research. Cullmann's "biblical history" is basically the biblical record of that history, not the modern historical-critical reconstruction it aims and claims to be. *Heilsgeschichte* would therefore be better translated and understood as "the story of our salvation," insisting that this story has a genuine historical basis but not claiming the prestige of modern historical research for a theological construction. Rethinking the category in this way would avoid the arbitrary selection of certain biblical events and could still do justice to the biblical data, only interpreting the data in a literary rather than a critical historical frame of reference. But this move was not made in the mid-twentieth century.

It is hard to deny that Cullmann's theologically loaded analytic tool leads him to misread the biblical data and that his New Testament theology is guilty on Wrede's charge of theological interests corrupting historical research. The idea of a divine plan is taken for granted by the New Testament writers and given prominence by Luke. It is surely more important for Paul than Bultmann was prepared to admit, but not the key to his theology or eschatology, and surely much less important for either John or Jesus than Cullmann claimed. Eschatology (however reinterpreted), not history, provides the key to how Jesus, Paul, and John think of God, essential as the history and faith of Israel was to all three (and to all the other New Testament writers and orthodox Christianity) and essential as a conception of history is to modern theology.

Cullmann's claim to be "carrying out [Barth's] Christocentric program on the field of New Testament exposition and by means of exegetical methods"[105] is unjustified. Seeing Jesus as the center of a "revelation history" (the "slender Christ-line of the Biblical history," or "a temporally connected historical series of a special kind"[106]), and faith as inserting oneself into that history, might provide an ideology for a triumphalist church, but membership of a great community and participation in a great tradition are different from Paul's or Luther's account of faith's saving relationship with God in Christ. But Cullmann's initial sympathy for the 1920s reaction against liberal theology was deflected by a sense that neither the early Barth's nor Bultmann's atemporal eschatology and understanding of revelation did justice to the biblical history or to historical reality.

These deficiencies were more effectively challenged in the 1960s by protestant systematic theologies such as J. Moltmann's *Theology of Hope* (1964, Eng. trans. 1967) and Pannenberg's seeing revelation in the "universal history" disclosed through the resurrection of Jesus, which anticipates the end. Roman Catholic theology revived at the Second Vatican Council (1962–1965) placed new emphasis on "salvation history" as a way of escaping from scholasticism but without expecting biblical theology to replace dogmatics. In New Testament theology, Bultmann remained central; and the most interesting criticisms of Bultmann, and the most stimulating New Testament theology, came from within the "school" of his pupils, most notably Ernst Käsemann (1906–1998), Günther Bornkamm (1905–1990), Hans Conzelmann (1915–1989), and Gerhard Ebeling (1912–2001). The leading Bultmannian to convert to Roman Catholicism, Heinrich Schlier (1900–1978), continued to make significant contributions to New Testament theology and to the methodological debate.[107]

The most significant New Testament theology of the 1950s was what James Robinson dubbed "the new quest of the historical Jesus." This differed from some more recent work in the field in its form-critical standpoint and by the strong and sophisticated theological commitment of the Bultmann school. Bornkamm's *Jesus of Nazareth* (1956, Eng. trans. 1960) is not very different from Bultmann's *Jesus* (1926) in its critical stance, but it is more interested in the historical person and more willing to acknowledge the present aspect of his eschatology. Dahl,[108] Käsemann,[109] and Ebeling,[110] among others, argued for the theological importance of historical research on Jesus, criticizing aspects of Bultmann's theology from a broadly similar kerygmatic theological standpoint. Käsemann in particular launched a series of missiles against Bultmann's interpretations of Paul,[111] John,[112] and New Testament eschatology, insisting on the primacy of Christology in Paul, John's heterodoxy, and the importance of futurist eschatology, which he called "apocalyptic." From outside the Bultmann school, the first and only volume of J. Jeremias's New Testament theology was on *The Proclamation of Jesus* (1971, Eng. trans. 1971). Whereas form critics had asked about each part of the synoptic tradition's "setting in the life of the early church," Jeremias asked also about its "setting in the life of Jesus." His theological stance was close to the old liberals who had also located the revelation of God in the history of Jesus as reconstructed by critical study rather than in the kerygma.[113]

Bornkamm[114] and Conzelmann[115] also pioneered the extension of Bultmann's history of the synoptic tradition to analyze further the evangelists' "redaction" or editing of their material, in order to understand their theological emphases.[116] Over fifty years' "redaction criticism" was sedimented in doctoral dissertations, but for the pioneers it was theologically vibrant, making modern theological judgments through its implied criticisms of evangelists whose "nomist" or salvation-history perspectives failed to match the Lutheran theology of the cross of Paul or Mark.[117]

In the Bultmann school's only textbook New Testament theology, intended to supplement but not replace Bultmann's, Hans Conzelmann[118] attached brief sections on the theologies of the synoptic evangelists to Part 2 on "The Synoptic Kerygma." The teaching of Jesus is appropriately included in this context, not as a separate section. His eschatology and ethics are rightly coordinated with and subordinated to his "idea of God," or rather to his belief in God. Conzelmann was surely right to insist that "the idea of God is not exhausted in statements about the coming kingdom of God."[119]

Conzelmann's New Testament theology recognizes the end of the Bultmannian hegemony in New Testament theology and in modern German protestant theology generally. He sees (and regrets) the new historicism and a new Biblicism,[120] and attempts to avoid the former while giving more prominence to the historical components of a New Testament theology than Bultmann had done. He understands theology "not only in general terms, as the interpretation of faith made at a particular time, but in a more special sense as an exegesis of the original *texts* of the faith, the oldest formulations of the creed."[121] The mainly German debate of the 1960s was admirably sifted and presented in a form accessible to non-German students by J. D. G. Dunn in *Unity and Diversity in the New Testament* (1977).

As the forty years of Bultmannian leadership in New Testament theology faded in the late 1960s, new presentations began to be published. None of these matched Bultmann's classic. From the Roman Catholic side, the four volumes of K. H. Schelkle's New Testament theology[122] provide thematically arranged redescriptions of the material. This has great practical value for those whose theological education takes place mainly outside biblical studies in fundamental and dogmatic theology but who need to know what scripture says on different doctrinal and moral topics. It is less ambitious than the New Testament theology that reshaped German protestant theology after each World War, but it has contributed to a reformed Roman Catholicism recovering its scriptural basis.

W. G. Kümmel's shorter work, *The Theology of the New Testament According to Its Main Witnesses*, joined the chorus against Bultmann's relegation of the message of Jesus to the presupposition of New Testament theology but goes further than most in emphasizing the significance that "Jesus ascribed to his person . . . in the context of his proclamation of salvation."[123] Placing Jesus alongside Paul and John as a "main witness" almost makes him a Christian and depends on a conservative view of the historical reliability of the synoptic tradition. His earlier book on "the eschatological message of Jesus," *Promise and Fulfillment*, had criticized both Dodd's "realized eschatology" and the dominant futurist account of J. Weiss and Schweitzer. Kümmel insisted on both a future and a present element in "the kingdom of God" and distinguished Jesus' "eschatological promise" from the "apocalyptic instruction" of Mark 13, despite his use of apocalyptic language. The meaning of Jesus' eschatological message is to be found in all he says about God, including the meaning he attached to his own person. In him "the Kingdom of God came into being, and in him it will be consummated."[124] The fulfillment has already taken place in Jesus, but it is provisional and concealed until the promised future, which is made certain by what has already happened. Kümmel will neither abandon the future hope by interpreting eschatology exclusively in terms of present-day human existence, nor accept that Jesus understood his message as "revealing apocalyptic secrets," as though the meaning of the present were to be found in "a divine reality beyond time."[125] Whether or not Kümmel's account of the union of hope and present experience persuades, it is clear that Jeremias was not alone in basing his Christianity very largely on his understanding of the teaching of Jesus.

In Kümmel's later *Theology* (1969), Paul is preceded by a chapter on the faith of the primitive community arguing that "the experience of Jesus' resurrection had convinced the disciples and other witnesses to the resurrection that Jesus' claim had indeed been true and had been confirmed by God."[126] "The proclamation of Jesus according to the first three gospels" differs from "the proclamation of Jesus" in Bultmann's *Primitive*

Christianity and in his New Testament theology.[127] Where Bultmann had placed Jesus firmly in his Jewish setting,[128] and most New Testament theology looks for *continuities* between Jesus and the early church, Kümmel found in their combinations of an "already" and a "not yet" a material *identity* between them, located in this pattern of history and eschatology. Several in the "new quest" had also found a present dimension in Jesus' proclamation of the kingdom of God and so related Jesus more closely to subsequent Christianity than to John the Baptist, but Kümmel goes further. He claims (with Jeremias) that Jesus also envisaged a time between his own death and the Parousia.

Unlike Cullmann, who advocated his biblical theology as a recipe for the 1940s church, Kümmel makes fewer explicit theological claims for his historical and exegetical descriptions, but the Christian standpoint and presupposition of his scholarly work is clear. Like most New Testament theology, he can say that "as Christians we do not come to the New Testament as to just any historical document of the past, but in the more or less clear conviction that in the writings of the New Testament we encounter the knowledge of God's revelation in Jesus Christ."[129]

What Kümmel claims to discover as an exegete is said to provide an account of the unity of the New Testament, and the basis for scripture functioning as a norm of Christianity. What is shared by the witnesses closest to the revelation event—Jesus; the earliest community; and the first reflective theologian, Paul—provides a criterion by which the other New Testament witnesses can be measured. John's "faith image of Jesus can be understood as an appropriate exposition of the divine action in the person of Jesus from the perspective of the believing community in the later period of primitive Christianity."[130] Kümmel's conclusion thus links his exegetical and historical conclusions to his own contemporary understanding of Christianity. The "quite definite divine eschatological history which Jesus sets before his hearers and [which] he challenges them to participate in" was enriched by a theological understanding of his death but in essentials was repeated ("extended") by his disciples, forming also today "the setting for the message of God's condescension in Jesus Christ."[131]

This account sees faith as believing the one message of all the major witnesses. Even though they "do not entirely agree in their interpretation of the person and the death of Jesus," they agree "that in Jesus God, the Lord of the world, has come to us."[132] Kümmel adds that "this coming of God can become a personal reality for us only if we so allow ourselves to be grasped by God's love that has come to us in Jesus Christ that we become new persons,"[133] but the way this happens is apparently by accepting the truth of the message about God's saving history. Despite his echoes of Bultmann's account of what faith means for Paul, Kümmel concludes that believers know themselves "to be transplanted into the time of salvation that has been begun through Christ's cross and resurrection."[134] This attempt to mediate between Bultmann and Cullmann finally sides with the latter. "Faith" is believing *that* the "eschatological history" is true. It is more a matter of accepting information about God and then responding to it in an appropriate way than of responding in obedience and trust to God, who addresses us through the Christian proclamation.

Bultmann's kerygmatic theology of the Word and faith is as foreign to some outside the Lutheran tradition as Cullmann's or Kümmel's theories of salvation history, but it aims to make what is central for Paul intelligible and credible by relating it to contemporary self-understandings, whereas the alternative looks like sheer assertion, perhaps believed on other grounds but not carrying conviction of itself. The eschatological language by which Paul communicated his message of God in Christ is interpreted by Bultmann in such a way as to invite a direct and total response to God rather than reducing faith to accepting information about God's long-term activity through history. That story is a necessary aspect of Christian faith and was underestimated by Bultmann, but making it central is to prefer Luke's theology to Paul's or John's.

The one-sidedness of Bultmann's account of Paul and John is open to correction, but his account of "what it means to speak of God" today[135] is what made his New Testament theology a modern theology, not simply a description of first-century theologies. The "salvation history" alternative was also a modern theology and offered some correction to Bultmann, but it did not make talk of God credible to those who were not already insiders. The theologies contained in the New Testament are all acknowledged by Christians as part of their heritage and some today will be content to define their Christian commitment in ecclesiological terms as joining the community and participating in "the eschatological history which Jesus sets before his hearers."[136] Those who claim a more direct relationship with the crucified and risen Jesus will see in that a weakening of the christological heart and center of Christianity.

It was the sense that the neo-Reformation theologies of the 1920s provided a more powerful and persuasive way of understanding the New

Testament message of God in Christ today that made Bultmann's New Testament theology central long after its weaknesses had been noted. Kerygmatic theologies recall Luther's christocentric concentration on the heart of the matter, whereas salvation-history theologies make more room for the church in history, and can sometimes appear triumphalist. The orientation of kerygmatic theologies to human existence gave them an experiential dimension, which seemed absent from the older dogmatics and from modern religious ideologies.

Making Christianity intelligible by understanding the Christ-event as answering the question of individual human existence was being challenged on different counts by the 1960s,[137] but the influence of Bultmann's conception remained strong in the short and balanced textbook of a pupil of Jeremias, E. Lohse, *Grundriss der neutestamentlichen Theologie* (Stuttgart: Kohlhammer, 1974). This, like Kümmel's, begins with "the proclamation of Jesus" (chap. 1), and discusses "the theology of the synoptic gospels" separately, after the chapter on Paul. As a compact and irenic presentation of how many scholars understood the contents of New Testament theology in the generation after Bultmann, concluding with an account of the unity of the New Testament, this one can scarcely be bettered. On the same scale, E. Schweizer's later *A Theological Introduction to the New Testament* (1989; Eng. trans. Nashville: Abingdon, 1991) is sufficiently similar to be classified as a popular New Testament theology.

These broadly Bultmannian lines of interpretation gained international and interconfessional recognition in the 1960s and have remained influential wherever theological interests have remained dominant, but the last third of the century was also characterized by more-conservative scholars producing equally impressive work. As some liberal scholars moved away from classical New Testament theology,[138] the balance within the discipline has shifted. This gives particular significance to the major New Testament theology of L. Goppelt (1911–1973), published posthumously in 1975–1976.[139]

Goppelt located himself in the "salvation history" tradition of "historical research on scripture," acknowledging Schlatter, von Rad, and Cullmann among his predecessors but relegating Kümmel and Jeremias to the conservative "positive historical" trend, along with B. Weiss, Beyschlag, and Stauffer. That classification of New Testament theologies is perhaps hard on Kümmel but signals Goppelt's call for greater hermeneutical sophistication than is found in New Testament theologies limited to historical reconstruction plus unargued personal beliefs. Goppelt is also right that New Testament talk of God is so rooted in the faith of Israel that a New Testament theology needs to say more about the Old Testament than most have done. While using modern critical methods responsibly, he knows that what he is trying to communicate cannot be done simply by critical historiography and so wants to bring his own theological perspective into "critical dialogue" with historical criticism.

Like Schlatter, he devotes his first volume to "Jesus' activity in its theological significance," but unlike Schlatter's, his presentation remains within the bounds of historical credibility. Volume 2 on "The Variety and Unity of the Apostolic Witness to Christ" does justice to the variety with fine presentations of Paul and Hellenistic Christianity, and the theology of some post-Pauline writings, notably 1 Peter, Revelation, James, Matthew, Hebrews, and Luke. Mark is absent and John incomplete, but this remains a textbook to ponder. It offers a reasoned alternative to Bultmann's classic, refusing to abandon either modern critical methods or the quasi-historical or narrative components of biblical talk of God.

From the same period comes the widely read conservative textbook of G. E. Ladd.[140] This is organized canonically rather than historically, except that Part I groups the Synoptic Gospels together to provide in effect a "historical Jesus" section based on accepting much of these Gospels as historically reliable. John is treated separately on account of its differences from the Synoptics and its "larger measure of theological interpretation."[141] At every point mainstream critical views are discussed, but traditional positions maintained. All thirteen Pauline Epistles are accepted, but the presentation is based mainly on those generally considered authentic. The quality of Ladd's scholarship places this work among the better textbooks despite its improbable critical judgments. However, it describes what is in the texts rather than interpreting it. The other large conservative New Testament theology from this period is by Donald Guthrie,[142] but this is organized thematically and does less justice to the historical diversity.

When George Caird died in post at Oxford in 1984, only a small part of his New Testament theology had been written, but the work was constructed from drafts and lecture notes and tapes.[143] The approach is thematic. The ecumenical churchman and chairman Caird thought that "to write a New Testament theology is to preside at a conference of faith and order. Around the table sit the authors of the New Testament, and it is the presider's task to engage them in a colloquium about theological matters which they themselves have placed on the agenda."[144] The "agenda" starts with "the Divine Plan" and ends with "the Theology of Jesus" since "the historical Jesus is recoverable and able to be seen as the starting-point and goal [!] of New Testament Theology."[145] Between these two chapters are six on the need, tenses, fact, experience, hope, and bringer of salvation. Caird's idiosyncratic presentation is closer to the older Anglo-American biblical theology than to the German textbooks, but the charisma of the Dodd disciple glimmers through his scribe's devoted *bricolage*, and the mantle or pallium was shortly to fall on his creative student N. T. Wright, whose unfinished project on *Christian Origins and the Question of God* (London: SPCK, 1992–) contains more New Testament theology than many more historically sophisticated New Testament theologies.

The social and cultural changes of the 1960s have impacted on New Testament studies, including New Testament theology, from the 1970s to the present. The expansion of North American scholarship outside seminary contexts encouraged interdisciplinary developments, especially the development of social-scientific and literary approaches to the biblical texts. Sometimes these have been undertaken with strong theological interests, overcoming the unproductive hostility between theology and the scientific study of religion,[146] but New Testament scholarship in the final quarter of the twentieth century also often moved away from its theological roots.[147] Social scientific research brought some antitheological baggage with it but, as Gerd Theissen showed, could become theologically fruitful. Humanistic literary study had been congenial to theology,[148] but the newer literary theory was not, and where adopted by biblical theo-logians has led in several different directions, some recognizably theological, others not, though what counts as theological is itself contested.[149] The change of climate and increased diversity has persuaded some biblical theologians working in secular contexts to become more explicit about their interests and standpoints, abandoning the restraint of New Testament theology done within the bounds of modern historical reason.[150]

The major traditional New Testament theologies from the last decade of the century and beyond have again come from Germany, where New Testament scholarship has remained predominantly theological and where the academic expectations placed on ordinands still require solid scholarly textbooks. The three volumes of H. Hübner's *Biblische Theologie des Neuen Testaments* (Göttingen: Vandenhoeck & Ruprecht, 1990–1995) were too distinctive to meet that need for textbooks representing a partial consensus. Its first volume is devoted to *Prolegomena*, discussing the canon and revelation, and Hübner remains an advocate of Bultmann's existential(ist) interpretation, but his "biblical theology" model is particularly concerned with the relationship between the Old and New Testaments, and focuses on the Old Testament as taken up in the New. This emphasis on each writer's debate with the Old Testament is one-sided and omits much that is normally found in a New Testament theology. Selected parts of Paul's epistles receive more attention than all the other New Testament writers combined.

A richer diet of theological reflection was projected by the Roman Catholic collaborator of Karl Rahner, Wilhelm Thüsing (1921–1998). The first volume of his New Testament theology appeared in 1981 (2d ed. 1996), the second in 1998, and the third (edited by Thomas Söding) in 1999. The fourth is still in unpublished fragments. The overall title, *The New Testament Theologies and Jesus Christ: Laying the Foundation of a Theology of the New Testament*, reflects Thüsing's concern to anchor the New Testament witness, recognized in all the diversity of its theologies, in the historical reality of Jesus. His sensitive New Testament scholarship is guided by strict theological aims, and the work has a scholastic theological texture untypical of biblical scholarship.

On a spectrum suggested by Wrede, stretching from his own exclusive concentration on the historical and exegetical tasks of biblical scholarship to the modern theological interests more or less clear in most New Testament theology, Thüsing stands at the theological end. At the opposite pole, the most impressive attempt to carry out Wrede's program is Klaus Berger, *Theologiegeschichte des Urchristentums. Theologie des Neuen Testaments* (Tübingen: Francke Verlag, 1994, 1995). As the double title suggests, Berger rejects any sharp distinction between history of theology and theology itself, and sees the historical task of New Testament scholarship itself as theology. This has not prevented him from writing a separate work on hermeneutics, and some profound essays relating exegesis and philosophy,[151] but his New Testament theology is a historical reconstruction embracing all available early Christian literature, much of it rejected by the early church as heretical. As Wrede had pointed out a century earlier, "no New Testament writing was born with the predicate 'canonical' attached."[152] Massive in scholarship, sometimes eccentric in judgment, this major monument to Wrede anticipates H. Räisänen's prospective realization of that same program.[153] Berger's nineteen "parts" are organized geographically from "earliest Palestinian theology," including a little on "the beginning of New Testament Theology with Jesus,"[154] through Antioch (260 pages show its centrality), Paul, Ephesus, back to Antioch for 137 more pages, and finally briefly Egypt, about which almost nothing is known.

Berger, like Räisänen, has modern theological interests that bring his historical reconstructions into the ambit of New Testament theology, and the same is true of another recent echo of Wrede's program in W. Schmithals's *The Theology of the First Christians*. Aware that "the fragmentary nature of our tradition does not allow us to write a developmental history of early Christian theology that is in any sense complete,"[155] Schmithals follows his hypothetical reconstructions of an apocalyptic Jesus and pre-Pauline traditions with a selective account of Paul and then some random insights into the later development. The book ends by discussing Luther's canon criticism and surprisingly rejects it, concluding that the New Testament canon united the different churches, "and when they are joined by the New Testament they are joined in the truth,"[156] thus confessing the Christian standpoint characteristic of New Testament theology, historical theology, and theological history.

Berger and Schmithals are such original scholars that specialists will long be stimulated, but their books are too individual to serve as textbooks. Most New Testament theologies are used in professional training where a rigorous theological study of scripture is still considered essential preparation for Christian ministry. Our survey, therefore, ends with four major textbooks from the decade 1992–2002 that meet this requirement well. It stops short of Ulrich Wilckens's impressive but still incomplete *Theologie des Neuen Testaments* (2002, 2005–). Jesus' work in Galilee, his death and resurrection are here included in the history of early Christian theology. Like I. Howard Marshall's admirable *New Testament Theology: Many Witnesses, One Gospel* (2004), it belongs to the new century, as do the textbooks of F. Thielman (2005), F. Matera (2007), and U. Schnelle (2007, Eng. trans. 2009), even though like the others its foundations were being laid from about 1960 onward. The four major textbooks from the end of our period represent (1) the new Tübingen conservatism, (2) an older Göttingen criticism, (3) Roman Catholic balance from Bavaria, and (4) the quality of the Bornkamm "school," which has made Heidelberg such a benchmark for New as for Old Testament theological scholarship.

The first volume of Peter Stuhlmacher's *Biblische Theologie des Neuen Testaments* (1992) is dedicated to his Tübingen colleague Martin Hengel, whose massive historical knowledge of early Judaism, yoked with theological conservatism, recalls Schlatter, Kittel, and Michel among his

Tübingen predecessors. Stuhlmacher also is indebted to Tübingen pietism, and as a former assistant of Käsemann, he too understands the Enlightenment critical scholarship his New Testament theology uses, even as he rejects the historical skepticism of classical form criticism. Like Goppelt, he wants to bring modern historical scholarship into conversation with the biblical writers' own understanding of their subject matter, which, as a Christian theologian, he himself shares. That need not be any different from what we have seen most New Testament theology doing when it approaches the texts from a Christian standpoint while hoping to prevent its theological interest from distorting historical judgment. Stuhlmacher aims to be subject to rational controls but open to the revelatory claim of the texts.[157] The conception of revelation he is working with seems closer to an older Biblicism than most New Testament theology today accepts, but the relationship between his own standpoint and the methods used is typical of the discipline.

The first "foundational" volume describes the proclamation of Jesus, that of the early church, and that of Paul. The second volume, "from the Paul school to the Revelation of John" (1999), is dedicated to his Old Testament colleague Hartmut Gese, whose history of traditions reflection on a complete biblical theology persuaded Stuhlmacher to write the New Testament half of a complete biblical theology based on the historically reconstructed continuum of tradition embracing both Testaments—a conception indebted to von Rad. All three want to show that the New Testament apostolic tradition follows on from and is open to the Old Testament. They therefore emphasize historical reconstruction rather than theological interpretation, leaving more for dogmatics to do than was typical of the Bultmann school—or of Anglo-American biblical theology. Despite this historical emphasis, Stuhlmacher restricts himself to the canonical writings and hopes to find in the apostolic tradition a norm for contemporary Christianity. He rightly finds this "center of scripture" in the revelation of the one God in Jesus Christ but controversially includes in this center the interpretation of Jesus' death as an atoning sacrifice,[158] and he insists (like Schlatter and Goppelt) that Jesus saw it that way too.[159] Others are unconvinced, and Wrede's suspicion of theological commitments influencing historical judgment illegitimately is back on target.

Stuhlmacher's textbook deserves a long life among evangelicals, and in English translation it could succeed G. E. Ladd (1974), and stand alongside I. H. Marshall (2004). A textbook closer to the German critical consensus of the middle and late twentieth century is the *Theology of the New*

Testament (1996; Eng. trans. Louisville: Westminster John Knox, 2000) by Georg Strecker (1929–1994), edited and completed by his student F. W. Horn. Like most New Testament theologies written over a long period, it reflects positions adopted over many years, such as the unusual hypothesis that the Johannine Epistles are older than the gospel.[160] Strecker sees the decisive starting point of the theological conceptions of the New Testament writers in the Christ-event witnessed to in the early Christian kerygma, and he resists subjecting this to a scheme of "biblical theology," such as that of Gese and Stuhlmacher. Like the history of religions school and Bultmann, he stressed the discontinuities between the two Testaments; and following Bultmann, he had absorbed the lessons of the 1920s dialectical theology.

Strecker's critical-historical presentation of New Testament theology begins with the theology of Paul and what that presupposes by way of Judaism, Gentile-Hellenistic influences, and earlier Christian traditions. Jesus' life and teaching, however, are set in the second section on early Christian tradition up to the composition of the Gospels. The resurrection traditions are analyzed here under "The Palestinian Church," and that is followed by "The Hellenistic Church" and by Q. This structure makes room for a section on the "historical Jesus" (interpreted as an apocalyptic prophet) but places this after Paul, and so gives Paul the prominence he has in Lutheranism, whereas a more canonical structure would subordinate "the apostle" to "the Lord." The hypothetical document Q would properly be absent from a canonical presentation too. In this critical-historical structure, a substantial one-hundred-page section on the theology of each synoptic evangelist in turn follows the gospel traditions. "The Johannine School" comes next, followed by the deuteropauline literature, which is seen as pointing to second-century Catholicism. The Catholic Epistles (including Hebrews here) come last, as "a message with a universal claim." This Göttingen synthesis is a worthy successor to Conzelmann's, and improved by being twice the length.

A similar structure to Strecker's, only omitting the proclamation of Jesus and saying little about the earliest community, is followed in Joachim Gnilka, *Theologie des Neuen Testaments* (1994). This belongs to the Herder commentary series, which best represents the revival of Roman Catholic biblical scholarship in the second half of the century. The absence of a section on the "historical Jesus" is justified here, not by that having no place in a New Testament theology or modern theology (as by Bultmann and Conzelmann) but by Gnilka's having already published in 1990 *Jesus of Nazareth: Message and History*. His more popular New Testament theology (1989) did contain a Jesus section. His Jesus book might therefore be seen as volume 1 of a New Testament theology, and his New Testament theology as volume 2. Gnilka pays close attention to historical description and exegetical elucidation of the theological conceptions of the biblical authors, and does not venture far into new theological interpretation. He does not include extracanonical material but does include sections on the precanonical hypothetical documents Q and an earlier Passion Narrative. If a New Testament theology is intended to assist modern Christians in defining their identity by reference to the canon, that is surely questionable, but Gnilka's lucid and reliable textbook is among the best. Second Thessalonians and James are curiously relegated to excursuses. A unity is found, behind the different theological conceptions, in the kerygma of the death and resurrection of Jesus, "the ground of our redemption,"[161] a phrase that reiterates the author's ecumenical Christian standpoint.

Another Roman Catholic textbook New Testament theology was only half completed, presumably because the author of the projected other half, H. Merklein, died in post. Alfons Weiser, *Theologie des Neuen Testaments II Die Theologie der Evangelisten* (1993) begins with Q, includes Acts with Luke, the Johannine Epistles with John, and a chapter on the Apocalypse. A final chapter on "The Underlying Ground of Unity: Jesus of Nazareth" offers a brief sketch of the contours of Jesus' life and work and brief reference to "foundational experiences with the raised Christ" at Easter and in early Christian community life.

The relative paucity of Roman Catholic textbooks is unsurprising in what has been for good reasons a mainly Protestant discipline, but the weight of solid monographs on topics in New Testament theology since the textbooks of M. Meinertz (1950) and J. Bonisirven (1951) is impressive. Most of these are doctoral dissertations supervised by A. Vögtle or R. Schnackenburg, or the second book usually required to qualify for a German university post. Also among Roman Catholic scholars, the theological penetration of W. Thüsing is matched by the writings of Heinz Schürmann, whose *Jesus—Gestalt and Geheimnis* (Paderborn: Bonifatius, 1994) is a masterpiece of New Testament theology. Schnackenburg's survey, *New Testament Theology Today* (New York: Herder & Herder, 1963), mapped the scene a generation ago, stimulated by the Second Vatican Council. In the United States, ecclesially committed biblical scholarship has been less closely wedded to systematic theology, but the commanding presence of R. E. Brown and J. Fitzmyer among the leading half dozen American biblical scholars of their day indicates that the flowering of Catholic biblical scholarship has not been limited to Europe. In the less-ecclesial settings of much North American biblical teaching and scholarship, the functions of New Testament theology textbooks are partly absorbed into more general introductions.[162]

The final major textbook of the period was published shortly after the twentieth century ended, but had been taking shape over the previous forty years, since its author Ferdinand Hahn's doctoral dissertation on *The Titles of Jesus in Christology* (1963; Eng. trans. 1969). In the two bulky volumes of his *Theologie des Neuen Testaments* (Tübingen: Mohr Siebeck, 2002), volume 1 shows the diversity of the New Testament in a history of early Christian theology, while volume 2 clarifies its unity by a thematic presentation. The "theological history" begins with John the Baptist, Jesus, and the early community, and ends with the apostolic fathers. Between these poles most New Testament books are treated separately, except that Paul's seven authentic Epistles are combined as sources for a theology of Paul, the Pastoral Epistles are homogenized, and 2 John is conjoined with 1 John. But the historical perspective is preserved by all that being prefaced with chapters on the earliest confessions, the Aramaic-speaking, and the early Hellenistic, Jewish communities. Most important, the Jesus chapter is not merely a "historical Jesus" chapter. It is called "Proclamation and Activity of Jesus and the Reception of the Jesus-Tradition Through the Early Community." The history is presented in a way that is alert to its continuities with what follows. The theological significance of asking behind the Gospels to the historical figure had already been discussed in the introductory methodological chapter as one of the two "questions of principle" for the whole enterprise. The other axiomatic question concerns the diversity and unity of the New Testament—and that is comprehensively addressed in the second volume.

The sheer scale of this New Testament theology (1,576 pages of text without footnotes and excluding bibliographies, overviews, and indices) allows more thorough discussion of the issues that have faced the discipline throughout the century than other New Testament theologies. That helps make it the best summation of twentieth-century work in the field. It offers little guidance on where the discipline has been going in the fractures of the past thirty years, but that also makes a point. These experiments are necessary and most valuable when combined with historical exegesis, but the modern (rather than postmodern) forms of the discipline remain fundamental for theological education aiming to clarify the identity of Christianity.

Hahn's account of the unity of the New Testament, already signaled at volume 1, pages 22–28, discusses the major contributions of Cullmann, Schlier, Thüsing, and several others.[163] A major advance in the development of New Testament theology textbooks, Part one of volume 2 provides 104 pages on "The Old Testament as the Bible of Early Christianity." This takes up what was right in the concerns of Hübner and Stuhlmacher, giving this its due place and proportions. New Testament theology is unthinkable without the witness to God in the faith of Israel as sedimented in the Old Testament, but that does not require the integration of the Testaments in a holistic biblical theology.

Part two (164 pages) discusses God's revelatory act in Jesus Christ (God, God's sovereignty, Christology, pneumatology, and the implicitly Trinitarian structure of the New Testament witness); part three (130 pages) discusses the soteriological dimension of God's revelatory act in Jesus Christ (anthropology, law, the rescue, the gospel as proclamation and making present of salvation). Part four (295 pages) discusses the ecclesiological dimension of God's revelatory act in Christ, and part five (50 pages) discusses its eschatological dimension. This whole second volume comes closer to a systematic theology than a history, but its shape is determined as much by the texts being interpreted as by the way these have come to be organized in dogmatics. The links with contemporary theology remain largely implicit, but a credible account is given of the presupposed unity of the New Testament. This work provides a high note on which to end our survey of the textbooks. It is not so creative as Bultmann's, but it develops the *genre*, taking full account of and contributing to the intensive discussions of New Testament theology since 1950. If there were any reason to suppose that the classical form of the modern discipline, spanning two hundred years from Bauer to Hahn, has been superseded, this work would mark its exodus with a bang, not a whimper.

ISSUES AND TEXTS

Definition

Summary attention to the major textbooks of New Testament theology does less than justice to the discipline as a whole over the last century.

More detailed research is found less in New Testament theologies than in monographs and articles on particular authors and themes, especially Christology,[164] and in commentaries on individual texts. Singling out some of this work in a more synoptic way and through book titles will allow reference to some significant contributions to New Testament theology outside the textbooks and draw together some threads.

The definition of New Testament theology has been complicated by an ambiguity in the word "theology." In a secular culture, religiously serious "talk of God" inevitably implies something about the speaker's own standpoint. This means that if New Testament theology is understood strictly as Christian "theology," a form of Christian talk of God, the aim of interpreters to speak of God must be included in its definition. But that is alien to the modern scholarly methods of New Testament theology's historical descriptions and reconstructions. Theological aims have been little discussed, even where they have been presupposed. Biblical hermeneutics has often been seen as a separate discipline with its own specialists rather than as integral to all biblical interpretation, as theory is to practice, and crucial in the practice of New Testament theology which combines theological interests with rational methods. Wrede's strict separation of the New Testament scholar's descriptive historical work, wrongly called New Testament theology from modern theological interests perhaps reduced the need for hermeneutical reflection. Perhaps not. In any case, this separation can be defended in terms of theological as well as historical integrity.[165] Clarity is then achieved by dropping the phrase "New Testament theology,"[166] rather than retaining it for the purely historical task. Those who claim to be doing New Testament theology today are usually declaring a modern theological interest while insisting that this must not distort their historical and exegetical scholarship.

The theological aims typical of those who write New Testament theology fluctuate between attempting to speak of God and the world through scriptural interpretation and merely providing material for Christian witness and further systematic reflection. Articulating Christianity through New Testament theology may be directly confessional or only indirectly supportive of contemporary Christianity (whether by reinforcing Christian witness or by criticizing inadequate expressions and defective practice). The latter does not require personal religious commitment, and many scholars insist that this is irrelevant to their work. They nevertheless operate within a tradition whose language may at any point become a vehicle of religious communication.

One result of including this reference to interpreters' aims is that more of the older scholarship can be classified as New Testament theology than is usual. The boundaries are indistinct, but most would see the linguistic work of Walter Bauer's dictionary[167] or most grammars of New Testament Greek[168] as an auxiliary discipline, whereas Kittel's *Theological Dictionary of the New Testament* (10 vols., 1933–1973, Eng. trans. 1964–1976) is (as the title indicates) more theological in orientation and contains some major contributions to New Testament theology. That is not merely on account of the theological concepts it clarifies. The theological aims of several scholars are apparent here as they were in its predecessor, the conservative Cremer's *Biblico-Theological Lexicon* (1874, 1886, Eng. trans. 1878, 1895), and its successors, especially the more compact *Dictionary of New Testament Theology* (1967–1971, Eng. trans. ed. C. Brown, 1975), and H. Balz and G. Schneider, editors, *Exegetical Dictionary of the New Testament* (3 vols., 1980–1983, Eng. trans. 1990–1993, the Roman Catholic C. Spicq, *Theological Lexicon of the New Testament* (1983, Eng. trans. 1994) and the IVP *Compendium of Contemporary Biblical Scholarship* (3 vols., 1990–1997). Theological arguments based on the biblical languages have been generally abandoned, but these dictionaries all contain New Testament theology as well as linguistic scholarship.

Jesus

The combination of scholarly methods and varying theological interests in New Testament theology is strongest in historical Jesus research, now widely agreed to be central to the discipline, even if best treated in a separate volume from New Testament theology textbooks. The latter are mainly concerned to interpret the biblical texts themselves, whereas historical research inquires *behind* the texts, often in a more suspicious or skeptical frame of mind. Christian theological reflection on Jesus calls for some historical Jesus research and makes this a task for New Testament theology. The attempt to exclude it from the discipline was overreaction to a trend that had made it central at the expense of the New Testament's own theological witness to God in Jesus. Traditional Christianity proclaims that, and is therefore more concerned with the biblical interpretations of Jesus than with modern historians' alternative narratives, but nothing that seems true in the latter can safely be ignored by theologians or educated believers. Their understandings of Jesus are typically mediated by tradition and witness, but theological reflection on the biblical

traditions requires historical investigation and attention to the continuities and discontinuities between Jesus and the early church. New
Testament theology may judge (historically) that any adequate historical
reconstruction will be speculative on account of the character of this fragmentary evidence, and may decline to go beyond what can be known
with very strong historical probability, but that is no reason to ignore or
reject what can be known in this way.

Arguments about the historical figure of Jesus have dominated New
Testament theology on account of Jesus' importance for Christianity and
the vulnerability of the doctrinal tradition to criticism at this point. The
gospel narratives of the Easter appearances, if not Paul's report, are vul-
nerable to historical criticism, as Reimarus demonstrated in the eighteenth century. On the other hand, the conviction that God vindicated
Jesus is foundational for Christian faith, and New Testament theology
has had to make sense of both the conflicting traditions and the eschatological event or mystery spoken of as resurrection (or alternatively, exaltation). Historically oriented New Testament theologies have treated
this as a question of the emergence of the resurrection faith, part of the
story of the first disciples, since it is no part of the historical life of Jesus.
On the other hand, a literary and canonical approach that interprets the
texts theologically must acknowledge that the Gospels see it as part of the
story of Jesus of Nazareth, not merely that of the early church. New
Testament theologies offering a "biblical Christ,"[169] must therefore build
into their presentations the texts' testimony to his resurrection. However
and wherever in a New Testament theology the resurrection of Jesus is
best discussed, its significance for early and subsequent Christian faith
must be made clear.

Paul

Historically oriented New Testament theologies have inevitably given
most attention to Paul's thought, on account of both the historical and
the theological quality of the sources. Paul is the only New Testament
author vividly known as a historical figure through primary sources, his
authentic Epistles. Their chronological priority among the New
Testament writings leads to the whole terrain being mapped by reference
to these relatively fixed points. That has made historical New Testament
theologies particularly attractive to Lutherans whose understanding of
Christianity owes more to the Apostle's supposed theology than is typical

of other denominations. One of the challenges for Roman Catholics writing a New Testament theology is to avoid allowing Paul a stranglehold on the presentation. One solution is to follow the canon in giving priority or prominence to the Gospels, despite their later dates.[170] Another is to start with a historical or biblical picture of Jesus.

From the days of F. C. Baur, the relationship between Paul and Jesus (or Jesus and Paul)[171] has been a major issue in modern understandings of Christianity and so an underlying issue in New Testament theology. It involves judgments about how important the earthly life and teaching of Jesus were for Paul. An example of how a small exegetical adjustment can deeply affect the total picture is the shift in much North American and British scholarship to interpreting Paul's phrase (seven times) "the faith of Jesus (Christ)" from "faith *in*" him, to his own faith, that is, faithfulness unto death.

The changing pictures of Paul in New Testament scholarship have been a barometer of New Testament theology. The major turn from liberal to neo-Reformation interpretations of Paul's theology after the First World War was both a cause and an effect of the wider revolution in theology, sparked by Barth's *Romans*. Toward the end of this period of fifty-odd years, some of the 1960s arguments about the details of a broadly Lutheran interpretation of Paul were at the same time a debate about Bultmann's theology.[172] The break with classical protestant interpretations of Paul initiated by Krister Stendahl's lecture in 1961 on "The Apostle Paul and the Introspective Conscience of the West"[173] was as much the product of good historical work[174] as of theological discontent, but it also became entangled with some growing dissatisfaction with biblical theology among many scholars.[175] The ebb and flow of historical debate can be charted in relation to its wider theological and cultural settings.

New Testament studies in the second half of the century, stimulated by the discoveries at Qumran in 1947 and by a growing awareness of the recent Holocaust, and also new opportunities for archaeology in Palestine and the State of Israel, gained a deeper knowledge of Second Temple Judaism. Albert Schweitzer had insisted on the importance of Jewish apocalyptic for understanding Paul,[176] but from Reitzenstein through Bultmann and his contemporaries, the emphasis had fallen on the Hellenistic Paul. It soon became clear that all the Judaism available in the sources for this period was more or less Hellenistic, but the fact that Paul (and all the New Testament writers) wrote in Greek and read the Septuagint had inclined scholars trained in the classics rather than Jewish studies to approach the texts from that background, including C. H. Dodd. Yet out of Dodd's Cambridge seminar there came W. D. Davies, *Paul and Rabbinic Judaism* (1948), and D. Daube's collection *The New Testament and Rabbinic Judaism* (1956), and a generation later a student of the Welshman Davies, E. P. Sanders, wrote *Paul and Palestinian Judaism* (1977). This redefined Paul's religious past and suggested a Schweitzerian interpretation of his new theology, with its emphasis on participation in Christ. Jewish historians of religion such as H. J. Schoeps[177] and later A. Segal[178] and the postmodern D. Boyarin[179] wrote on Paul, and J. Munck had challenged the dominant German models in *Paul and the Salvation of Mankind* (1954; Eng. trans. 1959), but it is E. P. Sanders who marks a turn of the tide against the Lutheran interpretations of Paul characteristic of the most creative New Testament theology of the century.

Older theological scholars, notably C. K. Barrett, the late N. A. Dahl, J. L. Martyn, L. E. Keck, the late J. C. Beker, U. Wilckens, J. Becker, and M. D. Hooker, were (and some still are) well aware of Paul's Jewishness, but succeeded in combining their Reformation theological insights with some outstanding historical scholarship in their New Testament theologies,[180] and the textbooks and commentaries of J. D. G. Dunn also integrate older theological insights with modern historical and exegetical research.[181]

New trends in biblical studies have often been launched in interpretations of Paul, and some of these fall within the ambit of New Testament theology. Even those seeking to break out of the older theological tradition have sometimes produced work full of theological potential, notably the social history of Wayne Meeks,[182] the social-scientific approaches of Gerd Theissen,[183] J. H. Schütz,[184] B. Holmberg,[185] and Philip Esler,[186] among others; the rhetorical criticism of H. D. Betz[187] and his Chicago student Margaret Mitchell,[188] and the political and liberationist perspective of N. Elliott.[189] The new literary theoretical approaches that have proliferated since the 1970s have contributed less to the study of Paul than to the gospel narratives. Linguistics have made a mark here as elsewhere,[190] and both postmodernity[191] and feminism[192] have visited Corinth. More traditional fields of New Testament theology were plowed by an American SBL seminar,[193] and of the making of many monographs there can be no end, while much study must prove itself in print. Most of what is written on Paul in Germany,[194] even in commentaries, is New Testament theology.

John

Paul is so pivotal in modern New Testament theology that other writers are in danger of receding from view, but John's gospel has been the central text for theological interpretation from Heracleon in the second century to Bultmann and Dodd[195] in the twentieth. Their literary and history of religions research was done in the service of their New Testament theology. The publication of Bultmann's Meyer commentary was completed in 1941, the year of his demythologizing manifesto,[196] which is also a significant document in the history of New Testament theology because this is where "existential(ist) interpretation" hit the fan.

The interpretation of John divided the theological spirits in the nineteenth century when some conservatives thought that to deny its historicity would destroy Christianity, but F. C. Baur made its theology the climax of the early Christian development. The theological character of its discourses and narrative was clear to most specialists by 1900, but the interpretation of these fluctuated as the history of religions background was variously assessed, with the tide ebbing from Hellenistic mysticism and even oriental Gnosticism to a recognition by the 1960s (clarified by the texts from Qumran) of its probably sectarian Jewish background. German protestant theology, where New Testament theologies flourished, has had less invested in John than in Paul, but the close affinity between Bultmann's existentialist theology and John's apparent individualism gave the discussion of this text (like Romans) a contemporary theological edge. The irony is that some of Bultmann's more orthodox theological critics found the Fourth Gospel less orthodox than Bultmann had claimed. Ernst Käsemann reverted to Baur's docetic picture of the Johannine Jesus as God bestriding the earth.[197] Whereas Bultmann accepted the Kierkegaardian christology he attributed to John, Käsemann could only subject what he found there to theological criticism or *Sachkritik*.

The subsequent discussion of John has been less obviously and directly theological, but the Anchor commentary (2 vols., 1966–1971) of the Roman Catholic R. E. Brown (1928–1998), and the monograph by J. L. Martyn, *History and Theology in the Fourth Gospel* (Nashville: Abingdon, 1968, 1979), which together mark a watershed in Johannine research, are theologically highly suggestive. They directed attention to the history of the Johannine community.[198] After Bultmann's relegation of the sacraments in John to an "ecclesiastical redactor," the recovery of a sense of the Johannine community opened a door to understanding their social importance.[199] Käsemann had intuited this community's sectarian character but done rather little with his insight. Like Bultmann, whose sociological insights in his form criticism had to wait for Gerd Theissen to be developed, Käsemann had reservations about social-scientific contributions to theology. But the theological potential of these new approaches was clear enough in Wayne Meeks's essay on "The Man from Heaven in Johannine Sectarianism,"[200] among the most suggestive articles ever written on this gospel. The theological relevance of literary approaches to John is evident in such monographs as G. R. O'Day, *Revelation in the Fourth Gospel* (Philadelphia: Fortress Press, 1986); M. M. Thompson, *The Humanity of Jesus in the Fourth Gospel* (Philadelphia: Fortress Press, 1988); C. R. Koester, *Symbolism in the Fourth Gospel* (Minneapolis: Augsburg Fortress, 1995); and in the narrative critical commentary of F. J. Moloney.[201] More traditional New Testament theology may be found in the many German monographs and commentaries on John[202] and in the best English work of the generation, John Ashton, *Understanding the Fourth Gospel* (Oxford: Clarendon, 1991, 2007). Monographs on particular theological themes run second only to those on Paul, and some attempts to interpret the text from different perspectives have been illuminating.[203] The burning question of anti-Judaism, or anti-Jewish potential in the New Testament, has been posed most insistently in Johannine study.[204]

The Synoptic Gospels

The interpretation of all three Synoptic Gospels has been a new epicenter of New Testament theology since the Second World War. The method called "redaction criticism," referring to the study of each evangelist's editing or "redaction" of his tradition of Jesus' words and actions, is not entirely new,[205] but has been pursued vigorously and relentlessly. The study of Matthew and Luke could build on the secure source-critical consensus that both evangelists had used Mark independently as their basic source. Distinguishing between tradition and redaction in Mark was less secure because the question of Mark's sources is quite uncertain, but form criticism had provided some basis for this by isolating originally independent units of tradition.

The beginnings of redaction criticism may be found much earlier, in the history of traditions research of Wrede's *Messianic Secret* (1901), in particular on Mark, and this theme was a nodal point of New Testament theology throughout the century, generating much reflection on Mark's theology.[206]

The focus of redaction criticism was on the *theology* of each evangelist. Studying this by analyzing how they interpreted their tradition (rather than simply collecting it and repeating it without alteration) corresponded to the findings of form critics (notably Martin Dibelius[207]) who located some traditions' "setting in the life of the early church" in preaching. The model of tradition being interpreted corresponded roughly to how protestant preachers interpret biblical traditions today, and dovetailed neatly with the account of revelation given by the "theology of the Word" and "kerygmatic theology." Revelation "happens" (where and when God wills) when the word is preached, that is, tradition is interpreted with an intention to proclaim the gospel. This correspondence accounts for the long popularity of a method of gospel criticism whose potential was rather limited. The scholarly seam was overworked because it seemed religiously useful.

The limited success of this method in the study of Mark[208] was perhaps responsible for the interpretation of this text in particular moving on into more-modern literary critical channels in the 1980s, especially in North America. These were generally less theologically motivated than German history of traditions research, and less directly linked to any particular theory of revelation, though reader-response criticism has affinities with kerygmatic theology.[209] Most of the best literary studies are rooted in historical-critical exegesis. Where this has been broken with, as in some structuralist interpretations and now deconstruction,[210] the results are less illuminating. The quantity, quality, and scope of recent monographs on Mark are without parallel in recent New Testament scholarship. Several of the authors would not expect their work to be classified as New Testament theology, but the category can be stretched to include most of it.

The title of the classic collection of redaction criticism on Matthew indicates its character. *Tradition and Interpretation in Matthew* (German 1960; Eng. trans London: SCM Press, 1963), by G. Bornkamm, G. Barth, and H. J. Held, contains Bornkamm's 1948 article on "The Stilling of the Storm in Matthew," which introduced the method. It carried further what Bultmann had sketched at the end of *The History of the Synoptic Tradition* (1921, 1931, Eng. trans. 1963, rev. 1968), 321–67: "The Editing (*Redaktion*) of the Traditional Material." Some of the best contributions were collected and where necessary translated in G. N. Stanton, ed., *The Interpretation of Matthew* (Philadelphia: Fortress Press, 1983, 1995).

The most important and influential redaction critical research was Hans Conzelmann's *The Theology of St Luke* (German 1954; Eng. trans. London: Faber, 1960). The German title, *Die Mitte der Zeit* (The Center of Time), points to the main thesis, that Luke has a distinctive theology, different from Paul's eschatological framework of thought. In the light of the experience of the delay of the Parousia, Luke developed a new conception based on history, or on that part of history understood as "salvation history," stretching from the Old Testament, centering on Christ, and fanning out into the history of the church guided by the Spirit, as indicated in Acts 1:9-11. Luke's "redaction" of Mark's account of Jesus' visit to Nazareth (Mark 6:1-6) in 4:16-30 is indicative. The "today" of salvation in 4:21 is clearly yesterday for Luke, who looks back to the time of salvation in Jesus' ministry, in striking contrast to Paul at 2 Cor 6:2: "*Now* is the day of salvation." Most revealing is Luke's "redaction" or rewrite of the "little apocalypse" (Mark 13:5-37) and its Introduction (see v. 4), in chapter 21. He clearly distinguishes between the fall of Jerusalem in A.D. 70, which for him is past history, and the eschatological coming of the Son of Man, which is no longer so imminent (see the polemic against those who say "the time is near" added at 21:8). References to the imminent end at Mark 9:1 and 14:62 are subtly altered at Luke 9:27 and 22:69.

The fact (or overwhelming probability) that Luke wrote Acts is proof positive of his historical perspective, and while the details of Conzelmann's presentation have been challenged, its main thesis has survived. One reason it was so intensely discussed and broadly supported by other Bultmannians, including Käsemann, Haenchen, and Vielhauer, and so dominated study of Luke for a generation,[211] was that it corresponded well to some wider contemporary theological debates, as the best New Testament theology often has done. Conzelmann and his colleagues did not approve of Luke's theology, which (allegedly) replaced eschatology with a view of history, rather than reinterpreting the futurist eschatology to fit a new situation as John had done. It was more like Cullmann's biblical theology and was labeled by Käsemann[212] "early catholic," which was not intended as a compliment. The third generation needed to readjust its thinking,[213] but in Käsemann's protestant view, the church was wrong to make this contingent historical development normative for subsequent generations. This is what happened with that very Lukan theologian, Irenaeus.

This recognition of Luke's theological significance if not stature was thus often accompanied by *Sachkritik*, and such theological criticism had implications for the New Testament canon, which could no longer be thought straightforwardly normative, since it contained some problematical theologies. In Käsemann's view, its theological diversity justified the pluralism of different denominations rather than (as was hoped throughout the ecumenical movement) the unity of the church.[214]

Luke as the father of second-century Catholicism might have been expected to provide a springboard for more Catholic and Anglican New Testament theologies, but the discipline remained firmly in German hands, and here the flourishing new Roman Catholic research centers were deeply indebted to their older protestant colleagues. Elsewhere the new interest in literary approaches[215] took the study of Luke–Acts further away from the maelstrom of 1960s theology, as did the growing interest in social history and sociological study.

In Matthean studies similarly, the redaction criticism that dovetailed so well with kerygmatic theology was successfully taken beyond Bornkamm by G. Strecker[216] and U. Luz,[217] but more historical and sociological[218] approaches have shifted the center of New Testament theology gravity from Christology to ecclesiology, here as elsewhere,[219] as questions about the relationship of Christianity and Judaism excited more attention. These studies benefited from recent advances in the study of Second Temple Judaism.[220]

Other Writings

Turning briefly and selectively to other New Testament texts, there has been increased interest in the Epistle of James and (as the millennium cast its shadow) in the Apocalypse. By contrast, there has been some decline in the estimation of Hebrews. The Epistle to the Ephesians excited interest where the argument between protestants and Roman Catholics loomed large.[221] Even the question of authorship is important here (as it is not in most New Testament theology), because if Paul had written it, one might draw a more "catholic" picture of Paul than the authentic Epistles permit.

Some have seen the author to the Hebrews as a major theological thinker, third only to Paul and John,[222] whereas most protestants are impatient with its symbolic world, even if admiring its rhetoric. Like Luther, many have been theologically critical of it for disallowing restoration following apostasy. Evidently theological judgments are interacting with historical description in such New Testament theology. Existentialist theologians can find little of value in this writing, whereas liturgical theologians can easily identify with the world they construct from this text, even if they are mistaken in attributing to the author their own understandings of "drawing near" to God. Like many sermons, this homily has generated unintended meanings, and lends itself to scholars developing one or another of its themes. Thus Ernst Käsemann's 1939 monograph, *The Wandering People of God* (Eng. trans.; Minneapolis: Augsburg, 1984), partly written in a Nazi prison, explores its ecclesiology and ethics effectively, even though the early Käsemann's history of religions hypothesis about the Gnostic background proved untenable.[223] Others have written on Hebrews' use of the Old Testament, its Christology, and individual concepts such as faith, confession, and perfection, but this text has not stood in the mainstream of New Testament theology, despite its rich symbolism.

General recognition that ethics is a part of New Testament theology, despite having formerly been treated in separate textbooks,[224] has given the Epistle of James a more positive place in New Testament theology than it enjoyed when discussed mainly in connection with its disagreement with Paul over faith and works.

Theology done as much through ethics as through doctrine brings increased attention to ecclesiology.[225] This is sometimes at the expense of Christology and soteriology, which have come to seem rather abstract in their traditional forms. This shift away from the classical Lutheran priorities that once dominated New Testament theology is evident in the work of R. B. Hays, who drew attention to the narrative substructure of Paul's theology and was among those who pressed for understanding "the faith of Jesus" in the subjective sense (Jesus' own faith)[226] and then clarified Paul's "ecclesiocentric hermeneutics"[227] and also wrote *The Moral Vision of the New Testament* (New York: HarperCollins, 1996), which is in itself almost a compact New Testament theology. The more social-historical descriptions of early Christian morality by Wayne Meeks,[228] informed by social-scientific theory, are also suggestive for New Testament theology, though less directly.

Renewed interest in the Apocalypse at the end of the century was encouraged by the approach of the millennium, but this text was also attractive to practitioners of new approaches, whether literary, social-scientific, or feminist, as well as to those wishing to reverse the negative judgments of many theologians, including the magisterial Reformers. The richness of this puzzling text has become more available through the century's further intensive study of Jewish apocalyptic, and it has provided unexpected resources for moral reflection in a consumer society[229] facing ecological crisis. Those more concerned with the reception of scriptural texts than with authorial intention have found here much to admire[230] and more to deplore. This could bring a new dimension to New Testament theology.

As New Testament studies became more varied in the final quarter of the twentieth century, New Testament theology was also drawn into new channels. As the boundaries between the churches and a pluralistic culture were more tightly drawn by some and became more porous in the work of others, it became more difficult to say what counted as New Testament theology. Any rational study of these texts that has a strong religious interest must be considered, but it has become harder to say what counts as rational and what is religious. Modern New Testament theology took shape within the critical-historical scholarship nourished by the Enlightenment, but as this has been challenged, and biblical scholarship has splintered, New Testament theology has become more fragmented. What counts as a "strong religious interest" can no longer be limited to those of conventional Christianity. The denominational allegiances that were once fairly clear in New Testament theology have given way to divisions of opinion that cut across confessional boundaries.

The new cultural interests in these texts are often religious, sometimes in ways unfamiliar to traditional believers. Biblical interpretation will not be constrained, and New Testament theology can no more shut itself off from what else is happening in biblical scholarship than from the wider culture. It has always been conditioned by the church and the society in which it has been practiced, and by the understandings of theology with which it has been associated. As societies become pluralist, a New Testament theology unconstrained by church authority is likely to follow, for better or worse. The main lines of twentieth-century New Testament theology have been critical and historical, whether linked with theologies of the word or of history. The new diversity of methods and interests toward the end of the century have complicated the picture but have not undermined the basic tasks of biblical studies. These remain linguistic, literary, and historical, and they continue to raise theological questions. The future shape of New Testament theology will depend on the tasks it is designed to fulfill. It continues to teach the churches how to read their scriptures, educating religious teachers in the meanings of these (for some) authoritative texts. If it is still to play a decisive role in determining the identity of religious communities or communions, then textual determinacy will remain indispensable, and the classical forms of New Testament theology provide essential guidelines.

C H A P T E R   F O U R

HERMENEUTICS

The Bible and the Quest for Theological Meaning

Leo G. Perdue

INTRODUCTION

Since its modern inception, beginning with the inaugural address of Johann Philipp Gabler at the University of Altdorf (March 30, 1787),[1] biblical theology has played an important role in the contemporary theological understanding of the church and culture. From the days of Gabler to the present, however, the dominant problem that has plagued biblical theology has been the distance between the past, sought to be understood through developing methods of historical criticism, and the present, in which the faith of the contemporary search is set forth in a variety of constructions, ranging from systematic presentations, to the forms of biblical narrative, to a variety of new formulations shaped by artistry, imagination, and postmodernism. The dichotomy of Gabler between historical-biblical theology and contemporary systematic formulation has collapsed during the past century. What have emerged are numerous contemporary expressions of modern faith that appropriate in some fashion biblical theology, however it may be expressed. Indeed, in the quest for hermeneutical appropriations of scripture, the very enterprise of biblical theology has been repeatedly redefined and differently understood. This essay seeks both to capture the major moments of this development and to characterize biblical theology as a larger part of the hermeneutical enterprise of the contemporary church within its various locations.

Neo-Orthodoxy, Biblical Theology, and Christian Hermeneutics

As I noted in my initial essay, Barth's *Der Römerbrief* in 1919 blazed the trail for a new theological approach that not only challenged and largely replaced liberal theology but also orchestrated new hermeneutical understandings of the two Testaments.[2] To adapt biblical interpretation to the use of the contemporary church, Barth contended that the Bible serves as a witness to the Word of God. Barth was aware of the method and interpretations of historical criticism, but he was more interested in enabling the church to view scripture as a canon. This Word of God, fully realized in Jesus Christ, speaks through the Bible in human words that in their essence are proclamation. Even so, the Word of God is not to be confused with human words, for God is not comprehended by anyone. The Word of God is known only through this text, while this knowledge allows for the proper interpretation of the text. For Barth, the biblical texts were to be understood in their relationship to Jesus Christ. This meant that he gave a christocentric interpretation to both the Old Testament and the New. Scripture witnesses to Jesus Christ, who becomes the one who is the active subject of the salvific narratives of the Christian story. Barth sought a hermeneutical understanding of scripture that assists the church in its encounter with Christ as the Word bringing salvation to believers.[3]

The previous essays have included numerous hermeneutical insights into the canon, including Jewish interpretations of the Tanakh and largely Christian views of the Old and New Testaments. The following attempts to sharpen some of these and to add what I would consider other, and often more recent, hermeneutical approaches to the Bible by contemporary Judaism and the modern church.

Hermeneutics in Jewish and Christian Biblical Theology

Hermeneutics as understood in this concluding chapter points to both construing the interpretation and meaning of the Bible in its various forms for contemporary faith and practice and engaging in the constructive task of enabling a text of the ancient past in its canonical forms to address the present communities of believers. As noted by Morgan at the end of his essay on New Testament theology, the Bible has always played an important role in the life of the church and contemporary culture. And this continues to be the case, regardless of the Christian community in which it functions. Yet, as Sommer cautions a Christian audience, the place of the Bible in Judaism varies significantly from that assigned to it by the various expressions of contemporary Christianity. In present Judaism, the Bible is but the beginning of a tradition that continues on through other formulations of Jewish texts, ranging from the Mishnah and Tosefta, to the Mekilta and other commentaries, to the Talmud, to contemporary interpretation.

Thus, in a volume that includes a summary of biblical theology as practiced in the churches during the twentieth and twenty-first centuries, we began, not arbitrarily, with Barth's *Epistle to the Romans*, for his theology has been the most important, contemporary hermeneutic in the past century. Of course, there cannot be and, in my judgment, ought not to be a single hermeneutic for interpreting the Bible. Rather, diversity, which I suggest reflects the many human cultures where Christianity has taken root, not uniformity, is the fundamental character of this enterprise in the current world. This is true as well for Judaism. For Jews and Roman Catholics, the Bible is but the first formation of teachings in a lengthy development of traditions over the centuries. For these two communities, their respective later traditions are given more religious authority than scripture. This marks the major difference from Protestant Christianity, since in the latter's various expressions the Bible holds the primary place of authority. This concluding chapter cannot but touch on the numerous examples of views and understandings of the Bible for present cultures and their many Christian and Jewish communities. Within these locations, traditions, and social groups that seek to engage the Bible, each community pursues the common enterprise of seeking to understand the Bible as an important, even if not final, word of God to human creatures.[4]

How one proceeds, of course, represents an important set of choices the hermeneut must make in interpreting the Bible for contemporary faith. It would seem to me that the following task of hermeneutics comprises the focus of the current exercise and serves as its first task: descriptions of academically informed interpretations that are representative of the classical Protestant churches (Anglican, Reformed, and Lutheran), the Roman Catholic Church, and Reformed Judaism. Of course, this delimitation will not be satisfactory to many. This would be true of churches that splintered from the major protestant denominations and non–Roman Catholic confessions, including Eastern Orthodoxy and Russian Orthodoxy. Their understandings of the Bible and its role in the construction of modern faith are often significantly different from those listed above. Space considerations make a more comprehensive and inclusive description of these additional articulations impossible. Nevertheless, the different confessions that are set forth may find some common ground, with obvious refinements and variations.

A second task is the possibility of constructing a hermeneutic that legitimates the authenticity of various forms of Judaism as well as the diverse expressions of Christianity, both Roman Catholic and Protestant, in this essay. The older approach of interfaith dialogue is not intended here, for it has long since run its once useful course. Rather, the expressions of different forms of Christianity and Judaism are each honored by being granted a voice that addresses their constituencies and the larger world that includes other religious communities. At the same time, every community's hermeneutic addresses openly, with honesty and engagement, each understanding within a global environment. There are wide variations here, but what must be avoided is the supercessionist claim that Christianity, born in the womb of Judaism, has somehow now replaced the chosen people to become the favored religion whose various communities together form the present people of God, while the children of Abraham have been stripped of their previous place of honor. What Roman Catholics and Jewish forms of institutional expression share, not surprisingly, is that tradition plays a greater role in the formulation of divine teaching than does the Bible. Protestants, by contrast, since the Reformation's clarion call of *sola scriptura* (scripture alone), while giving a significant place to continuing transformation and tradition (*simper Reformanda*), usually claim to privilege the Bible with first rank in the construction of modern faith and the place of authority. I would submit, however, that this claim is never followed in practice, even by fundamentalists, to adhere to the script of the text. However, all of these, to a greater or lesser extent, do have some investment in biblical hermeneutics, and thus cannot leave frozen in the ancient past the multiple teachings, often diverse, of the canonical documents.

Another task, the third, which comes into consideration in the writing of a biblical hermeneutic, is the issue of culture, from the time of the formation of the canon to the present. In contemporary theological discourse, Paul Tillich was especially important in noting and then constructing the relationship between theology and culture.[5] This existential religion, characterized by an ultimate concern, eliminates the gap between the sacred and the secular, for authentic religion must be at work in the sphere of everyday life. The existential situation of human beings involves anxiety and fear, which are to be addressed by the ultimate concern. Finally, Tillich points to the spirit of protest against the existential predicament of human beings. For Tillich this protest was against the industrial revolution, although now it would be against the technological world that dehumanizes. Humans make various efforts to escape emptiness, meaninglessness, and estrangement. The industrial and technological worlds have transformed humans into producers and consumers. It is the responsibility of the church to guard against this alienating, illegitimate anthropology.

However, the interaction of culture and religion needs to move from the constraints of Western paradigms of faith and culture to examine the religions of the world and their interaction with the diverse and multiple forms of human expressions of language, art, literature, values, and worldviews. Biblical theology must reject the illegitimate attempt of any religion, in particular Christianity with a missionary impulse, to foster the notion that its particular expression is superior to other global religions, not just Judaism, but also Chinese religions, Islam, Hinduism, and the myriad other religions practiced in the world. Biblical theology, based on the foundation of the notion of Christianity's superior position, becomes, in my judgment, illegitimate in attempting to foster religious and cultural preeminence. Conversion to Christianity and the delegitimizing of non-Christian religions, which some theologians of the church have at times sought to infuse into their formulations of biblical theology, become in themselves foreign to the most essential spirit of Christianity and Judaism.

Helpful in this task of hermeneutics, then, is the uncovering of the religious impulse, practice, or study of religion in its variety of forms in public discourse in diverse cultural expressions.[6] Throughout human history, in any and every region of the globe, the question of context is ever present in matters of interpretation of the Bible for contemporary communities, even those in which Christianity and Judaism are especially minority expressions. For each of these, the Bible not only addresses implicitly and at times directly its own immediate publics but also the cultures in which they are located. To do so requires that religions do not stand apart from the cultures in which they exist but rather interact with and engage their audiences. I doubt any biblical writer thought of composing for distant cultures far into the future, but there is no question that their faith, moral views, and sociopolitical values have greatly influenced the course of history, particularly that of the West and to a far lesser extent the East due to the unfortunate advent of Western colonialism. Indeed, without a critical biblical hermeneutic, emperors, kings, presidents, patriarchal males, racists, misogynists, and homophobes, to name only a few who negate the humanity of many based on gender, race, ethnicity, class, sexual identity, and geographical location, have often attempted to draw the Bible into the support of their own heinous and destructive ideologies. Thus, a proper biblical hermeneutic cannot simply concern itself with attempting to unveil the variety of theological views, moral values, and ritual practices of the ancient past. A proper biblical hermeneutic must address the present with an authentic voice, and if nothing else, deny the legitimacy of unjustified claims for barbarous practices that negate the humanity of people and endanger this good earth. Here, of course, we must boldly cross over into the area of this series that enters into conversation with contemporary theology. The failure of biblical scholars to undertake this necessary and important step relegates the Bible to the collections of ancient documents and artifacts from a long-dead civilization partially preserved in modern museums, but for the most part, buried in unexcavated and partially unearthed cities, unknown by present populations of people. This ignoring of the biblical text is compounded by allowing the abusers of Scripture to have their say in legitimating any action that is exploitative and destructive of the earth, its creatures, and human beings.

The fourth consideration has come into play in a much more apparent fashion, since the end of the global conflict of World War II and the subsequent decline of old-world empires (especially those of the British and French) and the emergence of American imperialism. This consideration is contextual theology.[7] Contextual theology places its primary focus on the numerous geographical and cultural locations of the church, which lead to a variety of formulations of Christian faith. The idea that there is some universal portrayal of a static theology that engages the church in all of its manifestations is patently absurd.

THE BIBLE AND THE CHURCH

This book and its subsequent volumes cannot rehearse the vast history of biblical theology, beginning in the biblical traditions themselves and moving into the present. This massive undertaking has been pursued and is being formulated by numerous scholars.[8] Additionally, it is not possible even in this series of books to survey in detail the numerous, important treatments of a variety of approaches to biblical hermeneutics by contemporary theologians and biblical scholars from Karl Barth to the present.[9] The most one may say is that those who engage in the construction of biblical theology and seek to fathom its possible hermeneutical implications are inevitably scholars who stand with one foot in the academy and the other in the church, synagogue, or temple. Thus, they bring to the table their own theological understandings, cultural locations, and ideological interests, which cannot simply be ignored or put aside in the interpretative and hermeneutical tasks. Hermeneuts should "come clean" in expressing who they are, what they think, and what they believe. Assuredly, these factor into the constructive work of the theologian. An example of this dual identity is the hermeneutical understanding of Brevard Childs, whose biblical theology emerges from both his academic and the churchly contexts.[10]

As a student, Childs wrote his Th.D. dissertation at Basel when two Old Testament theological giants, Walther Eichrodt and Walther Baumgartner, were on the faculty. Childs also attended the lectures of Karl Barth, who was in the systematics department, and he soon fell under the sway of his stimulating formulation of neo-orthodoxy. After initially working as a historical critic who was primarily interested in the history of religions in the earlier part of his career (through the 1970s), Childs spent the remainder of his time as a scholar and churchman dedicated to shaping a new understanding of biblical theology that would provide a compelling way for the church, and to a far lesser extent the synagogue, to appropriate the Bible by theological interpretation. Refusing to characterize his approach as another method, he developed a hermeneutical understanding of the formation of the canon and the reception of its faith as divine revelation. The core affirmation of Childs is that scripture is the theological context in which authentic affirmations of faith by the church are made.[11]

Childs's numerous works on biblical theology make use of his canonical approach, which he has described in detail in his many writings. He begins with the judgment that the historical-critical method is theologically bankrupt. This does not mean he discards traditional methods of exegesis, but, taken together, they face insurmountable difficulties in the attempt to produce a consensus of views about many specific issues.

Furthermore, they also are unable to construct a biblical theology that engages communities of faith, both past and present. It is the "Word" contained within the canonical text that for Childs is revelatory, not the particularities of the historical and social circumstances that may have influenced those authors, tradents, and editors of social communities who produced and preserved the tradition over many years or the historical events and social communities reconstructed by scholars. The focus of the theologian is the final form of the text that entered into the canon, not earlier traditions and sources that existed prior to the completion of a canonical book.

While his censure of historical criticism misses the mark (this collage of methods did not intend to express a theology for Judaism and Christianity), Childs does articulate in lucid and reasonable fashion his understanding of the canonical approach. First, the interpreter's focus is on the canonical form of the text that alone possesses authority and normative value. Second, the canonical process may be observed in the Bible as a hermeneutical articulation. Third, this process operated within the generations of faith communities in shaping the final form of the canon, both Old and New Testaments, and then enabling later communities to articulate their faith in response. Fourth and finally, the Bible is a normative, authoritative collection of texts *intentionally* shaped by communities of faith to address the divine Word to future generations. He names this intentionality a "canon consciousness." This theological meaning is located in the textual context for interpretation and not in the mind of the author or in how the original audience may have understood what was written.

When the two Testaments of the canon come into view, Childs argues that the Old Testament also speaks to the contemporary church as scripture. The authority and theological witness of the Old Testament are not found only in the New Testament's use of Old Testament theological themes and texts but rather both Testaments, taken together, continue to address the church in the present.[12] Thus, the Old Testament is and remains a part of Christian Scripture. What binds the Testaments together is their witness to the same divine reality, the Word of God.

Finally, in examining Judaism and Christianity, he concludes that the Old Testament is scripture and not simply a receptacle for the religious ideas of historical communities. Childs does not deny to Judaism the authenticity of the First Testament or the Jewish Bible. Furthermore, he does not insist that Christians must have the same canon in order to come to a theological presentation of the Bible (he recognizes there are different canons in historical communities of Judaism and Christianity). But he does insist, in following Barth, that theology is confessional and is not simply a collection of themes within the history of religion. The Bible is not a collection of ancient records, studied by contemporary historians to assist in their historical reconstructions, but rather a sacred canon that is normative and authoritative for the faith and practice of living religious communities.

THE BIBLE AND THE SYNAGOGUE[13]

Sommer's essay in this volume points clearly to the distinctions between Christian and Jewish hermeneutics in regard to the Bible. He notes that there cannot be a Jewish biblical theology in a precise sense. Expressions of Jewish theology, rather, base themselves on Judaism's rich postbiblical tradition and not simply scripture, and hence a Jewish theology cannot be chiefly biblical. Jewish postbiblical traditions include the Talmuds' midrashic collections, postrabbinic commentaries, the Mishnah, the Talmud, the mystical texts, and philosophy. The Protestant *sola scriptura* that is occasionally (and wrongly) understood as giving the Bible the primary place in contemporary hermeneutics is not true of Judaism.[14] Nevertheless, there can be such a thing as a Jewish theology that takes into consideration scripture along with these mentioned postbiblical texts.[15] According to Sommer, this Jewish theology would seek to recover or renew biblical voices that are often lost in Jewish thought and place them in the larger context of Jewish traditions. It is in the interaction or dialogue between biblical and postbiblical Jewish thinkers, then, that something Sommers loosely calls a Jewish biblical theology can arise. Sommer names this "dialogical biblical theology."

The most vociferous voice among Jewish scholars in the conversation about Jewish biblical theology is that of Jon Levenson, who has flatly rejected the very contention that Jews are interested one whit in this enterprise. His reasons, rehearsed in numerous issues and reissues of his essay, are as follows.[16] He begins with Gabler's address that distinguished biblical theology from dogmatic theology and indicates that it would appear this distinction would be maintained by all Protestant biblical theologians. However, this is not the case, for many biblical theologians openly emphasize that they approach the Hebrew Bible from the perspective of their faith and thus are obligated to relate the two Testaments theologically and to engage their own theological views. When this occurs, Gabler's clear distinction disappears. And for Levenson, this is where the difficulty for Jews finds its beginning. Levenson argues that the Hebrew Bible contains no dominant theme that may be consistently carried forth throughout the entire text and into the New Testament. And it is even more dubious when one takes into consideration the realization that themes change often and at times dramatically in the development of the canon. By contrast, many biblical scholars prefer the approach of the history of religions that sets forth the variety of beliefs and practices that exist both in the Tanakh and in the different cultures in which the Bible emerged. Levenson contends that, while some agreement among scholars may be obtained on the basis of historical research, this is not the case on the basis of biblical and contemporary theology. He writes: "The argument that Old Testament theology can maintain both an uncompromisingly historical character and distinction from the history of Israelite religion is therefore not valid."[17] If Christian Old Testament theologians are correct, that Christ is the fulfillment of the Hebrew Bible, then the reason Jews are not interested in this enterprise becomes only too obvious.

A second reason Jews are not interested in biblical theology, says Levenson, is the strong anti-Semitism that is explicit or at least implicit in Christian Old Testament theologies. He indicates that this is true of Walther Eichrodt's *Theology of the Old Testament*, especially in his characterization of Judaism as possessing only a "torso-like appearance . . . in separation from Christianity."[18] Reading Judaism through Pauline polemic, Eichrodt sees it as a legalistic, burdensome religion that negated any living relationship with God. When Eichrodt makes this callous assessment, Levenson notes that all pretense of scholarly objectivity is cast off. Levenson also criticizes the other Protestant giant of Old Testament theology, Gerhard von Rad, who writes as though Judaism did not exist. Von Rad sees the Old Testament absorbed into the New, which becomes the end of the Old Testament itself. This means essentially that Jesus Christ is the fulfillment of Israel's history of salvation.[19] Following the tack of earlier German scholarship, including that of Wellhausen, Judaism is distinguished from earlier Israelite religion in the writing down of the Torah, resulting in its spiritual death.[20] Subsequently, even many liberal Jews have at times rejected historical criticism as inherently anti-Semitic.

Third, since the large majority of Christian Old Testament theologians are Protestant, this also presents Jews with considerable difficulties. With *sola scriptura*, the Bible is at times given an anti-Semitic tinge.[21] What most Protestants have been interested to discover is the meaning of the Bible in the past and its import for contemporary faith, and not the tradition that exists between the Bible and the present.[22] The practice of tradition is more important for Jews than its set of beliefs. This, of course, stands in opposition to the important place of tradition not only in Catholicism but also in Protestantism.

Fourth, Jews are uneasy with any effort to systematize the Hebrew Bible, an approach often found in numerous works of Protestant Old Testament theology.[23] Jews accept the diversity of beliefs and practices in the Hebrew Bible as a matter of course.[24] Finally, Jews reject the approach of a systematic biblical theology based on a "center" (*Mitte*), since they agree there is none present in the Tanakh.

Fifth and finally, Levenson concludes that there are multiple contexts for Protestant interpretation of biblical texts: the author's, the redactor's, the canon's (or subsection's), and the church's. He states that Christian exegetes often fail to consider the Jewish contexts for interpreting biblical texts. For example, it is not the Reformation and Enlightenment that forged Christian interpretation but rather Auschwitz that has shaped the Jewish context of meaning for the present.[25]

However, one should note that Levenson's essay on the Jewish rejection of biblical theology was already seriously dated by the time of its first writing. Biblical theology since the 1960s has radically changed in its paradigms, compositions, and understandings. Instead, what we find in his essay is a view of biblical theology that stands closer to Eichrodt than its multiple expressions for the past half century. At a time when feminism, liberation theology, and postcolonialism were already significantly shaping biblical theology, his views not only ignore these developments but make his own position largely irrelevant. He does not take into consideration the multitude of contexts proposed by postcolonialism, feminism, literary approaches, and postmodernism. In addition, he even ignores Jewish contributions of theology, some of which are biblical in character, that were already clearly present in the 1980s.

One other important Jewish voice that merits a hearing in this present essay is that of Marvin Sweeney,[26] who has argued vigorously in making the case for a Jewish theology of the Bible. Sweeney notes that Jewish biblical scholars have been more interested in philology and historical reconstruction than in the theology of the Hebrew Bible, which has been, until now, an essentially Christian undertaking. However, while noting the hesitancy of some Jews to participate in this endeavor, he suggests we are witnessing a change among Jews. However, one of the most difficult challenges to making this an enterprise for both Jews and Christians is that of the different canons. Protestants have the following subsections: Pentateuch, the Historical Books, the Poetic and Wisdom Books, and the Prophetic Books. This structure suggests a look to the future for the fulfillment provided by Jesus Christ and the primitive church. The Jewish Tanakh, by contrast, has three parts: the Torah, the Prophets, and the Writings. This canonical arrangement suggests that Torah is the basis for life and moral action. And, in ending with the Chronicles, the Tanakh sees a restored Judaism as the fulfillment of history, ever open to new and important developments. Thus, these two different perspectives on canon, Sweeney indicates, color the way theology is undertaken.

CLASSICAL APPROACHES TO BIBLICAL THEOLOGY AND HERMENEUTICS[27]

A Systematic and Thematic Approach to Old Testament Theology and Hermeneutics

Walter Eichrodt (1890–1978), a colleague of Barth's at Basel, published the first section of his *Theology of the Old Testament* at the time Hitler assumed the role of chancellor of Germany (1933). Eichrodt's Old Testament theology in the years that followed became one of the classics of Old Testament theology. He sought to overcome the stagnation of Old Testament theology that was sought through the proof-texting method of orthodoxy and the historicism that made Israelite theology nothing but a compilation of themes. Casting aside the ahistorical use of the Old Testament by dogmatic theology, Eichrodt makes the successful transition from the history of Israelite religion to writing a theology of the Old Testament. He constructs, not a historical development of Israelite theological themes, but rather a systematic theology based on a cross section of the Old Testament. The center (*Mitte*) of this theology was the covenant. For him Old Testament theology witnessed the eruption of the kingship of God into human history. Israelite religion, which regarded biblical theology as divine revelation, may be divided into national, prophetic, and Jewish-legal religions. However, these may be discovered only by doing a cross section of the Old Testament that may be obtained through examination of Israelite faith in a systematic summary. The three circles related by covenant are God and the people of Israel, God and the world, and God and humanity.

This does not mean that Eichrodt dismissed the discipline of history. He set forth the view that Old Testament theology was in part a historical discipline that could point to the characteristic features of ancient Israelite existence. The history of Israel and the faith of Old Testament theology were closely to cohere. This was accomplished by placing each of the major theological themes within the content of the history of religion, allowing him to point to the plurality of understandings. As a Christian, Eichrodt also considered the Old Testament as essential for demonstrating the unity of the Bible and its theology. Overall, then, Eichrodt pointed to the legitimacy of the Old Testament as a discipline in a commanding way and gave an important place to its role in Christian hermeneutics. Yet it was still tied to history and firmly entrenched within the ancient Near Eastern context. What he achieved in addition was a way of finding unity within an evolving religion and its faith that underwent continual change.

The History of Tradition in Old Testament Theology and Typology

Gerhard von Rad's *Old Testament Theology* put into theological categories the themes of the method of tradition of history developed in Germany by Albrecht Alt and Martin Noth. Hermeneutically, this means revelation occurs within the "history or development" of traditions of faith. These traditions are expansions, according to von Rad, of themes articulated in confessions of faith, the earliest of which is Deut 26:5-9.[28] Surprisingly, however, von Rad abandons his Old Testament understanding of traditions by using typology in order to address the connection between the Old and New Testaments. For von Rad, tradition history contains three hermeneutical moves that are related: typology, promise-fulfillment, and reactualization. While acts of salvation were unrepeatable, once-for-all events, von Rad concluded that the events of Old Testament salvation history became the prototypes for the New

Testament's corresponding antitypes.[29] This means that salvific events in the Old Testament pointed beyond themselves to acts of redemption in the future, most important the Christ-event. Von Rad used the promise-fulfillment scheme to argue that the early event achieved an ever greater and more significant fulfillment, until the Christ-event provided the ulti-mate culmination of history.[30] This allows the Christian to read the Old Testament as a "book of ever increasing anticipation."[31] All of this means that the typological formulation of these themes foreshadows the final salvation history to which the New Testament gives testimony.[32]

Von Rad saw this hermeneutic as intrinsic to the Old Testament itself, since there were ever-new redemptive acts and fulfillments. The commu-nity of God always lived between the now and the not yet, in anticipa-tion of later, even grander fulfillments that resided still in the future. God was not held captive by the past but was ever active, willing and able to effectuate new acts of salvation in the present and future.[33]

Building on his teacher's (von Rad's) traditions history approach, Hartmut Gese has remarked that the mutual relationship between the two Testaments is essential to the task of biblical theology.[34] He points to the shortcomings of von Rad's biblical hermeneutics, including allegory, typology, and promise and fulfillment, although he seeks to continue von Rad's traditions history approach. The Bible is a continuum of two Testaments, and one cannot ignore the Apocrypha and other collections of the text including the Pseudepigrapha. For Gese, the canon is open-ended and continues beyond the Masoretic Text and the New Testament, something that is apparent in a variety of early Jewish and Christian communities. This means, of course, that revelation continues beyond the variety of early canons.

Biblical Theology, the History of Israelite Religion, and Hermeneutics

In Germany, many biblical theologians recently have used modernist interpretations of the history of religions as a way to resolve the tensions between history and theology. This tension was clearly articulated in Gabler's inaugural address at the University of Altdorf (1787).[35] Biblical theology, in his view, was to be a comprehensive description and sum-mary of biblical views that were set forth in chronological order regard-less of their innate theological value. "Pure" biblical theology was a compendium in which biblical theology provided views and understandings that were universal and divinely sanctioned. "Pure" biblical theology thus provided the foundation for the dogmatic theology of the church.

Beginning, then, with Gabler's historical understanding, historical criticism, the history of Israelite religion, and biblical theology assumed a decidedly historical cast that included both romanticism and positivism as their philosophical underpinnings. For the past two centuries, the debate between the tasks of simply describing the history of Israelite religion and the shaping of biblical theology has continued with one, then the other, gaining the upper hand, but rarely achieving a satisfactory compatibility. One was thought to exclude by its very nature the other.[36]

The appearance of the two-volume history of Israelite religion by Rainer Albertz has raised once again the significant differences between Old Testament theology and the history of Old Testament Theology.[37] Albertz rejects Old Testament theology as a self-contained enterprise and insists on an uncompromising history of religions approach to understand the development of ancient Israelite religion. The two methods cannot be totally separated, for Old Testament theology results ultimately in being a presentation of the religious ideas of ancient Israel.[38]

Albertz in the introduction to his two-volume religion of ancient Israel sets forth his basic methodological assumptions in concise fashion.[39] He asserts that the history of religions approach has more value for understanding the Old Testament than does Old Testament theology. These assumptions include: (1) the history of religions approach must have a historical construction devoid of "dogmatic principles of division and selection"; (2) this approach must allow later Judaism and Christianity to participate in the investigation. Terms like "Hebraism" are to be excised, along with the devaluations of the law as over against extolling the high point of prophetic religion; (3) this method is not a mere intellectual history of ideas but points instead to Israelites, both men and women, in their sociohistorical context; (4) this approach places side by side a political and a social history of Israel in order to determine the ideologies of those whose interests were at stake in certain beliefs and practices and to admit that there were substantive changes over the centuries; (5) the history of religions sets up a dialectical model in which the different, pluralistic views of the Hebrew Bible are brought into play; (6) this approach supports dialogue with non-Christian religions and does not attempt to formulate the uniqueness and thus the superiority of one religion over against another; and (7) the method must evaluate the postexilic period more appropriately and refrain from describing it as a decline, a Christian judgment that often has obviated dialogue between Jews and Christians.[40] It is also clear from reading Albertz that he contributes several other important assertions to this discussion. One major area of contention between the two is the making of value judgments. For Albertz, all scholars, including those engaging in the discipline of the history of religion, cannot be totally objective.[41] However, there must be controls established that keep the investigation from sinking into a subjective quagmire. Data must be brought into view and evaluated in an objective manner to set forth the dominant features of Israelite religion. While the historian of religion is not kept from making affirmations of truth about the normative, he or she still does not allow church dogmatics to influence the selection and evaluation of data for the reconstruction of Israelite religion. Albertz is critical of systematic presentations of Old Testament theologies, doubting there is any way of describing Israelite religion in a similar way in spite of Eichrodt's efforts to do so. It is extremely difficult, if not impossible, to discover any system for Old Testament theology that corresponds to Israelite religion. This is seen by the continuing failure to find a "center" for any systematic formulation.

It is important to note that Albertz does not withdraw from questions of Israel's religious relevance for the contemporary world. For him, the contrary is true. He argues that the history of religions allows for approaching theological controversies in the church that might well lead to a solution by noting that the religious history of Israel and early Christianity provides important insights into similar problems today. On theological grounds, the history of religions, more so than biblical theology, offers insight into problems of contemporary import.

While his positions have provoked considerable controversy,[42] Albertz asserts that these two disciplines share a great deal in their respective treatments of the Hebrew Bible. The scholar participates in both disciplines, although with different objectives defined by the purposes of each. Indeed, the history of religion provides Old Testament theology with insights and understandings that it otherwise would not be possible to obtain.[43]

Rudolf Bultmann and New Testament Hermeneutics[44]

The most important New Testament theologian of the twentieth century, who brought together the history of religions and theological hermeneutics in his numerous influential writings, was Rudolf Bultmann.

The major features of Bultmann's theology have been set forth above by Morgan. Bultmann's call to demythologize the New Testament is his key hermeneutical principle, for this allows the gospel, stripped of its mythological trappings, to address the contemporary church. Like Barth, Bultmann sought to proclaim the saving act of God in Christ, but this required the removal of the prescientific cosmologies of the ancient Jewish and Greek worlds. The kerygma, which he defined as "the message of God's decisive act in Christ,"[45] makes it possible for modern hearers to encounter the Word, and through faith, to appropriate and live an authentic life.[46] However, while he agreed with Barth's critique of liberalism and its limiting Christianity to morality and belief in steady progress, he could not agree with his largely uncritical acceptance of the biblical text, including its mythology. For Bultmann, faith that endorses the worldview of the New Testament "has not grasped the hiddenness and transcendence of divine action and . . . seeks God's act in the sphere of what is worldly."[47] In order for Bultmann accurately to translate the mythical language of the Bible, he relied heavily on a philosophy that deals "scientifically" with human existence rather than with natural science.[48] Bultmann noted, "What is involved here, is not only the criticism that proceeds from the world picture of natural science, but also—and even more so—the criticism that grows out of our self-understanding as modern persons."[49] Because Bultmann thinks that we cannot say God acts in the physical world without mistakenly "objectifying" God (that is, treating God like any human object), the interpretive task is to question what the text is saying about human existence. Theology, for Bultmann, is intimately tied to anthropology. Comparable to existentialism enabling humans to escape inauthenticity, Bultmann viewed the gospel as the liberation of humanity from fallenness. While humans may differentiate themselves from nature and perceive it as truly other, they cannot escape historical existence. History cannot be observed "objectively" in the sense used in the natural sciences, for every word spoken about history is at the same time said about the one who speaks.[50]

For Bultmann, the Old Testament must be proclaimed as the Word directed to humans so that it becomes a constituent of faith.[51] In presenting the Old Testament in a genuinely historical way, it enables humans to learn from the past those things that concern and disturb them. In so doing, it seeks to reactualize the understanding of human existence expressed in the Old Testament in order to gain an understanding of modern existence. Nevertheless, Bultmann contrasted the view of life expressed in the Old Testament with the Christian view under the antithesis: *Law and Gospel*. This means the Old Testament is the concrete expression of the demanding will of God. While Old Testament human beings stand under the divine demand, New Testament humans stand under divine grace, which accepts them as sinners. This demand of the divine will is the presupposition for existence under grace, making the Old Testament but the presupposition of the New. Christ becomes the end of the law. Even so, the Old Testament consists of documents that depict a history that is not our own. Rather, with Christ these become obsolete.

Most troubling is Bultmann's basic characterization of the Old Testament as the law, viewed through the eyes of Paul and Luther. The Old Testament allows humans to become aware of their nothingness and the consequential despair that obtains. This state of inauthentic life can be transformed only by the acceptance of the kerygma that issues from the eschatological reality of the Christ-event. The interpretation of the Old Testament enables humans to question their own self-understanding and to realize that their redemption comes, not from their own actions, but rather by faith in Christ. The salvific character of the Christ-event is not a historical list of God's saving acts for Israel articulated in the Old Testament or a group of laws requiring strict adherence. Rather, the saving event of Christ is the Word of God, grounded in divine grace, which enables modern believers to experience salvation. Christ is the ultimate and final eschatological act of divine redemption that leads to an end of one history and the beginning of a new one. Thus, for the church the history of Israel is a closed chapter, a movement from divine wrath and the historical events of salvation based on God's transmission of the law to Israel to a new history of God's forgiveness actualized by grace. The faith of the church seizes the Old Testament, understanding it as provisional and limited. It is only the Christ-event that allows the Old Testament to be heard. But this means that in the true sense, the Old Testament cannot be God's word. It becomes revelation only by being viewed through the lens of the kergyma. The salvation, prophecies, and laws of the Old Testament are provisional and only now receive their true meaning in the appropriation of the Christian faith. The elements of the Christ-event were portrayals of the Jewish hope for the future. Christ speaks in the Old Testament only when it presents the promise of what will become the proclamation of the good news.

THE ADVENT OF LITERARY APPROACHES TO BIBLICAL THEOLOGY[52]

More recent literary studies have questioned many of the assumptions of historical criticism's efforts to capture the meaning of texts. These approaches are based on the idea that the Bible is composed of literature, and, as such, should be read in ways similar to other literary works. A large variety of literary methods have been taken up by different biblical scholars who favor a literary approach over that of history. These ways of engaging the text offer hermeneutical insight that history can never do. Biblical literary critics make use of numerous theories and theorists: new criticism (Cleanth Brooks,[53] John Crowe Ransom[54]);[55] Russian formalism and its critics (Viktor Shklovskii,[56] M. M. Bakhtin);[57] reader-response theory (David Bleich,[58] Jonathan Culler,[59] and Umberto Eco[60]);[61] and speech-act theory (J. L. Austin[62]).[63] The literary approach to biblical theology focuses on individual pieces of literature in the Bible and moves away from a systematic articulation of its basic theological ideas shaped by the original social and historical contexts and by the new context of its interpreters in the present. Important questions that arise include: Why was the text written? How does the text's form contribute to its meaning? What purposes did the author have in mind for the text? Or, alternatively, eschewing the emphasis on the author and his or her location, how did (or does) the text invite its readers to participate in the text itself? Thiselton notes that the application of literary theory to biblical interpretation is one of the most important developments of the last third of the twentieth century in the study of the Bible and biblical theology, even though some scholars either remain hostile to it or operate as if it had not occurred.[64]

Narrative Criticism

Narrative criticism is a particularly interesting literary approach, because it has been used by theologians and biblical scholars to articulate the theology or better the theologies of the Bible. One of its defining features is that it finds within the text an "implied author," a "narrative," and an "implied reader." The identity of the reader helps us distinguish narrative criticism from related fields. Whereas rhetorical criticism is concerned with how a document affected original readers, reader-response criticism places emphasis on the reader as the key contributor to the meaning of a text, and deconstruction is concerned with the ideal reader who can decipher the work's codes. However, narrative criticism is concerned with the reader who is "implied" by the text. The text itself determines what this reader knows, and this knowledge serves the story's emplotment, enabling its meaning to take full effect.

One may place the theologies of story into two broad areas. Theology and literature pursues the interaction between religious meaning and modern literature, while theology as literature focuses on biblical stories themselves and places their features within the narrative character of theology.[65] The second area has been especially prominent in literary treatments of biblical theology.[66]

Simply defined, theological narrative is "discourse about God in the setting of story."[67] Narrative theologians strongly censure biblical scholars' adoption of systematic theology's strong dependence on philosophical paradigms to approach questions of "truth," to conceptualize beliefs in discursive language, to identify a unifying center, and to discuss themes of belief at the expense of ignoring the nature and character of narrative.[68]

While there are a variety of distinctions among literary scholars, there are several common features.[69] The key insight is, of course, the recognition of the fundamental importance of narrative as a subject of theological inquiry. Narrative is indispensable in the presentation of the characterization of God and the formation of religious themes, including particularly divine action in history and individual existence as unfolded in the plots of stories. Particular emphasis is also placed on the different types and functions of narratives.

Biblical Narrative as "History-like"

Influenced by Erich Auerbach,[70] the Yale school's narrative theology, initiated especially by Hans Frei and developed by George Lindbeck and then by the Duke ethicist Stanley Hauerwas, has presented an approach to biblical hermeneutics in the form of "story." In his now classic volume, *The Eclipse of Biblical Narrative*,[71] Frei analyzed the hermeneutical difficulties presented by traditional historical criticism and proposed recapturing the older hermeneutical appropriation of the church, that is, retelling the Christian story and the individual narratives that comprised it. This precritical reading was not only doctrinal, as viewed by the doctors of the church at the time (the pre-Enlightenment period), but also literal, historical, and revealing of the divine word and action. The Christian story, from Genesis to Revelation and the end of time, was the "real world,"[72] thus removing any distance between the reader and the text.[73]

The misfortune for the church, hermeneutically speaking, was the development of historical criticism, beginning with the Enlightenment, which led to the distance between present history and story. The scholarly, critical history replaced the precritical reading of the biblical story, removing the sense of actuality and even the possibility of revelation.

What this meant for Frei was the loss of both the "history-like" quality of biblical narrative and the Bible's reality and unity. In constructing a new hermeneutic, he concludes the Bible contains "history-like," realistic narratives, which should be read on their own terms and not evaluated as to whether they refer to real, historical events or to generalized moral teachings and universal truths.[74] The reference of the story is internal, not external (i.e., actual history or systematic doctrines of faith) to its literary form.

Thus, for Frei narrative becomes the means for the expression and affirmation of faith. Taking a page from Hans-Georg Gadamer,[75] he argues that his understanding of hermeneutics seeks to merge the readers' own stories with the larger story of the Christian faith. This convergence allows readers to make sense of their own lives. Indeed, this process of engagement and merger becomes the means by which Christ is encountered.[76]

The Close Reading of Biblical Narrative

Important for biblical interpretation since the 1980s is the paradigm[77] of new criticism, sometimes called "close reading,"[78] which appeared initially in American literary circles during the 1930s. The important emphases are, first, viewing the biblical text as an object of aesthetics and meaning, and not concentrating on the author and his or her intention or self-perceived meaning; and second, recognizing that texts possess numerous cultural fields of reference that affect their meaning. Even so, the specificity of a text's meaning, not widely diffused cultural values that may be present in its language, is the object of interpretation.

Characterization, the development of plot, important themes and motifs, the determination of mood, literary structure, the point of view, repetition, and the interaction of dialogue and narration are important elements of close reading. Biblical narrative is also replete with numerous techniques, including irony, satire, paradigmatic type scenes, repetition, and even flashbacks.[79] Robert Alter correctly notes that biblical historians have often missed the literary features of narrative in interpreting the biblical sources. For him it is the artistry of biblical narrative that draws its careful readers into the world of the text and redescribes reality.[80] Prose fiction becomes the means by which sacred history is hermeneutically actualized. Entering the world of this narrative fiction, readers may become transformed.

Metaphorical Theology

Another literary approach that provides a lens for hermeneutical insight into the biblical text is metaphorical theology. By necessity, language about God is metaphorical.[81] Metaphor interfaces two distinct objects (tenor and vehicle) within a sentence or saying.[82] The tenor is the principal subject that is conveyed by a vehicle, or secondary subject.[83] The vehicle, better known than the tenor, describes the latter, which is obscure. Thus the vehicle though this interaction gives some new insight into the tenor. Metaphors become especially important in construing God. These include God as the Divine Warrior, the Judge, the Redeemer (or *gô'êl*), and the Lover. These vehicles become ways of understanding the mysterious God who serves as the tenor.

McFague reminds us that metaphors construct a tension between the "is" and the "is not."[84] While there is similarity, there is also difference, meaning that a literal interpretation is wrongheaded. Finally, metaphors after frequent use in a culture have a tendency to become sterile, even dead, requiring then the creation of new and provocative ones.

Ricoeur asserts that the absurdity inherent in metaphors is a "strategy of discourse" that destroys the literal meaning of a statement and transforms it into a meaningful contradiction that allows for new perspectives to emerge.[85] Compelling metaphors even allow the hearer/reader to be transformed.[86] While frequently encountered, metaphors lack "steno-meanings" that are accepted by all members of a culture. Inevitably, metaphors include a range of possible understandings.[87]

The Artistry of Imagination[88]

A literary concentration on imagination has offered a rather innovative way to engage in biblical hermeneutics in the construction of contemporary faith. While imagination refers to the capacity of the conscious and unconscious mind to create basic images,[89] it may be understood as the means by which perception and thought or sensation and conception are experienced that lead to insight and its articulation.[90] As an act of creativity, imagination may present mimetic portrayals of an object or subject. When applied to theology, imagination sets forth images of the mysterious "God," who is not known by ordinary sense perceptions. Amos Wilder has correctly observed that people are more motivated by images than ideas. The way lives are conducted and goals pursued are grounded in the imaginative construal of reality and our place within it.[91]

The Intersection of Narrative History and Narrative Fiction[92]

A theologian and philosopher who provides a significant role for the imagination is Paul Ricoeur. His objective is a complete narrative hermeneutics, and it is his work that has provided significant insights to the hermeneutical quest for biblical theology and its input in contemporary theology. Especially insightful for biblical hermeneutics is his comparison of narrative fiction with narrative history, for he overcomes many of the limitations inherent in Frei's understanding of biblical narrative and its presumed difficulties with theological insights. Where Ricoeur disagrees with Frei is the important matter of truth.[93]

The critical problem raised by Frei is the question of meaning and reference. For Frei stories hold meaning by reference to their internal operation. The story is the meaning. They do not hold meaning by reference to something that is external to their own narrative structures. While narrative theologians and literary critics argue the Bible should be interpreted according to literary, not historical, canons, historical critics examine the Bible to reconstruct the history of Israel that resides outside the text. Their narrative history replaces biblical narratives. These two groups of scholars also disagree over what is true: something that has happened historically as opposed to the validity of an idea or event by reference to the internal workings of a narrative.

Ricoeur offers a way out of this impasse by recognizing the important role that imagination plays in both types of narrative.[94] His argument is that narrative history and narrative fiction have something in common at the *level of sense*, that is, the form of the story. Where they differ is at the level of reference. Is the reference a perceived "fact" or an invention?

Historical narrative refers to events outside the narrative in ways that fictional narrative does not. For Ricoeur, the unity of historical and fictional narratives is found in the plot: events and experiences are sequenced and placed in clusters of related configurations. Not only do people react to events that reveal their character; the results of plot lead to climax and conclusion.

Ricoeur also suggests that history and fiction intersect at the point of the historical nature of humanity. Not only do humans live in history, they are history. Their nature is radically historical, but that reality comes to expression only when they organize their experiences in the form of narrative. Thus, in narrative history, the attempt is made to describe the human world in ordinary discourse with the use of data and interpretation. By contrast, narrative fiction attempts to redescribe the human world, that is, to suspend conventional language and re-create the world according to the symbolic structures of meaning within the story.

The Theology of Imagination[95]

It is Walter Brueggemann who has been most responsible for shaping a theology of the imagination in his treatment of Old Testament texts.[96] While distinguishing between reconstructing Old Testament theology and the enterprise of hermeneutics, he notes that while "the two are distinct tasks, they cannot be completely separated."[97] In two seminal essays,[98] Brueggemann introduces the theological task with two affirmations that have provided the impetus for Old Testament theology since the work of Gabler. First, the Old Testament is a normative collection of texts that moves the interpreter beyond critical analysis and historical location to contemporary hermeneutics that allows the text to speak to the church in the present age. Second, "A theological statement is not concerned with *the process and character of the text*, but with *the process and character of the God* met in the text."[99]

To understand both the process of bringing together historical past and contemporary present requires understanding the basic structure of Old Testament theology. This consists of a dialectic of "structure legitimation" and the "embrace of pain." The Old Testament not only imagines God participating in the "common theology" of its world (thus, "structure legitimation") but also struggling to be free from it by entering into the particularities of social interaction and conflict (i.e., the "embrace of pain"). Thus, for Brueggemann God is both "above the fray," that is, transcends the everyday struggles of human life, and participates "in the fray," that is, is present and active in Israel's historical experiences. These two fundamental polarities are present in a Christian theology of imagination.

The threat of structure legitimation, present in a theology of creation and providence, is that it may be abused by becoming the basis for total-itarianism, in which representatives of God in public institutions rule by fiat and not by compassion. Thus, it becomes a theology of the elite and powerful.[100]

To counter this possibility of constructing an authoritarian theology, the Old Testament also sets forth a theology of dissent that originates in the "embrace of pain." Since historical experience often fails to corre-spond to the expectations of structure legitimation, a theological crisis ensues, leading to the cry for liberation from suffering. Pain experienced in history and experience also leads to alienation from God.[101] Thus, this theology of dissent counters that of order and provides very different images of the pain that characterizes the nature of God and human exis-tence (cf. Job, the Laments, and the Prophets). Neither of these two alternative theologies cancels out the other but rather both exist in cre-ative tension.

In his Old Testament Theology,[102] Brueggemann sets forth his view of the Hebrew Bible, which he sees as a series of "story-worlds" that arise from the imagination of the writers and speakers of the Old Testament canon. His most important insight is his recognition that the language of the Hebrew Bible, issuing from the imagination, does not seek only to legitimate an existing social order but rather also deconstructs a debili-tating power structure. Theologically this means that Israel's God is sub-ject, not to the norms of classical theology, but rather operates according to the rules of the drama itself. Often this God acts in ways to counter the existing power structure when it becomes oppressive. Yet this divinity does not leave reality in the disarray of chaos. In shaping his own hermeneutic, Brueggemann sees Old Testament theology as part of a rev-olutionary struggle against the possession of goods, power, and control, and yet also offers a strategy that would enable global communities to sur-vive in a life-giving structure.

Using the metaphors of imagination and the grammar of faith, Brueggemann presents his theology by using the theme of a trial or court-room drama. He investigates the nature of God as revealed by Israel's tes-timony, countertestimony, unsolicited testimony, and embodied testimony. Brueggemann's key points in this work include the understanding that

Old Testament theology, while primarily a Christian enterprise, does not exclude hearing and giving authenticity to non-Christian voices, including Jewish ones. He adds that pluralism is a major characteristic that disallows any systematic presentation, that the cultural contexts of interpreters play an important role in interpretation, that voices from the margin in both scripture and the contemporary world are important to hear, that they must have a role in the world of authentic faith, that a "grammar of faith" construing God through various parts of speech takes precedence over ontology and acts of salvation, and that scripture is not to be demeaned by reading it only through the eyes of Christianity and the New Testament.

THEOLOGIES OF LIBERATION

Feminism[103]

Feminist theology became important in the 1960s in the context of the struggle for civil rights and the more intense efforts to undermine patriarchy. While there are common features in the numerous expressions of feminism, there is also significant diversity. Feminism is a consciousness emerging from identity constructed by place, experience, and gender. Early feminism targeted the evil of patriarchy and theologies, which failed to subvert misogyny and to take seriously women's issues and experiences. Some feminists like Mary Daly concluded the church was far too entrenched in patriarchy to dismantle sexism, with the result that her own efforts became secular. However, some later feminists have moved to a more positive and systematic presentation of key affirmations. Phyllis Trible, for example, attempted to recover the stories of women in the Bible in order to present either examples of those who struggled against and at times lessened the destructiveness of misogyny or who fell victim to the horrors of patriarchy. Other feminists, including Sallie McFague,[104] have drawn on Christian tradition to shape new theological possibilities for envisioning God, the human community, and the church. Then there are feminists, like Elizabeth Johnson, who reinterpret traditional theological doctrines to envision a feminine Godhead.[105] At present, feminism in various expressions is taking root in non-Western cultures and embracing new social and linguistic codes emerging from these different locations.

Feminism especially seeks to undermine sexism by means of a variety of strategies to effectuate social, economic, political, cultural, and religious change that will result in the recognition of the full humanity of women and their egalitarian participation in human institutions.[106] In religious discourse, feminism questions and subverts the interpretations of sexist male scholars and their misconstrual of history and the Bible. By recovering women's stories in the Bible and Christian tradition as well as those in the larger culture, patriarchy is suppressed.

Feminists, while noting that traditional theological language in the Bible is largely patriarchal (God is father, king, lord, and warrior), emphasize that God is beyond gender (male or female). Thus, metaphorical ways of talking about God include both male and female titles and names that are present in the text and the cultures from which it issued.[107] Inclusive language moves beyond the issue of speaking of God and seeks to embrace both male and female by authenticating genderless language. Thus, titles and pronouns of humans are abandoned in the description of a social reality that places women in subordinate roles.

Feminist Interpretations of History

It is possible to place feminist interpretation of the Bible into two types of expression: those that are historical and others that are literary. While Schüssler Fiorenza is critical of this bipolarity, since it represents to her a dualism that she seeks to dislodge from human thought, this approach to postmodern feminist biblical scholars remains, in my judgment, heuristically useful in understanding feminist biblical scholarship.[108] Feminist historians take two separate directions in interpreting Israelite religion, society, and biblical texts. The first direction involves recognizing the significance of women in Israelite and early Jewish history in order to attempt to recover their voices and roles in biblical history. At the same time, because so much of biblical knowledge has been produced by males, feminists are "suspicious" of past studies. These secondary studies may be cleansed of sexism by replacing them with feminist interpretations that are geared to discovering the place of women in the sociopolitical and religious world of ancient Israel, early Judaism, and primitive Christianity. To assist in this task, feminist historians include the importance of noncanonical texts and data from material culture that also reveals the important status and roles of women. It is impossible to shape a biblical theology that engages contemporary faith without considering patriarchy and feminism.[109]

A second bearing taken by feminist interpreters of scripture concentrates on the literary construction and meaning of texts. This approach often dispenses to a large degree with history, considering it to be a largely useless enterprise in liberating women. Since history has been written by males who have ignored women of the past, the historical approach has little to offer women. The male codes of reading the Bible, particularly those that privilege the interpretations of white Western men to the exclusion or even shameful debasing of feminist, womanist, egalitarian, postcolonial, and postmodernist ways of understanding and interpreting scripture, are inherently based on the patriarchal history of the (largely male) persons who not only wrote and redacted the Bible but also have been responsible for most of the modern histories of the primitive church.

We begin with feminist history. There are several biblical scholars who have shaped important historical methodologies and interpretations of the past and have gained significant attention because they not only foster historical interpretations that recapture the role of women but also offer key articulations of feminist hermeneutics in historiography and for theology. I shall mention only two: Elisabeth Schüssler Fiorenza and Carol Meyers.

In Memory of Her[110]

In the work of Elisabeth Schüssler Fiorenza, one discovers a rather different reading of early Christian history and theology than the ones constructed by males in western Europe and North America. Not since Karl Barth's *Der Römerbrief* appeared in 1919 to counter the dominant approach of the history of religions in biblical interpretation and to shape a new theological discourse in what became neo-orthodoxy has a book had the impact of her reconstruction of early Christianity.

In Memory of Her was published originally in 1983, and then revised and reissued in 1995. Here she lays out the features of a clearly articulated feminist critical method, a feminist model of historical reconstruction, and a feminist critical hermeneutic.

She contends her book has two essential purposes: the reconstruction of early Christian history as women's history to remember and reclaim their story and to reclaim this history as the events that have importance for both women and men in every contemporary social, political, religious, and geographical location. Self-consciously and openly, she conceives of herself as both a feminist historian and a feminist theologian. Patriarchy in the New Testament and white male elitism in contemporary New Testament interpretation are the two objects of her criticism. But her approach is not simply reactionary. Rather, she reshapes the nature of historiography and rediscovers the place of women in the primitive church.

She asserts that all interpreters are caught up in their own biases, partisan politics, and self-interests. This means that the tasks of historiography are referential, having been shaped by these frames of orientation. In addition, the frequent elimination of women in Eurocentric biblical interpretation has distorted the early history of the beginnings and expansion of early Christianity. Fiorenza also strongly contests the patriarchal authority of revelation avowed by church officials in post–Vatican II understandings of scripture. She engages the biblical texts by a hermeneutic that concludes not all texts in the canon are by necessity authoritative in the lives of women, including those who participate in the church. What she ultimately seeks is a historiography and a hermeneutic that enable contemporary women to unite in sisterhood with their women ancestors in the faith. This does not happen without struggle prior to the fullness of time when authentic discourse provides both meaning and direction for the church and the larger world. The New World comes, not with a whimper, but with the loud shout of captives set free.

In her historical reconstruction, Schüssler Fiorenza identifies the locus of revelation and therefore authority not in scripture but rather in the ministry of Jesus and the *ekklēsia* of the women who are called to become Jesus' disciples. The goal of the feminist critical method is to "break the silence" developed by androcentrism, which will result in the reconstruction of women's roles in the history of the origins and expansion of early Christianity. This suppression is obvious in such things as Luke's Gospel, where the origins of Christianity are almost totally a male enterprise. This and other examples of androgenous characterization of the early church are followed by the process of canonization, occurring during the time of significant conflict over the role of women in the primitive church. With the patriarchal supremacy that emerged from these conflicts, canonization led to the inclusion of some books that were largely patriarchal. This led to the doctrine of apostolic succession by which men of power and privilege exerted control over offices, liturgies, and doctrines. Alternative voices were silenced, including those of the

Montanists; gnostics of different kinds; women who pointed to Mary Magdalene, Salome, and Martha as belonging to the line of succession of disciples and apostles; and to prophetesses who continued to speak divine messages. Deuteropauline household codes placed women in roles of subjection. This antifeminist view continued into the church fathers (cf. especially Tertullian), whose polemics against women continued well into the third century. Women were responsible for the entrance of sin in the world through the fall, for the temptation of the angels who fell from heaven, and ultimately for the most damnable heresies. Patriarchy won this battle of the book in the history of primitive Christianity. The way to break this code of enforced silence is for feminist historians to do their work with a hermeneutics of suspicion to uncover male bias in the Bible and in the institutional church. Other voices, including those of heretics and noncanonical texts, must be heard critically and openly.

Schüssler Fiorenza then articulates her model of historical reconstruction that facilitates the rewriting of early Christianity. Historians no longer work naively with the positivistic philosophy of history designed to uncover the "facts." By giving birth to a new "unifying vision" born of the imagination, different philosophies of history are embraced, applied, and scrutinized. Her feminist model provides an important place for the voices of the disinherited to whom the gospel was preached and who formed the core of the early communities. A feminist historiography recognizes and delegitimates the developing patriarchalization of the Christian community. Women, including those who lived in the past, engaged in this assault on patriarchy, often to their peril. Hellenistic mystery cults, for example, were at times subversive of patriarchy in the household and the larger society. Yet these associations provided the contexts for women's symbolic deconstruction of patriarchy and independence. This also was found in expressions of early Christianity and Judaism, leading to their attraction of women who had been marginalized by society and family. Uncovering and deconstructing the patriarchal character of the hierarchic, male-centered Greco-Roman world both symbolically and actually provides a witness with which modern feminists can find common cause.

A Feminist Reconstruction of Early Christianity

Schüssler Fiorenza's identification of three salient points required of any feminist historian shapes this aspect of her work. These have significant implications for hermeneutics that seeks to align itself with the witnesses of the early church. The first is the problem posed by pluralism. Putting matters into two major possibilities, she asks if there are two very different understandings and practices concerning the role and place of women in the Jesus movement into the early second century of primitive Christianity.

Second, a problem that has perplexed and continues to occupy the attention of Christian theology and New Testament theologians is the reconstruction of the historical Jesus and the earliest beginnings of the Jesus movement. Since Christianity has placed its primary theological emphasis on Christology, how does this development historically take shape and what implications does it have on latter formulations of the church's varied understandings of this pivotal figure? Third, what is most difficult is encountering the vexing problem of the sparsity of texts about the lives of Jewish and Gentile women during the origins of primitive Christianity; and how is it possible to reconstruct their lives? Even more difficult is the realization that there are various views of women in these ancient texts. The turn to texts outside the New Testament confronts a vast array of literatures from different cultures and communities. When one adds the many thousands of epigraphic sources, the problem becomes even especially difficult.

The roles and places of women in Roman, Hellenistic, and Jewish communities in the first century C.E. are rather varied and unclear. At times this is due to pluralism in these various cultures. Thus, for example, what were the different views of women among Jewish sects, including the community at Qumran? Some very influential Wisdom and apocalyptic texts were especially misogynistic in their views of women (e.g., cf. Philo, Ben Sira, and the collection of Enoch texts). On the other hand, there are also texts that extol the heroism and virtues of women who held prominent social roles.[111]

The Jesus movement, in Schüssler Fiorenza's assessment, viewed humanity in terms of wholeness, not gender differentiation, meaning that all people—regardless of sexual identity, social class, and ethnic and racial difference—could participate in the new Israel and enjoy the common table fellowship that broke down these barriers. In the early movement, a community of equals shattered all gender and social barriers, including those caused by patriarchy.

One important view of Schüssler Fiorenza that has dramatic implications for New Testament theology and Christian hermeneutics is her representation of the "Sophia-God" of Jesus and the following of women who were counted among his closest disciples.[112] For Schüssler Fiorenza, the early Jesus traditions present a message of a gracious God in the image of divine Sophia (see Luke 7:35). Sophia is at first identified with God and then, later, with Jesus, since he originally understood himself as the prophet and child of Wisdom (cf. Matt 11:28-30). Her envoys, originally understood as John and Jesus, are persecuted and killed (Luke 13:34).

In Paul, however, Jesus becomes Sophia (see 1 Cor 1:24; cf. Phil 2:6-11; 1 Tim 3:16; Col 1:15-20; Eph 2:14-16; Heb 1:3; 1 Pet 3:18, 22; and John 1:1-14). Believers "in Christ" are possessed by God's spirit and the spirit of Wisdom. Faith becomes the basis for salvation, not works possible only for the well-to-do. In these texts, the Lord of the Jesus movement is no longer a prophet of divine Sophia but is now identified with divine Sophia herself. In the baptismal formula of Gal 3:28, the tension between the early Christian community and the larger society begins to be removed. This is noted in Paul's missionary activities with women who are among his colaborers: Prisca, Apphia, Phoebe, and Junia (apostle). Commended specifically for their laboring in the missionary efforts were Mary, Tryphaena, Tryphosas, and Persis. Euodia and Syntyche "raced" alongside Paul, while Phoebe was a minister to the community of Cenchreae. There were, in addition, missionary couples, including Prisca and Aquila and Andronicus and Junia. These women are not mentioned as wives," but rather are called colaborers with their husbands. An apocryphal text, "The Acts of Paul and Thecla," presents a woman missionary to whom as late as the third century women in Carthage appealed for their authority to teach.

Schüssler Fiorenza traces the steady rise of patriarchy in the faith and practice of the churches in the later communities. A theology of accommodation emerged in which churches adopted a patriarchal caste to find a more accepting place in the larger society of the empire. Even so, there are texts, especially Mark and John, that enable women to assume roles of apostolic and ministerial leadership. This leads to a clash of understandings about women that finally culminates in the patriarchy of most of the churches in the third and later centuries.

In her final section, "Toward a Feminist Biblical Spirituality: The Ekklēsia of Women," Schüssler Fiorenza speaks hermeneutically of a sisterhood that creates a means of empowerment for women leading to a discipleship of equals. This feminist community will no longer allow itself to be relegated to the margins of the church but rather, in solidarity with all the oppressed, will help form a new community destined to transform the world. She uses the term *ekklēsia* with new meaning to speak of egalitarian communities that make their own decisions in reshaping a just world.

Later, in *Miriam's Child and Sophia's Prophet*,[113] she constructs more graphically a feminist Christology that seeks to empower all marginals, victims, and oppressed peoples to oppose the dictatorship of capitalist Western nations whose lives of ease are built on the backs of those they subjugate and exploit. Two worlds stand before us: one of a radicalized democracy in which all participate to improve their lives; and one of a dictatorship of controlling and privileged nation states, whose policies advance the well-being of only a small percentage of the global population. A critical feminist liberationist hermeneutic seeks the promise of a radical democracy and economic justice for all. Her theoretical model, a "critical feminist liberationist hermeneutics," consists of four strategies. First, a hermeneutics of tradition rejects male, traditional interpretations of the Bible and theology that limit full participation of women and other marginals in the human image of God.

Second, the actualization of "memory" enables interpreters to discover biblical and nonbiblical sources for constructing discourse that opposes sexist narratives. Third, the evaluative procedure affirms the authentic and disconfirms the inauthentic in texts and interpretations. And fourth, the activity of the imagination recognizes the legitimacy of this gospel of inclusion through the participation of women in liturgy and ritual. In its full empowerment, this hermeneutic moves away from and dismisses the paradigm of the modern "malestream"[114] of tradition and replaces it with the new feminist consciousness that transforms all sociopolitical and religious realities into ones that liberate. This means that biblical theology is a "public deliberative discourse of the *ekklēsia*."[115] This discourse must be constructed by a pluriform community of all peoples, who are not differentiated on the basis of class, wealth, education, gender, and geography. Each member of this community must be free to speak in shaping the theological understanding of scripture. She writes:

> Biblical theology that understands itself as a politics of ekklēsia attempts to trace and revalorize the early Christian egalitarian traditions. At the same time it seeks to displace the politics and rhetorics of subordination and otherness that is inscribed in the "Pauline" correspondence with a politics and rhetorics of equality and responsibility. It conceives of early Christian writings as taking sides in the emancipatory struggles of antiquity and conceptualizes early Christian community as

a radical democratic assembly (ekklēsia) of differing theological voices and socio-rhetorical practices.[116]

This radical, democratic politics of equality sets forth a theology of the divine *politeuma*, or city of citizens that becomes its theological basis and structure. The kyriarchic power structures of elitist males vying for domination of the kingdom is resisted and defeated. This hermeneutic does not privilege elitist spokesmen, such as Paul, to define authoritatively and once and for all what is true or false theologically but rather turns to the victims whose voices may be rediscovered, if only in fragmented form, in the canon and other Christian writings. Finally, Schüssler Fiorenza fashions theology that engages and incorporates authentic discourse of other religions.

Remembering Eve: A Feminist Social History of Ancient Israel[117]

Carol Meyers's use of feminist historiography and "ethnoarchaeology"[118] to reconstruct ancient Israelite history and society, especially during the pre-state period, also pays rich dividends in discovering the roles of women in ancient Israel. While she does not engage in biblical theology in the sense outlined by Barr, her insights are of importance for the work of feminist biblical study and theological articulation.

Meyers's historical work is shaped by several basic factors regarding the gender roles of women in premodern societies, including those of ancient Israel and Judah. The fundamental principle is the recognition that there is no universal set of rules governing gender roles in these societies, for variation, at times significant, is present among human groups. Yet there are also several other important principles: all societies participate in the distribution of labor, including at times the consideration of gender. Thus women's roles vary from being primarily engaged in nurturing and child rearing to the physical labor required of subsistence farming to a combination of both. But especially interesting is the principle that the more involved women are in subsistence labor, the higher is their status. However, this begins to reverse itself after women reach a level of providing forty percent of the labor force.

Meyers's study of Iron Age I Israel's material culture, when combined with social science methodologies, aids in the understanding of pre-state, tribal society. On the basis of archaeological data construed through the method of ethnoarchaeology, Meyers contends there were three major tasks of households in this tribal constellation of social communities. The first was participation in military activities by largely male citizen warriors of clan villages whose subsistence economies were based on agriculture and the herding of small groups of cattle or sheep. When war was pursued, more responsibility for labor that led to the production of food and other essentials fell to women. While the goods and land of each household was owned by its family, the dominant male was the major authority. Second, land reclamation through the construction of terraces and cisterns and the removal of trees, shrubs, and stones was a collective effort of households. This required increased participation of women and older children in the workforce. And third, there were the actions necessary to enable a frontier society to transition from dependence on to independence from nearby Canaanite feudal city-states. Altogether, these household requirements produced, if not an egalitarian society regarding the dismissal of gender differentiation, the active participation of women in tasks necessary for the subsistence of familial households. This gave women greater status.

Theologically speaking, the increased status of women due to their participation in physical labor would explain a text like Gen 1–2, which emphasizes the equality of men and women in conceiving the image of God (1:26-28). Further, the emphasis on the worship of one deity did not allow for the introduction of numerous goddesses. Polytheism and the pairing of the gods and goddesses were replaced by an emphasis on the equality of men and women in early Israel. While the status of women declined significantly in Iron Age II Israel with the establishment of the state, this early emphasis on gender equality became a part of Israel's historical memory that was to shape part of its religious and social understanding.

Meyers's historical work offers an important contribution to biblical theology.[119] While the depiction of women in the creation narratives in Gen 1–3 may be more of an ideological depiction than a description of social reality, it still allows greater clarity about the continuing conflict of egalitarianism with the patriarchy of statehood ushered in by the Israelite monarchy.[120]

Literary Criticism and the Rhetoric of Language[121]

Another feminist scholar whose work has been important for construing Old Testament theology and its contemporary meaning is Phyllis

Trible. By means of rhetorical criticism, she has provided significant explanations of the Bible's literary force. She interprets a text by defining the boundaries of literary units (prose or poetry), revealing their component parts and structural patterns, and pointing to the literary techniques used in ordering the text's artistic composition. The focus of this interpretative method is placed on the literary text itself, not the narrator, the composer, the original audience, or later interpreters. For her, the literary artistry of a text construes its meaning.

Trible sees her interpretative work as that of a feminist theologian. In speaking about her understanding of feminism, Trible defines it rather broadly as a "critique of culture in light of misogyny."[122] This critique focuses on gender but it is extended, as is the work of Schüssler Fiorenza, to widen its scope to address larger "issues of race and class, psychology, ecology, and human sexuality."[123] Patriarchy, in its various social, cultural, and political manifestations, has damaged severely the bond of common humanity of all oppressed groups in the United States and indeed the entire globe. Thus, in a penetrating article on biblical theology, she writes that "feminism not only describes but convicts. It opposes the paradigm of domination and subordination in all forms, most particularly male over female, but also master over slave and humankind over the earth. Sex, race, class, and ecology intertwine as issues."[124]

In *God and the Rhetoric of Sexuality*, she touches on a variety of topics concerning justice and draws important theological insights from narratives, words, and poems, including creation and anthropology ("male and female" bear the *Imago Dei*, and *'âdâm* is not man, but rather "earth creature"), "compassion" (plural of *reḥem*, "womb"), the fall and the refusal to allow the expulsion from Eden to be the final word on the human condition, including the relationship between the sexes, the story of Ruth and Naomi in which two women "work out their own salvation" in a world of patriarchy, and the poem of Rachel's "weeping for her children" (Jer 31:15-22), in which Yahweh consoles the grieving mother by speaking of their future in a new creation. In that day, a new reality appears: the virile male is surrounded and protected by the feminine: the weeping mother, Rachel, Yahweh, the divine mother, and the daughter Israel, who surpasses the son. Indeed, each of these is highlighted in the strophes of the poem that for Trible is the new reality, artistically depicted, in which a woman (God, mothers, and humans) metaphorically embraces/protects the man.

Womanist Biblical Interpretation[125]

African American women, along with African women in other cultures, read the Bible differently from more-privileged, white European and American feminists. They and other ethnic women of marginalized peoples also will at times make use of the artistry of rhetoric and the theology of story in the shaping of their theological discourse. But more important is the focus on social context, especially that of the interpreter, in articulating both biblical and contemporary theology. The struggle against slavery, colonialism, and racism has shaped a different hermeneutic than that offered by most theologians who work with the Bible and contemporary faith. Even the black church has often engaged in patriarchy leading to the demeaning of African American women.

African American women identify with the women who are exploited and victimized in biblical narratives. For example, Hagar, the Egyptian (thus, African) concubine of Abraham, is seen as reflecting the experiences of African American women who were slaves and even after emancipation have continued to be marginalized not only by white society but even in a patriarchal black church. A "concubine" owned by Abraham, Hagar's labor, offspring, and body were his to claim and to control. Envied and maltreated by Abraham's "barren" wife, Sarah, Hagar takes her child, and, together, they flee into the wilderness. They survive through the compassionate oversight of God, and she even receives what seems to be the impossible promise that her son will be the founder of a great nation.[126] African American women also long with hopeful anticipation for salvation from a violent and uncaring world and church. Thus the God and the Savior who speaks of the redemption and release of the destitute, the maligned, the exploited, and the victims, who include in particular women, offers them hope in a world of shameful exploitation.

Renita Weems has written important works of narrative and literary criticism from a womanist perspective.[127] She takes up metaphorical literary analysis and theology in her study of the Prophets, Hosea in particular, but also Jeremiah and Ezekiel as well. Most convincingly, she shreds the superficial veneer of scholars' attempts to justify the actions of these abusive males and their mistreatment of women. She especially reveals the lurid fascination of these prophets with women's bodies and the dishonor done to shame them by the "men of God."

As a womanist scholar, she recognizes that interpretation takes shape within a framework of power that dispels the notion of "innocent" readings of the biblical text. Her book on Hosea and Gomer sets forth interpretative dimensions of her major topic, violence done to women. While chapter 1 describes the nature of metaphor, the more important chapter is the second, which sets forth the sociohistorical context of the metaphors of sexual violence within the interaction of dread and desire and the power structures of Israelite society and especially patriarchal marriage. The third chapter raises the theological questions of the portraits of God, which are captured by prophetic metaphors. And most important for our work on hermeneutics, the fourth chapter raises question of how to engage these texts that write of the brutal actions taken against marginalized women. Yet not all is hopeless, for behind and in front of her writings is the anticipation of gender relationships based on shared love and loyalty.

The prophets use feminine metaphors to describe the social and religious infidelity of Israel and Jerusalem as promiscuous women who deserve the violence done to them. Real women and their presentation as theological metaphors in the Old Testament portray the daughters of Israel as victims of predatory behavior, rape, dishonor, and mutilation. Hosea, Jeremiah, and Ezekiel stimulated through their language the sexual fantasies of their male audiences and their power over women, marriage, and family. They contributed to the frequently encountered cultic view of women as polluted and requiring a ritual of cleansing following menstruation, as sexually deviant, and as dangerous to males.

To deconstruct the authority of these and other insidious texts in the Bible that dishonor and do violence to women, we as readers must recognize how significant they have been in shaping our own social world. The prophets' use of sexual metaphors is not to go unchallenged. While they may have led to the "shock of recognition" among men in Israel who saw themselves as faithless women, they also have assisted in helping provoke a sexist social, political, and religious reality that must now be confronted and rejected.

Mujerista Biblical Interpretation[128]

Another type of feminist interpretation coming from the margins is *mujerista* biblical interpretation. The term "*mujerista*" is an "invented" word, although it obviously echoes the Spanish word *mujer* (woman). Thus, *mujerista* theology is Latina "women's theology," but even more it is Latina "women's liberation theology." This theology sets forth a theological basis for Latinas to speak from their marginal experiences in the United States. These voices cry out for a liberating praxis that enables them to engage in the struggle (*en la lucha*) to bring an end to oppression and to enable Latinas to be regarded as valued human beings in their communities. *La lucha* is the struggle to end oppression, not only of Latinas and the larger Latino community, but also of all marginalized persons and groups in the world. This theology provides a model that may be used by all victimized peoples in obtaining the "space" they need for existence with dignity.

The oppression of Latinas began, of course, with the conquistadors who decimated the native populations and enslaved those who survived. And it has continued with Latinas not only exposed to racism and patriarchy from the dominant white male controlled social order but also to the machismo of Latino men. In their history in the Americas, Latinas have developed through their religious experience, nurtured particularly in the Roman Catholic Church, a popular piety that centers on the heritage of women who have struggled to survive, some of whom became saints, and on the Virgin Mary in her various appearances (e.g., "Our Lady of Guadalupe"). The Bible is a second resource, but the Latina knowledge of scripture has often been limited to what they have heard in their churches. Isasi-Díaz explains that Latinas in America understand the "Word of God" to be, not scripture, but rather the belief that God is in their midst in their struggles. This is the experience, then, that provides the framework for *mujerista* theology.

In her book on *mujerista* theology, Ada Maria Isasi-Díaz sets forth the major features of this woman's theology from a Latina perspective. First, this theology gives Latinas the right to name themselves in ways that provide identity and the conceptual framework used in thinking, understanding, and relating to others. Thus she coins the word *mujerista*, which expresses Latina theology as differentiated from feminism. Latinas have a distaste for feminist theology, because it does not seek to share power among all groups, regardless of differences, and because it seems to promote, at least among white middle-class women, benefits for only some women, often at the expense of other marginalized peoples, including the poor, regardless of gender, and people of color. Thus, "a *mujerista* is someone who makes a preferential option for Latina women, for our struggle for liberation." *Mujeristas* engage in this struggle, not as individuals, but as members of a Latino community who are called to bring forth a new anthropology of women and men who are made in the image of God and to repudiate anything that degrades them.

Second, *mujerista* theology is not only a systematic articulation of faith but also a liberating praxis, that is, "reflective action that has as its goal liberation." This theological praxis enables Latinas to understand and appreciate who they are and seeks to influence mainline theologies that undergird the largely non-Latino churches in the United States. This theology seeks to enable Latinas to discover God in their community and especially in their struggles.

Third, *mujerista* theology seeks to enable Latinas to envision their future, their new community, and their common values in ways that lead to their proleptic realization in Latina life. This theology seeks to assist Latinas to recognize how much they have internalized victimization and thus are obligated to understand that self-effacement is not a virtue.

Fourth, *mujerista* theology stresses the importance of social location in the doing of theology. Isasi-Díaz explains that the "place" involves Latinas' *mestizaje* and *mulatez*, that is, "our condition as racially and culturally diverse people" and as people living in two cultures, Hispanic and Anglo, in the United States. This racial and cultural diversity is reflected in the struggle to live a new future into being, one in which boundaries are removed. Finally, these terms refer to both pluralism and to Latinas' social location in the U.S., one that embraces the past and views the future as one in which all people and peoples may participate.

Fifth, this theology stresses the perspective that issues out of Latino shared experiences and the community in which life is lived. *Lo cotiadiano*, the life experiences of Latinas, has not only a descriptive implication but also a hermeneutical purpose. Thus Latinas see the world in ways that are different from non-Latinas. *Lo cotiadiano* has to do with Latinas, struggling as marginalized people, who construct themselves theologically in regard to meaning and identity as well as to the larger world. While it is not normative, liberation becomes the value that construes the legitimacy and truthfulness of certain beliefs and actions over against those that are oppressive and destructive to the community of humankind. *Lo cotiadiano* is subversive of oppressive structures, whether social or theological, and serves as a reminder that Latinas are not the object of *mujerista* theology but rather its subjects and more especially its agents.

Mujerista justice involves a variety of factors. The objective is not the construction of theory but rather acting in ways that will bring about a righteous social order. Isasi-Díaz places emphasis on reflective action. Thus, while rational thinking is involved, the goal is to establish justice through actions that are largely communal. She places her emphasis on contextualization in understanding that justice is a concrete reality existing within the lives of real people. The institution of justice comes through struggle within the Latina context. Thus, sociopolitical and economic understanding of the Hispanic community is essential in understanding and then devising a strategy to obtain justice.

The Latino family is changing because increasingly women are unwilling to live with abusive men. The patriarchal family is slowly dying. The features of *machismo* (patriarchy) and *hembrismo* (passivity projected onto women) are dissolving. In the family, women have been able to claim their voice and to influence larger Latino society. The Latino community is an extension of the family, so that as the family changes for the good, while maintaining the values of Latinas, the larger society is to be transformed for the better.

How, then, does *mujerista* theology approach biblical interpretation? And beyond that, what would a *mujerista* biblical theology look like? Since the majority of Latinas are practitioners of the religion of their conquerors, the *conquistadores*, that is, Roman Catholicism, there is not a strong tradition in the reading of the Bible. However, the fact that more recently Latinos and Latinas are joining Protestant churches where the Bible is read indicates the need for all churches to understand a *mujerista* interpretation of the Bible.

Once again *la lucha* ("struggle") plays a key role in the Latina reading of the Bible. The difficulty of understanding the Bible and the critical methods used to interpret it can be an overwhelming challenge for many Latinas. This is one reason why spirituality, praying to God, and worship have usually taken priority over reading the Bible. Even so, struggle is to serve as the lens through which the Bible is understood. Thus, the struggle of women and other marginalized people in biblical narratives becomes especially important for Latina readers. Also important is the theme of liberation within stories of survival and of release from bonds of oppression in Egypt and, later, Babylonia. The Bible is understood as inspired only when it contributes to the struggle for liberation. It helps in shaping the *proyecto histórico*, that is, the desired future in which Latinas will participate as God continues to bring about the "kin-dom" in which all share. This future involves the rejection of the present as a time of oppression and domination by the wealthy and powerful. Biblical eschatology helps Latinas construct a future in which the injustices of the present will give way to a reality of well-being and righteousness. The Bible also is used by Latinas to discover hope and inspiration, not to find the word of God that tells them what to do. The people in the Bible who struggled, including Jesus, become those with whom Latinas identify. Their struggles and the struggles of their communities allow Latinas to come into contact with those who have had similar experiences. Latinas learn to enter into conflict with other oppressed and exploited groups in order that they may overcome the domination they have experienced.

Thus, for *mujerista* theology, the word of God (*palabra de Dios*) is not the Bible but rather the faith that God is a participant in daily struggles. It is an incarnation in social life that pursues a transformation of the world. What Latinas have to say about the Bible is to be heard, not dismissed. Their biblical interpretation allows them to determine what it is that the church believes in contrast to interpretations of the hierarchical church that are forced upon them.

Postcolonial Feminist Theology

Describing herself as an Asian postcolonial feminist theologian, Kwok Pui-lan, like Brueggemann, places significant emphasis on the imagination in constructing biblical theology and contemporary hermeneutics. She writes:

> The term *dialogical imagination* describes the process of creative hermeneutics in Asia. It attempts to convey the complexities, the multidimensional linkages, and the different levels of meaning that underlie our present task of relating the Bible to Asia. This task is dialogical, for it involves ongoing conversation among different religious and cultural traditions. . . . Dialogical imagination attempts to bridge the gaps of time and space, to create new horizons, and to connect the disparate elements of our lives into a meaningful whole.[129]

Thus postcolonial feminists must decolonize the mind and the soul, not only of their patriarchal exploiters, but also of themselves. To do this they cannot simply rely on the very different experiences of white women in the West but must come to an understanding and appreciation of themselves as Asian, along with other, postcolonial groups. To decolonize the mind means to rid the oppressors of the desire to conquer, control, and hierarchically rule over others. To decolonize the mind of the oppressed and the victims who dwell in the shadows of the margins means to remove the complicity of the feelings and actions of victimage, subordination, and inferiority. The use of the imagination theologically allows us to have new images of God, the world, and the human community, which lead to new patterns of both understanding and action. God is construed as the God of the oppressed, and humans strive in their relationships and institutions to create a reality of egalitarianism.

Postcolonial theology, including the form that takes on feminist issues, does not reject *in toto* historical criticism, because it reveals the "worldliness" of the texts, that is, the material and ideological backgrounds from which the texts emerged and to which they responded. Even so, as Sugirtharajah has noted, historical criticism has often been the handmaiden of colonialism and its new expression, neocolonialism. Indeed, the method formed during the period of Western imperialism and was inappropriately used to justify Western translations and interpretations of the Bible as superior to those of the colonial nations.[130] Once historical criticism, viewed through the lens of the West, became the norm, it excluded indigenous ways of reading the text through the cultures of the two-thirds world. What is particularly different now, however, is that postcolonial theology allows theologians to articulate and examine new questions about the historical and literary contexts of both the past and the present and thereby enlarge the moral imagination of interpretation.

For Kwok, there are several types of imagination that come into play theologically in the decolonization of the mind. The first she discusses is "historical imagination."[131] She rejects the simplistic construal of history as a factual recording of data, and supplants it with the perspective of one who actualizes the memory of the past for present understanding and life. This requires us to rewrite history as though women and other oppressed groups and nations exist in order to give them their rightful place in the world. Each oppressed group, including women, becomes a "historical subject." This means they have an identity as humans of worth. The tenacious and complex problem with doing this remembering is to determine how this occurs for the marginalized who have left behind in the historical records almost no trail. The so-called Western China experts in universities in the West have interpreted Chinese history according to a Eurocentric model of Western impact and Chinese response. Thus, the influences of Western powers on other peoples is stressed, while the Chinese were not the actors but the acted-upon. Marxist interpretation offers no better solution. It rewrites history according to an ideology often foreign to indigenous peoples. After all, Marx was a European. He too ignored women and colonized nations. Even in the postcolonial Asian context, Kwok reminds us, Wong Wai Ching has argued Asian women theologians have wrongly presented women as either victims of oppression or national heroines who engage in struggles against unjust male rulers. The problem for Wong is that in these depictions, Asian feminist theologians have supported inadvertently the nationalist politics and agendas of Asian identities and the priorization of Western academic theory.[132]

More important in Kwok's view are the insights of Chung Hyun Kyung and Mary John Mananzan,[133] who reject the binary constructs of "heroine" and "victim." In their view, Asian women do not rely on male theologians or institutions that champion forgetfulness. Rather, the historical imagination seeks, not only to reconstitute the past, but also to release the past in order to make the present livable.

Kwok then moves to assess "Dialogical Imagination" as an element of her hermeneutical appropriation of the Bible.[134] This creative type of imagination seeks to display the many complexities and levels of meaning that exist in relating the Bible to an Asian context. It is dialogical, for it includes conversation between different cultures and a variety of religions. The misuse of the Bible by Western powers in the colonization of much of Asia has led many to experience alienation from this book. It cannot speak with conviction to Asians until the metanarratives of Western superiority, supported by the church and the Western interpretation of the Bible, are diassembled. Kwok notes that dialogical hermeneutics involves ongoing conversation among different cultures and their religions. Asian theologians affirm that divine revelation and acts of redemption are present in the revelation and actions of the histories and cultures of Asian peoples. This includes the many different Asian religions. Of course there is enormous diversity in culture in each Asian country. In East Asia, the alliance of capitalism, patriarchy, and its support by some traditional religions like neo-Confucianism provides a growing economy that establishes the hierarchy of patriarchal, wealthy males over women who provide cheap labor. This patriarchy must be rejected in the attempt to establish an egalitarian world of many different cultures and social groups, as well as the equality of the genders.

The "Diasporic Imagination" also plays an important role in Kwok's theological hermeneutic. This may refer either to the discourse of people who have experienced forced dispersion, or to those who harbor a longing to return to their homeland. While appropriating the ideas of such diasporan theologians as Segovia, she gives them a feminist twist. Women, she contends, possess an ambivalent past, having fragments of memories, cultures, and histories that usually reflect the misogyny of their home countries. Thus, feminists must deal not only with displacement, usually finding themselves located in a strange and different culture that is oppressive but also with the patriarchy of their past in homelands not receptive to them as fully free and valued as human beings.[135] The diasporic experience of women is more complex, for it not only must come to a knowledge of history that often has excluded them and religious traditions that have marginalized them but also must deal with the additional factors of class, race, and ethnicity. Women are required to reimagine their own cultural traditions in order to shape them into a positive receptacle for human worth.

In her treatment of postcolonialism and feminist biblical studies, Kwok contends that this approach creates space for women in colonial, postcolonial, and patriarchal settings, both in the past and in the present, by stimulating historical and moral imagination.[136] Marginalized women have often turned to the Bible, in spite of its frequent sexism, to discover examples of women who are liberated, enabling them to experience the freedom of human dignity and thus participate fully in the social worlds of past and present. Thus, postcolonial feminist interpreters of the Bible investigate how the symbolization of women and gender in the text and its appropriation may legitimately relate to the dispelling of class interests, unequal gender modes of production, the concentration of state power in the hands of men, and colonial domination by powerful males.[137] To deconstruct the paradigm of male power, counter-narratives are shaped that negate the sexism of many biblical stories.

Toward a Postcolonial Interpretation

Asia is multicultural and multiracial. The Continent has seven major linguistic zones and numerous religious scriptures that have shaped its many cultures. The task of Asian postcolonial theologians and biblical interpreters is not to abstract dogmas as universal truths but rather to respect the particularity of these various stories. Biblical study must destabilize all imperialistic claims for truth in order to achieve the liberation of all. Asia is multiple, fluid, changing. It is not to serve as the "Other" in Western theology. Due to the multiplicity of languages, cultures, and religions in Asia, postcolonial interpreters cannot see the world through the Western paradigms of history and culture. Indeed, Asian theologians must demythologize the authority and sacrality of the Bible as the single norm for theology. They must demystify the ideology of the text that the West continues to use to dominate the peoples of the East, and especially its marginals, and draw on their own resources in order to achieve a syncretistic theology. The test of any theology is how it is able to lessen human suffering, promote justice and egalitarianism, bring about liberation, and build community among all groups.

Postcolonial Feminism in the Two-Thirds World[138]

There are also significant women's voices who speak to us from the Third World, including Africa, Central America, and Asia, and the Western countries to which some have migrated. I have necessarily limited my examples to a few, keenly aware that other voices have been and continue to be heard.[139] Among African feminists who are biblical scholars, one of the most provocative has been Musa Dube. For her, women in the two-thirds world call for the decolonization of colonial education, languages, culture, methods of reading, including a dependence on historical criticism, the metanarratives of Western imperial ideology, and hierarchy.[140]

In her contributions to postcolonial readings of the Bible, she has argued that too many Western biblical interpreters read the Bible as a text that relates to and has meaning only for the past. In many cases, these boundaries between past and present become barriers incapable of being crossed. Yet these must be crossed, if the Bible is to have any contemporary significance. In doing so, she advocates postcolonial readings that decolonize imperialist tendencies in the Bible that have been wittingly or unwittingly used to support colonization.

> For me to read the Bible as an African woman and from my experience . . . is to be inevitably involved with the historical events of imperialism. Indeed, to read the Bible as an African is to take a perilous journey, a sinister journey, that spins one back to connect with dangerous memories of slavery, colonialism, apartheid, and neo-colonialism. To read the Bible as an African is to relive the painful equation of Christianity with civilization, paganism with savagery.[141]

Commenting on Dube's words above, Makhosanda Nzimande had this to say:

> This melancholic assertion made by the Motswana woman, Musa Dube, the doyen of postcolonial feminist Biblical criticism in Africa, is indeed

an irrefutable truism that speaks for the multitudes of African women in the African continent. Yet, the winds of postcolonial Biblical criticism have reached the shores of the South African hermeneutical arena, beckoning the attention of Biblical scholars. It remains my deepest conviction . . . that postcolonial Biblical criticism is a mandatory and valuable interpretive tool that could provide fresh insights on Biblical interpretation in the post-apartheid era.[142]

A sub-Saharan Motswana woman, Dube uses a postcolonial interdisciplinary approach and employs "a strategy of resistance" aimed at opposing the colonizer's interpretation of the canon and to demonstrate how the Bible has been abused to support Western views of imperialism.[143] Dube argues that issues of land, race, power, international connection, contemporary history, and gender need to be given serious attention by biblical scholars seeking hermeneutically to approach the Bible. She cautions that the term "postcolonial" does not mean that colonization and its aftereffects have reached their conclusion. Rather, this perspective regards the methods and effects of imperialism as a continuing reality in global relations. Dube makes the important point, also made by others, that both colonized peoples and colonized women are categorized as oppressed. However, colonized women are subjected to greater abuse because two patriarchal systems have been superimposed on them, that of the colonizer and that of the postcolonial, largely male governments that have emerged in the former colonies. Men have benefited the most from the new world of postcolonialism.[144] Like Sugirtharajah, she proposes a syncretizing reading strategy whereby the colonized reread the master's canon to decolonize both it and the societies in which it functions.[145]

Storytelling in Postcolonial Lands[146]

Mercy Amba Oduyoye, of Ghana, has been active in the World Council of Churches, initiated the "Decade of Churches in Solidarity with Women," and, in addition to her own writing, helped to mentor a community of African women in theology. She operates from the social location of the background of colonization and slavery and confronts the continuing effects of racism, misogyny, and poverty within the context of African patriarchy, globalization, and neocolonialism. Her approach is the power of story, understood by Hans Frei and the Yale school as narrative theology. This storytelling tradition from Africa draws on traditions of myth, culture, and women's experiences. Like many other women in feminist interpretation, she notes that the Bible has been used to oppress women. However, it also has been an important resource for women in resisting the violence done to them by patriarchy. Female circumcision, AIDS, rape and abuse, and genocidal murder have been experienced by women in their own tribal societies. Thus, for the theologian who is concerned with biblical theology, narratives of women in the Bible who survived abuse may set forth encouragement and hope for their contemporaries. Women's theology in Africa has the additional responsibility of unveiling the systemic violence of colonialism and missionary activity.

Significant for her hermeneutics are several principles. The first handles life lived in Africa in which global challenges must be addressed. This is its context. The theology is that of the living women of this continent in the form of stories, prayers, and songs. These depict a God of marginalized people, including women. The second does not allow life to be separated into the secular and the holy. Rather, all of life is the subject of reflection and articulation. It is not merely spirituality that is of interest but also economic exploitation, the political instability of nations, the destruction caused by epidemics and famine, and the militarism of African leaders and groups competing for control that results in war, even genocide. Thus, how is God present and active in the midst of these trials? And how do Christians, Muslims, and practitioners of other religions join forces to reach a common accord in achieving liberation? The third recognizes that women in Africa engage in the mothering not only of families and children but also of those who are more destitute than they. This image of "mothering" has become the dominant one in African feminist theology.

Oduyoye looks at the religio-cultural context of Africa as primary for the development of women's theology and mentions the following features of religion. "Africans live in a spiritual universe." Traditional culture and religion that see the spiritual essence of life are connected to Christianity. Thus, for example, how may communication with controlling and directing spirits be obtained? How do women maintain the importance of marriage and childrearing in the face of patriarchal abuse? How does the strong identity given by community continue in a tribal existence that has often led to violence against women? These and similar questions must be addressed by African feminists.

For Oduyoye, stories convey important values and present gender roles that break from patriarchy. In addition, African feminist theologians point to the importance of rituals reflecting phases and aspects of women's lives, including marriage and motherhood. African women by tradition are socialized to nurture others, a central value, yet it may be abused by the notion that women are to be subservient to men. Deconstructing the power of the mythic structure of subservience is perhaps the greatest challenge to feminists in Africa.

The key to feminist theology in Africa, of course, is the construction of language about God. Central are the nature and activity of God in relationship to humanity, the spirits, and nature. While the Creator is known by many names in African religions, the one Oduyoye prefers is "Source Being." Divine presence gives life to all that exists, but its withdrawal leads to the devastations that afflict humans. For Oduyoye, the dominant metaphor for God is "mothering." The dominant role for women in Africa is that of the mother who nurtures and cares for her children as well as others who are in need. Thus, God is the mother who gives to and cares for the needy, who extends to them hospitality, and is active in nature to bring the abundant life.

Oduyoye also speaks, in conclusion, of the mutuality of women's experience of oppression that enables them to find a mutuality common to their gender. Thus, feminists are to tell the stories of the past and new ones that create a community that does not regard gender as a line of separation.

OTHER FORMS OF LIBERATION THEOLOGY

Liberation Theology in Latin America

Since the 1960s, a number of Latin American theologians have written books that support marginals in their countries, in particular the poor. Many Latin American governments have victimized their own people, especially the poor, by continuing policies of European and American colonialism. While there are diverse expressions of liberation theology, there is the collective recognition of the importance of context. Thus, they, like many postcolonial scholars, have shaped a contextual theology that pertains to their own sociocultural settings, and not those of Europe and North America.[147] They hold in common as well the need not only to articulate the language of liberation but also to shape its teachings in practice. The philosophical and religious backgrounds for liberation theology have been varied, ranging from neo-Marxism to the prophetic corpus of the Bible in order to provide a social-critical basis. Indeed, for most liberation theologians, orthopraxis takes precedence over orthodoxy as the primary consideration for theological reflection.[148]

The message and practice of liberation for the oppressed is also actualized in the divine commands to love and care for their neighbors by joining with them in solidarity. All people, including the poor, are fully human, a fundamental view that is often denied by oppressive social and political systems.[149] Liberation theologians write, teach, and act to enable the downtrodden to achieve their full human dignity. Yet liberation theology does not only speak and act for marginals. It also points to them as practicing a spirituality that is to be emulated. Their solidarity, love, serenity, and piety become expressed in ways that provide examples of faithful living. In turn, God expresses partiality toward the poor:

> God is especially close to those who are oppressed; God hears their cry and resolves to set them free (Exod 3:7-8). God is Father of all, but most particularly Father and defender of those who are oppressed and treated unjustly. Out of love for them, God takes sides, takes their side against the repressive measures of all the pharaohs.[150]

In Christian liberation theology, Jesus Christ joined in solidarity with the poor, suffered their misfortunes, opposed repressive rulers, and through his ministry and proclamation initiated the dawning of the kingdom of God in which justice would reign supreme. Liberation theology's manifesto is to act in justice to free the oppressed from bondage until the final culmination of the kingdom, when a new heaven and a new earth appear. It is in the church's transformation of oppressive structures that all people are able to achieve their full humanity, regardless of race, color, creed, national and geographical location, gender, or sexual orientation.[151]

A Theology of the Diaspora[152]

In recent years, Fernando Segovia has shaped a theology of the diaspora that builds upon the foundations of liberation theology, intercultural studies, and postcolonialism. Although he has not written a biblical theology that emanates from this perspective, he has published several important books and composed a number of key essays that illustrate clearly his thinking. *Decolonizing Biblical Studies* is a collection of eight of his previously published essays, while another, *Reading from this Place*, consists of a collection of essays of leading Asian American and Hispanic scholars, which he introduces and to which he contributes his own essay.

In *Decolonizing Biblical Studies*, he initially explains clearly the "competing modes of discourse" that characterize the methods of contemporary biblical studies. Segovia discusses historical criticism's view of the Bible under the rubric "The Text as Means." Historical criticism, which has enjoyed a long and unrivaled history, has experienced a "broad retreat" during the last quarter century. Some of these more recent approaches have occurred due to changing political and economic realities in the globe, in particular, the end of colonialism and the emergence of post-colonialism. This has allowed the voices of the Third World to speak and be heard for the first time in the history of biblical interpretation.

Historical criticism, in Segovia's view, has lacked theoretical sophistication and a critical self-consciousness. For this approach, the meaning of the biblical text is located in the world that it projects, in the reconstruction of the author, or in a combination of both. There was generally little appreciation for or way of getting at the artistic and ideological disposition of the text. Historical positivism has been the theoretical base of traditional historical criticism, since the text has been viewed as "univocal and objective." The ideology of the interpreter was not considered, since she or he approached the text "objectively" and interpreted it according to "scientific" canons of understanding. The text itself was an object, and its worldviews could be understood by the historical critic.

Segovia then turns to consider more recent literary criticism in a variety of modes (rhetorical, formalistic, new, and so on) under a different rubric: "The Text as Medium." These literary approaches, highly diverse as they are, are much more self-consciously theoretical and have not only strongly criticized historical criticism but also have offered new paths to understanding. These literary approaches of recent vintage are united in their understanding that meaning emerges from the interaction of text and reader. Except for the arrogance of some historical critics' claim to extrapolate only the original meaning that issues from the text, this is true, in my judgment of historical criticism. Only those who work from the folly of thinking that their views are objective and scientific fail to realize this. For Segovia, the transition from original author and audience to implied author and audience, both in the past and the present, along with the understanding that meaning derives from the interaction of text and reader, gave room to the issues of narratology, characterization, and point of view. Instead of viewing the text as a collection of sources and redactions shaped over centuries, now it is understood as a unified whole that had and continues to have meaning and importance. Recent literary critics have also recognized that the text has many, often competing, meanings.

Segovia notes that the next stage in interpretation involves the analysis of texts by means of social science. Under the heading "The Text as Means and Medium," he contends that this approach not only possesses a necessary self-conscious awareness of its ideology but also points beyond the goal of historical criticism's attempt to understand a text in its original setting to a broader understanding of the social and cultural codes at work in its location. Problematic for Segovia, however, is the realization that the reader is a universal, nameless, sophisticated intellectual who still offers the authoritative interpretation. While attempting to get at the meaning of the text by understanding the culture that produced it, this approach is still flawed by seeking the elusive original background of the text. Thus, meaning is supposed to be in the interaction between the text and the context that produced it, while the interpreter's ideology and social location in the present are not taken into consideration. This failure to consider the interpreter's social location and own ideology weakens severely the effort to derive the meaning of the text.

For Segovia, the best approach to determine meaning is to recognize that it comes from the interaction of text, its social and cultural context, the reader, and his or her location and ideology. He derives this approach from the general area of cultural studies, which he discusses under the heading "The Text as Construction." This approach rejects as naive the possibility of a disinterested writer and an unidentified audience. Rather, the readers of a text are people who have their own stake in the meaning pursued. No longer is the reader's own voice silenced by the "expert" scholar but now is heard in both the questions addressed to the text and the answers received. Increasingly, reading is influenced by postmodernist theory with the goal being the construction of both text and meaning. This involves dialogue that occurs among the various readers from different social locations, that of the text itself, the generations of interpreters, and the various audiences over the centuries. This has led to a global hermeneutic in the mode of the postcolonial world and postcolonial approaches to biblical criticism.

In the second chapter of *Decolonizing Biblical Studies*,[153] Segovia begins to outline in detail his own hermeneutic born of cultural studies and, in particular, postmodernism. He begins by noting that in recent studies emerging from the margins, not one but rather multiple meanings of texts arise. In addition, "progress" in the text and its understanding is not linear but rather multidirectional. Further, the ideological interests of the text join those of the interpreter. Interpretation is not value-free but rather political in its assertions. The approach of the interaction of text, interpreter, and context liberates the text from the elitism that had imprisoned it and from the claims of unchallengeable assertions of intellectuals and their elitist methods. Interpretation now moves among marginals who heretofore have been excluded from participation in the construction of meaning because of race, color, gender, status, and location. The notion of some overarching metanarrative, shaped by metropoles and their elitist supporters, is dismissed.

In this book and elsewhere, Segovia's own contribution to hermeneutics is his understanding of the "diaspora" (meaning "scattering," or "dispersion"), a biblical Greek term that originally referred to Jews living outside Eretz Israel. These were the Jews forced into exile by the imperial conquerors (Assyrians, Babylonians, Greeks, and Romans) and economic necessity. However, the diasporic experience has continued to occur throughout history and the many human societies and cultures.[154] For Segovia, the diaspora refers to people who reside in a country other than the one of their birth. While some may choose to live in another country, others are forced to do so against their will. The reasons for displacement vary, but generally are due to economics and politics. The experience shared by people of the diaspora is migration. Furthermore, he understands diasporic studies as a subdiscipline of postcolonialism. Consequently, the term should not refer only to the Jewish experience but rather to marginals in many different locations who are in exile. Discrimination in their new locations often keeps these displaced persons in marginalized positions of servitude.

Segovia in the remainder of this book and elsewhere sets forth his understanding of biblical studies as a Latino in a diasporic location. Born in Cuba, he now lives in the United States and teaches at Vanderbilt University. His self-revelation is critical for understanding both the ideology of the text and that of his work as interpreter. The fact that other interpreters from different settings will render the meaning of the text in different ways is important in the act of interpretation. The various readers are "others" to be "acknowledged," "respected," and "engaged," not simply as individuals but rather as members of communities, which have their own social, cultural, and ideological constructs. Reading and writing as a Latino, he speaks not only as one who is a member of the diasporic

Hispanic community but also as one who lives among people in North America who are multicultural. This means, then, that he dwells in two worlds at times in a conflictual tension that he embodies and experiences. In his view, Hispanic Americans are eternal "others" in both the dominant American, Eurocentric culture in which they are not valued and respected and the marginal world of Latinos who often regard people like himself as "outsiders."

A final dimension of Segovia's hermeneutic is "The Text as Other." The text by necessity is contextualized. This means it is a body of literature that had its own social location among people who themselves were often marginalized as "others." The voice of the biblical text they hear seeks to liberate and empower them by addressing them in their experience as "others." The theory residing behind this hermeneutic is reader-response criticism, in which meaning derives from the interaction of reader and what is read. Both the text and the reader have their own social locations that shape their identities, worldviews, and meanings. Meaning cannot help but be socially constructed. For him, the Hispanic experience of "otherness" becomes the lens through which to interpret the Bible, even as the Bible in turn is able to transform the lives of the "others." This means that cultural criticism demonstrates that reality is not only constructed, it is to be engaged. The world of the text and the world of the dominant culture are to be critically engaged. According to Segovia, "a hermeneutics of otherness," coupled with one of engagement, becomes the essence of a hermeneutics of the diaspora.

African American Liberation Theology and Biblical Interpretation

Another important social and cultural context for hermeneutics in the United States that makes significant use of the Bible is African American liberation theology (or simply, black theology). The specificity of this particular form of liberation theology is the fact that it has emanated from people who are the descendants of slaves, kidnapped by traffickers in human slaves and sold for profit, transported to colonies, in particular those in what is now the southern United States, and forced to work on plantations as slaves. This long and often tragic history, paralleled perhaps only by the genocide and theft of the lands of indigenous peoples in the Americas, has been a long and arduous march toward freedom, which has yet to be fully achieved. Lincoln's Emancipation Proclamation, issued in 1863, was followed by a century of a trying struggle for civil rights, culminating in the civil rights legislation of 1964. While discrimination on the basis of race is illegal, the attendant poverty and covert discrimination have continued to diminish the humanity of African Americans throughout the United States. To address these evils and to keep hope alive, African Americans have often turned to the Bible for inspiration.

Vincent Wimbush has written and edited several volumes that speak theologically to an American society still rife with racism.[155] His hermeneutical approach is set forth in his essay "Reading Texts as Reading Ourselves." Like Segovia, he also points to the hermeneutical necessity of the interaction of both text and reader from their respective social locations. Classics of any kind, including a religious canon, honored in a culture, always need to be approached with suspicion. This hermeneutics of suspicion is important, since distance is necessary to assess critically the ideological assumptions of both text and interpreter. One interpretation or one ideology should not be given the status of the true one for all times and every social community. While premodern views of fundamentalists and the perspectives of imperial nations are to be rejected, just as important is the necessity to shape the traditions of the past into an engaging and transformative vehicle to move the society and its culture to new heights of a responsible faith.

The Bible has been a text that for several centuries has spoken directly to the trials and hopes of African Americans, marginalized socially and politically, and yet fellow combatants in the struggles for freedom from the destructive power of racism and for human dignity. This requires that they interpret the world in view of their own experiences and self-understandings and speak prophetically against the abuse of marginalized people and to oppose the misuse of the text to legitimate racism, slavery, apartheid, and colonialism.

Wimbush speaks of the key role that orality has played in articulating the justice contained in pages of scripture, necessitated in part by the prohibition of the education of black slaves by white masters and racists in the eighteenth and nineteenth centuries. He also reminds us that literalism did not enter African American interpretations of scripture until the transition of some black churches to fundamentalism. He then enters into a clear and cogent articulation of African American biblical hermeneutics. First, a hermeneutic embracing African American interpretations of scripture must be set forth by those who at least are aware of the historical experiences of this community and its readings of the Bible.

This provides a necessary basis for engaging in a critically reflective approach to biblical texts that is relevant to contemporary America. Second, as already noted, this hermeneutic emanating from African Americans requires an understanding of both the culture of the Bible and the reader. Third, the text and its reader must critically engage each other. This demands that the theme of the oneness of God's human creation challenges the distortions caused by racism. Yet the text must also be subjected to criticism, especially when it engages in racist talk about the legitimacy of slavery and patriarchy. These are to be countered by the critical awareness that these views corrupt the biblical teaching of justice. Those who ignore this particular community and its concerns can only be regarded as misguided and illegitimate interpreters of the text.

African Americans and the Bible

Finally, the major points raised by the contributors to *The Bible and American Myth*, the majority of whom are African American authors, provide a stimulating response to the question *How might putting African Americans at the center of the study of the Bible affect the study of the Bible?* The major conclusion reached in this collection is the contention that the "crux of interpretation is not words, but worlds."[156] Central to these essays is the common view that it is critical for interpretation to understand not only what people have done to the text but what the text has done to people. Further, they argue that the context of interpretation is not the ancient past but rather the social and cultural locations of the African American communities in the present. While Wimbush does not dispense with his work in historical criticism, he recognizes that lay communities in the church must be allowed to appropriate the Bible in shaping their own understanding of the world. In his own contribution in this collection, Wimbush contends that enabling African American biblical interpretation to become the major approach of the academy would lead to a more critical focus on the social and cultural role of sacred texts. The result would be the elucidation of the relationship between society, culture, and text in reaching interpretative judgments. He concludes that the metaphor "darkness" has become a way of seeing, understanding, and living in a world of pain inhabited by the marginals of human societies. Scripture has contributed to this darkness. But it can be overcome only by the light of critical minds ensconced within communities of pain and suffering, enabling those who suffer to see eventually the dawning of hope.

NOTES

1. Dialogical Biblical Theology: A Jewish Approach to Reading Scripture Theologically

1. The question of whether something like such a notion may have motivated some Jewish groups in antiquity (in particular the Sadducees and their offshoot, the Essenes) or a group that still exists (the Karaites) is complex. It is not clear that these groups in fact held a position truly analogous to the Protestant principle of *sola scriptura* (see Moshe Goshen-Gottstein, "Tanakh Theology: The Religion of the Old Testament and the Place of Jewish Biblical Theology," in *Ancient Israelite Religion: Essays in Honor of Frank Moore Cross* [ed. Patrick D. Miller, Paul D. Hanson, and S. Dean McBride; Philadelphia: Fortress Press, 1987], 627), and even if they did, they nevertheless relied heavily on oral traditions regardless of their pretensions to the contrary. See, for example, the discussion of the Karaites' *sēbel hayyĕrūšâ* in Daniel Frank, "Karaite Exegesis," in *The Middle Ages* (vol. 2 of *Hebrew Bible/Old Testament: The History of Its Interpretation*, ed. Magne Sæbø; Göttingen: Vandenhoeck & Ruprecht, 2000), 115. In any event, my concern in this essay is not those groups but the many varieties of Judaism in the ancient, medieval, and modern worlds that evolved out of the ancient rabbinic movement, including all four modern forms of religious Judaism (Reform, Orthodox, Conservative, and Reconstructionist).

2. One might argue that even in Protestantism, tradition has always played a role alongside scripture, but at least the ideal of an exclusively or primarily biblical doctrine nevertheless deeply affected Protestantism. Leo Perdue points out that "Protestant systematic theology in no way is obligated to give priority to the biblical view, as Sommer suggests," in carefully critiquing one of my earlier discussions of biblical theology. See Leo Perdue, *Reconstructing Old Testament Theology: After the Collapse of History* (Minneapolis: Fortress Press, 2005), 207. Perdue's critique is well-taken. I should not be understood to suggest that all Protestant theology is supposed to be exclusively biblical. The question remains, why would one want to create a biblical theology at all, even if a systematic thinker would reserve the right to disagree with its teachings? It is no coincidence that the desire to create such a theology arose neither in Judaism nor in Catholic or Orthodox settings but in Protestant settings in the eighteenth century, and that it remained an exclusively Protestant undertaking for so long. The view that the theology of the Bible is of particular significance (though not necessarily having ultimate authority) results in large part from the notion of *sola scriptura*.

3. On scripture as a part of tradition (rather than a wholly distinct category) in rabbinic Judaism, see Abraham Joshua Heschel, *Torah Min Ha-Shamayim b'Aspaqlarya Shel Ha-Dorot* [in Hebrew] (3 vols.; London and New York: Soncino and the Jewish Theological Seminary, 1965 and 1990), 3:45–47 (an English translation by Gordon Tucker is available); Yochanan Silman, *The Voice Heard at Sinai: Once or Ongoing?* [in Hebrew] (Jerusalem: Magnes, 1999), 26–27; and my own remarks in "Unity and Plurality in Jewish Canons: The Case of the Oral and Written Torah," in *One Scripture or Many? Perspectives Historical, Theological and Philosophical* (ed. Christine Helmer and Christof Landmesser; New York: Oxford University Press, 2004), 108–50, esp. 123–26.

4. First published in Jacob Neusner, ed., *Judaic Perspectives on Ancient Israel* (Philadelphia: Fortress Press, 1987), and reprinted in a slightly revised version in Jon Levenson, *The Hebrew Bible, the Old Testament, and Historical Criticism: Jews and Christians in Biblical Studies* (Louisville: Westminster John Knox, 1993). References here will be to the later version.

5. See especially Goshen-Gottstein, "Tanakh Theology," 621–22. Goshen-Gottstein had begun publishing some of his ideas on Jews' relationship to biblical theology during the preceding decade; for example, Moshe Goshen-Gottstein, "Jewish Biblical Theology and the Study of Biblical Religion" [in Hebrew], *Tarbiz* 50 (1981): 37–50; Moshe Goshen-Gottstein, "Christianity, Judaism, and Modern Bible Study," VTSup 28 (1975): 69–88.

6. See especially Isaac Kalimi, "History of Israelite Religion or Old Testament Theology?" *SJOT* 11 (1997): 110–18; and Ziony Zevit, "Jewish Biblical Theology: Whence? Why? and Wither?" *HUCA* 76 (2005): 289–316.

7. See Shimon Gesundheit, "Gibt es eine jüdische Theologie der Hebräischen Bibel?" in *Theologie und Exegese des Alten Testaments / der Hebräischen Bibel. Zwischenbilanz und Zukunftsperspektiven*, ed. Bernd Janowski; SBS (Stuttgart: Verlag Katholisches Bibelwerk, 2005), 73–86, esp. 75–76. Gesundheit refers to Leo Adler, *Der Mensch in der Sicht der Bibel* (Munich/Basel: E. Reinhardt, 1965). An English translation of Adler's book by Daniel Schwartz, with a forward by Gesundheit, will be published soon.

8. Abraham Joshua Heschel, *The Prophets*, 2 vols. (New York: Harper Torchbooks, 1962), recently reprinted in one volume as Abraham Joshua Heschel, *The Prophets* (New York: HarperCollins Perennial Classics, 2001). Among the relevant works by Buber, we might note in particular Martin Buber, *Moses: The Revelation and the Covenant* (New York: Schocken, 1958); Martin Buber, *The Prophetic Faith* (New York: Macmillan, 1949); and Martin Buber, *The Kingship of God*, trans. Richard Schiemann (New York: Harper & Row, 1967).

9. Of the three, Buber is in fact the only one who might be described as a biblical scholar, since his studies of biblical Hebrew narrative style remain significant to this day. Nonetheless, his work on Bible comprises a small percentage of his output.

10. Yehezkel Kaufmann, *Toledot Ha-Emunah Ha-Yisraelit* [in Hebrew] 4 vols. (Jerusalem and Tel Aviv: Bialik & Devir, 1937–56). The first three volumes are available in an English abridgment: Yehezkel Kaufmann, *The Religion of Israel: From Its Beginnings to the Babylonian Exile*, trans. and abridged by Moshe Greenberg (Chicago: University of Chicago Press, 1960); parts of the final volume are available in English as Yehezkel Kaufmann, *The Babylonian Captivity and Deutero-Isaiah*, trans. C. W. Efroymson (New York: Union of American Hebrew Congregations, 1970).

11. Most of the key works considered examples of Jewish biblical theology are deeply influenced by Kaufmann, but many contemporary observers overlook this facet of those

works. Leo Perdue devotes more than a third of his recent discussion of Jewish biblical theology to Michael Fishbane; see Perdue, *Reconstructing*, 215–36. In his fine discussion Perdue never mentions the relation of Kaufmann's work to Fishbane's. Much of Fishbane's *ouevre* (and in particular the works that Perdue discusses) consists of a lengthy response to Kaufmann's assertion that the religion of biblical Israel had no place for myth and magic (a judgment famously seconded by Fishbane's other significant interlocutor, Gershom Scholem; see Gershom Scholem, *Major Trends in Jewish Mysticism* [New York: Schocken, 1941], esp. 7–8). A similar relationship to Kaufmann is found in the work of Levenson, who repeatedly takes issue with him in Jon Levenson, *Sinai and Zion: An Entry Into the Jewish Bible* (San Francisco: Harper & Row, 1987), and even more crucially in regard to questions of the presence or absence of myth in Jon Levenson, *Creation and the Persistence of Evil: The Jewish Drama of Divine Omnipotence* (San Francisco: Harper & Row, 1988). While both Fishbane and Levenson disagree with Kaufmann on specifics, the research agenda they take as assertively Jewish biblicists is the one given to them by Kaufmann in his role as the leading Jewish biblical scholar of the twentieth century. A different sort of relationship is evinced by Israel Knohl, *The Divine Symphony: The Bible's Many Voices* (Philadelphia: Jewish Publication Society, 2003), and also his earlier work, Israel Knohl, *The Sanctuary of Silence: The Priestly Torah and the Holiness School* (Minneapolis: Fortress Press, 1995). Both works may be characterized as lengthy attempts to reconfigure and hence to reinforce some of Kaufmann's main findings concerning ancient Israelite perceptions of God. Yochanan Muffs, *The Personhood of God: Biblical Theology, Human Faith and the Divine Image* (Woodstock, Vt.: Jewish Lights, 2005), is suffused throughout with Kaufmann's understanding of the gulf between Israelite and Mesopotamian religion. Muffs takes Kaufmann, however, in a startling direction: he integrates Kaufmann's antimythological insights with the very different ideas of Abraham Joshua Heschel concerning divine pathos and with Thorkild Jacobsen's approach to the development of Sumerian and Babylonian religion. In so doing, Muffs creates what is at once a remarkably agile historical overview and a breathtakingly creative theological synthesis. (For especially clear examples, see Muffs, *Personhood of God*, 39–40 and 83–87.)

12. To be sure, not every paragraph of the work directly discusses this central idea. In order to present his argument regarding monotheism, Kaufmann must attend to questions of the dating of biblical documents (in particular, the early dating of the Priestly source, but also the early dating of many psalms and the unified nature of various prophetic corpora such as Isa 1–33), questions regarding history (for example, the nature of the Israelite conquest of Canaan), and comparisons with ancient Near Eastern literature. These issues lead Kaufmann into extended debates with (and sharp polemics against) other biblical scholars. Thus, large parts of these four volumes deal with historical and textual issues. Nonetheless, the many long discussions dealing with these topics are all marshaled to support one central idea regarding monotheism and its consequences. Kaufmann's treatise, despite its length, is a highly unified composition. In this regard it differs from many works on the history of Israelite religion that are much shorter but much more diffuse.

13. Walther Eichrodt, *Theology of the Old Testament*, 2 vols., trans. J. A. Baker, OTL (Philadelphia: Westminster Press, 1961–1967).

14. Gerhard von Rad, *Old Testament Theology*, 2 vols., trans. D. M. G. Stalker (Edinburgh: Oliver & Boyd, 1962–1965). It is sometimes claimed that von Rad rejected the idea of a *Mitte* or central concern of Old Testament theology (see von Rad's own statements in 1:114 and 2:362; see also Ben Ollenberger, Elmer Martens, and Gerhard

Hasel, eds., *The Flowering of Old Testament Theology: A Reader in Twentieth-Century Old Testament Theology, 1930–1990* [Winona Lake, Ind.: Eisenbrauns, 1992], 121). Von Rad's own claim notwithstanding, it is not quite the case that von Rad really moved away from the notion of a *Mitte*. The notion of salvation does pervade his work: though it does not provide the structure, it nevertheless serves as the criterion according to which he makes exegetical and critical judgements. A telling example is his insistence on the existence of a Hexateuch that ends with salvation in the form of entry into the land under the leadership of Joshua (=Jesus="Yhwh saves"). Further, James Barr notes that von Rad's emphasis on transmission and transformation (or, to phrase it differently, God's self-revelation in history) serves as a *Mitte*, though this *Mitte* involves a process rather than a theme; see James Barr, *The Concept of Biblical Theology* (Minneapolis: Fortress Press, 1999), 47; 339–40; see also David Carr, "Passion for God: A Center in Biblical Theology," *HBT* 23 (2001): 1–2.

15. Samuel Terrien, *The Elusive Presence: Toward a New Biblical Theology* (San Francisco: Harper & Row, 1978).

16. Walter Brueggemann, *Theology of the Old Testament: Testimony, Advocacy, Dispute* (Minneapolis: Fortress Press, 1997). Here, even more strongly than in von Rad's case, process comes to the fore as the central structuring principle behind the canon and the work of the biblical theologian.

17. Muffs, *Personhood of God*. See especially 22–25, 176–78, and his call for a remythologization of theology in 192–93.

18. Carr, "Passion," 2–3, makes this point: "Perhaps it would be even better to speak of 'nodal points' in biblical theology: that is, multiple points where various traditions converge, all treating a comon conceptual structure (often differently)."

19. To be sure, the idea of covenant is absent in parts of the Hebrew Scriptures, such as Wisdom literature, and it occurs in very different forms in, say, P and D. But Eichrodt was correct to assert that the idea of covenant pervades the Old Testament. We might better phrase the thesis: several competing ideas of covenant occur throughout most, though not all, of Hebrew Scripture, and the tensions among them represent one of the main engines that produce theological meaning in these texts. On this approach to covenant as a unifying theme, see especially Levenson, *Sinai and Zion*, and note Goshen-Gottstein's positive evaluation of Eichrodt's stress on covenant in Goshen-Gottstein, "Tanakh Theology," 642n52. Critiques of Eichrodt on this point are rather petty; they miss the forest by focusing on a few clearings or by insisting on talking only about how motley the trees are.

20. On the relationship between Cohen's work and Kaufmann's, see Eliezer Schweid, "Biblical Critic or Philosophical Exegete? The Influence of Herman Cohen's *The Religion of Reason* on Yehezkel Kaufmann's *History of Israelite Religion*" [in Hebrew], in *Massu'ot: Studies in Qabbalah and Jewish Thought in Memory of Professor Efraim Gottlieb* (ed. Michal Oron and Amos Goldreich; Jerusalem: Mosad Bialik, 1994), 414–28; and also Benjamin Uffenheimer, "Myth and Reality in Ancient Israel," in *The Origins and Diversity of the Axial Age*, ed. S. Eisenstadt (New York: SUNY Press, 1986), 136–37.

21. Similarly, in his earlier work, Yehezkel Kaufmann, *Exile and Alienation* [in Hebrew] (Tel Aviv: Devir, 1954–1961), portions of which are available in Yehezkel Kaufmann, *Judaism and Christianity: Two Covenants*, trans. C. W. Efroymson [Jerusalem: Magnes Press, 1988]), Kaufmann maintains that Christianity and Islam continue Judaism's ancient fight against paganism, and Kaufmann acknowledges the integrity of the religious polemics of

each of these three monotheistic faiths. In his somewhat positive approach to Christianity, Kaufmann recalls not only Cohen but also Cohen's student, the leading Jewish philosopher of the modern era, Franz Rosenzweig. Kaufmann's positive evaluation of Islam differs significantly from, and may provide a crucial corrective to, Rosenzweig's work.

22. On similarities between Kaufmann and biblical theologians, see Moshe Greenberg, *Studies in the Bible and Jewish Thought* (Philadelphia: Jewish Publication Society, 1995), 175–88; and Gesundheit, "Gibt es," 86. Goshen-Gottstein points out (Goshen-Gottstein, "Tanakh Theology," 622) that "the very idea of 'Tanakh theology' never occurred to [Kaufmann], since there existed only one area of inquiry." Whether Kaufmann conceived of himself as a biblical theologian, however, is irrelevant to the question of whether in fact he was one. (For forty years Moliere's bourgeois gentleman was speaking prose without knowing he did so, yet what he spoke was prose just the same.) The fact that for Kaufmann, unlike his Christian counterparts, there existed only one area of inquiry rather than two, history of religion and biblical theology, points not necessarily to the absence of the latter among Jews but perhaps to a potential unity of the two for them. I will return to the absence of a divide between the two subfields in the next section.

23. See in particular the reviews and discussions in Barr, *Concept*, 286–311; and Perdue, *Reconstructing*, 183–238. Important recent publications include Joel Kaminsky and Alice Ogden Bellis, eds., *Jews, Christians, and the Theology of the Hebrew Scriptures*, Symposium (Atlanta: Society of Biblical Literature, 2000); and Isaac Kalimi, ed., *Jewish Bible Theology: Perspectives and Studies* (Winona Lake, Ind.: Eisenbrauns, forthcoming).

24. Richard Elliot Friedman, *The Disappearance of God: A Divine Mystery* (Boston: Little, Brown, 1995). The book was reprinted as Richard Elliot Friedman, *The Hidden Face of God* (New York: HarperCollins, 1997).

25. In taking the canon so seriously, Friedman has accomplished the goals of Brevard Childs more than any other scholar. Indeed, I would argue, Friedman is probably one of the only scholars, Jewish or Christian, who has produced a genuinely Childsean biblical theology. The only other work I know of that genuinely works with canon is Michael Fishbane, *Haftarot: The Traditional Hebrew Text with the New JPS Translation* (Philadelphia: Jewish Publication Society, 2002); for a description of its canon-critical dimension, see my remarks at http://www.arts.ualberta.ca/JHS/reviews/review114.htm.

26. On this tendency of Jewish theology, see Gesundheit, "Gibt es," 76. For another example of this phenomenon, see Abraham Joshua Heschel, "The Concept of Man in Jewish Thought," in *Comparative Philosophy*, eds. S. Radhakrishnan and P. Raju (Lincoln, Nebr.: Johnsen, 1966), 122–71, esp. 127, 137, 142; Abraham Joshua Heschel, *God in Search of Man: A Philosophy of Judaism* (New York: Farrar and Giroux, 1955), 412–13 and passim.

27. James Kugel, *The God of Old: Inside the Lost World of the Bible* (New York: Free Press, 2003).

28. Knohl, *Divine Symphony*.

29. Another candidate for the apogee of this trajectory in Jewish thought, incidentally, is the twentieth-century Jewish thinker Yeshayahu Leibowitz. Leibowitz himself commented on the similarity between theological apperceptions of the Priestly Torah and his own work when he saw a draft of *Sanctuary of Silence* shortly before his death.

30. See Mordecai Breuer, *Pirqei Bereshit* [in Hebrew] 2 vols. (Alon Shevut: Tevunot, 1999), especially the programmatic statements in 1:11–19 and 48–54; and also Mordecai Breuer, *Pirqei Mo'adot* [in Hebrew] 2 vols. (Jerusalem: Horeb, 1993), esp. the chapters "The Ten Plagues" (1:193–232) and "The Splitting of the Reed Sea" (233–65).

31. See, for example, Breuer, *Pirqei Mo'adot*, 1:211–12. My extremely brief summary of Breuer's work succeeds in conveying its temerity but fails to divulge its literary and philosophical subtlety.

32. It should be acknowledged that one reason Levenson's claim is no longer true is because so many scholars responded to his essay by producing distinctively Jewish contributions to biblical theology—in particular Levenson himself in both *Sinai and Zion* and *Creation*. On the other hand, some of the works I describe as examples of Jewish biblical theology predate Levenson's provocative essay of 1987: Kaufmann, Heschel, Buber, Adler, most of the essays by Greenberg and Milgrom, and some of the original publications of essays by Breuer.

33. See also Isaac Kalimi, "History of Israelite Religion or Old Testament Theology?" 114–15, which is discussed in Perdue, *Reconstructing*, 198. On the other hand, one wonders whether Levenson overstates this point. It is true that Jewish scholars showed little interest in writing synthetic times covering all of biblical theology resembling the multivolume works by von Rad and Eichrodt. Nonetheless, James Barr and Ziony Zevit rightly note that many Jewish biblical scholars were interested in reading those works and regarded them highly, at least if we can judge from the evidence of the well-thumbed copies of the standard Protestant biblical theologies at the Hebrew University library. See Barr, *Concept*, 292; and Zevit, "Jewish Biblical," 316–17, n. 56.

34. See especially Levenson, *Hebrew Bible, Old Testament*, 16–23, 40–42.

35. See Barr, *Concept*, 277, 298, critiquing Levenson's phrasing in Levenson, *Hebrew Bible, Old Testament*, 40. For a similar critique, see Perdue, *Reconstructing*, 191–92.

36. Eichrodt's place along the continuum of anti-Semitisms and anti-Judaisms, intense or innocuous, is the topic of a conversation between two characters in Chaim Potok's novel *In the Beginning* (New York: Knopf, 1975), 389. An Orthodox Jew named David Lurie, living in the Bronx in 1945, complains to his younger brother Alex about Eichrodt's description of "the torsolike appearance of Judaism in separation from Christianity" [in *Theology*, 1:26]:

> I looked up at Alex. "How do you like being called a torso?"
> "I've been called worse things than that by goyim."
> "But he's supposed to be a great scholar, Alex."

It is true that Eichrodt and von Rad were very far from associating in any way with the violent anti-Semitism of their time and place. The anti-Judaism of these great scholars, as David's remark suggests, remains a mistake at both scholarly and moral levels.

37. Perdue, *Reconstructing*, 211.

38. Alexander Rofé, "Third Isaiah, After All" [in Hebrew], in *Studies in the Composition of the Torah and Prophetic Books*, ed. Alexander Rofé (Jerusalem: Akademon, 1985), 108–26. The article also appeared in *'Al Ha-Perek* 2 (1986).

39. Paul D. Hanson, *The Dawn of Apocalyptic* (Philadelphia: Fortress Press, 1975). For a critique of Hanson's compositional analysis within Isaiah 56–66, see, among others, Brooks Schramm, *The Opponents of Third Isaiah: Reconstructing to Cultic History of the Restoration* JSOTSup (Sheffield: Sheffield Academic Press, 1995); and, more briefly, Benjamin Sommer, *A Prophet Reads Scripture: Allusion in Isaiah 40–66*, Contraversions (Stanford: Stanford University Press, 1998), 190–91.

40. Bernard Levinson and Douglas Dance, "The Metamorphosis of Law into Gospel: Gerhard von Rad's Attempt to Reclaim the Old Testament for the Church," in *Recht und Ethik im Alten Testament*, eds. Bernard Levinson, Eckart Otto, and Walter Dietrich (Münster: Lit-Verlag, 2004), 83–110.

41. Hermann Spieckermann, "Mit der Liebe im Wort: Ein Beitrag zur Theologie des Deuteronomiums," in *Liebe und Gott: Studien zum Deuteronomium. Festschrift zum 70. Geburtstag von Lothar Perlitt*, eds. Reinhard Kratz and Hermann Spieckermann (Göttingen: Vandenhoeck & Ruprecht, 2000), 190–205.

42. Spieckermann, "Mit der Liebe," 191–92.

43. Ibid., 200.

44. Precisely the same notion is common in rabbinic Judaism. Cf. the opening words of the second benediction before the Shema in the rabbinic liturgy for the evening: "With eternal love You have loved Your people the house of Israel: You have taught us Torah and commandments, laws and statutes." Similarly, the second benediction before the Shema in the morning liturgy begins its discourse on revelation, Torah, and commandments with the words, "With great love you have loved us, O Lord our God; You have showered us with great mercy." Love and mercy are not opposed to law here; as in Deuteronomy, law is the expression of God's love and mercy. Cf. the similar viewpoint in *m. Makkot* 3:16: "The Holy one wished to provided Israel with merit; therefore He gave them law and commandments, as it is said (Isaiah 42:21), 'The LORD wants to make Israel victorious; therefore He gave Israel much law, so that Israel would gain honor.'" One wonders whether this passage may be a direct response to Paul's notion of the law as a stumbling block; see the remark of I. Epstein in Joseph Hertz, *The Authorised Daily Prayer Book. Hebrew Text, English Translation with Commentary and Notes* (New York: Block Publishing Company, 1955), 627. On the notion that law, given for the benefit of Israel, is a token of divine mercy and not simply judgement, see further Solomon Schechter, *Aspects of Rabbinic Theology* (New York: Schocken, 1961), 146-47, and E. E. Urbach, *The Sages: Their concepts and Beliefs*, trans. Israel Abrahamson (Jerusalem: Magnes, 1975), 365–67.

45. By way of contrast, see S. Dean McBride, "The Yoke of the Kingdom: An Exposition of Deuteronomy 6:4–5," *Int* 27 (1973): 299–301, for an outstanding example of a Christian biblical theologian who recognizes that love and law are intimately related in Deuteronomy; indeed, that the former finds expression precisely through the latter.

46. Georg Braulik, "Gesetz als Evangelium. Rechtfertigung und Begnadigung nach der deuteronomischen Tora," in *Studien zur Theologie des Deuteronomiums* (Stuttgart: Verlag Katholisches Bibelwerk, 1988), 123–60, esp. 126.

47. See the famous rabbinic dictum found in *S. 'Eli. Zut.* 17:9; *m. Mak.* 3:15; and at the end of each chapter of *m. 'Abot* in standard editions. On the centrality of grace in rabbinic Judaism, see R. J. W. Werblowsky, "Tora als Gnade," *Kairós* 15 (1973): 156–63; and Solomon Schechter, *Aspects of Rabbinic Theology* (New York: Schocken, 1961), 133–34, 278–79, 306-7.

48. Braulik, "Gesetz als Evangelium," 145, 149.

49. Raymond Brown, *The Message of Deuteronomy: Not by Bread Alone*, BST (Leicester: InterVarsity Press, 1993), 23–25.

50. Henning Graf Reventlow, *Gebot und Predigt im Dekalog* (Gütersloh: Gerd Mohn, 1962), 15–21.

51. Brevard S. Childs, *Introduction to the Old Testament as Scripture* (Philadelphia: Fortress Press, 1979), 211–12, 224; Dennis Olson, *Deuteronomy and the Death of Moses*,

OBT (Minneapolis: Fortress Press, 1994), 3, 174–76, who maintains that "Deuteronomy in the end holds together law and human responsibility with promise and divine mercy" (3). Their view is quite similar to that of the rabbis. An unusually sensitive treatment of love and law in Deuteronomy that at once defends both Deuteronomy's own positions and rabbinic understandings of Deuteronomy against antinomian attacks is found in McBride, "Yoke." Another attempt to show the connection between law and gospel in Deuteronomy is found in Lothar Perlitt, "'Evangelium' und Gesetz im Deuteronomium," in *The Law in the Bible and Its Environment*, ed. Timo Veijola (Göttingen: Vandenhoeck & Ruprecht, 1990), 23–38.

52. Levenson, *Hebrew Bible, Old Testament*, 48–51.

53. Ibid., 56. Cf. Moshe Greenberg, "On the True Meaning of Scripture" [in Hebrew], in *'Al Hammiqra' Ve'al Hayyahadut* (Tel Aviv: 'Am 'Oveid, 1984), 344–49; and also Benjamin Sommer, "The Scroll of Isaiah as Jewish Scripture, Or, Why Jews Don't Read Books," *SBL Seminar Papers* (Atlanta: Scholars Press, 1996), 240–41.

54. See Perdue, *Reconstructing*, 193, 206. For a sensitive reflection on the tension between discerning coherence and acknowledging dissonance in the work of a Protestant biblical theologian who is also a historian of religion, see Patrick D. Miller, "Deuteronomy and Psalms: Evoking a Biblical Conversation," *JBL* 118 (1999): 17.

55. Brueggemann, *Theology*.

56. Erhard Gerstenberger, *Theologies of the Old Testament* (Minneapolis: Fortress Press, 2002).

57. Concerning this issue, see also S. Tamar Kamionkowski, "A Dialogic Model for Jewish Biblical Theology," (forthcoming) and Marc Brettler, "Psalms and Jewish Biblical Theology," in *Jewish Bible Theology: Perspectives and Studies*, ed. Isaac Kalimi (Winona Lake, Ind.: Eisenbrauns, forthcoming).

58. I refer to *Sinai and Zion* and *Creation* respectively. On the importance of discussing particular themes, see also the methodological statement in Barr, *Concept*, 52–56.

59. For the former, see James Barr, *Biblical Faith and Natural Theology* (Gifford Lectures, 1991; Oxford: Oxford University Press, 1993); (and, more briefly, Barr, *Concept*, 468–96); and the parallel but more restrained conclusions of John J. Collins, *Encounters with Biblical Theology* (Minneapolis: Fortress Press, 2005), 91–104 and 117–26. For the latter, see Yochanan Muffs, *Love and Joy: Law, Language and Religion in Ancient Israel* (New York and Cambridge: Jewish Theological Seminary and Harvard University Press, 1992), 9–49; Meir Weiss, "Concerning the Doctrine of Retribution in the Bible" [in Hebrew], *Tarbiz* 31–32 (1962–1963): 236–63, 1–18; and Joel Kaminsky, *Corporate Responsibility in the Hebrew Bible* JSOTSup (Sheffield: Sheffield Academic Press, 1995).

60. Stephen Geller, "The God of the Covenant," in *One God or Many? Conceptions of Divinity in the Ancient World*, ed. Barbara Nevling Porter (Casco Bay, Maine: Casco Bay Assyriological Institute, 2000), 273–319. In addition, Stephen Geller, *Sacred Enigmas: Literary Religion in the Hebrew Bible* (London: Routledge, 1996), represents its own style of theological cross section (à la Eichrodt) done from a literary point of view rather than a cross section forced into a mold that ultimately comes from the categories of doctrinal theology.

61. Sara Japhet, *The Ideology of the Book of Chronicles and Its Place in Biblical Thought* (Frankfurt: Peter Lang, 1989); Ronald E. Clements, *God's Chosen People: A Theological Interpretation of the Book of Deuteronomy* (London: SCM Press, 1968); Hans-Joachim Kraus, *Theology of the Psalms* (Minneapolis: Augsburg, 1986). On Psalms, see also Brettler, "Psalms and Jewish Biblical Theology." On the need for biblical theology to concentrate

on discrete texts, see also Manfred Oeming, Gesamtbiblische Theologien der Gegenwart: *Das Verhältnis von AT und NT in der Hermeneutischen Diskussion Seit Gerhard von Rad* (Stuttgart: Verlag W. Kohlhammer, 1985), 252; and cf. Barr, *Concept*, 140–45.

62. For an example of how secular Jews relate to the Bible as scripture, see Yair Zakovitch, "The Goal: Strengthening Our Cultural Identity," in *Minds Across Israel: Conversations with Thinkers and Authors on Judaism, Zionism, and Israel* [in Hebrew] (Jerusalem and Tel Aviv: Jewish Agency and Yedi'ot Aharonot, 2003), 265–80.

63. The following four sections are largely taken from Benjamin Sommer, "Ein neues Modell für Biblische Theologie," trans. Goenke Eberhardt, in *Theologie und Exegese des Alten Testaments / der Hebräischen Bible. Zwischenbilanz und Zukunftsperspektiven*, ed. Bernd Janowski, Stuttgarter Bibelstudien (Stuttgart: Verlag Katolisches Bibelwerk, 2005), 187–212.

64. Ibid., 25

65. Otto Eissfeldt, "The History of Israelite-Jewish Religion and Old Testament Theology," in *The Flowering of Old Testament Theology: A Reader in Twentieth-Century Old Testament Theology, 1930–1990*, eds. Ben Ollenberger, Elmer Martens, and Gerhard Hasel (Winona Lake, Ind.: Eisenbrauns, 1992), 21.

66. Johann Gabler, "On the Proper Distinction Between Biblical and Dogmatic Theology and the Specific Objectives of Each," in *The Flowering of Old Testament Theology*, 502 (=John Sandys-Wunsch and Laurence Eldredge, "J. P. Gabler and the Distinction Between Biblical and Dogmatic Theology: Translation, Commentary, and Discussion of His Originality," *SJT* 33 [1980]: 144).

67. See Gabler (ed. Ollenburger et al., p. 500/Sandys-Wunsch and Eldredge, 142): "When these opinions of the holy men have been carefully collected from Holy Scripture and suitably digested, carefully referred to the universal notions, and cautiously compared among themselves, the question of their dogmatic use may then profitably be established, and the goals of both biblical and dogmatic theology correctly assigned. Under this heading one should investigate with great diligence which opinions have to do with the unchanging testament of Christian doctrine, and therefore pertain directly to us; and which are said only to men of some particular era or testament." I understand "Under this heading" to refer to the second of the two theologies referred to in the previous sentence, viz., dogmatic theology.

68. Sandys-Wunsch and Eldredge, "Gabler and the Distinction," 158, notes, "Gabler has perhaps a better claim to be considered the father of the study of biblical religion than the father of biblical theology." The role of the biblical theologian for Gabler goes beyond purely diachronic description, in that the biblical theologian also should note which biblical doctrines are unique to a particular book or writer and which are common throughout the Bible. For Gabler, as Sandys-Wunsch points out (148), only the latter "are true doctrines of religion. Having once separated these doctrines biblical theology then has the task of ordering them into a coherent whole." Thus the description is not exclusively historical; it entails a higher-order task as well. But discussions of the relevance of these ideas to contemporary religion are the exclusive domain of the dogmatic theologian.

69. For a representative example of this thinking, see the clear statement in Isaac Kalimi, "History of Israelite Religion or Old Testament Theology?"

70. Walter Eichrodt, "Does Old Testament Theology Still Have Independent Significance within Old Testament Scholarship?" in *The Flowering of Old Testament Theology*, 36–37. Cf. the similar reasoning in Eichrodt, *Theology*, 1:27.

71. Eichrodt, "Does Old Testament Theology Still Have Independent Significance," 33. Eichrodt differs only slightly from Gabler in this respect. For Gabler, the biblical theologian describes the particulars and then notes which doctrines appear throughout the Bible, thus articulating something similar to what Eichrodt has in mind when he speaks of the Bible's essence. In any event, the biblical theologian's task remains descriptive for both thinkers.

72. See Goshen-Gottstein, "Tanakh Theology," 617.

73. Jean Bottéro, *Religion in Ancient Mesopotamia* (Chicago: University of Chicago Press, 2001).

74. See Kaufmann, *Toledot*; William Foxwell Albright, *Yahweh and the Gods of Canaan: An Historical Analysis of Two Contrasting Faiths* (Garden City: Doubleday, 1968).

75. Such a reading of the inscription is not the only one possible, of course, but it is accepted by many biblicists, and it is heuristically helpful for present purposes. The literature on the finds from Kuntillet 'Ajrud and the related finds at Khirbet el-Qom is enormous. For the texts, see the helpful edition and brief commentary in Shmuel Aḥituv, *Handbook of Ancient Hebrew Inscriptions* [in Hebrew] (Jerusalem: Bialik, 1992), 111–15, 152–61. Of the many studies, note especially Patrick D. Miller, *The Religion of Ancient Israel* (Louisville: Westminster John Knox, 2000), 31–36, with recent bibliography.

76. See the discussion of this question in Levenson, "Why Jews Are Not Interested," 37–38; and Goshen-Gottstein, "Tanakh Theology," 629.

77. Bertrand Russell, *A History of Western Philosophy* (New York: Simon & Schuster, 1945).

78. Cf. Oeming, *Gesamtbiblische Theologien*, 225: "Gesamtbiblische Theologie im Sinne einer einheitlichen, von der ganzen Bibel konstant bezeugten Lehre gibt es nicht und wird es nicht geben. Die Hoffnung auf die endliche Entdeckung eines geistigen Bandes, das die vielgestaltige biblische Welt im Innersten zusammenhält, ist illusorisch. Wie die Physiker werden auch die Exegeten bei der Suche nach der biblisch-theologischen 'Weltformel' scheitern." On the ill-defined nature of the field of biblical theology, see also the trenchant remarks of Zevit, "Jewish Biblical," 305.

79. On the relation between biblical theology and history of Israelite religion, see also Levenson, "Why," 35–38; Barr, *Concept*, 100–139; Collins, *Encounters*, 24–33. Barr and Collins emphasize the substantial overlap between these fields in practice. I would go a step further and assert that it is often impossible to distinguish them at all—except in cases where the biblical theology turns out to be a particular sort of dogmatic theology or apologetics. My assertion that the two fields are perhaps identical is true on practical grounds (much of what claims to belong to one field looks identical to material in the other) and on theoretical grounds (no clear definition for biblical theology has emerged, and some of the many hazy ones in fact do describe a particular type of the history of Israelite religion). To be sure, some histories have much less in common with a biblical theology (for example, Ziony Zevit, *The Religions of Ancient Israel: A Synthesis of Parallactic Approaches* [New York: Continuum, 2001]). Nonetheless, many monographs or articles could easily be classified in the one field or the other, regardless of the author's intentions. This is the case, for example, of treatments of a particular aspect of biblical theology or religion. Marc Brettler, *God Is King: Understanding an Israelite Metaphor*, JSOTSup (Sheffield: Sheffield Academic Press, 1989) could belong to either field, even though its rhetorical style is more historical. The same is true of H. W. F. Saggs, *The Encounter with the Divine in Mesopotamia and Israel* (London: Athlone Press, 1978), which disregards any

artificial distinction between the fields. On a single page Saggs is happy to enter into dialogue with von Rad, *Old Testament Theology*, and with Frank Moore Cross, *Canaanite Myth and Hebrew Epic)*, and Saggs's work is the more enriching for his readiness to do so. Similarly, Bernd Janowski, *Gottes Gegenwart in Israel* (Neukirchen: Neukirchener, 1993), was published, quite appropriately, in the Beiträge zur Theolgie des Alten Testaments, but it could just as easily have been published by a series on the history of Israelite religion, without any changes being necessary. Kaufmann's work provides an excellent example of this overlap. Similarly, the words "biblical theology" appear, appropriately, in the subtitle of Muffs's *Personhood of God*, but Muffs's frequent comparisons of Mesopotamian and Israelite religion (which draw deeply on the works of Yehezkel Kaufmann and Thorkild Jacobsen) render the book worthwhile for historians of ancient Near Eastern religion.

80. Zevit, "Jewish Biblical," 339, characterizes the goal very well: "The issues on which most Jewish scholars focus seem to proceed under a motto that is a reversal of Anselm's, to wit: '(critical) understanding in search of faith.'"

81. See Krister Stendahl, "Biblical Theology, Contemporary," in *The Interpreter's Dictionary of the Bible*, 4 vols. (Nashville: Abingdon, 1962), 1:418–32.

82. Ibid., 1:419.

83. See his study, Krister Stendahl, *The Bible and the Role of Women: A Case Study in Hermeneutics*, trans. Emilie T. Sander, vol. 15; Facet Books Biblical Series (Philadelphia: Fortress Press, 1966), and also Barr's comments in *Concept*, 196–97.

84. Barr, *Concept*, 199.

85. Indeed, Stendahl, having noted that there is no basis in the New Testament for the ordination of women, did not terminate his work there—that is, he did not limit that book to a description of what the New Testament meant. Rather, he went on to discuss what this New Testament situation did and did not mean for the contemporary Church of Sweden, arguing that ordination of women was acceptable to a church based on the New Testament nevertheless. Thus he himself embraced both the role he names "biblical theologian" and the unnamed role of the person who follows the biblical theologian in that work, sometimes on a single page. See further Barr's discussion of Stendahl's mixing of the two activities in *Concept*, 196–98.

86. In the last chapter of Oeming, *Gesamtbiblische Theologien*, 232–41.

87. Ibid., 232.

88. Ibid., 233–34. Further, Oeming acknowledges that there are multiple measures of value suggested by both the New Testament and Christian theology, and thus many possible Christian theologies of the Old Testament are possible, necessary, and desirable. See his remarks on 235.

89. Von Rad, *Old Testament Theology*, 2:428–29 and passim. Cf. the similar remarks in Walther Eichrodt, *Theology*, 1:26: "To our general aim of obtaining a comprehensive picture of the realm of OT belief we must add a second and closely related purpose—*to see that this comprehensive picture does justice to the essential relations with the NT. . . .* In expounding the realm of OT thought and belief we must never lose sight of the fact that the OT religion, ineffaceably individual though it may be, can yet be grasped in this essential uniqueness only when it is seen as completed in Christ" (emphasis added).

90. Oeming does not use this Kantian terminology, but it suits his project well.

91. Oeming, *Gesamtbiblische Theologien*, 237.

92. Ibid., 234–35.

93. Ibid., 238–39.

94. Ibid., 239.

95. Oeming's contribution to Christian theology here is very similar to Brueggemann's. In particular, both discuss the deep skepticism, doubt, and complaint against God that the Old Testament legitimates; see Oeming, *Gesamtbiblische Theologien*, 240, and Brueggemann, *Theology*, 400–403.

96. Oeming, *Gesamtbiblische Theologien*, 235.

97. Rainer Albertz, *A History of Israelite Religion in the Old Testament Period*, 2 vols. (Louisville: Westminster John Knox, 1994). Albertz discusses the potential relationship between the study of the history of Israelite religion and biblical theology in greater detail in Rainer Albertz, "Religionsgeschichte Israels statt Theologie des Alten Testaments! Plädoyer für eine forschungsgeschichtliche Umorientierung," *JBTh* 10 (1995): 3–24.

98. Albertz, *History*, 1:17.

99. Ibid., 1:12.

100. For example, Martin Noth, *A History of Pentateuchal Traditions* (Englewood Cliffs, N.J.: Prentice Hall, 1972).

101. For example, Gerhard von Rad, "The Problem of the Hexateuch," in *The Problem of the Hexateuch and Other Essays*, trans. E. Trueman Dicken (London: SCM Press, 1984).

102. Michael Fishbane, *Biblical Interpretation in Ancient Israel* (Oxford: Oxford University Press, Clarendon, 1985).

103. Paul D. Hanson, *The Diversity of Scripture: A Theological Interpretation* (Philadelphia: Fortress Press, 1982).

104. Albertz, *History*, 1:17. For another example of a historical work whose author notes its theological use, see Mark Smith, *The Origins of Biblical Monotheism: Israel's Polytheistic Background and the Ugaritic Texts* (New York: Oxford University Press, 2001), 18-19.

105. On the relation between Albertz's work and Old Testament theology, see further Barr, *Concept*, 122–23; and John Barton, "Alttestamentliche Theologie nach Albertz?" *JBTh* 10 (1995): 25–34.

106. Barr, *Biblical Faith and Natural Theology*.

107. In *Concept*, he makes this argument more explicit. See, for example, *Concept*, 586: "Work in biblical theology . . . can furnish indications and suggestions to doctrinal theology; and likewise it can indicate, among the many options of doctrinal theology, those which are amenable to its own work, and provide a space and a conceptual area which gives room for its own operations." Cf. *Concept*, 64–65.

108. Cf. Oeming, *Gesamtbiblische Theologien*, 237: "Biblische Theologie ist somit weder eine bloß historische, noch eine bloß dogmatische Disziplin, sondern beides zugleich."

109. John Collins also discusses biblical wisdom literature in relation to natural theology in Collins, *Encounters*, 91–104 ("The Biblical Precedent for Natural Theology"), and 117–26 ("Natural Theology and Biblical Tradition"); the former (originally published in 1977) was a crucial predecessor for Barr's work, while the latter provides important reflections on the limitations of Barr's book. Collins's approach matches the dialogical model I propose here somewhat less than Barr's, since he does not spend as much time specifically engaging the work of modern theologians.

110. In particular, Moshe Greenberg, *'Al Hammiqra' Ve'al Hayyahadut* [in Hebrew] (Tel Aviv: 'Am 'Oveid, 1984); and Moshe Greenberg, *Hassegullah Vehakkoah* [in Hebrew] (Oranim: Hakkibbutz Hameuhad, 1986); see also Greenberg, *Studies*.

111. "Postulates of Biblical Criminal Law," originally published in *Yehezkel Kaufmann Jubilee Volume*, ed. Menahem Haran (Jerusalem: Magnes, 1960); reprinted in many collections, including Greenberg, *Studies*, 25–42.

112. The only explicit reference to these rabbinic laws occurs in footnotes 28 and 29 there.

113. The degree to which the rabbinic laws concerning capital punishment represent an evolution or a revolution in relationship to biblical law can be debated. For the latter view, see especially Moshe Halbertal, *Interpretive Revolutions in the Making* [in Hebrew] (Jerusalem: Magnes Press, 1997); but see other view in Yair Lorberbaum, *The Image of God: Halakhah and Aggadah* [in Hebrew] (Tel Aviv: Schocken, 2004).

114. These appear in Greenberg, *Hassegullah Vehakkoah*, 11–18 and 49–67. Material approximating the former appears in English as "A Problematic Heritage: The Attitude Toward the Gentile in the Jewish Tradition—An Israeli Perspective," *Conservative Judaism* 48 (1996):22–35. Some of the latter article appears in English as "On the Political Use of the Bible in Modern Israel: An Engaged Critique," in *Pomegranates and Golden Bells*, eds. David P. Wright, David Noel Freedman, and Avi Hurvitz (Winona Lake, Ind.: Eisenbrauns, 1995), 461–71. See also Moshe Greenberg, "You Are Called Human" [in Hebrew], in *'Al Hammiqra' Ve'al Hayyahadut* (Tel Aviv: 'Am 'Oveid, 1984), 55–67.

115. Thus Greenberg provides what Oeming would call *Sachkritik* (Oeming, *Gesamtbiblische Theologien*, 238)—or rather, he notes that the rabbis engaged tentatively in *Sachkritik*.

116. Zachary Braiterman, *(God) After Auschwitz: Tradition and Change in Post-Holocaust Jewish Thought* (Princeton: Princeton University Press, 1998).

117. See Braiterman's discussion of what he calls "antitheodicy" in Braiterman, *(God) After Auschwitz*, 4–5, 31–38, 47–59. This notion closely resembles what Brueggemann calls "countertestimony." See Brueggemann, *Theology*, 317–32.

118. For three additional examples of a dialogical biblical theology at work, see Benjamin Sommer, "Revelation at Sinai in the Hebrew Bible and Jewish Theology," *JR* 79 (1999):422–51; Sommer, "Unity and Plurality"; and Benjamin Sommer, "Prophecy as Translation: Ancient Israelite Conceptions of the Human Factor in Prophecy," in *Bringing the Hidden to Light: The Process of Interpretation. Studies in Honor of Stephen A. Geller*, eds. Diane Sharon and Kathryn Kravitz (Winona Lake, Ind.: Eisenbrauns, 2007) 271-90.

119. The following subsection is based on Benjamin Sommer, "Psalm 1 and the Canonical Shaping of Jewish Scripture," in *Jewish Bible Theology: Perspectives and Studies*, ed. Isaac Kalimi (Winona Lake, Ind.: Eisenbrauns, forthcoming).

120. Incidentally, these rules are of little practical relevance for a community selling its religious objects or properties, since the Talmud explains that these rules do not apply when the items are sold by the seven leading members of the congregation in the presence of the congregation. See Rava's comment in *b. Meg.* 26a and *Orah H ayyim* 153:8.

121. See Rashi's comment on 28b to *hespēd šel rabbīm*.

122. Also in y. *Šab.* 1:1 (3a) and, in a slightly different version, *b. Šab.* 11a.

123. Cf. Rashi's commentary on *b. Šab.* 11a to *h bērîm hā'ôsēqim*.

124. Many other passages can be cited; in the aggregate, they evince both the tension between these two important values and the greater respect for study, though not without some complexities. See, for example, *b. Šab.* 10a (concerning which cf. *b. Roš Haš.* 35a); *b. Šab.* 127a; in *b. Ber.* 8a, the teachings of Ḥisda, of Ḥiyya in the name of 'Ulla (note

the complexity of his view, which implies that temple service was greater than study; cf. m. 'Abot 1.2, where the two seem to be of equal value, and see also the attempt to reach a mediating position in b. Meg. 3a–b), of Abbaye, and of Ammi and Assi in b. Ber. 8a (apparently contradicting Abbaye's different perspective in b. Meg. 29a, but note that this opinion ought to be attributed not to Abbaye but to Rava according to Rabbeinu Hananel and Gilyon Hašas); b. Ber. 31a–b. On the paramount value of Torah study over all other religious values (including prayer), see especially the debate involving Rabbi Tarfon, Rabbi Akiva, and the elders in b. Qidd. 40b and also the teaching of Rabbi Yosi there, and see further m. Pe'ah 1:1 (=b. Qidd. 40a), and note also the texts collected in m. 'Abot, chapter 6. For a later rabbinic voice valorizing study over prayer, see Maimonides' Code, Laws of Prayer, 8:3—a passage whose higher valorization of study is noteworthy, because it appears in a chapter that emphasizes the great importance of prayer. For further discussion of the value of Torah study in classical rabbinic literature, see E. E. Urbach, The Sages: Their Concepts and Beliefs, trans. Israel Abrahamson (Jerusalem: Magnes, 1975), 612–14; and Shmuel Safrai, "Oral Torah," in The Literature of the Sages, Part One, ed. Shmuel Safrai, CRINT (Philadelphia: Fortress Press, 1987), 35–119, esp. 102–6; Marc Hirshman, "Torah in Rabbinic Thought: The Theology of Learning," in The Cambridge History of Judaism: The Late Roman-Rabbinic Period, vol. 4, ed. Steven Katz (Cambridge: Cambridge University Press, 2006), 899–924.

In light of the consistent tendency of these texts to weigh the relative value of prayer and prophecy, I cannot agree with the claim in Lawrence Hoffman, "Hallels, Midrash, Canon, and Loss: Psalms in Jewish Liturgy," in Psalms in Community: Jewish and Christian Textual, Liturgical and Artistic Traditions, eds. Harold Attridge and Margot Fassler (Atlanta: Society of Biblical Literature, 2003), 33-57 that "the presumed dichotomy between prayer and study exists more in the minds of twentieth- and twenty-first-century critics than it did in the rabbinic imagination" (54). Hoffman is right to point out that for the rabbis, prayer was not limited to "the current popular notion of prayer as personal conversation with God" but also includes "the midrashic linking of biblical text to the expression of theological realia" (55) so that prayer was itself, in part, a form of sacred and salvific study; the very fact that prayer in rabbinic culture is conceptualized this way itself points to the rabbinic understanding of the religious value of study.

125. To be sure, Mitnagdim continued to value prayer, and Hasidim eventually began to reemphasize study, a trend evident as early as the development of Chabad. But the pronounced tendencies are clear. For discussions of these differing religious sensibilities, see Norman Lamm, "Study and Prayer: Their Relative Value in Hasidism and Mitnagdism," in Samuel K. Mirsky Memorial Volume: Studies in Jewish Law, Philosophy, and Literature, ed. Gersion Appel (New York: Yeshiva University, 1970), 37–52; Mordecai Wilensky, Hasidim Umitnagdim: Letoldot Hapulmus Beyneyhem [in Hebrew] 2d. ed. (Jerusalem: Mossad Bialik, 1990), 15–26; and Allan Nadler, The Faith of the Mithnagdim: Rabbinic Responses to Hasidic Rapture (Baltimore: Johns Hopkins University Press, 1997), 50–77, 151–70.

126. Wilensky, Hasidim Umitnagdim, 1:17–19. See further the comments of Nadler, Faith, 151, 232–33.

127. Already in its early period Hasidism began to develop a model of leadership in which the rebbe is treated as the group's king. This royal model of leadership is most prominent in the Ruzhin/Boyaner groups, and it has also become conspicuous in the Chabad sect, but to some degree it is present in all Hasidic groups. The model usually involved dynastic mechanisms for the transfer of leadership. On the development of the

dynastic model during Hasidism's first century, see David Assaf, *The Regal Way: The Life and Times of Rabbi Israel of Ruzhin*, Stanford Series in Jewish History and Culture (Stanford: Stanford University Press, 2002), 47–68. Further, it focused on particular leaders who, like ancient Near Eastern monarchs, served as an axis mundi. See Arthur Green, "The Zaddiq as Axis Mundi in Later Judaism," in *Essential Papers on Kabbalah*, ed. Lawrence Fine (New York: New York University Press, 1995), 291–311.

The question of messianism among Hasidim is more complex. To be sure, some scholars (e.g., Martin Buber and Simon Dubnow) argue that early (pre-1800) Hasidism constituted an attempt to do away with messiansim, but others (Ben Zion Dinur, Isaiah Tishby) regard early Hasidism as thoroughly messianic in orientation, and some (Gershom Scholem, Joseph Weiss) take a middle ground, regarding messianism as an accepted doctrine but not an area of intense focus among early Hasidim. For a review of the literature and a defense of the last position, see Gershom Scholem, "The Neutralization of the Messianic Element in Early Hasidism," in *The Messianic Idea in Judaism and Other Essays on Jewish Spirituality* (New York: Schocken, 1971), 176–202, 359–63. All scholars would agree, however, that intense messianic speculation became more common among some Hasidic leaders by about 1800; see Scholem, 179.

128. For a highly readable treatment of the different styles of leadership in each community, see Amnon Levi, *The Haredim* [in Hebrew] (Jerusalem: Keter, 1989), 150–64, 176–77, who also notes the tendency among Mitnagdim in recent decades to exalt leading Talmudic scholars in a manner that begins to approach the royal model of the Hasidim. On the even more extreme movement among recent Mitnagdim toward insistence that scholars are the ultimate leaders, see Haym Soloveitchik, "Migration, Acculturation, and the New Role of Texts in the Haredi World," in *Accounting for Fundamentalisms: The Dynamic Character of Movements*, eds. Martin Marty and R. Scott Appleby (Chicago: University of Chicago Press, 1994), 197–235, esp. 216–21.

129. Or, in the actual world of Mitnagdim, any male.

130. The identification of wisdom psalms is a matter of some controversy, but even by the broadest definitions they amount to less than a tenth of the psalms found in the Psalter. See Avi Hurvitz, *Wisdom Language in Biblical Psalmody* [in Hebrew] (Jerusalem: Magnes, 1991); R. N. Whybray, "The Wisdom Psalms," in *Wisdom in Ancient Israel: Essays in Honour of J. A. Emerton*, eds. John Day, Robert Gordon, and H. G. M. Williamson (Cambridge: Cambridge University Press, 1995), 152–60; Roland Murphy, "A Consideration of the Classification, 'Wisdom Psalms,'" VTSup 9 (1963): 156–67.

131. This phenomenon is well known in narrative literature. See Adele Berlin, *Poetics and the Interpretation of Biblical Narrative* (Winona Lake, Ind.: Eisenbrauns, 1994), 102.

132. The same point was made by Whybray, "The Wisdom Psalms," 155.

133. One might compare the comment of Rabbi Shimon bar Yoḥai quoted above from y. Ber. 1:5 (3b), where studying is presumed to be an activity that one performs with one's mouth; reading or contemplating a text is done out loud. Study involves mouth and mind simultaneously.

134. Both ibn Ezra and Gunnel André note the similarity of vocabulary in Ps 1:1-2 and Deut 6:4-9, on the basis of which they suggest that the psalmist alludes to that passage from Deuteronomy. See Gunnel André, "'Walk,' 'Stand,' and 'Sit' in Psalm 1:1–2," VT 32 (1982): 327; Stefan Reif, "Ibn Ezra on Psalm I 1–2," VT 34 (1984): 232–36.

135. So far as I know, this approach to the canonical function of Psalm 1 was first expressed, rather in passing, both by Meir Weiss, "The Way of Torah in Psalm 1," in

Miqra'ot Kekhavvanatam [in Hebrew] (Jerusalem: Mosad Bialik, 1988), 111 (originally published in the journal *Ma'ayanot* 6 [1957]); and by Claus Westermann, *Praise and Lament in the Psalms* (trans. Keith R. Crim and Richard N. Soulen; Edinburgh: T&T Clark, 1981), 253 (first published in German in 1964). This insight is developed in greater depth by Joseph Reindl, "Weisheitliche Bearbeitung von Psalmen; ein Beitrag zum Verständnis der Sammlung des Psalters," VTSup 32 (1981):333–56, esp. 339–41; and by Gerald Wilson, *The Editing of the Hebrew Psalter*, SBLDS (Chico, Calif.: Scholars Press, 1985), 143, 204–7. Reindl pays particular attention to form-critical questions, noting the difference between the setting of psalms and the setting of the Psalter. For brief treatments of the canon-shaping role of Ps 1, see also Childs, *Introduction*, 513; Johannes Marböck, "Zur frühen Wirkungsgeschichte von Ps 1," in *Freude an der Weisung des Herrn. Beiträge zur Theologie der Psalmen. Festgabe zum 70. Geburtstag von Heinrich Groß*, ed. Ernst Haag and Frank-Lothar Hossfeld, SBB 13 (Stuttgart: Verlag Katholisches Bibelwerk, 1986), 207–22, esp. 211; J. Clinton McCann, "The Psalms as Instruction," *Int* 46 (1992):117–28, esp. 119.

136. On this conversion of human response into divine revelation, see also Childs, *Introduction*, 513–14; Wilson, *Editing*, 206; McCann, "The Psalms as Instruction," 119. Already in the tenth century, Saadia Gaon viewed the Psalter as a revealed text rather than a humanly authored one. In light of the canon-shaping role of Ps 1, it becomes clear that the attempt to convert the Psalter into a revelatory text is much older than Saadia; Saadia's seemingly radical reading in fact reflects the *peshat* of Ps 1, or at least the *peshat* of Ps 1's editorial role. On Saadia's view of the Psalter, see Uriel Simon, *Four Approaches to the Book of Psalms*, trans. Lenn Schramm (Albany: SUNY Press, 1991), 2–5. Another text that views the psalms this way is found in the Dead Sea Scrolls in 11Q 27:2–11.

137. The only strong examples are Pss 35:28 and 62:7. In three cases (Pss 62:7; 77:13; and 143:5) the verb refers to the worshiper's utterance describing divine works. In these cases the verb is always parallel to some form of the verbal root *zkr* (="mention"), so that the verb *hāgâ* does not itself denote prayer but refers to a verbalization of some idea that happens to occur in the context of prayer.

138. On the significance of this parallel, see Alexander Rofé, "The Piety of the Torah-Disciples at the Winding-up of the Hebrew Bible: Josh 1:8; Ps 1:2; Isa 59:21," in *Bibel in jüdischer und christlicher Tradition: Festschrift für Johann Maier zum 60. Geburtstag*, eds. Helmut Merklien, Karlheinz Muller, and Gunter Stemberger (Frankfurt: Anton Hain, 1993), 78–85, esp. 81–82.

139. The last passage in the Nevi'im makes the same point; see Mal 3:22. One might see the reference to Elijah in 3:23 as a response that attempts to defend prophecy after the lower ranking it received in 3:22. This defense reserves an eschatological role for prophecy, even if in the here-and-now prophecy has surrendered its role to Torah.

140. On this characterization of the Jewish canon, cf. John Barton, *Oracles of God: Perception of Ancient Prophecy in Israel After the Exile* (London: Darton, Longman & Todd, 1986), 21. To be sure, Jewish tradition posits a distinction between the Prophets and the Writings (see Radak's introduction to his commentary on Psalms), but those two sections remain functionally similar for Jewish readers: they are both primarily aids to understanding the Pentateuch and spurs to observing its law.

141. On the ceaseless nature of study as envisioned by this psalm, see also Weiss, "The Way of Torah," 126.

142. On the emphasis of a life of nearly uninterrupted Torah-study in contemporary Mitnagdism, see Soloveitchik, "Migration, Acculturation," 216–17.

143. On the contrast between the two, see also the rather different treatment of Walter Brueggemann, "Bounded by Obedience and Praise: The Psalms as Canon," *JSOT* 50 (1991): 63–92, esp. 66, which is carefully critiqued in Gerald Wilson, "The Shape of the Book of Psalms," *Int* 46 (1992): 129–42, esp. 136–37.

144. On the democratizing trend of study implied in Ps 1, see Rofé, "Piety," 81.

145. Wilson points out that the two apparent exceptions, Pss 10 and 33, are in fact no exceptions at all, since these psalms are simply continuations of the poems found in Pss 9 and 32 respectively, both of which have a Davidic superscription. See Wilson, *Editing*, 155; and the similar argument in Jesper Høgenhaven, "The Opening of the Psalter: A Study of Jewish Theology," *SJOT* 15 (2001): 169–80, esp. 173.

146. Similarly, Ps 145 may be the conclusion of the last division of the Psalter; its first and last verses contain the characteristic language of the doxologies that conclude the four earlier divisions. The five hymns of praise in Pss 146–150 would then be a concluding set of hymns that cap off the Psalter as a whole. See Wilson, *Editing*, 185; and Wilson, "Shape," 132–33.

147. See Wilson, *Editing*, 204; Patrick D. Miller, "The Beginning of the Psalter," in *The Shaping of the Psalter*, ed. J. Clinton McCann, JSOTSup (Sheffield: Sheffield Academic Press, 1993), 83–92, esp. 85; Gerald Sheppard, *Wisdom as Hermeneutical Construct: A Study in the Sapientializing of the Old Testament*, BZAW (Berlin: De Gruyter, 1980), 139–41.

148. For a listing of the relevant MT manuscripts, see Wilson, *Editing*, 207. Some manuscripts of Acts 13:11 cite Ps 2:7 as 1:7. It must be admitted that the reference in some manuscripts of Acts might imply not that what we usually call Ps 1 is unnumbered but that what we usually call Pss 1 and 2 are a single psalm.

149. In arguing that these two texts contend with each other, I regard them as separate texts. On the other hand, many scholars argue that Pss 1–2 are a single unit. (The view that Pss 1–2 is a unified text is already evident in *b. Ber.* 9b–10a. See Miller, "Beginning," 85; and, for further verbal links between these psalms, Marböck, "Frühen Wirkungsgeschichte," 211; J. Kenneth Kuntz, "Wisdom Psalms and the Shaping of the Hebrew Psalter," in *For a Later Generation: The Transformation of Tradition in Israel, Early Judaism, and Early Christianity [Essays in Honor of George Nickelsburg]*, eds. Randal Argall, Beverly Bow, and Rodney Werline [Harrisburg, Pa.: Trinity Press International, 2000], 152.) On the basis of this apparent unity, Sheppard attempts to read the unified text that is now Pss 1–2 as functioning together to form a single introduction to the Psalter (see Sheppard, *Wisdom*, 136–44), an attempt that I do not regard as holding together. In spite of the verbal connections between these two psalms, the distinct nature of each psalm should not be overlooked. An inclusio marks Ps 1 as a discrete text, as noted by Robert Alter, *The Art of Biblical Poetry* (New York: Basic Books, 1985), 116. For a defense of reading Ps 1 as its own text (rather than just part of Pss 1–2), see J. T. Willis, "Psalm 1—an Entity," *ZAW* 91 (1979): 381–40. It seems unnecessary to me to attempt to interpret away the manifest tension between what clearly were (as even Sheppard acknowledges, 139–41) originally two separate texts. Rather, we should note the dialectic that has been created by the placement of these two texts, a dialectic that is not explicitly resolved in the Psalter. For another approach that acknowledges these tensions without artificially resolving them, see Miller, 88–92.

150. Two recensions exist, but the differences between them do not affect my argument. All subsequent references are to the Buber edition (Solomon Buber, ed., *Midrash*

Tehillim, Which Is Called Shocher Tov [Vilna: Romm, 1891]). For an overview of the textual history, see Isaac Kalimi, "*Midrash Psalms Shocher Tov*: Some Theological and Methodological Features and a Case Study—the View of God," in *God's Word for Our World: Theological and Cultural Studies in Honor of Simon John De Vries* (ed. J. Harold Ellens et al.; London: T&T Clark, 2004), 63–76, esp. 63–65.

151. The themes we see in this section are not unique within *Midr. Tehillim*. As Esther Menn points out, *Midr. Tehillim* frequently goes "far beyond the biblical sources themselves in portraying Israel's greatest king as a founding figure for its holiest site"; see Esther Menn, "Prayerful Origins: David as Temple Founder in Rabbinic Psalms Commentary (*Midrash Tehillim*)," in *Of Scribes and Sages: Early Jewish Interpretation and Transmission of Scripture*, ed. Craig Evans (London: Continuum, 2004), 77–89, esp. 77. Thus this passage fits a larger pattern found later in this work. Similarly, the comparison between Moses and David found in *Midr. Tehillim* 1§1–2 occurs elsewhere in this work; see Menn, 81, and references there. It remains important to ask why these themes are brought forward in a comment on Ps 1, which seems to deal with neither David nor the temple.

152. In Eli's case, the verb clearly means "sit," as is evident from the following phrase, "upon his chair." The absence of this phrase in the parallel verse concerning David in 2 Sam 7:28 suggests to the rabbis that the verb in this case has its secondary meaning, "to lean."

153. See *b. Soṭah* 40b, *b. Soṭah* 41b, *b. Yoma* 25a, *b. Yoma* 69b, *y. Pesah* 5.10 (7d), *y. Yoma* 3.2 (4b), *y. Soṭah* 7.7 (8a). An exception is *Midr. Sam.* 27 §1–2, which contain an extremely abbreviated form of the midrash as found in *Midr. Tehillim*.

154. Some modern biblical scholars believe that the Eli was in fact a direct descendant of Moses himself; see Julius Wellhausen, *Prolegomena to the History of Ancient Israel* (trans. Black and Menzies; New York: Meridian, 1957), 142–43, and Cross, *Canaanite Myth*, 195–217. The Chronicler implies that Eli was descended from Aaron in 1 Chr 24:3 (cf. 1 Sam 22:9-20), and the rabbis follow this view. Either way, the connection of any high priest to the theme of Torah is clear.

155. My translation follows the standard printed edition rather than Buber. On the textual issue, see Buber's note ad loc.; and William Braude, trans., *The Midrash on Psalms*, Yale Judaica Series (New Haven: Yale University Press, 1959), 2:397n10.

156. I suspect that Rabbi Joshua proposed an alternative because he was troubled by one aspect of Eliezer's suggestion: Eliezer substituted the commandment of tefillin, which is observed only in the daytime, for the study of Torah, which, according to Ps 1:2, should take place day and night. Joshua's alternative is a commandment observed both morning and evening, which is a more appropriate substitute for Torah study as described in the psalm.

157. For example, see Sheppard, *Wisdom*, 136–44.

158. See Wilson, "Shape," 137–38.

159. For an argument that it is inappropriate for Jewish interpreters to privilege the redactors, see Sommer, "The Scroll of Isaiah as Jewish Scripture, Or, Why Jews Don't Read Books"; and more briefly Sommer, "Revelation," 423. Some Christian thinkers express similar qualms about the canon criticism and its theological application; see, for example, James Barr, *Holy Scripture: Canon, Authority, Criticism* (Philadelphia: Westminster, 1983), 49–74.

160. The following subsection expands on my article, Benjamin Sommer, "The Source Critic and the Religious Interpreter," *Int* 60 (2006): 11–16.

161. See John Hayes, "The Tradition of Zion's Inviolability," *JBL* 82 (1963): 419–26; Ben Ollenberger, *Zion, the City of the Great King: A Theological Symbol of the Jerusalem Cult*, JSOTSup (Sheffield: JSOT Press, 1987), 107–29.

162. For the view that this ideology in Isaiah 1–39 stems from the historical Isaiah, see Kaufmann, *Toledot*, 3:147–256 (and see, more generally, 14–38); von Rad, *Old Testament Theology*, 155–75; John Hayes and Stuart Irvine, *Isaiah, Eighth Century Prophet: His Times and His Preaching* (Nashville: Abingdon, 1987), 54–56. For the view that these notions largely stem from a later redactor, see the especially clear presentations in R. E. Clements, *Isaiah 1–39*, NCB (Grand Rapids: Eerdmans, 1980), 16–19; James Ward, *Amos and Isaiah* (Nashville: Abingdon, 1969), 228–56.

163. For a lengthier discussion of the allusion, see Sommer, *Prophet*, 86–87.

164. See Otto Eissfeldt, "The Promises of Grace to David in Isaiah 55:1–5," in *Israel's Prophetic Heritage*, eds. B. Anderson and W. Harrelson (New York: Harper & Bros., 1962), 202–7.

165. For a lengthier discussion of the relationship between these passages, see Sommer, *Prophet*, 115–17. For other examples of Deutero-Isaianic revision of preexilic royal prophecies, see 84–88, 112–15, 153–54.

166. See Marc Brettler, "The Book of Judges: Literature as Politics," *JBL* 108 (1989): 412–15; Yairah Amit, *Hidden Polemics in Biblical Narrative* (Leiden: Brill, 2000), 178–88.

167. I borrow this term from Amit, *Hidden Polemics*. Neither Amit nor Brettler, in their excellent treatments of the hidden polemic against Saul in Judg 19–21, take note of the way these chapters work with the last half of 2 Samuel to present a hidden polemic against David as well.

168. On the ambivalent attitudes toward the monarchy in Samuel, see Robert Polzin, *Samuel and the Deuteronomist: A Literary Study of the Deuteronomistic History, Part Two*, Indiana Studies in Biblical Literature (Bloomington: Indiana University Press, 1989), esp. 22–49. On this book's complex view of David—at once admiring and cynical—see Robert Alter, *The Art of Biblical Narrative* (New York: Basic Books, 1981), 114–30.

169. See John J. Collins, *The Scepter and the Star: The Messiahs of the Dead Sea Scrolls and Other Ancient Literature*, ABRL (New York: Doubleday, 1995), 29–34, 49–56.

170. Reuven Kimelman, "The Messiah in the Amidah: A Study in Comparative Messianism," *JBL* 116, no. 2 (1997): 313–20.

171. Private communication. Leifer maintains that the rabbinic prayer book serves as a *summa* of rabbinic theology, refuting the view that the rabbis never produced a statement of core beliefs.

172. Chaim Stern, ed., *Gates of Prayer: The New Union Prayerbook: Weekdays, Sabbaths, and Festivals, Services and Prayers for Synagogue and Home* (New York: Central Conference of American Rabbis, 1975); Chaim Stern, ed., *Gates of Prayer for Shabbat and Weekdays: A Gender Sensitive Prayerbook* (New York: Central Conference of American Rabbis, 1994).

173. *Siddur Va'Ani Tefillati* [in Hebrew] (Jerusalem: Kenesset Harabbanim Beyisrael and Hattenu'ah Hamsoratit, 1998), 68. Another recent Conservative prayer book includes two versions of the first paragraph, both of which are royalist, but it also includes a meditation on the *Amidah* by Rabbi André Ungar, which clearly can function as an alternative text. The first paragraph of this meditation speaks of God's "redeeming love" rather than of a "redeemer." See *Siddur Sim Shalom for Shabbat and Festivals* (New York:

Rabbinical Assembly and United Synagogue for Conservative Judaism, 1998), 35a–b, 39, 115a–b, 121.

174. Of course, the same tends to be true of biblical theologies that do attempt a cross-cut; one of the characteristics that differentiates dialogical biblical theology is simply its self-reflective honesty.

175. This approach may be more readily acceptable to Jews and Catholics, with their emphasis on tradition as a religious category that has independent value alongside scripture. Such notions are not entirely absent in Protestant tradition, however; for example, one might note the Wesleyan quadrangle, which embraces not only scripture but tradition, reason, and experience. Further, in some ways the role of *sola scriptura* in contemporary Protestant thought has become more limited. See the discussions of Avery Dulles, "Reflections on 'Sola Scriptura,' " in *Revelation and the Quest for Unity* (Washington: Corpus Books, 1968), 67–74; and Robert Gnuse, *The Authority of the Bible: Theories of Inspiration, Revelation, and the Canon of Scripture* (New York: Paulist Press, 1985), 116–17; but see also the more traditional Protestant approach of Stephen Chapman, "The Old Testament Canon and Its Authority for the Christian Church," *ExAud* 19 (2003). On the greater affinity of Jewish and Catholic scholarship in this regard, see my comments in Sommer, "Unity and Plurality," 109–11.

176. See Collins, *Encounters*, 2.

177. See Brueggemann, *Theology*, 62.

178. Collins rightly criticizes Brueggemann's claim that biblical theology must be based exclusively on the text itself and that the only legitimate countertestimony to biblical testimony is found in the Bible itself. Collins notes that other testimonies can in fact have a voice: he mentions the findings of archaeology and historical scholarship and modern ethical sensibilities that stem from the Enlightenment tradition to which we all are heir (see Collins, *Encounters*, 5). Collins does not point out the possibility of countertestimony from religious tradition. As a result, his own model of a nonconfessional biblical theology remains, as Levenson would argue, without clear moorings: how can one decide whether a biblical testimony or a contemporary ethical countertestimony takes precedence? For the dialogical biblical theologian, on the other hand, the model provided by countertestimony found in tradition provides a guide to answering this sort of question. For a study of how countertestimony in tradition sets aside scriptural teaching, see "Using Rabbinic Exegesis as an Educational Resource When Teaching the Book of Joshua" in Greenberg, *Hassegullah Vehakkoaḥ*, esp. 11–18.

179. Here it is crucial to recall that modern biblical scholarship (especially in its composition-critical and form-critical manifestations) has demonstrated that tradition is not subsequent to scripture. Rather, tradition grew up alongside scripture and indeed preceded scripture. See Dulles, "Reflections," 70–72 and 80.

180. Here again I find myself in disagreement with Collins, whose cogent descriptions of the problems at hand nevertheless do much to clarify the fundamental issues. "The very appeal to dogmatic principles cuts off the possibility of dialogue with those who do not share those principles," he writes (Collins, *Encounters*, 25). It is not at all clear why this should be the case. On the contrary, by acknowledging at the outset what confessional principles inform one's evaluation of scripture, one can avoid the self-deceptive claim to objectivity made by theologians such as Eichrodt, von Rad, and Wellhausen. The sometimes offensive nature (not to mention speciousness) of those claims tends to preclude dialogue. On the other hand, the specifically Christian nature of Barr's (and to some

degree Collins's) attempts to find natural theology in the Old Testament does not prevent their findings in this regard from being interesting and theologically useful to Jews.

181. For example, some modern and medieval interpretations of revelation at Sinai that might seem radical turn out to be strikingly similar to the understanding of revelation in some of the pentateuchal sources, which were obscured by the process of redaction. See Sommer, "Revelation."

2. Old Testament Theology Since Barth's Epistle to the Romans

1. Hans Joachim Kraus, *Die Biblische Theologie: Ihre Geschichte und Problematik* (Neukirchener Verlag, 1970); James D. Smart, *The Past, Present and Future of Biblical Theology* (Philadelphia: Westminster, 1979); F. F. Bruce, "The Theology and Interpretation of the Old Testament," in *Tradition and Interpretation* (ed. G. W. Anderson; Oxford: Clarendon, 1979), 385–416; H. Graf Reventlow, *Problems of Old Testament Theology in the Twentieth Century* (Philadelphia: Fortress Press, 1985); John H. Hayes and Frederick Prussner, *Old Testament Theology: Its History and Development* (Atlanta: John Knox, 1985); George Coats, "Theology of the Hebrew Bible," in *The Hebrew Bible and Its Modern Interpreters* (ed. Douglas A. Knight and Gene M. Tucker; Philadelphia and Chico, Calif.: Fortress Press and Scholars Press, 1985), 239–62; Jesper Høgenhaven, *Problems and Prospects of Old Testament Theology* (Biblical Seminar; Sheffield: JSOT, 1987); John J. Collins, "Is a Critical Biblical Theology Possible," in *The Hebrew Bible and Its Interpreters* (ed. William Henry Propp et al.; Winona Lake, Ind.: Eisenbrauns, 1990), 1–17; Gerhard Hasel, *Old Testament Theology: Basic Issues in the Current Debate*, 4th rev. ed. (Grand Rapids: Eerdmans, 1991); James Barr, *The Concept of Biblical Theology: An Old Testament Perspective* (Minneapolis: Fortress Press, 1999).

2. For the text of the speech, see Otto Merk, *Biblische Theologie des Neuen Testaments in ihrer Anfangszeit* (Marburger Theologische Studien 9; Marburg: N. G. Elwert, 1972), 273–84.

3. For a recent discussion of Gabler's proposal, see Ben C. Ollenburger, "Biblical Theology: Situating the Discipline," in *Understanding the Word: Essays in Honor of Bernhard W. Anderson* (ed. James Butler et al.; JSOT 37; Sheffield: JSOT, 1985), 37–62.

4. Barr, *The Concept of Biblical Theology*, 1–18.

5. *The Epistle to the Romans* (London: Oxford, 1933; based on the 1919 German original); and *Church Dogmatics* (Edinburgh: T&T Clark, 1936–1977). Important studies of Barth and his work include David Ford, *Barth and God's Story: Biblical Narrative and the Theological Method of Karl Barth in the Church Dogmatics* (Studien zur interkulturellen Geschichte des Christentums 27; Frankfurt am Main: Peter Lang, 1981); Johannes Rau and Eberhard Busch, *Karl Barth: Gedenkfeier zum 100. Geburtstag am 20. April 1986 in Düsseldorf* (Düsseldorf: Presse- und Informationsamt der Landesregierung Nordrhein-Westfalen, 1986); Otto Bächli, *Das Alte Testament in der Kirchlichen Dogmatik von Karl Barth* (Kirchen-Vluyn: Neukirchener Verlag, 1987); and Rudolf Smend, "Karl Barth als Ausleger der Heiligen Schrift," *Theologie als Christologie*, ed. Heidelore Köchert und Wolf Krötke (Berlin: Evangelische Verlagsanstalt, 1988), 9–37.

6. Paul McGlasson, "Barth, Karl," *Dictionary of Biblical Interpretation* I, ed. John H. Hayes (Nashville: Abingdon, 1999), 1:99–100.

7. Brevard Childs is the best example of an Old Testament scholar who incorporates many of the features of dialectical theology into his theology (*Biblical Theology of the Old*

and New Testaments: Theological Reflection on the Christian Bible [Minneapolis: Fortress Press, 1993]). When doing Old Testament theology, Childs rejects the approach of the history of religion.

8. See the essays in "Part I.2: A Discussion of Barth's Epistle to the Romans," in *The Beginnings of Dialectic Theology,* ed. James M. Robinson (Richmond: John Knox, 1968), 61–130.

9. Rudolph Bultmann, "Karl Barth's Epistle to the Romans in Its Second Edition," in *The Beginnings of Dialectic Theology,* 100; emphasis added. Thus Barth follows the tradition of Schleiermacher's *On Religion* and Otto's *The Idea of the Holy,* both of which seek to demonstrate a "religious a priori."

10. George Ernest Wright, *God Who Acts: Biblical Theology as Recital* (SBT 8; London: SCM, 1952).

11. The most important, early covenant theologian was the Dutch scholar Johannes Cocceius. See W. J. van Asselt, *The Federal Theology of Johannes Cocceius (1603–1669)* (Leiden: Brill, 2001).

12. Otto Eissfeldt, "Israelitisch-jüdische Religionsgeschichte und alttestamentliche Theologie," ZAW 55 (1926) 1–12 = "The History of Israelite-Jewish Religion and Old Testament Theology," in *The Flowering of Old Testament Theology: A Reader in Twentieth-Century Old Testament Theology, 1930–1990,* ed. Ben C. Ollenburger, Elmer A. Martens, and Gerhard F. Hasel (Winona Lake, Ind.: Eisenbrauns, 1992), 20–29.

13. Eissfeldt, "The History of Israelite-Jewish Religion and Old Testament Theology," 20–21.

14. Ibid., 29.

15. Among the various studies of the history of the religion of ancient Israel, see Patrick Miller, "God and the Gods: History of Religion as an Approach and Context for Bible and Theology," in *Affirmation* 1 (1973): 37–62; idem, "Israelite Religion," in *The Hebrew Bible and Its Modern Interpreters,* ed. Douglas A. Knight and Gene M. Tucker (Philadelphia: Fortress Press and Chico, Calif.: Scholars Press, 1985), 201–37; and Karel van der Toorn, *Family Religion in Babylonia, Syria and Israel: Continuity and Change in the Forms of Religious Life* (Studies in the History and Culture of the Ancient Near East 7; Leiden: Brill, 1996). For the importance of archaeology for Israelite religion, see William D. Dever, "The Contribution of Archaeology to the Study of Canaanite and Early Israelite Religion," in *Ancient Israelite Religion,* 209–47; idem, "Archaeology and the Religions of Israel," BASOR 301 (1996): 83–90; and Beth Alpert Nakhai, *Archaeology and the Religions of Canaan and Israel* (ASOR Books 7; Boston, Mass.: American Schools of Oriental Research, 2001). The importance of iconography for understanding Israelite religion in its ancient Near Eastern context is demonstrated by the numerous publications of Othmar Keel and his students. Important works include *Die Welt der altorientalischen Bildsymbolik und das Alte Testament. Am Beispiel der Psalmen* (Göttingen: Vandenhoeck & Ruprecht, 1996); and, with Christoph Uehlinger, *Gods, Goddesses, and Images of God in Ancient Israel* (Minneapolis: Fortress Press, 1998). For the importance of ancient Near Eastern religions and their impact on Israelite religion, see Fritz Stolz, "Probleme westsemitischer und israelitischer Religionsgeschichte," ThR 56 (1991): 1–26. E. A. Knauf is one who argues along with several other historians that archaeology is more important than the biblical texts in writing a history of religion. ("From History to Interpretation," in *The Fabric of History, Text, Artifact and Israel's Past,* ed. D. V. Edelman [JSOTSup 127; Sheffield: Sheffield Academic Press, 1991], 26–64).

16. Barr, *The Concept of Biblical Theology*, 100–101.

17. This conservative trend has been endemic to the Albright school, including not only Albright himself but some of his more distinguished former students (e.g., see Frank Cross, *Canaanite Myth and Hebrew Epic* [Cambridge, Mass.: Harvard University Press, 1973]), who argues that Israel historicized Canaanite myth.

18. Eichrodt, "Does Old Testament Theology Still Have Independent Significance?" 34.

19. Ibid., in *The Flowering of Old Testament Theology*, ed. Ben C. Ollenburger, et al. (Winona Lake, Ind.: Eisenbrauns, 1992), 38.

20. Julius Wellhausen, *Prolegomena zur Geschichte Israels* (2d ed.; Berlin: G. Reimer, 1883) and idem, *Israelitische und Jüdische Gerschichte* (2d ed.; Berlin: G. Reimer, 1895).

21. Heinrich Ewald, *The History of Israel* (4th ed., thoroughly revised and corrected; London: Longmans, Green, 1876–1886).

22. Wilhelm Martin Leberecht de Wette, *Beiträge zur Einleitung in das Alte Testament 1 & 2* (Halle: Schimmelpfennig, 1806–1807); *A Critical and Historical Introduction to the Canonical Scriptures of the Old Testament* (4th ed.; New York: D. Appleton and Co., 1864); and *Lehrbuch der historisch-kritischen Einleitung in die Bibel Alten und Neuen Testaments* (ed. Eberhard Schrader, 8th ed.; Berlin: G. Reimer, 1869).

23. Wilhelm Vatke, *Die biblische Theologie wissenschaftlich dargestellt. 1: Die Religion des Alten Testaments nach den Kanonischen Büchern entwickelt* (Berlin: G. Bethge, 1835).

24. Eduard Wilhelm Eugen Reuss, *History of the Canon of the Holy Scriptures in the Christian Church* (2d ed.; Edinburgh: R. W. Hunter, 1891).

25. Karl Heinrich Graf, *Die geschichtlichen Bücher des Alten Testaments zwei historisch-kritische Untersuchungen* (Leipzig: T. O. Weigel, 1866).

26. Rudolf Smend, *Lehrbuch der alttestamentlichen Religionsgeschichte* (2d ed.; Freiburg: J. C. B. Mohr, 1899). "The history of religion will demonstrate how this religion originated among the people of Israel, how they lived within its structure, how they experienced especially their fortunes through its strongest influences, and how they created and maintained their life through it, how it ruled their life, how it required their subjection, and how it allowed the people of the Jewish community to re-emerge" (p. 7).

27. Abraham Kuenen, *Historisch-kritische Einleitung in die Bücher des Alten Testaments: hinsichtlich ihrer Entstehung und Sammlung* (3 vols.; Leipzig: Otto Schulze, 1887–1894). A partial translation of his three-volume Dutch introduction, first edition (1861–1865), was produced in 1865, and then later the entire introduction was translated into German.

28. Hermann Gunkel, *Schöpfung und Chaos in Urzeit und Endzeit: Eine religions-geschichtliche Untersuchung über Gen 1 und Apoc Joh 12* (Göttingen: Vandenhoeck & Ruprecht, 1895). Also see his *Genesis* (3d ed.; Göttingen: Vandenhoeck & Ruprecht, 1910), now translated and published in English as *Genesis* (Mercer, Ga.: Mercer University Press, 1997); idem, *Die Religionsgeschichte und die alttestamentliche Wissenschaft* (Berlin: Protestantischer Schriftenvertrieb, 1910); and idem, *Israel und Babylonien: Der Einfluss Babyloniens aud die israelitische Religion* (Göttingen: Vandenhoeck & Ruprecht, 1903); J. J. Scullion, "Gunkel, Johannes Heinrich Hermann," in *Dictionary of Biblical Interpretation*, ed. John H. Hayes (Nashville: Abingdon, 1999), 1:472–73. For important studies of Gunkel, see Werner Klatt, *Hermann Gunkel. Zu seiner Theologie der Religionsgeschichte und zur Entstehung der formgeschichtlichen Methode* (FRLANT 100; Göttingen: Vandenhoeck & Ruprecht, 1969); and Rudolf Smend, *Deutsche Alttestamentler in drei Jahrhunderten: mit 18 Abbildungen* (Göttingen: Vandenhoeck & Ruprecht, 1989).

29. Albert Eichhorn, *Das Abendmahl im Neuen Testament* (Leipzig: J. C. B. Mohr [Paul Siebeck], 1898).

30. William Wrede, *Über Ausgabe und Methode der sogennanten neutestamentlichen Theologie* (Göttingen: Vandenhoeck und Ruprecht, 1897); and idem, *The Messianic Secret* (Cambridge: J. Clarke, 1971).

31. Wilhelm Bousset, *Religionsgeschichtliche Studien: Aufsätze zur Religionsgeschichte des hellenistischen Zeitalters* (Leiden: Brill, 1979); and idem, *Die Religion des Judentums im späthellenistischen Zeitalter*, ed. Hugo Gressmann; 3d ed. (Tübingen: J. C. B. Mohr, 1926).

32. Hugo Gressmann, *Entwicklungsstufen der Jüdischen Religion* (Giessen: Alfred Töpelmann, 1927); and idem, *Die Älteste Geschichtsschriebung und Prophetie Israel* (2d ed.; Göttingen: Vandenhoeck & Ruprecht, 1921).

33. Hugo Gressmann, *Albert Eichhorn und die religionsgeschichtliche Schule* (Göttingen: Vandenhoeck & Ruprecht, 1914).

34. Emil Schürer, *The History of the Jewish People in the Age of Jesus Christ (175 B.C.–A.D. 135)* (Edinburgh: T&T Clark, 1973–1987).

35. For the bibliography of Wilhelm Baudissin, see Wilhelm Frankenberg and Friedrich Küchler, eds., *Abhandlungen zur semitischen Religionskunde und Sprachwissenschaft, Wolf Wilhelm Grafen von Baudissin zum 26. September 1917 überreicht von Freunden und Schülern und in ihrem Auftrag und mit Unterstützung der Strassburger Cunitzstiftung* (BZAW 33; Giessen: A. Töpelmann, 1918).

36. Paul de Lagarde, *Semitica* (Göttingen: Dieterich, 1878–1879).

37. See Hans Rollmann, "William Wrede, Albert Eichhorn, and the 'Old Quest' of the Historical Jesus," in *Self-Definition and Self-Discovery in Early Christianity: A Study in Changing Horizons. Essays in Appreciation of Ben F. Meyer*, ed. David J. Hawkin and Tom Robinson (Lewiston, N.Y.: E. Mellen Press, 1990), 79–99; and, idem, "Eichhorn, Karl Albert August Ludwig," *Dictionary of Biblical Interpretation* I, ed. John H. Hayes (Nashville: Abingdon, 1999), 1:324–25.

38. Sigmund Mowinckel, *Psalmenstudien I-VI* (Kristiana: J Dybwad, 1921–1924); and idem, *He That Cometh* (New York: Abingdon, 1954).

39. For a review of Mowinckel's understandings, see H. M. Barstad and M. Ottosson, eds., "The Life and Work of Sigmund Mowinckel," *SJTh* (1988): 1–91.

40. Hugo Gressmann, ed., *Altorientalische Texte und Bilder zum Alten Testament* (2d ed.; Berlin: Walter de Gruyter, 1926–1927); and, idem, *Die ältteste Geschichtsschreibung und Prophetie Israels* (2d ed.; Göttingen: Vandenhoeck & Ruprecht, 1921).

41. James G. Frazer, *The Golden Bough: A Study in Magic and Religion*, 2 vols. (London: Macmillan, 1890).

42. S. H. Hooke, ed., *Myth and Ritual: Essays on the Myth and Ritual of the Hebrews in Relation to the Culture Pattern of the Ancient East* (London: Oxford University Press, 1933).

43. S. H. Hooke, ed., *The Labyrinth; Further Studies in the Religion between Myth and Ritual in the Ancient World* (London: Society for Promoting Christian Knowledge, 1938).

44. W. O. E. Oesterley, *Sacrifices in Ancient Israel: Their Origin, Purposes and Development* (New York: Macmillan, 1937); and Theodore H. Robinson, *Hebrew Religion: Its Origin and Development* (2d ed.; London: Society for Promotion of Christian Knowledge, 1937).

45. T. H. Robinson and W. O. E. Oesterley, *Hebrew Religion: Its Origin and Development* (New York: Macmillan, 1930); and Robinson, *A Short Comparative History of Religions* (2d ed.; London: Duckworth, 1951).

46. E. O. James, *History of Religions* (New York: Harper, 1957); and *Myth and Ritual in the Ancient Near East: An Archeological and Documentary Study* (New York: Praeger, 1958).
47. S. H. Hooke, ed., *Myth, Ritual, and Kingship* (Oxford: Clarendon Press, 1958).
48. A. R. Johnson, *The Cultic Prophet in Ancient Israel* (Cardiff: Wales University Press, 1944; 2d ed. 1962); and idem, *Sacral Kingship in Ancient Israel* (2d ed., Cardiff: Wales University Press, 1967).
49. Ivan Engnell, *Divine Kingship in the Ancient Near East* (2d ed.; Oxford: Blackwell, 1967).
50. Helmer Ringgren, *Israelitische Religion* (2d ed.; Stuttgart: W. Kohlhammer, 1982).
51. Alfred Ossian Haldar, *Associations of Cult Prophets among the Ancient Semites* (Uppsala: Almqvist & Wiksells, 1945).
52. Sigmund Mowinckel, *Psalmenstudien*; and *He That Cometh*.
53. Johannes Pedersen, *Israel: Its Life and Culture* 1–4 (Atlanta: Scholars Press, 1991).
54. Aage Bentzen, *King and Messiah* (2d ed.; Oxford: Blackwell, 1970).
55. Of the numerous studies impacted by more modern anthropological methods, one may mention the book of Frank Gorman, who used the theories of Victor Turner, Mary Douglas, and Clifford Geertz in his analysis of priestly ritual (*The Ideology of Ritual: Space, Time and Status in the Priestly Theology* [JSOTSup 91; Sheffield: Sheffield University, 1990]).
56. Albertz, *Persönliche Frömmigkeit und offizielle Religion. Religionsinterner Pluralismus in Israel und Babylon* (Stuttgart: Calwer, Verlag, 1978).
57. Albertz, *A History of Israelite Religion in the Old Testament Period* I, 1–21. In his paper given at the Society of Biblical Interpretation International meeting in 1993, Albertz called for the reorientation of biblical studies with the major focus being placed primarily on the history of Israelite religion instead of on biblical theology. Later, in 1994, in his discussions in the SBL International meeting at Leuven, he expressed regret that he had been misunderstood. He emphasized that he was not calling for a dismissal of Old Testament theology but rather was contending that the discipline of the history of religion should have priority. Also see his essays in *Geschichte und Theologie: Studien zur Exegese des Alten Testaments und zur Religionsgeschichte Israels* (BZAW 326; Berlin: Walter de Gruyter, 2003).
58. Frank Crüsemann argues that neither biblical theology nor the history of religion may be completely objective. To claim the contrary, in his view, is pseudo-objectivity. In addition, he is rather skeptical of the hope of Albertz that an increasing consensus about Israel's religion will emerge, for there is as much variation in this field as there is in Old Testament theology ("Religionsgeschichte oder Theologie? Elementare Überlegungen zu einer falschen Alternative," *JBTh* 10 [1995]: 69–77).
59. The so-called minimalist historians argue that "Israel" of the Old Testament is a fiction that cannot be identified with a sociohistorical community (see Niels Peter Lemche, "Warum die Theologie des Alten Testaments einen Irrweg darstellt," *JBTh* 10 [1995]: 79–92; and Thomas L. Thompson, "Das Alte Testament als theologische Disziplin," *JBTh* 10 [1995]: 157–73). See also Philip R. Davies, *In Search of Ancient Israel* (JSOTSup 148; Sheffield: Sheffield Academic Press, 1992); Thomas Thompson, *Early History of the Israelite People from the Written and Archaeological Sources* (SHANE IV; Leiden: Brill, 1992); and N. P. Lemche, *The Canaanites and Their Land: The Tradition of the Canaanites* (JSOTSup 110; Sheffield: Sheffield Academic Press, 1991).

60. Erhard Gerstenberger, *Theologies of the Old Testament* (Minneapolis: Fortress Press, 2002).

61. Leo G. Perdue et al., *The Family in Ancient Israel* (Louisville: Westminster John Knox, 1997).

62. Gerstenberger, *Theologies in the Old Testament*, 25–91.

63. See Albrecht Alt, "The God of the Fathers," in *Essays on Old Testament History and Religion* (New York: Blackwells, 1968), 1–77; Bernd-Jörg Diebner, "Die Götter des Vaters," *DBAT* 9 (1975): 21–51; and Matthias Köckert, *Vätergott und Väterverheissungen: Eine Auseinandersetzung mit Albrecht Alt und seinen Erben* (FRLANT 142; Göttingen: Vandenhoeck & Ruprecht, 1988).

64. Gerstenberger, *Theologies in the Old Testament*, 93–110.

65. Ibid., 111–60.

66. Gottwald, *The Tribes of Yahweh*.

67. Keel, *Die Welt der altorientalischen Bildsymbolik und das Alte Testament*.

68. Smith, *The Early History of God*.

69. Patrick Miller, *The Divine Warrior in Early Israel* (HSM 5; Cambridge, Mass.: Harvard University, 1973).

70. Gerstenberger, *Theologies in the Old Testament*, 161–205.

71. Gerhard von Rad, "Royal Ritual in Judah," *The Problem of the Hexateuch and Other Essays* (New York: McGraw-Hill, 1966), 222–31.

72. See Niehr, "Auf dem Weg zu einer Religionsgeschichte Israels und Judas. Annäherungen an einen Problemkreis," 57–78. He adds that two types of religion existed entwined in Israelite culture and history: primary religions speak of the order of the cosmos and stress a hierarchal society in which authority moves from gods to kings to the bureaucracy and eventually to the lowest social stratum, while secondary religions place in the foreground the personal relationship of humans to God and express themselves through confessional worship. In contrast to theology, the purpose of the history of religions is to engage in reconstruction on the basis of material culture and texts and not in retelling the biblical religion.

73. See his *Erinnerungen aus der Kriegsgefangenschaft Frühjahr 1945*.

74. Gerhard von Rad, *Old Testament Theology* (2 vols.; New York: Harper & Row, 1962, 1965).

75. Manfred Oeming, *Gesamtbiblische Theologien der Gegenwart* (2d ed.; Stuttgart: Kohlhammer, 1987).

76. Von Rad, *Old Testament Theology*, 1:105-15.

77. *Old Testament Theology*, 2:357.

78. For important studies of von Rad, see Martin Honecker, "Zum Verständnis der Geschichte in Gerhard von Rad's Theologie des Alten Testaments," *EvTh* 23 (1963): 143–68; H. W. Wolf, Rolf Rendtorff, and Wolfhart Pannenberg, *Gerhard von Rad: Seine Bedeutung für die Theologie* (München: Chr. Kaiser, 1973); and the volumes published from papers presented in Heidelberg, Oct. 18–21, 2001, in celebration of his one-hundredth birthday, *Das Alte Testament und die Kultur der Moderne*, eds. Manfred Oeming, Konrad Schmid, and Michael Welker (*Altes Testament und Modern* 8; Münster: LIT Verlag, 2003).

79. Von Rad, "The Theological Problem of the Doctrine of Creation." See Walter Brueggemann, "The Loss and Recovery of 'Creation' in Old Testament Theology," *Today* 53 (1996): 177–90, for an assessment of von Rad's early view.

80. Von Rad, "The Theological Problem of the Old Testament Doctrine of Creation," 131–43.

81. Ibid., 133f. Gunneweg emphasizes that for von Rad, even as early as this essay, creation is also a part of salvation. Indeed, the Old Testament speaks of the two in the same breath (Isa 43:1f.; Gunneweg, *Biblische Theologie des Alten Testaments. Eine Religionsgeschichte Israels in biblisch-theologischer Sicht*, 142).

82. Bernhard M. Levinson and Douglas Dance, "The Metamorphosis of Law into Gospel," in *Recht und Ethik im Alten Testament*, ed. Bernard M. Levinson and Eckart Otto with the collaboration of Walter Dietrich; *Altest Testament und Moderne* 13; Münster: LIT, 2004), 83–110.

83. BWANT 47 (Stuttgart: 1929).

84. Gerhard von Rad, "Die levitische Predigt in den Büchern der Chronik," *Die Bezeichnungen für Land und Volk im alten Testament*, ed. L. Rost; Festschrift Otto Procksch; Leipzig: A. Deichert, 1934), 113–24.

85. Von Rad, *Deuteronomium-Studien* (FRLANT 58; Göttingen: Vandenhoeck & Ruprecht, 1947).

86. *Old Testament Theology*, 1:219–31.

87. Ibid., 187–289.

88. Gerhard von Rad, "The Theological Problem of the Old Testament Doctrine of Creation," 140.

89. *Old Testament Theology*, 2:357.

90. *Old Testament Theology*, 1:3–102.

91. For a detailed assessment of von Rad as an Old Testament theologian, see James L. Crenshaw, *Gerhard von Rad* (Makers of the Modern Theological Mind; Waco, Tex.: Word Books, 1978).

92. See James Barr's devastating critique of this assumption in his important book, *The Semantics of Biblical Language* (Oxford: Oxford University Press, 1961).

93. This creed found expression in cultic lyrics (Pss 78; 105; 106; 135; and 136), again demonstrating its liturgical setting.

94. "The Form-Critical Problem of the Hexateuch," 54.

95. *Old Testament Theology*, 1:105.

96. Ibid., 106.

97. Unlike Rudolph Bultmann, who contrasts Old Testament law with New Testament grace and points to the failure of Old Testament promises as a serious hermeneutical dilemma ("The Significance of the Old Testament for the Christian Faith," in *The Old Testament and Christian Faith* [ed. B. W. Anderson; New York: Harper & Row, 1963], 8–35).

98. See *Old Testament Theology*, 2:364–87.

99. We shall examine Levenson's criticism of Protestant Old Testament theology in a later chapter.

100. *Old Testament Theology*, 2:319–35, 357–87.

101. Ibid., 2:319.

102. Gerhard von Rad, *Wisdom in Israel*, 307. Von Rad argued: "All that the wise men say, especially also what they have to say about the beneficent turning of the world towards men, only has meaning if one places one's trust in the orders, and that means, in the last resort, in Yahweh. This is a trust to which Yahweh is entitled and which has long since been justified by experience."

103. Gerhard Hasel, *Old Testament Theology: Basic Issues in the Current Debate* (rev. and exp. 4th ed.; Grand Rapids: Eerdmans, 1972), 139–71.

104. Leonardo Boff and Phillip Berryman, *Cry of the Earth, Cry of the Poor* (Ecology and Justice Series; Maryknoll, N.Y.: Orbis Books, 1997); Dieter T. Hessel and Rosemary Radford Ruther, *Christianity and Ecology: Seeking the Well-being of Earth and Humans* (Harvard University Center for the Study of World Religions; Cambridge, Mass.: Harvard University Press, 2000); Catherine Keller, *The Face of the Deep* (London: Routledge, 2003); and Denis Edwards, *Ecology at the Heart of Faith* (Maryknoll, N.Y.: Orbis Books, 2006).

105. For studies on the history of religion, see the earlier chapter. Overviews of social scientific studies include Gary A. Herion, "The Impact of Modern and Social Science Assumptions on the Reconstruction of Israelite History," *JSOT* 34 (1986): 3–33; and *Ancient Israel's Faith and History: Introduction to the Bible in Context. Essays in Honor of George E. Mendenhall*, ed. Gary A. Herion (Louisville: Westminster John Knox, 2001); Charles E. Carter, "A Discipline in Transition: The Contributions of the Social Sciences to the Study of the Hebrew Bible," in *Community, Identity, and Ideology: Social Science Approaches to the Hebrew Bible*, ed. Charles F. Carter and Carol Meyers (Winona Lake, Ind.: Eisenbrauns, 1996), 3–36; and idem, "Social Scientific Approaches," in *The Blackwell Companion to the Hebrew Bible*, 36–57.

106. For a survey of myth, see J. W. Rogerson, *Myth in Old Testament Interpretation* (BZAW 134; Berlin: W. de Gruyter, 1974). Also see, Brevard S. Childs, *Myth and Reality in the Old Testament* (SBT 27; London: SCM Press, 1960); and H.-P. Müller, *Mythos, Tradition, Revolution: Phänomologische Untersuchungen zum Alten Testament* (Neukirchen-Vluyn: Neukirchener Verlag, 1973).

107. See S. H. Hooke, ed., *Myth and Ritual* (London: Oxford, 1933); *The Labyrinth* (London: SPCK, 1935); and *Myth, Ritual and Kingship* (Oxford: Clarendon, 1958); Sigmund Mowinckel, *Psalmenstudien* I (reprint; Amsterdam: P. Schippers, 1961); and I. Engnell, *Studies in Divine Kingship in the Ancient Near East* (Oxford: Basil Blackwell, 1967).

108. Benedikt Otzen, Hans Gottlieb, and Knud Jeppesen, *Myths in the Old Testament* (London: SCM, 1980).

109. See especially Wright, *God Who Acts*. Other important works of Wright include *The Old Testament Against Its Environment* (SBT 2; London: SCM, 1950); and with an ecumenical committee in Chicago, *The Biblical Doctrine of Man in Society* (Ecumenical Biblical Studies 2; London: SCM, 1954).

110. Henri and H. A. Frankfort, John A. Wilson, and Thorkild Jacobsen, *The Intellectual Adventure of Ancient Man (Before Philosophy)* (Chicago: University of Chicago Press, 1946).

111. Ernst Cassirer, *Language and Myth* (New York: Harper & Brothers, 1946); and Lucien Levy-Bruhl, *Primitive Mentality* (New York: Macmillan, 1923).

112. Also see Henri Franfort's *Kingship and the Gods: A Study of Ancient Near Eastern Religion as the Integration of Nature and Society* (Chicago: University of Chicago Press, 1978). This understanding impacted dramatically the work of T. H. Gaster, a scholar of ancient folklore, who compiled numerous parallels to Old Testament myths, rituals, and customs. Gaster contrasted the personal God of Israel with the personification of natural forces in Near Eastern religion (*Myth, Legend, Custom in the Old Testament*, 2 vols. [New York: Harper & Row, 1969]).

113. See *Canaanite Myth and Hebrew Epic* (Cambridge: Harvard, 1973). The processes of the mythologization of history and the historization of myth are addressed by J. J. M.

Roberts ("Myth Versus History," *CBQ* 38 [1976]: 1–13). Roberts is a former student of Wright and Cross.

114. See especially H.-H. Schmid, "Schöpfung, Gerectigkeit und Heil," *Altorientalische Welt in the alttestamentlichen Theologie* (Zurich: TVZ Verlag, 1974), 88. The English translation, "Creation, Righteousness, and Salvation: 'Creation Theology' as the Broad Horizon of Biblical Theology," *Creation in the Old Testament*, ed. B. W. Anderson, Issues in Religion and Theology 6 (Philadelphia: Fortress Press, 1984).

115. "Schöpfung, Gerectigkeit, und Heil," 24.

116. Anderson, ed., *Creation in the Old Testament*. His essay "Introduction: Mythopoeic and Theological Dimensions of Biblical Creation Faith" is found on pp. 1–24.

117. B. W. Anderson, *From Creation to New Creation*, Overtures to Biblical Theology (Minneapolis: Fortress Press, 1994). See his earlier *Creation Versus Chaos: The Reinterpretation of Mythical Symbolism in the Bible* (New York: Association Press, 1967).

118. *From Creation to New Creation*, 3–4.

119. Ibid., 7.

120. Ibid., 11–16.

121. Ibid., 207–32.

122. Ibid., 233–45.

123. Rolf Knierim, "Cosmos and History in Israel's Theology," *Werden und Wirken der Alten Testaments* (Göttingen: Vandenhoeck & Ruprecht, 1980), 59–123; "The Task of Old Testament Theology," in *Horizons in Biblical Theology* 6 (1984): 25–57.

124. "History fails or is justified to the extent that it is in step with the just and righteous order of the world" ("Cosmos and History," 94).

125. Thus, the attempted violation of this separation in the Tower of Babel episode in Gen 11:1-9 leads to the alienation of the nations from one another and from God.

126. Jon Levenson, *Creation and the Persistence of Evil: The Jewish Drama of Divine Omnipotence* (San Francisco: Harper & Row, 1988).

127. Ibid., 148.

128. Ibid., 153.

129. Claus Westermann, *Elements of Old Testament Theology* (Atlanta: John Knox, 1982); and idem, "Creation and History in the Old Testament," in *The Gospel and Human Destiny*, ed. Vilmos Vajta; A Continental Commentary (Minneapolis: Augsburg, 1971), 11–38. Also see "Biblical Reflections on Creator-Creation," in *Creation in the Old Testament*, ed. B. W. Anderson (Issues in Religion and Theology 6 (Philadelphia: Fortress Press, 1984), 90–101; idem, *Creation* (Philadelphia: Fortress Press, 1974); idem, *Blessing in the Bible and the Life of the Church* (Philadelphia: Westminster, 1978); idem, *Genesis 1–11* (A Continental Commentary; Minneapolis: Augsburg, 1984); and idem, *Genesis 12–36*, Continental Commentary (Minneapolis: Augsburg, 1995). For several examinations of Westermann as theologian and hermeneut, see Manfred Oeming and Gerd Theissen, eds., *Claus Westermann: Leben—Werk—Wirkung* (Beiträge zum Verstehen der Bibel 2; Münster: LIT Verlag, 2003). Richard J. Clifford has also argued that creation is a significant theological theme in the Hebrew Bible as well as in the ancient Near East. He denies this theme is a late one in Israel (*Creation Accounts in the Ancient Near East and in the Bible* (CBQ 26; Washington, D.C.: Catholic Biblical Association, 1994). For an overview of the relationship between history and creation that focuses on important Old Testament texts, see Karl Eberlein, *Gott der Schöpfer—Israels Gott* (2d, expanded ed., Beiträge zur

Erforschung des Alten Testaments und des antiken Judentums 5; Frankfurt A. M.: Peter Lang, 1989).

130. For example, see Claus Westermann, *Praise and Lament in the Psalms* (Richmond: John Knox Press, 1981); idem, *Basic Forms of Prophetic Speech* (Louisville: Westminster John Knox, 1991); idem, *Roots of Wisdom: The Oldest Proverbs of Israel and Other Peoples* (Louisville: Westminster John Knox, 1995); and idem, *Das mündliche Wort: Erkundungen im Alten Testament* (Arbeiten zu Theologie 82; Stuttgart: Calwer Verlag, 1996).

131. For a survey of his life and work, see James Limburg, "Old Testament Theology for Ministry: The Works of Claus Westermann in English Translation," in *Word and World* 1/2 (1981): 169–78.

132. Westermann, "Creation and History in the Old Testament," 23.

133. See Hans-Peter Müller, "Claus Westermann—ein theologischer Denker zwischen Altem Testament und Moderne," *Claus Westermann*, 96–98.

134. Westermann, *Elements of Old Testament Theology*, 9.

135. Ibid., 53.

136. "Biblical Reflection on Creator-Creation," 90–93.

137. Claus Westermann, *Blessing in the Bible and the Life of the Church* (OBT; Philadelphia: Fortress Press, 1978); and idem, *Genesis 12–36*, 436.

138. Westermann, *Blessing in the Bible and the Life of the Church*, 6.

139. Claus Westermann, *What Does the Old Testament Say about God?* (Atlanta: John Knox Press, 1979), 42.

140. Gösta Lindeskog has argued that creation and history form two separate traditions that eventually came together ("The Theology of the Creation in the Old and New Testaments," in *The Root of the Vine: Essays in Biblical Theology*, ed. Anton Fridrichsen [Philadelphia: Westminster, 1953], 1–22). Helga Weippert contends that the first to bring together the concept of Yahweh as Creator of the world and the Lord of history was Jeremiah (Helga Weippert, *Schöpfer des Himmels und der Erde. Ein Beitrag zur Theologie des Jeremiabuches* [SBS 102; Stuttgart: Kohlhammer, 1981]). Eckart Otto has suggested that the effort to correlate human experience and divine transcendence led to the development of creation theology ("Erwägungen zu den Prolegomena einer Theologie des Alten Testaments," *Kairos* 19 [1977]: 53–72).

141. Westermann, "The Blessing of God and Creation," *What Does the Old Testament Say About God?*, 39–52.

142. Ibid.

143. See Westermann, *Elements of Old Testament Theology*, 118–52.

144. Ibid., 153–216.

145. Ibid., 217–32.

146. Westermann, "The Interpretation of the Old Testament: An Historical Introduction," in *Essays on Old Testament Hermeneutics*, ed. Claus Westermann (Richmond: John Knox Press, 1963), 41.

147. The first part of this emphasis was undertaken by one of his students, Rolf Knierim, who noted that creation supersedes history in that creation is both before and after the temporal period of world history ("Cosmos and History in Israel's Theology," *Werden und Wirken der Alten Testaments* [Göttingen: Vandenhoeck & Ruprecht, 1980], 59–123; and idem, "The Task of Old Testament Theology," *Horizons in Biblical Theology* 6 [1984]: 25–57. For the latter part of the emphasis, see Jon Levenson, *Creation and the Persistence of Evil: The Jewish Drama of Divine Omnipotence* (San Francisco: Harper &

Row, 1988). Also see my chapter on Job in *Wisdom Literature: A Theological History* (Louisville: Westminster John Knox, 2007).

148. Childs, *Biblical Theology of the Old and New Testaments*, 70–71.

149. See especially *Introduction to the Old Testament as Scripture* (Philadelphia: Fortress Press, 1979); *Old Testament Theology in a Canonical Context* (Philadelphia: Fortress Press, 1985); and *Biblical Theology of the Old and New Testaments* (Minneapolis: Fortress Press, 1992).

150. Childs, *Biblical Theology of the Old and New Testaments*, 107–22.

151. Ibid., 110–12.

152. Ibid., 112–13.

153. Ibid., 113–14.

154. Ibid., 77–79.

155. Ibid., 85–88.

156. See especially Perdue, *The Collapse of History*, 155–86; and Barr, *The Concept of Biblical Theology*, 37–39, 47–51.

157. Rolf Rendtorff, *Theologie des Alten Testaments. Einkanonischer Entwurf* 1 & 2 (Neukirchen-Vluyn: Neukirchener Verlag, 1999, 2001).

158. Rolf Rendtorff, "'Wo warst du, als ich die Erde gegrundete?' Schöpfung und Heilsgeschichte;" "'Bund' als Strukturkonzept in Genesis und Exodus," *Kanon und Theologie: Vorarbeiten zu einer Theologie des Alten Testaments* (Neukirchen-Vluyn: Neukirchener Verlag, 1991), 94–122 and 123–31.

159. Gustaf Friedrich Oehler, *Theologie des Alten Testaments*, 2 vols. (Tübingen: Heckenhauer, 1873–1874).

160. Ernst Andreas Heinrich Hermann Schultz, *Alttestamentliche Theologie: Die Offenbarungsreligion auf ihrer vorschristlichen Entwicklungsstufe* (Frankfurt: Heyden & Zimmer, 1869). Schultz continued to change his views, resulting in four editions, the last of which traced the history of Israelite religion and then arranged the materials into systematic categories. The 4th ed. was translated into English by J. A. Patterson and is entitled *Old Testament Theology: The Religion of Revelation in its Pre-Christian Stage of Development*, 2 vols. (Edinburgh: T&T Clark, 1892).

161. Bernhard Stade, *Biblische Theologie des Alten Testaments, 1: The Religion Israels und die Entstehung des Judentums* (Tübingen: J. C. B. Mohr [Paul Siebeck], 1905).

162. Frank Crüsemann, "Die Eigenständigkeit der Urgeschichte: Ein Beitrag zur Diskussion um den 'Jahwisten,'" in *Die Botschaft und die Boten: Festschrift für H. W. Wolff*, ed. Jörg Jeremias and Lothar Perlitt (Neukirchener-Vluyn: Neukirchener Verlag, 1981), 11–29.

163. Rendtorff, *Canon and Theology*, 94.

164. Rendtorff, "'Wo warst du als ich die Erde gegrundete?' Schöpfung und Heilsgeschichte," and "'Bund' als Strukturkonzept in Genesis und Exodus," 94–122 and 123–31.

165. Rendtorff, "Theologie des Alten Testaments: Überlegungen zu einem Neuansatz," *Kanon und Theologie*, 9–12. Also see his "Creation and Redemption in the Torah," in *The Blackwell Companion to the Hebrew Bible*, ed. Leo G. Perdue (Oxford: Basil Blackwell, 2001), 311–21.

166. Rendtorff, *Theologie des Alten Testaments* 2, 7.

167. Ibid., 8–9.

168. Ibid., 12–13. He notes that the plural in Gen 1:26-28 ("let us") may refer to the divine court (1 Kgs 22:19; Job 1:6; 2:1, and perhaps Isa 6:8; pp. 14–15).

169. Rendtorff, *Theologie des Alten Testaments* 2, 233–35. For his views of creation theology in the Hebrew Bible, see pp. 7–18.

170. He notes the reference to Solomon as the king of Israel in Prov 1:1 and the fiction of Solomon ("son of David, king in Jerusalem") in Qoh 1:1.

171. For introductions to postmodernism, see especially Linda Hutcheon, *A Poetics of Postmodernism: History, Theory, Fiction* (New York: Routledge, 1988); Frederic Jameson, *Postmodernism, or the Cultural Logic of Late Captialism* (Durham, N.C.: Duke University Press, 1991); John McGowan, *Postmodernism and Its Critics* (Ithaca, N.Y.: Cornell University Press, 1991); Alaine Touraine, *Critique of Modernity* (Oxford: Blackwell Publishers, 1995); David Harvey, *Justice, Nature and the Geography of Difference* (Oxford: Blackwell Publishers, 1996); and Paul Cilliers, *Complexity and Postmodernism: Understanding Complex Systems* (London: Routledge, 1998). Helpful postmodernist introductions to theology and the Bible include Elisabeth A. Castelli, Stephen D. Moore, Gary A. Phillips, and Regina M. Schwartz, *The Postmodern Bible* (New Haven, Conn.: Yale University Press, 1995); Graham Ward, *The Postmodern God* (Oxford: Blackwell Publishers, 1998); and his edited work, *The Blackwell Companion to Postmodern Theology* (Blackwell Companions to Religion; Oxford: Blackwell Publishers, 2001); Other important insights are made by Robert A. Segal and Thomas Ryba, "Religion and Postmodernism: A Review Symposium," *Religion* 27 (1997): 101–49; and Burke O. Long, "Ambitions of Dissent: Biblical Theology in a Postmodern Future," *JR* 96 (1996): 276–89. Finally, two important books on theology and scripture that are postmodern in approach are those by Timothy K. Beal, *Religion and Its Monsters* (London: Routledge, 2002; and Catherine Keller, *Face of the Deep: A Theology of Becoming* (London: Routledge, 2003).

172. Jacques Derrida, *L'Écriture et différence* (Paris: Éditions du Seil, 1967); *Dessimination* (Chicago: University of Chicago Press, 1981); *L'Écriture et différence* (Paris: Éditions du Seil, 1967); and *Of Grammatology* (corrected ed.; Baltimore: Johns Hopkins Press, 1998).

173. Jean-François Lyotard, *The Post-Modern Condition: Le defferend* (Paris: Minuit, 1983); *The Inhuman: Reflections on Time* (Cambridge: Polity Press, 1991); and *Toward the Postmodern* (Atlantic Highlands, N.J.: 1993). Also see Stanley E. Fish, *Is There a Text in this Class?* (Cambridge, Mass.: Harvard University Press, 1980).

174. For a clear summary of Foucault's thinking, see the essay by Mark Poster, "Foucault, Michel," in *The John Hopkins Guide to Literary Theory and Criticism*, 277–80. Among his most substantial writings, see *The Archaeology of Knowledge and the Discourse on Language* (New York: Pantheon Books, 1982); *Death and the Labyrinth: The World of Raymond Roussel* (London: Continuum, 2004); *The History of Sexuality* 1–3 (London: Penguin, 1990–1992); and *Power* (ed. James Faubian; London: Penguin, 2002); for interpretations of Foucault, see J. G. Merquior, *Foucault* (Berkeley: University of California, 1987).

175. Roland Barthes, *Writing Degree Zero* (New York: Hill & Wang, 1968); *S/Z: An Essay* (New York: Hill & Wang, 1974); *Elements of Semiology* (New York: Hill & Wang, 1968); *Structural Analysis and Biblical Exegesis: Interpretational Essays* (Pittsburgh: Pickwick Press, 1974); *The Pleasure of the Text* (New York: Hill & Wang, 1975); *Empire of Signs* (London: Jonathan Cape, 1983); *The Rustle of Language*, 1986; *Criticism and Truth* (London: Athlone) 1987; *The Semiotic Challenge*, 1988; *On Racine* (Berkeley: University of California Press, 1992); *The Eiffel Tower, and Other Mythologies* (Berkeley: University of California Press, 1997); and *The Language of Fashion* (Oxford: Berg, 2006).

176. Cf. Roland Barthes' important essay "The Death of the Author," in *Image, Music, Text* (London: Fontana Press, 1977), 142-48. Here he joins Derrida and other post-modern theorists in arguing the attempt to point to the author's intent or understanding as the ultimate meaning of a text is nothing more than the illegitimate endeavor of the claim to have the single, correct view. For Barthes, the death of the author leads to the birth of the reader, who, through textual analysis, imposes multiple meanings upon a text (See *S/Z: An Essay*). Readers are the sources of numerous meanings given to a piece of literature.

177. Barthes chooses to speak of major mythologies, which contain the values and authoritarian place of the bourgeoisie that are imposed upon others. The ideology of texts is contained in the effort to force bourgeois culture's emphases upon its readers and hearers (see *The Eiffel Tower and Other Mythologies*).

178. This is one of the important assertions of Jean-François Lyotard, *The Post-modern Condition: A Report on Knowledge* (Minneapolis: University of Minnesota Press, 1984). Also see his *The Postmodern Explained* (Minneapolis: University of Minneapolis Press, 1993).

179. Graham Ward, "Introduction: 'Where We Stand,' " in *The Blackwell Companion to Postmodern Theology*, ed. Graham Ward (London: Blackwell Publishers, 2001), xii.

180. Graham Ward, "Introduction: 'Where We Stand,'" xiii.

181. Postmodern historiography, known as "New Historicism," objects to what it considers to be a false claim of modernist historiography, that is, the reconstruction of the past through the objective interpretation of retrievable data. New Historicism allows for the subjective interplay of the imagination with texts and other data in the setting forth of a variety of historical interpretations. See A. K. M. Adam, *What Is Postmodern Biblical Criticism?* [Guides to Biblical Scholarship; Minneapolis: Fortress Press, 1995), 46f.; Gina Hens-Piazza, *The New Historicism* (Guides to Biblical Scholarship; Minneapolis: Fortress, 2002); and John Brannigan, *New Historicism and Cultural Materialism: Transitions* (New York: St. Martin's Press, 1998).

182. See Walter Brueggemann, *Texts Under Negotiation: The Bible and Postmodern Imagination* (Minneapolis: Fortress Press, 1993); *Theology of the Old Testament* (Minneapolis: Fortress Press, 1997); and "Biblical Theology Appropriately Postmodern," *Jews, Christians, and the Theology of the Hebrew Scriptures*, ed. Alice Ogden Bellis and Joel S. Kaminsky; Symposium 8 (Atlanta: Scholars Press, 2000), 97–108. His theology has now appeared in paperback with only a few changes:

183. See, for example, *Prophetic Imagination* (2d ed.; Minneapolis: Fortress Press, 2001); and *David's Truth in Israel's Imagination and Memory* (2d ed.; Minneapolis: Fortress Press, 2002).

184. *An Introduction to the Old Testament* (Louisville: Westminster/John Knox, 2003), 4.

185. Ibid., 8.

186. He writes that "acts of imaginative construal that admit of no single reading but that generate many possible futures" ("Biblical Theology Appropriately Postmodern" 105).

187. Gayatri Chakravorty Spivak, "Can the Subaltern Speak?" in *Marxism and the Interpretation of Culture*, ed. Cary Nelson and Lawrence Grossberg (Chicago: University of Chicago Press, 1988), 271–313. Her important publications include: *In Other Worlds: Essays in Cultural Politics* (New York: Routledge, 1988); edited with Ranajit Guha, *Selected Subaltern Studies* (Oxford: Oxford University Press, 1988); *A Critique of Postcolonial*

Reason: Toward a History of the Vanishing Present (Cambridge, Mass.: Harvard University Press, 1999); and *Death of a Discipline* (New York: Columbia University Press, 2003).

188. Laura Chrisman and Benita Parry, eds., *Postcolonial Theory and Criticism* (English Association, Rochester, N.Y.: D. S. Brewer, 2000); and Ankie M. M. Hoogvelt, *Globalization and the Postcolonial World: The New Political Economy of Development* (2d ed.; Baltimore: Johns Hopkins University Press, 2001).

189. For definitions of colonialism, postcolonialism, neocolonialism, and imperialism, see Robert J. C. Young, *Postcolonialism: An Historical Introduction* (Oxford: Blackwells, 2001), 13–69; Peter Childs and Patrick Williams, *An Introduction to Post-Colonial Theory* (London: Harvester & Wheatsheaf, 1997); and idem, Jean Jacques Weber and Patrick Williams, *Post-Colonial Theory and Literatures: African, Caribbean, and South Asian* (WVT; Trier: Wissenschaftlicher Verlag, 2006).

190. John McLeod, *Beginning Postcolonialism* (Manchester: Manchester University Press, 2000), 19.

191. Recent studies of Fanon and his work include Alice Cherki, *Frantz Fanon: A Portrait* (Cornell, N.Y.: Cornell University Press, 2006); and Joseph Young and Jana Evans Braziel, eds., *Race and the Foundations of Knowledge: Cultural Amnesia in the Academy* (Urbana: Illinois University Press, 2006).

192. Biodum Jeyifo, "Fanon, Frantz," *The John Hopkins Guide to Literary Theory and Criticism* (Baltimore: John Hopkins University Press, 1994), 229. For a similar tracing of stages, see Justin S. Ukpong, *Sacrifice, African and Biblical: A Comparative Study of Ibibio and Levitical Sacrifices* (Rome: Urbaniana University Press, 1987).

193. Edward W. Said, *Orientalism* (London: Routledge & Kegan Paul, 1978); *Covering Islam: How the Media and the Experts Determine How We See the Rest of the World* (London: Routledge & Kegan Paul, 1981); *The World, the Text, and the Critic* (Cambridge, Mass.: Harvard University Press, 1988); *Culture and Imperialism* (New York: Knopf, 1994); and *Beginnings: Intention and Method* (London: Granta Books, 1997). In *Postcolonialism* (383–94), Young has provided a well-written, succinct introduction to Said.

194. See the important observations on ideologies of text and interpreter in the writings of Pui-lan Kwok (*Introducing Asian Feminist Theology* [Cleveland: Pilgrim Press, 2002]; and *Postcolonial Imagination and Feminist Interpretation* [Louisville: Westminster John Knox, 2005]).

195. Itumeleng Mosala, *Biblical Hermeneutics and Black Theology in South Africa* (Grand Rapids: Eerdmans, 1989), 40.

196. West, *The Academy of the Poor*, 108.

197. See most recently, *The Bible and Empire: Postcolonial Explorations* (Cambridge, Mass.: Cambridge University Press, 2005); and *Voices from the Margin: Interpreting the Bible in the Third World*, ed. R. S. Sugirtharajah; rev. and expanded 3d ed. (Maryknoll, N.Y.: Orbis Books, 2006).

198. R. S. Sugirtharajah, *Postcolonial Criticism and Biblical Interpretation* (Oxford: Clarendon Press, 2002), 13. Also see Homi Bhabha, *The Location of Culture* (London: Routledge, 1994).

199. R. S. Sugirtharajah, series ed., *The Postcolonial Bible: The Bible and Postcolonialism*, vol. 1 (Sheffield: Sheffield Academic Press, 1998), 94.

200. R. S. Sugirtharajah, "A Postcolonial Exploration of Collusion and Construction in Biblical Interpretation," in *The Postcolonial Bible*, ed. R. S. Sugirtharajah (Sheffield: Sheffield Academic Press, 1998), 91–116.

201. Ibid.

202. R. S. Sugirtharajah, "Introduction: The Margin as a Site of Creative Re-visioning," in *Voices from the Margin: Interpreting the Bible in the Third World*, new ed., ed. R. S. Sugirtharajah (Maryknoll, N.Y.: Orbis, 1995), 1–8.

203. Ibid.

3. New Testament Theology in the Twentieth Century

1. William Wrede, "On the Task and Method of New Testament Theology So-Called," in *The Nature of New Testament Theology* (ed. and trans. Robert Morgan; SBT 25; London: SCM Press, 1973), 68–116 and 182–93. Revised edition forthcoming.

2. Heinrich Julius Holtzmann, *Lehrbuch der Neutestamentlichen Theologie* (2d ed.; 2 vols.; Tübingen: J. C. B. Mohr [Paul Siebeck], 1911).

3. B. Weiss, *Biblical Theology of the New Testament* (2 vols.; German 1868, 1903; Eng. trans. Edinburgh: T&T Clark, 1896).

4. W. Beyschlag, *New Testament Theology* (2 vols.; German 1891–1892; Eng. trans. Edinburgh: T&T Clark, 1896).

5. Wrede, "Task," 75.

6. Ibid., 116.

7. Ibid., 68f.

8. Ibid., 116.

9. Heikki Räisänen, *Beyond New Testament Theology* (2d ed.; London: SCM Press, 1990, 2000).

10. Wayne Meeks, "Why Study the New Testament?" *NTS* 51 (2005): 155–70, 167–68.

11. For example, James Barr, *The Semantics of Biblical Language* (Oxford: Oxford University Press, 1961); Langdon Gilkey, "Cosmology, Ontology, and the Travail of Biblical Language," *JR* 41 (1961): 194ff.; Brevard S. Childs, *Biblical Theology in Crisis* (Philadelphia: Westminster Press, 1970).

12. See the title of Hans Conzelmann's collection, *Theologie als Schriftauslegung* (Munich: Kaiser, 1974).

13. Meeks echoes much of what was said by Krister Stendahl at the centenary meeting of the Society for Biblical Literature. See J. P. Hyatt, ed., *The Bible and Modern Scholarship* (London: Carey, 1965), 196–209.

14. Meeks, "Why Study," 168.

15. Ibid.

16. Ibid., 164.

17. Ibid., 166.

18. I have argued that New Testament theology makes a contribution to this in "Can the Critical Study of Scripture Provide a Doctrinal Norm?" *JR* 76 (1996): 206–32; and "The New Testament Canon of Scripture and Christian Identity," in *The Unity of Scripture and the Diversity of the Canon* (ed. J. Barton and M. Wolter; Berlin: Walter de Gruyter, 2003), 151–94.

19. Meeks, "Why Study," 166.

20. Ibid., 168.

21. Ibid. He refers to George Lindbeck's "helpful typology" in *The Nature of Doctrine: Religion and Theology in a Post-Liberal Age* (Philadelphia: Westminster, 1984) and evidently prefers Lindbeck's "cultural linguistic" model of religion.

22. Meeks, "Why Study," 166.

23. Ibid., 163.

24. Ibid.

25. Ibid.

26. Ibid., 163f.

27. Ibid.

28. Ibid., 155, 167.

29. Ibid., 167.

30. Ibid.

31. For example, the recent writings of Francis Watson and Stephen Fowl, but above all Karl Barth, *Römerbrief* (2d ed.; Munich: Chr. Kaiser, 1922; Eng. trans. London: Oxford University Press, 1933).

32. On Rothe's pious, speculative, and secular theology, see Claude Welch, *Protestant Thought in the Nineteenth Century* (New Haven, Conn.: Yale University Press, 1972), 282–91.

33. Meeks, "Why Study," 169.

34. Ibid., 167.

35. Ibid.

36. Ibid.

37. Räisänen, *Beyond New Testament Theology*, 203–9.

38. In Christopher Rowland and Christopher Tuckett, eds., *The Nature of New Testament Theology* (Oxford: Blackwell, 2006), 207.

39. J. P. Gabler, "On the Proper Distinction Between Biblical and Dogmatic Theology and the Specific Objectives of Each" (Eng. trans. *SJT* 33 (1980): 133–58; reprint forthcoming. Otto Merk, *Biblische Theologie des Neuen Testaments in ihrer Anfangszeit* (Marburg: N. G. Elwert Verlag, 1972), is the best account.

40. In 1756 A. F. Büsching published in Göttingen his *Thoughts on the Character of Biblical-dogmatic Theology and Its Advantage over the New Scholastic Theology.*

41. Otto Merk's account of the origins of the modern discipline surveys its textbooks down to 1971 (*Biblische Theologie*).

42. Bultmann wrote of "the interpretation of the New Testament writings under the presupposition that they have something to say to the present" in *Theology of the New Testament* (Eng. trans. vol. 2; New York: Scribner, 1955; London: SCM Press, 1955), 251.

43. See A. H. M. Jones, *Independence and Exegesis* (Tübingen: Mohr, 1983).

44. Strauss, *The Christ of Faith and the Jesus of History* (1865; Eng. trans. L. E. Leck, Philadelphia: Fortress Press, 1977).

45. Weiss, *Biblical Theology*, 1:9.

46. F. C. Baur, "Die Christuspartei in der korinthischen Gemeinde . . ." (1831, reprinted Stuttgart: Frommann, 1963) saw conflict in the early church a few years before interpreting it theologically with help from Hegel's dialectic.

47. F. Hahn, *Theologie des Neuen Testaments* (2 vols.; Tübingen: Mohr Siebeck, 2002); U. Wilckens, *Theologie des Neuen Testaments* (vol. 1, parts 1–2; Neukirchen-Vluyn: Nekirchener, 2002).

48. Wrede, "Task," 69.

49. Ibid., 183.

50. Ibid. ". . . the question of revelation is one for dogmatics, and no concern of biblical theology."

51. Ibid., 69

52. Ibid., 183.

53. Meeks, "Why Study," 168.

54. See G. Theissen, *Theory* and *passim*. Now also *Erleban und Verhalten der ersten Christen* (Gerd Mohn: Gütersloh, 2007).

55. Wrede, "Task," 69.

56. Paul Feine, *Theologie des Neuen Testaments* (2d ed.; Leipzig: Hinrichs, 1911).

57. Ibid., 1.

58. Ibid., viii.

59. Ibid., ix.

60. Ibid.

61. T. Zahn, *Grundriss der Neutestamentlichen Theologie* (Leipzig: Deichert, 1928).

62. J. Kaftan, *Neutestamentliche Theologie. Im Abriss dargestellt* (Berlin: Warneck, 1927).

63. In addition to Schlatter's New Testament theology (Eng. trans. 1995 and 1997), his commentary on Romans (1935, Eng. trans. 1995), *Do We Know Jesus?*, and the essays in W. Nuer, *Adolf Schlatter* (Eng. trans. 1995), more is planned.

64. Schlatter, 1905. Eng. trans. in Neuer (1995), 211–25.

65. Ibid., 219.

66. Ibid., 220.

67. Schlatter, "New Testament Theology and Dogmatics," Eng. trans. in R. Morgan, *The Nature of New Testament Theology* (London: SCM Press, 1973), 117–66. A new edition is forthcoming.

68. Ibid., 118.

69. Ibid., 117.

70. Ibid., 155.

71. Cf. Käsemann *Questions*, 4–5, 235. Making him the Godfather of the "new quest" was surely romanticism.

72. Bultmann, *Theology*, 2:248–50.

73. Ibid., 237–39, 239–41.

74. Cf. Rudolf Bultmann, *Faith and Understanding* (vol. 1; London: SCM Press, 1969), 28–52. The essay is from 1924.

75. See Rudolf Bultmann, "The Problem of a Theological Exegesis of the New Testament," in *The Beginnings of Dialectic Theology* (ed. J. M. Robinson; Richmond: John Knox, 1968), 236–56 . The essay is from 1925.

76. The German word *existential* is not exactly "existential" (which is *existentiell*) or "existentialist" (which refers to a philosophical movement) but means "relating to human existence." This was analyzed phenomenologically by Heidegger.

77. See J. Macquarrie, *An Existentialist Theology* (London: SCM Press, 1955).

78. Eng. tr. *Existence and Faith* (Cleveland: World Publishing, 1960), 111–46; (London: Collins Fontana ed., 1964), 130–72.

79. Eng. tr. *The Gospel of John* (Oxford: Blackwell, 1971).

80. In a penetrating 1954 review of the New Testament theology, reprinted in *The Crucified Messiah* (1954; Eng. trans. Minneapolis: Augsburg, 1974), 90–128, Nils Dahl

implied that Bultmann's *Sachkritik* and his "existential" interpretation transgress these limits. See pp. 93–95, 127–128.

81. Bultmann, *Theology* 1, 3.

82. Rudolf Bultmann, *Jesus and the Word* (Eng. trans. New York: Scribner, 1934).

83. "Theological Exegesis", 256.

84. For example, by Barth in correspondence, and E. C. Hoskyns in a review in *JTS* 38 (1927): 106–9.

85. His important reply to Kuhlmann, "Die Geschichtlichkeit des Daseins und der Glaube" (1930), is available in *Existence and Faith*.

86. "New Testament and Mythology" has been retranslated by Schubert Ogden, following Bultmann's anarthrous title, in *New Testament and Mythology and Other Basic Writings* (Philadelphia: Fortress Press, 1984), 1–43.

87. Braun, "The Problem of a New Testament Theology" (German 1961; Eng. trans. in *Journal for Theology and the Church* 1 (1965): 169–83. See also vol. 5, 88–127, on "The Meaning of New Testament Christology" (German 1957).

88. Exceptions include the untranslated Finnish works of E. G. Gulin (1940) and A. T. Nikolainen (1971), and the untranslated Swedish contribution of R. Kieffer (1977). For information, see Räisänen, *Beyond*, 57–60, 69–73. Like the Vienna contribution of K. Niederwimmer (2003), and from French Switzerland, F. Vouga (2001), these all are influenced by German New Testament theology.

89. E. C. Hoskyns's Cambridge lectures on New Testament theology inspired C. K. Barrett, A. M. Ramsey, and C. F. Evans, among others, and *The Riddle of the New Testament* (with F. N. Davey) (London: Faber, 1931) stimulated "biblical theology." Their *Crucifixion and Resurrection* was published in 1981 (ed. G. S. Wakefield; London: SPCK).

90. E. F. Scott, *The Varieties of New Testament Religion* (New York: Scribner, 1947).

91. F. C. Grant, *An Introduction to New Testament Thought* (New York/Nashville: Abingdon, 1950).

92. Alan Richardson, *An Introduction to the Theology of the New Testament* (London: SCM Press, 1958).

93. A. M. Hunter, *The Unity of the New Testament* (London: SCM Press, 1943; German 1952); and *Introducing New Testament Theology* (London: SCM Press, 1957).

94. C. H. Dodd, *The Parables of the Kingdom* (London: Nisbet, 1935).

95. J. Weiss, *Jesus' Proclamation of the Kingdom of God* (1892; Eng. trans. Philadelphia: Fortress Press, 1971).

96. Albert Schweitzer, *The Mystery of the Kingdom of God* (1901; Eng. trans. London: Macmillan, 1914).

97. For criticism see W. G. Kümmel, *Promise and Fulfilment* (1945, 1953; Eng. trans. London: SCM Press, 1957).

98. Jeremias, especially *The Parables of Jesus* (1947; Eng. trans. London: SCM Press, 1954, 1963); and *The Eucharistic Words of Jesus* (1935; Eng. trans. London: SCM Press, 1966).

99. F. Büschel, *Theologie des Neuen Testaments* (Gütersloh: Bertelsman, 1935).

100. M. Albertz, *Die Botschaft des Neuen Testamentes* (4 vols. Zurich: Evang., 1947–1957).

101. M. Meinertz, *Theologie des Neuen Testaments* (2 vols.; Bonn: Hanstein, 1950).

102. J. Bonsirven, *Théologie du Nouveau Testament* (Paris: Aubier, 1951).

103. Oscar Cullmann, *Christ and Time* (London: SCM Press, 1962), xii.

104. Ibid.

105. Ibid., xiii.

106. Ibid., 20, 21.

107. See Heinrich Schlier, *The Relevance of the New Testament* (German 1964; Eng. trans. New York: Herder, 1968), 1–75. The key article is from 1957.

108. Dahl's Norwegian 1953 (German 1955) article on "The Problem of the Historical Jesus" was translated in 1962 and reprinted in 1974 and in *Jesus the Christ* (Minneapolis: Fortress Press, 1991), 81–111.

109. Käsemann, *Essays on NT Themes* (German 1954; original lecture 1953; Eng. trans. London: SCM Press, 1964), 15–47; *New Testament Questions of Today* (Eng. trans. London: SCM Press, 1969), 23–65 (German 1964); 101–2 (German 1960); 111–16 (German 1962); *Jesus Means Freedom* (London: SCM Press, 1969), 16–41; German 1968.

110. Ebeling, *Word and Faith* (German 1960; Eng. trans. London: SCM Press, 1963). Key articles were published in 1958 and 1959; *Theology and Proclamation* (German 1962; Eng. trans. London: Collins, 1966). E. Fuchs's writings are less clear.

111. Käsemann, *Questions*, 13–15, 168–235; *Perspectives on Paul* (London: SCM Press, 1971).

112. Käsemann, *The Testament of Jesus* (German 1966; Eng. trans. London: SCM Press, 1968); also *Questions*, 15–17, 138–67.

113. For trenchant criticism of Jeremias, see E. Käsemann in *Questions*, 23–65, esp. 24–35. Käsemann's picture of the Jesus of history was closer to Harnack's than was that of Jeremias, but his view of revelation and theology was very different.

114. G. Bornkamm, G. Barth, and H. J. Held, *Tradition and Interpretation in Matthew* (German 1960; Eng. trans. London: SCM Press, 1963).

115. Conzelmann, *The Theology of St Luke* (London: Faber, 1960); German: *Die Mitte der Zeit*, 1954.

116. See also W. Marxsen, *The Evangelist Mark* (German 1956; Eng. trans. Nashville: Abingdon, 1969). For an early survey, see E. Rohde, *Rediscovering the Teaching of the Evangelists* (German 1966; Eng. trans. London: SCM Press, 1968).

117. This "theological criticism" of Luke in particular was pressed by Käsemann, whose slogan "early catholicism" highlighted the theological interests in New Testament theology. See also S. Schulz, *Die Mitte der Schrift* (Munich: Kaiser, 1976).

118. Hanz Conzelmann, *An Outline of the Theology of the New Testament* (German 1967; Eng. trans. London: SCM Press, 1969).

119. Ibid., 99. A most impressive subordination of Jesus' eschatology and ethics to his sense of God is found in H. Schürmann, *Jesus—Gestalt und Geheimnis* (Paderborn: Bonifatius, 1994).

120. Conzelmann, *Outline*, xiv.

121. Ibid., xv. That un-Pauline move was opposed by Käsemann, "Konsequente Traditionsgeschichte?" *ZThK* 62 (1965): 137–52.

122. K. H. Schelkle, *Theology of the New Testament* (German 1968–1976; Eng. trans. Collegeville, Minn: Liturgical Press, 1971–1978).

123. W. G. Kümmel, *The Theology of the New Testament According to Its Main Witnesses* (1969; Eng. trans. Nashville: Abingdon, 1973), 58.

124. W. G. Kümmel, *Promise and Fulfillment* (1945; London: SCM Press, 1957), 155.

125. Ibid.

126. Kümmel, *Theology*, 106.

127. Bultmann's *Jesus* (1926) was more theological, presenting the "complex of ideas in the oldest layer of the synoptic tradition" (Eng. trans., p.18), and through that encountering history, thus making history and theology coincide.

128. Unlike some Jesus research, Bultmann the theologian added that Jesus' call to decision implied a Christology. *Theology* 1, 43. Also *Faith and Understanding* (1929).

129. Kümmel, *Theology*, 322, cf. 16. Elsewhere he sees the task of New Testament *Wissenschaft* as relating historical research to the "divine message" of these texts, confirming the theological character of the whole discipline. See *The New Testament: The History of the Investigation of Its Problems* (German 1958; Eng. trans. Nashville: Abingdon, 1972), 405.

130. Kümmel, *Theology*, 266.

131. Ibid., 326, 330.

132. Ibid., 333.

133. Ibid.

134. Ibid., 201–2.

135. See Bultmann, *Faith and Understanding*, 53–65 (German originally 1925).

136. Kümmel, *Theology*, 326.

137. In 1961 U. Wilckens noted that since many now rejected Bultmann's account of revelation, "the structure of a theology of the New Testament must be thought through anew from the ground up." See *Revelation as History* (ed. W. Pannenberg; London: Sheed & Ward, 1969), 115.

138. The 1960s Germanophilia of New Frontiers in Theology, Journal for Theology and the Church, Twentieth-Century Theology in the Making, etc., gave way to a more American self-determination. See J. M. Robinson and H. Koester, *Trajectories through Early Christianity* (Philadelphia: Fortress Press, 1971).

139. Edited by Goppelt's pupil J. Roloff, *Theology of the NT* (Eng. trans. Grand Rapids: Eerdmans, 1981–1982).

140. G. E. Ladd, *A Theology of the New Testament* (Grand Rapids: Eerdmans, 1974).

141. Ibid., 221.

142. Donald Guthrie, *New Testament Theology* (Leicester: InterVarsity, 1981).

143. George Caird, *New Testament Theology* (ed. L. D. Hurst; Oxford: Oxford University Press, 1994).

144. Ibid., 18.

145. Ibid., 44. Although the resurrection does not appear in the index, it receives some brief mention on pp. 239–41.

146. Most brilliantly in the work of G. Theissen. Among many books see especially *A Theory of Primitive Christian Religion* (London: SCM Press, 1999). See also P. F. Esler's "socio-theological" model in *New Testament Theology: Communion and Community* (Minneapolis: Fortress Press, 2005).

147. See n. 138. J. M. Robinson and H. Koester had been trained in European theology in Basle and by Bultmann but, stimulated partly by the archaeological discoveries at Nag Hammadi, accentuated the history of religions and history of traditions dimensions of their European past. R. W. Funk also discoursed on his shift of interest from theological hermeneutics in the 1960s to extramural work on Jesus in the 1980s.

148. Amos N. Wilder, *The Language of the Gospel* (New York: Harper & Row, 1964); and William B. Beardslee, *Literary Criticism of the New Testament* (Philadelphia: Fortress

Press, 1970), provided early signs of a new trend. Dan Via's *The Parables* (Philadelphia: Fortress Press, 1967), is subtitled *Their Literary and Existential Dimension*.

149. A. Thiselton, *New Horizons in Hermeneutics* (New York: HarperCollins, 1992), provides a judicious survey, and analysis. S. D. Moore, *Literary Criticism of the Gospels* (New Haven, Conn.: Yale University Press, 1989), offers some sparkling analysis and some "misadventures in postcriticism."

150. Liberation theologians led the way. The postmodern theologies of F. B. Watson, A. K. M. Adam, and S. E. Fowl offer new directions.

151. Klaus Berger, *Exegese und Philosophie* (Stuttgart: KBW, 1986); *Hermeneutik des Neuen Testaments* (Gütersloh: Mohr, 1988).

152. Wrede, "Task," 70.

153. A taster may be found in C. Rowland and C. Tuckett, eds., *The Nature of New Testament Theology* (Oxford: Blackwell, 2006), 167–85.

154. Berger, *Exegese*, 114–16.

155. W. Schmithals, *The Theology of the First Christians* (1994; Eng. trans. Louisville: Westminster John Knox, 1997). A point made emphatically by E. Käsemann, "The Problem of a New Testament Theology," *NTS* 19 (1972–1973): 235–45.

156. Schmithals, *Theology*, 369.

157. Stuhlmacher, *Biblische Theologie des Neuen Testaments* 1 (Göttingen: Vandenhoeck & Ruprecht, 1992), 154.

158. Ibid., 2:310.

159. Ibid., 1:123–43.

160. See Strecker's Hermeneia Commentary, *The Johannine Letters* (German 1989; Eng. trans. Minneapolis: Fortress Press, 1995).

161. Joachim Gnilka, *Theologie des Neuen Testaments* (Freiburg: Herder, 1994), 463.

162. Notable are those of L. T. Johnson, *The Writings of the NT* (Philadelphia: Fortress Press, 1986, 1999); R. E. Brown, *An Introduction to the New Testament* (New York: Doubleday, 1997); and C. R. Holladay, *A Critical Introduction to the New Testament* (Nashville: Abingdon, 2005).

163. Including Dodd (1936), Dunn (1971), and J. Reumann (1991) writing in English. Like Dunn's, Reumann's *Variety and Unity in New Testament Thought* (Oxford: Oxford University Press, 1991), is in effect a New Testament theology.

164. Including soteriology, for example, K. Grayston, *Dying We Live* (London: DLT, 1990); and H. J. Hultgren, *Christ and His Benefits* (Philadelphia: Fortress Press, 1987).

165. For example, K. Stendahl, "Method in the Study of Biblical Theology," in *The Bible in Modern Scholarship* (ed. J. P. Hyatt; Nashville: Abingdon, 1965), 196–209; and James Barr, "The Theological Case against Biblical Theology," in *Canon, Authority and Old Testament Interpretation* (ed. G. M. Tucker et al.; Philadelphia: Fortress Press, 1988), 3–19.

166. Wrede, "Task," 116.

167. The English translation, *A Greek-English Lexicon of the New Testament and Early Christian Literature*, is now called BAGD (Bauer, Arndt, Gingrich, Danker); (Chicago: Chicago University Press, 1979).

168. For example, J. H. Moulton, vol. 1 (1906), vol. 2 with W. F. Howard (1919–1929), vol. 3 and 4, N. Turner (1963 and 1976); F. Blass and A. Debrunner, (1913, 1947;

trans. R. W. Funk; 1959); Chicago: Chicago University Press; German subsequently revised by F. Rehkopf, 1976.

169. Schlatter and Goppelt may be said to offer constructions of this, and Wilckens sees "the appearances as self-revelation of the Risen One" (*Theologie*, I.2, 133).

170. Although he starts with Paul, Gnilka allows him only a quarter of the available space.

171. For example, W. Wrede, *Paul* (1904; Eng. trans. 1907); H. Windisch (1934); R. Bultmann (1936) in *Existence and Faith*; E. Jüngel (1962); J. Blank (1968); D. Wenham (1995); and the survey of V. Furnish in the *Bulletin of the John Rylands Library*, 1964.

172. Especially Käsemann's resistance to understanding "the righteousness of God" exclusively as a gift from God (and so emphasizing the human recipient more than the power of God the Giver). For example, *Questions*, 168–82 (originally 1961).

173. Krister Stendahl, "The Apostle Paul and the Introspective Conscience of the West" (1961), in *HTR* 56 (1963): 199–215. Reprinted in *Paul Among Jews and Gentiles* (Philadelphia: Fortress Press, 1976).

174. Notably E. P. Sanders, *Paul and Palestinian Judaism* (London: SCM Press, 1977); and *Paul, the Law and the Jewish People* (London: SCM Press, 1983).

175. H. Räisänen, *Paul and the Law* (Tübingen: Mohr Siebeck, 1983). New Testament Theology defenses of the Lutheran perspective included H. Hübner, *Law in Paul's Thought* (German 1978; Eng. trans. Edinburgh: T&T Clark, 1984); S. Westerholm, *Israel's Law and the Church's Faith* (Grand Rapids: Eerdmans, 1988).

176. Albert Schweitzer, *The Mysticism of Paul the Apostle* (German 1930; Eng. trans. London: Macmillan, 1931). This might have been better called "the theology of," or "the eschatology of." It hinged on Schweitzer's novel category of "eschatological mysticism," not mysticism as usually understood.

177. H. J. Schoeps, *Paul: The Theology of the Apostle in the Light of Jewish Religious History* (German 1959; Eng. trans. Philadelphia: Westminster, 1961).

178. A. Segal, *Paul the Convert* (New Haven, Conn.: Yale University Press, 1990).

179. D. Boyarin, *A Radical Jew* (Berkeley: University of California Press, 1994).

180. For example, C. K. Barrett's commentaries and *From First Adam to Last* (London: A&C Black, 1962); and *Paul* (London: Chapman, 1994); N. A. Dahl, *Studies in Paul* (Minneapolis: Augsburg, 1977); *Studies in Ephesians* (Tübingen: Mohr; 2000); J. L. Martyn's Anchor Commentary on *Galatians* (New York: Doubleday, 1997); Leander E. Keck's Abingdon Commentary on *Romans* (2005, but incorporating the substance of essays from 1965); J. C. Beker, *Paul the Apostle* (Philadelphia: Fortress Press, 1980). U. Wilckens, EKK Commentary on Romans (3 vols.; 1978–1982); J. Becker, *Paul: Apostle to the Gentiles* (German 1989; Eng. trans. Louisville: Westminster John Knox, 1993); M. D. Hooker, *From Adam to Christ* (Cambridge, Mass.: Cambridge University Press, 1990).

181. See Dunn's Word Commentary on *Romans* (1988), *Jesus, Paul and the Law* (Louisville: Westminster John Knox, 1990), *The Theology of Paul the Apostle* (Grand Rapids: Eerdmans, 1998) and *The New Perspective on Paul* (Tübingen: Mohr Siebeck, 2005).

182. Wayne Meeks, *The First Urban Christians* (New Haven, Conn.: Yale University Press, 1983), provides as important insights into Pauline ecclesiology as his colleague Nils Dahl, *Das Volk Gottes* (1940) did.

183. Gerd Theissen, *The Social Setting of Pauline Christianity* (German 1974–1975; Eng. trans. Philadelphia: Fortress Press, 1982); *Psychological Aspects of Pauline Theology* (German 1983; Eng. trans. Philadelphia: Fortress Press, 1987); *Social Reality and the Early Christians* (German 1974–1987; Eng. trans. Minneapolis: Fortress Press, 1992).

184. J. H. Schütz, *Paul and the Anatomy of Apostolic Authority* (Cambridge: Cambridge University Press, 1975).

185. B. Holmberg, *Paul and Power* (Philadelphia: Fortress Press, 1978).

186. Philip Esler, *Galatians* (London: Routledge, 1998); *Conflict and Identity in Romans* (Minneapolis: Fortress Press, 2003); and *New Testament Theology: Communion and Community* (Philadelphia: Fortress Press, 2005).

187. H. D. Betz, *The Epistle to the Galatians* (Hermeneia; Philadelphia: Fortress Press, 1979). See also G. A. Kennedy, *New Testament Interpretation through Rhetorical Criticism* (Chapel Hill: University of North Carolina Press, 1984).

188. Margaret Mitchell, *Paul and the Rhetoric of Reconciliation* (Tübingen: Mohr, 1992; Louisville: Westminster John Knox, 1993).

189. N. Elliott, *Liberating Paul* (New York: Orbis, 1994). For a brilliant combination of literary and sociological approaches, see N. R. Petersen, *Rediscovering Paul: Philemon and the Sociology of Paul's Narrative World* (Philadelphia: Fortress Press, 1985).

190. For example, several works of D. Patte. Also H. Boers, *The Justification of the Gentiles* (Peabody, Mass.: Hendrickson, 1994); and earlier German writings of E. Güttgemanns.

191. Dale B. Martin, *The Corinthian Body* (New Haven, Conn.: Yale University Press, 1995). See also Sandra H. Polaski, *Paul and the Discourse of Power* (Sheffield: Sheffield Academic Press, 1999), more on Galatians.

192. Antoinette Clark Wire, *The Corinthian Women Prophets* (Minneapolis: Augsburg Fortress Press, 1990, 1995). For feminist history with strong New Testament theology implications, see E. S. Fiorenza, *In Memory of Her* (New York: Crossroads, 1983); and for good collections of essays, see R. S. Kraemer and M. R. D'Angelo, eds., *Women and Christian Origins* (New York: Oxford University Press, 1999); E. Schlüssler Fiorenza, ed., *Searching the Scriptures: A Feminist Commentary* (2 vols.; New York: Crossroads, 1995); and the various *Feminist Companion* volumes edited by A.-J. Levine.

193. *Pauline Theology* (ed. J. M. Bassler et al.; 4 vols.; Minneapolis: Fortress Press, 1991, 1993, 1995, 1997).

194. See, for example, such surveys as Otto Merk, *Paulus-Forschung, 1936–1985*, in *ThR* 53 (1988).

195. Rudolf Bultmann, *The Gospel of John* (1941. Eng. trans. Oxford: Blackwell, 1971); C. H. Dodd, *The Interpretation of the Fourth Gospel* (Cambridge: Cambridge University Press, 1953). From the same period, E. C. Hoskyns's posthumous commentary deserves mention as the product of "a time when we are struggling back with great difficulty to a theological interpretation of the gospels," *The Fourth Gospel* (ed. F. N. Davey; London: Faber, 1940), 47.

196. English translation in H. W. Bartsch, ed., *Kerygma and Myth* (vol. 1; London: SPCK, 1953), and see n. 43.

197. See Ernst Käsemann, *The Testament of Jesus* (Philadelphia: Fortress Press, 1968); and Bornkamm's criticism in J. Ashton, ed., *The Interpretation of John* (Philadelphia: Fortress Press, 1986), 79–98, 2d ed. 1996 (German 1968) 2007. Also Käsemann, *Questions*, 15–18, 138–67 (German 1957).

198. See also: R. E. Brown, *The Community of the Beloved Disciple* (London: Chapman, 1979); J. L. Martyn, *The Gospel of John in Christian History* (New York: Paulist Press, 1979).

199. See D. Rensberger, *Johannine Faith and Liberating Community* (Philadelphia: Westminster, 1988).

200. Wayne Meeks, "The Man from Heaven in Johannine Sectarianism," *JBL* 91 (1972): 44–72. Reprinted in Ashton, *Interpretation.*

201. F. J. Moloney, *Belief in the Word* (vol. 1; Minneapolis: Augsburg Fortress, 1993); vol. 2, *Signs and Shadows* (1996); vol. 3, *Glory Not Dishonor* (1998).

202. For example, J. Blank, *Krisis* (Freiburg: Lambertus, 1964); H. Leroy, *Rätsel und Missverständnis* (Bonn: Hanstein, 1968); J. Frey *Die Johanneische Eschatologie* (3 vols.; Tübingen: Mohr Siebeck, 1997–2000).

203. For example, the political: R. J. Cassidy, *John's Gospel in New Perspective* (Maryknoll, N.Y.: Orbis Books, 1992). The dialogue with Pilate in John 18:29–19:21 has proved fascinating in this regard. For a cultural anthropological perspective, see J. H. Neyrey, *An Ideology of Revolt* (Philadelphia: Fortress Press, 1988).

204. For example, *Anti-Judaism and the Fourth Gospel* (25 papers from the Leuven Colloquium, 2000; Assen: Van Gorcum, 2000, with bibliography).

205. F. C. Baur's "tendency criticism" had in the 1840s analyzed the theology of each evangelist in order to position it in the development of early Christian thought, but without the hypothesis of Markan priority could not develop redaction criticism.

206. See C. M. Tuckett, ed., *The Messianic Secret* (Philadelphia: Fortress Press, 1983); H. Räisänen, *The "Messianic Secret" in Mark* (German 1976; Eng. trans. Edinburgh: T&T Clark, 1990). R. H. Lightfoot was also a forerunner.

207. Martin Dibelius, *From Tradition to Gospel* (German 1919; Eng. trans. New York: Scribner, 1934).

208. For example, W. Marxsen, *Mark the Evangelist* (German 1956; Eng. trans. Nashville: Abingdon, 1969); coining the term *"Redaktionsgeschichte,"* C. C. Black, *The Disciples according to Mark* (Sheffield: JSOT, 1989), provides an insightful analysis of the method; and W. R. Telford, *The Interpretation of Mark* (Philadelphia: Fortress Press, 1985, 1995), offers a comprehensive survey.

209. Stephen Moore's introduction to these approaches (above, n. 149) is invaluable, and the second edition of Telford, *Interpretation* (1995), gives examples from the best applications of it to Mark, including Joanna Dewey, Robert Tannehill, Robert Fowler, Andrew Lincoln, Elizabeth Struthers Malbon, Willem Vorster, and Frank Matera. Malbon's *In the Company of Jesus: Characters in Mark's Gospel* (Louisville: Westminster John Knox, 2000), provides an excellent route into this; and R. A. Horsley, *Hearing the Whole Story* (Louisville: Westminster John Knox, 2001), shows how different approaches can be fruitfully combined.

210. For example, S. Moore, *Mark and Luke in Poststructuralist Perspectives* (New Haven, Conn.: Yale University Press, 1992).

211. For example, L. E. Keck and J. L. Martyn, *Studies in Luke–Acts* (Philadelphia: Fortress Press, 1966). See also Joseph Fitzmyer's majestic Anchor Bible commentary on Luke (2 vols.; New York: Doubleday, 1981 and 1985).

212. Conzelmann objected to this as anachronistic, even though he too dated Luke–Acts around A.D. 100; *Outline*, xvi.

213. See also Käsemann, "Paul and Early Catholicism" (German, 1963) in *Questions*, 236–51; and earlier, "Ministry and Community in the New Testament" (originally 1949) in *Essays on New Testament Themes* (London: SCM Press, 1964), 62–94.

214. See Käsemann, *Essays*, 95–107 (original lecture, 1951); *Questions*, 252–59 (original lecture 1963). The mid-century German debate on the canon and "the center of scripture" was an important chapter in the history of New Testament theology and remains a live issue. See E. Käsemann, ed., *Das Neue Testament als Kanon* (Göttingen: Vandenhoeck & Ruprecht, 1970).

215. Notably R. Tannehill, *The Narrative Unity of Luke–Acts* (2 vols.; Philadelphia: Fortress Press, 1986 and 1990), and several studies of Luke's parables.

216. G. Strecker, *Der Weg der Gerechtigkeit* (Göttingen: Vandenhoeck & Ruprecht, 1962).

217. See U. Luz's essay "The Disciples in the Gospel according to Matthew" (German 1971); Eng. trans. in G. N. Stanton, ed., *Interpretation*. His monumental *Evangelisch-Katholische Kommentar* (EKK), 1985–2003, became in translation the Hermeneia commentary (1989–2004).

218. J. A. Overman, *Matthew's Gospel and Formative Judaism* (Minneapolis: Fortress Press, 1990).

219. J. Roloff, *Die Kirche im Neuen Testament* (Göttingen: Vandenhoeck & Ruprecht, 1993), shows how rich this focus can be.

220. W. D. Davies, *The Setting of the Sermon on the Mount* (Cambridge: Cambridge University Press, 1964), was groundbreaking. See also A. J. Saldarini, *Matthew's Christian Jewish Community* (Chicago: Chicago University Press, 1994); D. C. Sim, *The Gospel of Matthew and Christian Judaism* (Edinburgh: T&T Clark, 1998).

221. H. Schlier's commentary (1957) was debated from a confessional stance by E. Käsemann, *TLZ* 86 (1961): 1–8. Reprinted in *Exegetische Versuche und Besinnungen* (vol. 2; Göttingen: Vandenhoeck & Ruprecht, 1964), 253–61.

222. Among recent New Testament theologies, K. Niederwimmer (2003) gives it prominence.

223. Robert Jewett's popular commentary, *Letter to Pilgrims* (New York: Pilgrim, 1981), applied this motif to contemporary circumstances, showing again how close New Testament theology may stand to Christian practice.

224. For example, W. Schrage, *The Ethics of the New Testament* (German 1982; Eng. trans. Philadelphia: Fortress Press, 1988); W. Marxsen, *New Testament Foundations for Christian Ethics* (German 1989; Eng. trans. Minneapolis: Augsburg Fortress, 1993); E. Lohse, *Theological Ethics of the New Testament* (German 1988; Eng. trans. Minneapolis: Augsburg Fortress, 1991); F. J. Matera, *New Testament Ethics* (Louisville: Westminster John Knox, 1996), is limited to the Gospels and Pauline Epistles, "the legacies of Jesus and Paul."

225. J. Roloff, *Kirche*, is the standard textbook. The reissue of Paul Minear, *Images of the Church in the New Testament* (1952, rev. printings, 1960, 1970, 1977, 2004, 2005) is indicative.

226. R. B. Hays, *The Faith of Jesus Christ* (Chico, Calif.: Scholars Press, 1983).

227. R. B. Hays, *Echoes of Scripture in the Letters of Paul* (New Haven, Conn.: Yale University Press, 1989).

228. Wayne Meeks, *The Moral World of the First Christians* (Philadelphia: Westminster, 1986); and *The Origins of Christian Morality* (New Haven, Conn.: Yale University Press, 1993).

229. R. Bauckham, "The Economic Critique of Rome in Revelation 18," is highly suggestive. See *The Climax of Prophecy* (Edinburgh: T&T Clark, 1993), 338–83.
230. See J. L. Kovacs and C. C. Rowland, *Revelation* (Oxford: Blackwell, 2004).

4. Hermeneutics: The Bible and the Quest for Theological Meaning

1. According to Gabler, there must be a differentiation between dogmatic (systematic) theology and biblical theology. He spoke at a time when biblical theology was viewed as setting forth universal, eternal truths, which dogmatic theology was to arrange in systematic order. In rejecting this understanding, Gabler contended that biblical theology was a historical enterprise that sought to portray the theology of the biblical authors. The appropriate method to follow was historical criticism. Gabler distinguished between true biblical theology that is the limited, conditional theology of the biblical writers, and pure biblical theology, which seeks to discover the eternal theological truths of divine revelation. He attempted to mediate between biblical theology as a historical exercise to reconstruct the history of Israelite religious ideas and biblical theology as a tool of systematic theology that was to incorporate the salient, universal ideas of the Bible into a systematic form addressing current situations. Gabler's distinction largely prevailed until the rise of neo-orthodoxy, when Barth and others recognized that historical criticism built a wall between the past and present, effectively prohibiting the voices of scripture to address the present. Instead, they were locked within a past that at best might be viewed from a distant future.
2. See the brief comments by P. McGlasson, "Barth, Karl," *Dictionary of Biblical Interpretation*, ed. John H. Hayes (Nashville: Abingdon, 1999), 99–100.
3. Brevard Childs is the best example of an Old Testament scholar who incorporates many of the features of dialectical theology into his theology (*Biblical Theology of the Old and New Testaments: Theological Reflection on the Christian Bible* [Minneapolis: Fortress Press, 1993]). Childs rejects as invalid anything that has to do with the history of religion when applied to Israel and the Old Testament.
4. There are numerous studies of hermeneutics and biblical theology that have appeared in the twentieth and twenty-first centuries. Among these, I recommend the Scripture and Hermeneutics series, published by Zondervan and representing evangelical biblical hermeneuts. In my judgment, the best volume in this series is Craig Bartholomew et al., eds., *Canon and Biblical Interpretation* (Scripture and Hermeneutics Series 7; Grand Rapids: Zondervan, 2006). More mainline interpretations include Donald K. McKim, *A Guide to Contemporary Hermeneutics: Major Trends in Biblical Interpretation* (Grand Rapids: Eerdmans, 1986); Klaus Berger, *Hermeneutik des Neuen Testaments* (Tubingen: Francke, 1999); Fernando F. Segovia, *Decolonizing Biblical Studies: A View from the Margins* (Maryknoll, N.Y.: Orbis, 2000); Christoph Dohmen und Günter Stemberger, *Hermeneutik der Jüdischen Bibel und des Alten Testaments* (Kohlhammer Studienbücher Theologie 1.2; Stuttgart: Kohlhammer, 1996); Walter Dietrich and Ulrich Luz, *The Bible in the World Context: An Experiment in Contextual Hermeneutics* (Grand Rapids: Eerdmans, 2002); Oda Wischmeyer, *Hermeneutik des Neuen Testaments* (Neutestamentliche Entwürfe zur Theologie 8; Tübingen: Francke, 2004); Bernd Janowski, *Kanonhermeneutik: Vom Lesen und Verstehen der christlichen Bibel* (Neukirchen-Vluyn: Neukirchener Verlag, 2007); Timo Veijola, *Offenbarung und Anfechtung. Hermeneutisch-theologische Studien zum Alten Testament* (Neukirchen-Vluyn: Neukirchener Verlag, 2007); David A. Holgate and

Rachel Starr, *SCM Studyguide to Biblical Hermeneutics* (SCM Studyguides; London: SCM Press, 2006); Manfred Oeming, *Biblische Hermeneutik*, 2d rev. ed. (Darmstadt: Primus, 2007); Manfred Oeming and Joachim F. Vette, *Contemporary Biblical Hermeneutics: An Introduction* (London: Ashgate, 2007); J. Edwin Hartill, *Principles of Biblical Hermeneutics* (Grand Rapids: Zondervan, 2007); and Jeannine K. Brown, *Scripture as Communication: Introducing Biblical Hermeneutics* (Grand Rapids: Baker, 2007).

5. Paul Tillich, *Systematic Theology*, 3 vols. (London: SCM Press, 1978); *The Courage to Be* (2d ed. with an Introduction by Peter J. Gomes; Yale Nota bene; New Haven, Conn.: Yale University Press, 2000); *Dynamics of Faith* (First Perennial Classics; New York: HarperPerennial, 2001); *Love, Power and Justice: Ontological Analyses and Ethical Implications* (New York: Oxford University Press, 1960); and *Theology of Culture* (New York: Oxford University Press, 1970).

6. For a legitimate approach to this area, both socially and theologically, see the Public Religion Project carried out by the Martin Marty Center at the University of Chicago. The goal of this project has been to promote the numerous efforts to illuminate and to interpret the forces of faith within a pluralistic society, in particular American society in the contemporary world. For a full description of this projection, with a careful definition of terms, see their website, http://martycenter.uchicago.edu/research/publicreligion_today.shtml.

7. Among recent biblical theologies that recognize the importance of context for both the descriptive and hermeneutical tasks is Erhard Gerstenberger, *Theologies of the Old Testament* (Minneapolis: Fortress Press, 2002), esp. 25–91. He begins by setting forth his assumptions in describing Old Testament theology. "Any theological 'approach,' including any exegesis of the Old Testament and any 'theology' of the Old Testament based on it, is subject to its own limited, concrete, contextual conditions and therefore cannot be absolutized." Modern interpreters cannot help but read and make judgments from their own different contexts when doing biblical theology. This is even more true in the hermeneutical enterprise.

8. Henning Graf Reventlow, *Epochen der Bibelauslegung: Epochen der Bibelauslegung*, 4 vols. (München: C. H. Beck, 1990–2001); Christoph Dohmen and Günter Stemberger, *Hermeneutik der Jüdischen Bibel und des Alten Testaments* (Studienbücher Theologie 1/2; Stuttgart: W. Kohlhammer, 1996); Magne Sæbø, ed., *Hebrew Bible, Old Testament: The History of Its Interpretation* (Göttingen: Vandenhoeck & Ruprecht, 1996–); and William Baird, *History of New Testament Research*, 4 vols. (Minneapolis: Fortress Press, 1992–).

9. Several of the most significant treatments include Robert Morgan and John Barton, *Biblical Interpretation* (Oxford Bible; Oxford: Oxford University Press, 1988); and Oeming, *Contemporary Biblical Hermeneutics*.

10. Brevard Childs, *Biblical Theology of the Old and New Testaments: Theological Reflection on the Christian Bible* (Minneapolis: Fortress Press, 1993); *Introduction to the Old Testament as Scripture* (Philadelphia: Fortress Press, 1979); *Old Testament Theology in a Canonical Context* (Philadelphia: Fortress Press, 1985); and *Biblical Theology of the Old and New Testaments* (Minneapolis: Fortress Press, 1992). Also see Christoph Dohmen and Manfred Oeming, *Biblischer Kanon, warum und wozu?: eine Kanontheologie* (Freiburg: Herder, 1992); and Rolf Rendtorff and David E. Horton, *The Canonical Hebrew Bible: A Theology of the Old Testament* (Tools for Biblical Study; Blandford Forum, England: Deo Press, 2006).

11. Childs, *Biblical Theology of the Old and New Testaments*, 70–71.

12. Ibid., 77–79. Rolf Rendtorff also focuses on the canon in approaching Old Testament theology, although, unlike Childs, he does not attempt to write a comprehensive biblical theology. *Theologie des Alten Testaments. Einkanonischer Entwurf* 1 & 2 (Neukirchen-Vluyn: Neukirchener Verlag, 1999, 2001). See especially his last section of the second volume for his view of canon and its implications for hermeneutics.

13. Among the Jewish scholars who have developed at least elements of a Jewish biblical theology, see Moshe Weinfeld's essay "Theologische Trends in der Tora-Literatur," *Beth Mikra* 16 (1971): 10–22 (Heb.); Mattitiahu Tsevat, "Theology of the Old Testament—A Jewish View," *HBT* 8 (1986): 33–49; M. H. Goshen-Gottstein, "Tanakh Theology: The Religion of the Old Testament and the Place of Jewish Biblical Theology," *Ancient Israelite Religion: Essays in Honor of Frank Moore Cross*, ed. Patrick D. Miller Jr., Paul D. Hanson, and S. Dean McBride (Philadelphia: Fortress Press, 1987), 587–644; Yochanan Muffs, *Love and Joy: Law, Language and Religion in Ancient Israel* (New York and Cambridge: Jewish Theological Seminary and Harvard University Press, 1992); Isaac Kalimi, "Religionsgeschichte Israels oder Theologie des Alten Testaments? Das jüdische Interesse an der Biblischen Theologie," *JBTH* 10; Neukirchener Verlag, 1995, 45–68; Moshe Greenberg, *Studies in the Bible and Jewish Thought* (Philadelphia: Jewish Publication Society, 1995); and, of course, the chapter by Benjamin Sommer in this volume. Sommer also reminds us that Yehezkel Kaufmann set the stage and the tone for Jewish biblical theology with *Toledot Ha-Emunah Ha-Yisraelit* [in Hebrew] 4 vols. (Jerusalem and Tel Aviv: Bialik and Devir, 1937–1956). The first three volumes are available in an English abridgement: Yehezkel Kaufmann, *The Religion of Israel: From Its Beginnings to the Babylonian Exile* (Chicago: Chicago University Press, 1960); and parts of the final volume are found in English in Kaufmann, *The Babylonian Captivity and Deutero-Isaiah* (New York: Union of American Hebrew Congregations, 1970). Sommer remarks that one whose theological work is infused with Kaufmann is Yochanan Muffs. See in particular his *The Personhood of God: Biblical Theology, Human Faith and the Divine Image* (Woodstock, Vt.: Jewish Lights, 2005).

14. According to Sommer, it is not clear that early Jewish groups, such as the community at Qumran, held any position truly analogous to the Protestant principle of *sola scriptura* (see Moshe Goshen-Gottstein, "Tanakh Theology," 627). Even if any did hold to such a view, they still depended very much on oral traditions. See, for example, Daniel Frank, "Karaite Exegesis," *Hebrew Bible/Old Testament: The History of Its Interpretation I/2: The Middle Ages*, ed. Magne Sæbø (Göttingen: Vandenhoeck & Ruprecht, 2000), 115. Sommer's concern is not in these early communities, but rather in the many varieties of Judaism in the ancient, medieval, and modern world that developed from the early rabbinic movement and now find expression in all four modern forms of religious Judaism (Reform, Orthodox, Conservative, and Reconstructionist).

15. For a discussion of scripture as a part of Jewish tradition in rabbinic Judaism, see Benjamin Sommer, "Unity and Plurality in Jewish Canons: The Case of the Oral and Written Torah," *One Scripture or Many? Perspectives Historical, Theological and Philosophical*, eds. Christine Helmer and Christof Landmesser (New York: Oxford University Press, 2004), 108–50.

16. See Jon A. Levenson, "Why Jews Are Not Interested in Biblical Theology," *The Hebrew Bible, the Old Testament, and Historical Criticism: Jews and Christians in Biblical Studies*; Louisville: Westminster John Knox, 1993), 33–61. This is a revision of the arti-

cle originally published in *Judaic Perspectives on Ancient Israel*, ed. Jacob Neusner (Philadelphia: Fortress Press, 1987).

17. Levenson, "Why Jews Are Not Interested in Biblical Theology," 37.

18. Ibid., 40–41. See Eichrodt, *Theology of the Old Testament*, 1:26.

19. Levenson, "Why Jews Are Not Interested in Biblical Theology," 41. See von Rad, *Old Testament Theology*, 2:321.

20. Julius Wellhausen, *Prolegomena to the History of Israel* (Atlanta: Scholars Press, 1944).

21. Levenson, "Why Jews Are Not Interested in Biblical Theology," 45; see Amy Jill Levine, who makes a similar argument about the Christian portrayal of Jesus as the great liberator and prophet of social justice, while Judaism of his period is wrongly portrayed as legalistic and sexist. She also calls on postcolonial biblical interpreters to recognize their at least implicitly anti-Semitic biases ("Anti-Judaism and Postcolonial Biblical Interpretation," *Journal of Feminist Studies in Religion* 20 [2004]: 91–132).

22. Jon D. Levenson, "Theological Consensus or Historicist Evasion? Jews and Christians in Biblical Studies," *Hebrew Bible or Old Testament? Studying the Bible in Judaism and Christianity*, ed. Roger Brooks and John J. Collins (Christianity and Judaism in Antiquity 5; Notre Dame: University of Notre Dame Press, 1990), 131f.

23. Levenson, "Why Jews Are Not Interested in Biblical Theology," 51–54.

24. Jon Levenson, "The Eight Principles of Judaism and the Literary Simultaneity of Scripture," *The Hebrew Bible, The Old Testament, and Historical Criticism* (Louisville: Westmninster John Knox, 1993), 62–81. In this essay, Levenson describes Maimonides' argument for the unity and divinity of the Torah, even though he believed Moses wrote the Torah and that God did not dictate it to him. "The authority of the Torah does not require faithful exegetes to deny the contradictions within it, but the frank recognition of the contradictions does not allow them to base religious life and practice on something less than the whole" (pp. 79–80).

25. Jon D. Levenson, *Creation and the Persistence of Evil: The Jewish Drama of Divine Omnipotence* (Princeton: Princeton Theological Seminary, 1994).

26. Marvin A. Sweeney, "Tanak versus Old Testament: Concerning the Foundation for a Jewish Theology of the Bible," *Problems in Biblical Theology. Essays in Honor of Rolf Knierim*, ed. Henry T. C. Sun and Keith L. Eades with James M. Robinson (Grand Rapids: Eerdmans, 1997), 353–72; and idem, "Reconceiving the Paradigms of Old Testament Theology in the Post-Shoah Period," *Jews, Christians, and the Theology of Hebrew Scriptures*, ed. Alice Ogden Bellis and Joel S. Kaminsky (Symposium 8; Atlanta: Scholars Press, 29-2000), 155–72.

27. James Barr, *The Concept of Biblical Theology: An Old Testament Perspective* (Minneapolis: Fortress Press, 1999).

28. Gerhard von Rad, *Old Testament Theology*, 2 vols. (New York: Harper & Row, 1962, 1965), 19.

29. Ibid., 2:364–87.

30. Ibid., 319–35, 357–87.

31. Ibid., 319.

32. See von Rad's essay on hermeneutics, 17-39, in Claus Westermann, ed., *Essays on Old Testament Hermeneutics*, 2d ed. (Atlanta: John Knox, 1964). For important studies of von Rad, see James L. Crenshaw, *Gerhard von Rad* (Makers of the Modern Theological Mind; Waco, Tex.: Word Books, 1978); Martin Honecker, "Zum Verständnis der

Geschichte in Gerhard von Rad's Theologie des Alten Testaments," *EvTh* 23 (1963): 143–68; and H. W. Wolf, Rolf Rentdorff, and Wolfhart Pannenberg, *Gerhard von Rad: Seine Bedeutung für die Theologie* (München: Chr. Kaiser, 1973).

33. See the criticism of von Rad by Manfred Oeming, *Gesamtbiblische Theologien der Gegenwart: Das Verhaltnis von AT und NT in der hermeneutischen Diskussion seit Gerhard von Rad*, 2d ed. (Stuttgart: Kohlhammer, 1987). Now see his more recent formulation of hermeneutics in his *Contemporary Biblical Hermeneutics*.

34. Hartmut Gese, *Zur biblischen Theologie: Alttestamentliche Vorträge* (München: Chr. Kaiser, 1986); and *Vom Sinai zum Zion: Alttestamentliche Beiträge zur biblischen Theologie*, 3rd ed. (Gütersloh: Gütersloher Verlagshaus, 1990).

35. Johann Phillip Gabler, "An Oration on the Proper Distinction between Biblical and Dogmatic Theology and the Specific Objectives of Each," in *The Flowering of Old Testament Theology*, ed. Ben C. Ollenburger, Elmer A. Martens, and Gerhard F. Hasel (Sources for Biblical and Theological Study 1; Winona Lake, Ind.: Eisenbrauns, 1992). For studies of Gabler, see Otto Merk, *Biblische Theologie des Neuen Testaments in ihrer Anfangszeit* (Marburg: Elwert, 1972); Robert Morgan, "Gabler's Bicentenary," *ET* 98 (1987): 164–68; Magne Saebø "Johann Philipp Gablers Bedeutung für die biblische Theologie," *ZAW* 99 (1987): 1–16; and John Sandys-Wunsch and Laurence Eldredge, "J. P. Gabler and the Distinction between Biblical and Dogmatic Theology: Translation, Commentary, and Discussion of His Originality," *SJTh* 33 (1980): 133–58.

36. See the historical surveys of literature by G. W. Anderson, "Hebrew Religion," in *The Old Testament and Modern Study: A Generation of Discovery and Research*, ed. H. H. Rowley (London: Oxford University Press, 1951), 283–310; Walther Zimmerli, "The History of Israelite Religion," *Tradition and Interpretation*, ed. G. W. Anderson (London: Oxford University Press, 1979), 351–84. For earlier studies of this relationship and opposition, see C. R. North, "Old Testament Theology and the History of Hebrew Religion," *SJT* 2 (1949): 113–26; William A. Irwin, "The Study of Israel's Religion," *VT* 7 (1957): 113–26; James Barr, "The Problem of Old Testament Theology and the History of Religion," *CJTh* 3 (1957): 141–49; and C. J. Bleeker, "Comparing the Religio-Historical Method and the Theological Method," *Numen* 18 (1971): 9–29.

37. Rainer Albertz, *A History of Israelite Religion in the Old Testament Period*, 2 vols. (Minneapolis: Fortress Press, 1994).

38. Rolf Rendtorff is doubtful that a debate concerning the value of one of the two methods over the other is necessary. Indeed, he sees them as different methods ("Die Hermeneutik einer kanonischen Theologie des Alten Testaments," *JBTh* 10 (1995): 35–44. He notes that Old Testament theology has two major presuppositions. One is that the Old Testament is a theological book (cf. Rudolf Smend, "Theologie im Alten Testament," *Verifikation*, FS Gerhard Ebeling, ed. Eberhard Jüngel [Tübingen: J. C. B. Mohr, 1982], 104–17). The second is that the subject matter of Old Testament theology is the final form of the canon (cf. his *Theologie des Alten Testaments. Ein kanonischer Entwurf* I & II [Neukirchen-Vluyn: Neukirchener Verlag, 1999], 2001). By contrast, he argues that the history of religion is concerned to reconstruct the life and religious thought of the ancient community in a diachronic process. Rendtorff is joined by Isaac Kalimi, who agrees that the difference between the two points to two different methods with distinct goals and procedures (e.g., see "Religionsgeschichte Israels oder Theologie des Alten Testaments?, 45–68).

39. Albertz, *A History of Israelite Religion in the Old Testament Period*, 1:1–21.

40. Ibid., 11–12.

41. Frank Crüsemann argues that biblical theology and the history of religion cannot be completely objective. To claim the contrary, in his view, is pseudo-objectivity. In addition, he is rather skeptical of the hope of Albertz that an increasing consensus about Israel's religion will emerge ("Religionsgeschichte oder Theologie? Elementare Überlegungen zu einer falschen Alternative," *JBTh* 10 [1995]: 69–77).

42. Albertz, *Jahrbuch für biblische Theologie* 19 (1995). This collection of critical responses to Albertz also contains two essays. The first sets forth his basic positions for preferring the history of religions over Old Testament theology ("Religionsgeschichte Israels statt Theologie des Alten Testaments! Plädoyer für eine forschungsgeschichtliche Umorientierung," *JBTh* 10 [1995]: 3–24). The second contains his response, in which he argues that Old Testament theology, while it ought to be an exegetical, historical, and systematic enterprise, belongs to the sphere of the church, whereas the history of Israelite religion offers Old Testament theology a concrete material basis, even while having to dispense with normative judgments ("Hat die Theologie des Alten Testaments doch noch eine Chance?" *JBTH* 10 [1995]: 177–87).

43. Gerstenberger, *Theologies in the Old Testament*, 16. Gerstenberger makes ready use of the methods of the history of religions and numerous sociological methods in constructing his theologies. He differentiates five major social constructions that influence their varying views of God and social ethics. These are the family and clan, the village and small town, the tribal alliances, the monarchial state, and confessional and parochial communities. These divergent theologies are present throughout the Old Testament. While Gerstenberger's hermeneutical insights are not fully developed, his tracing of the divergent theologies points by implication to the fact that there would also by necessity be various hermeneutical understandings.

44. Rudolf Bultmann, *Faith and Understanding* (Philadelphia: Fortress Press, 1969); *New Testament & Mythology and Other Basic Writings* (Philadelphia: Fortress Press, 1984); *Jesus and the Word* (New York: Scribner, 1991 [1987]). Also see *Rudolf Bultmann: Interpreting Faith for the Modern Era*, ed. Roger Johnson (Minneapolis: Fortress Press). This is a collection of essays from throughout Bultmann's career, ranging from 1917 to 1958.

45. Bultmann, *New Testament & Mythology*, 12.

46. Bultmann, *Faith and Understanding*, 30.

47. Ibid., 122.

48. Ibid., 324.

49. Bultmann, *New Testament & Mythology*, 5.

50. Rudolf Bultmann, *Interpreting Faith for the Modern Era*, 92.

51. Rudolf Bultmann, "The Significance of the Old Testament for Christian Faith," in *The Old Testament and Christian Faith: A Theological Discussion*, ed. B. W. Anderson (New York: Harper & Row, 1963), 8–35.

52. Samuel Terrien, *Till the Heart Sings: A Biblical Theology of Manhood and Womanhood* (Biblical Resource Series; Grand Rapids: Eerdmans, 1994).

53. See especially Robert Alter, *The Art of Biblical Narrative* (New York: Basic Books, 1981); idem, *The Art of Biblical Poetry* (New York: Basic Books, 1985); and *The Literary Interpretations of Biblical Narratives*, ed. Kenneth R. R. Gros Louis, with James S. Ackerman and Thayer S. Warshaw (Nashville: Abingdon, 1974).

54. John Crowe Ransom, *The New Criticism* (Norfolk, Conn.: New Directions, 1941).

55. Michael Groden and Martin Kreiswirth, eds., *The Johns Hopkins Guide to Literary Theory & Criticism* (Baltimore: Johns Hopkins University Press, 1994).

56. Viktor Shklovskii, *Theory of Prose* (Elmwood Park, Ill.: Dalkey Archive Press, 1990). Also see Karen A. McCauley, "Russian Formalism," in *Johns Hopkins Guide*, 634–38.

57. M. M. Bakhtin, *Problems of Dostoevsky's Poetics*, 2d ed. (Ann Arbor, Mich.: Ardis, 1973); ibid, *Speech Genres and Other Late Essays* (Austin: University of Texas Press, 1986). An important example of the application of Bakhtin has been set forward by Carol A. Newsom in her article "Bakhtin, the Bible, and Dialogic Truth," *JR* 76 (1996): 290–306.

58. David Bleich, *Readings and Feelings: An Introduction to Subjective Criticism* (Urbana, Ill.: National Council of Teachers of English, 1975); and ibid., *Subjective Criticism* (Baltimore: Johns Hopkins University Press, 1978).

59. Jonathan Culler, *The Pursuit of Signs: Semiotics, Literature, Deconstruction* (augmented ed.; Ithaca, N.Y.: Cornell University Press, 2002).

60. Umberto Eco, *The Role of the Reader: Explorations in the Semiotics of Texts* (Bloomington: Indiana University Press, 1979).

61. A handy introduction is Jane P. Tompkins, ed., *Reader-Response Criticism: From Formalism to Post-Structuralism* (Baltimore: Johns Hopkins University Press, 1980). Especially important is the book of essays by Stanley Fish, *Is There a Text in This Class?* (Cambridge, Mass.: Harvard University Press, 1980). Also see Wolfgang Iser, *The Act of Reading: A Theory of Aesthetic Response* (Baltimore: Johns Hopkins University Press, 1978). In biblical studies, see Edgar V. McKnight, "Reader-Response Criticism," in *To Each Its Own Meaning*, ed. Stephen R. Haynes and Steven L. McKenzie (Louisville: Westminister John Knox Press, 1993), 197–219; and J. Cheryl Exum and David J. A. Clines, *The New Literary Criticism and the Hebrew Bible* (JSOTSup 143; Sheffield: JSOT Press, 1993). Also see David J. A. Clines, "Why Is There a Book of Job and What Does It Do to You If You Read It?" in *The Book of Job*, ed. W. A. M. Beuken (BEThL 114; Leuven: Leuven University Press, 1994), 1–20; Kathryn Pfisterer Darr, *Isaiah's Vision and the Family of God* (Louisville: Westminster John Knox Press, 1994); Daniel Patte, "Speech Act Theory and Biblical Exegesis," *Semeia* 41 (1988): 85–102; Hugh C. White, "Introduction: Speech Act Theory and Literary Criticism," *Semeia* 41 (1988): 1–24; ibid, "The Value of Speech Act Theory for Old Testament Hermeneutics," *Semeia* 41 (1988): 41–63.

62. J. L. Austin, *How to Do Things with Words* (Cambridge, Mass.: Harvard University Press, 1962); ibid., *Philosophical Papers* (Oxford: Clarendon Press, 1961); and ibid, *Sense and Sensibilia* (Oxford: Clarendon Press, 1962).

63. Among biblical scholars who discuss this approach, see Daniel Patte, "Speech Act Theory and Biblical Exegesis," *Semeia* 41 (1988): 85–102; Hugh C. White, "Introduction: Speech Act Theory and Literary Criticism," *Semeia* 41 (1988): 1–24; ibid, "The Value of Speech Act Theory for Old Testament Hermeneutics," *Semeia* 41 (1988): 41–63.

64. Anthony C. Thiselton, *New Horizons in Hermeneutics: the Theory and Practice of Transforming Biblical Reading* (Grand Rapids: Zondervan, 1992), 471.

65. Kliever, *The Shattered Spectrum*, 157. Ronald Thiemann remarks: "Narrative highlights both a predominant literary category within the Bible and an appropriate theological category for interpreting the canon as a whole" (*Revelation and Theology: The Gospel as Narrated Promise* [Notre Dame: University of Notre Dame Press, 1985], 83).

66. The scholarly literature is immense. Among the most important expressions of narrative theology are Frei, *The Eclipse of Biblical Narrative; The Identity of Jesus Christ: The Hermeneutical Bases of Dogmatic Theology* (Philadelphia: Fortress Press, 1975); George

Lindbeck, *The Nature of Doctrine. Religion and Theology in a Postliberal Age* (Philadelphia: Westminister, 1984); Paul Ricoeur, *Time and Narrative*, 2 vols. (Chicago: University of Chicago Press, 1984, 1985); "Biblical Hermeneutics," *Paul Ricoeur on Biblical Hermeneutics*, ed. John Dominic Crossan; idem, *Semeia* 4 (1975): 29–146; idem, "The Narrative Function," *Semeia* 13 (1978): 177–202; *Essays on Biblical Interpretation* (ed. Lewis Mudge; Philadelphia: Fortress Press, 1980), 75–79; David Tracy, *Analogical Imagination* (New York: Crossroad, 1981); especially his analysis of the religious "classic"; Stephen Crites, "The Narrative Quality of Experience," and "The Spatial Dimensions of Narrative Truth Telling," in Michael Goldberg, ed., *Theology and Narrative: A Critical Introduction* (Nashville: Abingdon, 1981–1982); idem, *Jews and Christians, Getting Our Stories Straight: The Exodus and the Passion-Resurrection* (Nashville: Abingdon, 1985); Garrett Green, ed., *Scriptural Authority and Narrative Interpretation* (Philadelphia: Fortress Press, 1987); Stanley Hauerwas, *Vision and Virtue* (Notre Dame: Fides, 1974); Stanley Hauerwas and L. Gregory Jones, eds., *Why Narrative?* (Grand Rapids: Eerdmans, 1989); A. E. Harvey, ed., *God Incarnate: Story and Belief* (London: SPCK, 1981); and George W. Stroup, *The Promise of Narrative Theology* (Atlanta: John Knox, 1981). According to Goldberg, narrative theologians generally subscribe to the following elements: the form of the biblical narrative reflects the structure of reality; the meaning of the story is of central importance; and the ethic expressed in and through the narrative is significant (*Theology and Narrative*, 155). Important overviews of narrative theology are provided by Michael Goldberg, *Theology and Narrative*; Kliever, *The Shattered Spectrum*, 153–84; Mark Allan Powell, *What Is Narrative Criticism* (Guides to Biblical Scholarship; Minneapolis: Fortress Press, 1990); and George Stroup, "Theology of Narrative or Narrative Theology? A Response to *Why Narrative?*" *TToday* 47 (1991): 424–32.

67. Fackre, "Narrative Theology: An Overview," 343.

68. Two important though distinctive "schools" of narrative theology have developed, one primarily associated with Yale (Hans Frei, Stanley Hauerwas, David Kelsey, and George Lindbeck) and the other largely identified with Chicago (Paul Ricoeur, David Tracy, and Julian Hartt). For a comparison of the two, see Gary Comstock, "Two Types of Narrative Theology," *JAAR* 55 (1987): 687–717.

69. See Fackre, "Narrative Theology: An Overview," 340–52.

70. Erich Auerbach, *Mimesis: The Representation of Reality in Western Literature* (Princeton, N.J.: Princeton University Press, 2003).

71. See Frei, *The Eclipse of Biblical Narrative*; and *The Identity of Jesus Christ*. For a careful and cogent critique, see James Duke, "Reading the Gospels Realistically: A Review of Hans Frei's 'Eclipse of Biblical Narrative' and 'Identity of Jesus Christ,'" *Encounter* 38 (1977): 296–306.

72. Similar is the view of George Lindbeck, who argues that the literary genre of the Bible is "an overarching story that has the specific literary features of realistic narrative" (*The Nature of Doctrine*, 120–21).

73. See Stroup, *The Promise of Narrative Theology*, 63–65.

74. Frei's assessment is clearly dependent on Auerbach.

75. Hans-Georg Gadamer, *Truth and Method*, 2nd. rev. ed. (London: Continuum, 2004).

76. See Comstock, "Two Types of Narrative Theology," 690.

77. The literature in this area is vast. Among the more important treatments that have impacted biblical studies are Wayne Booth, *The Rhetoric of Fiction* (Chicago: University

of Chicago Press, 1961); Northrop Frye, *Anatomy of Criticism* (Princeton, N.J.: Princeton University Press, 1957); Frank Kermode, *The Genesis of Secrecy: On the Interpretation of Narrative* (Cambridge, Mass.: Harvard University Press, 1979); and Robert Scholes and Robert Kellogg, *The Nature of Narrative* (New York: Oxford University Press, 1966). Important literary treatments of biblical narrative include James Ackerman and Kenneth Gros-Louis, eds., *Literary Interpretations of Biblical Narratives* (Nashville: Abingdon, 1974); Michael Fishbane, *Text and Texture* (New York: Schocken, 1979); J. P. Fokkelman, *Narrative Art in Genesis* (Assen: Van Gorcum, 1975); David Gunn and Danna Fewell, *Narrative in the Hebrew Bible* (Oxford: Oxford University Press, 1993); and Danna Fewell, ed., *Reading Between Texts* (Louisville: Westminster John Knox, 1992); Jacob Licht, *Storytelling in the Bible* (Jerusalem: Magnes, 1978); and Meir Sternberg, *The Poetics of Biblical Narrative: Ideological Literature and the Drama of Reading* (Bloomington, Ind.: Indiana University Press, 1987). For the approach to texts in the New Testament, see especially the excellent book by Joanna Dewey, *Mark as Story: An Introduction to the Narrative of a Gospel* (with David Rhoads and Donald Michie; 2d ed. (Minneapolis: Fortress Press, 1999).

78. See Barton, *Reading the Old Testament*, 140–98.

79. Robert Alter, *The Art of Biblical Narrative* (New York: Basic Books, 1981). He explains: "By literary analysis I mean the manifold varieties of minutely discriminating attention to the artful use of language, to the shifting play of ideas, conventions, tone, imagery, syntax, narrative viewpoint, compositional units, and much else; the kind of disciplined attention, in other words, which through a whole spectrum of critical approaches has illuminated, for example, the poetry of Dante, the plays of Shakespeare, the novels of Tolstoy" (pp. 12–13). We are focusing largely on narrative in this section, although, as Alter among others has demonstrated, poetry is also a literary form that may be interpreted in a similar way (*The Art of Biblical Poetry* [New York: Basic Books, 1985]).

80. Alter, *The Art of Biblical Narrative*, 24.

81. Among the many important studies on metaphor, see: Ian Barbour, *Myths, Models and Paradigms* (New York: Harper & Row, 1974); Max Black, *Models and Metaphors* (Ithaca, N.Y.: Cornell University Press, 1962); Frederick Ferré, "Metaphors, Models, and Religion," *Soundings* 51 (1968): 327–45; George Lakoff and Mark Johnson, *Metaphors We Live By* (Chicago: University of Chicago Press, 1980); I. A. Richards, *The Philosophy of Rhetoric* (New York: Oxford University Press, 1936); Paul Ricoeur, "The Metaphorical Process," 75–106; *Interpretation Theory: Discourse and the Surplus of Meaning* (Fort Worth: TCU, 1976); *The Rule of Metaphor* (Toronto: University of Toronto Press, 1977); Sheldon Sacks, ed., *On Metaphor* (Chicago: University of Chicago Press, 1979); and Phillip Wheelwright, *Metaphor and Reality* (Bloomington: Indiana University Press, 1962). For a detailed application of metaphorical theory to the theology of the book of Job, see my *Wisdom in Revolt: Metaphorical Theology in the Book of Job* (JSOTSup 112; Sheffield: Almond Press, 1991).

82. Richards, *The Philosophy of Rhetoric*, 96.

83. Wayne Booth, *A Rhetoric of Irony* (Chicago: University of Chicago Press, 1974) 22.

84. McFague, *Metaphorical Theology*, 18.

85. Ricoeur, "The Metaphorical Process," 77–78.

86. Ibid., 75.

87. Wheelwright, *Metaphor and Reality*, 33.

88. John Dominic Crossan, ed., "Biblical Hermeneutics," Paul Ricoeur on Biblical Hermeneutics, *Semeia* 4 (1975): 29–146; Amos Wilder, *Theopoetic: Theology and the Religious Imagination* (Philadelphia: Fortress Press, 1976; idem, *Jesus' Parables and the War of Myths: Essays on Imagination in the Scripture* (Philadelphia: Fortress Press, 1985); Robert Murray, "Exegesis and Imagination" (Ethel M. Wood lecture, delivered at the Senate House, University of London on 1 March 1988); David Brown, *Tradition and Imagination: Revelation and Change* (Oxford: Oxford University Press, 1999); Walter Brueggemann, *The Prophetic Imagination* (Philadelphia: Fortress Press, 1987); Garrett Green, *Imagining God: Theology and the Religious Imagination* (San Francisco: Harper & Row, 1989); and idem, "Myth, History, and Imagination: The Creation Narratives in Bible and Theology," HBT 12 (1990): 19–38.

89. Mary Warnock, *Imagination* (Berkeley: University of California, 1978), 10.

90. Robert Scharlemann, "Transcendental and Poietic Imagination," *Morphologies of Faith* (ed. Mary Gerhart and Anthony Yu; AAR Studies in Religion 59; Atlanta: Scholars Press, 1990), 109–22.

91. Wilder, *Theopoetic.*

92. See *Time and Narrative*, 2 vols. (Chicago: University of Chicago Press, 1984, 1985); "Biblical Hermeneutics," *Paul Ricoeur on Biblical Hermeneutics*, ed. John Dominic Crossan; *Semeia* 4 (1975): 29–146; "The Narrative Function," *Semeia* 13 (1978): 177–202; and *Essays on Biblical Interpretation* (ed. Lewis Mudge; Philadelphia: Fortress Press, 1980) 75–79.

93. See Comstock, "Truth or Meaning," 117–40.

94. For a brief discussion of imagination, see A. R. Manser, "Imagination," *Encyclopedia of Philosophy* 4 (1967): 136–38. Manser stresses Kant's point that imagination is the ability to "form mental images, or other concepts not directly derived from sensation." Since the data of the senses are fragmentary and incomplete, imagination enables one to perceive the whole at once. Kant extended this understanding to argue that productive imagination combines human experiences into a single, connected whole, thereby making the world and human experience of the world coherent.

95. Walter Brueggemann, *The Land* (Philadelphia: Fortress Press, 1977); *Living Toward a Vision* (Philadelphia: United Church Press, 1982); *Hopeful Imagination*; *The Prophetic Imagination* (Philadelphia: Fortress Press, 1987); *Hope Within History* (Atlanta: John Knox, 1987); *Power, Providence and Personality: Biblical Insight into Life and Ministry* (Louisville: Westminister John Knox, 1990); and *Interpretation and Obedience* (Minneapolis: Fortress Press, 1991).

96. In addition to Brueggemann, see the works of John Collins, *Apocalyptic Imagination: An Introduction to the Jewish Matrix of Christianity* (New York: Crossroad, 1984); and "Is a Critical Biblical Theology Possible?," *The Hebrew Bible and Its Interpreters*, ed. William Henry Propp, et al. (Winona Lake, Ind.: Eisenbrauns, 1990), 1–17.

97. Walter Brueggemann, *Hopeful Imagination: Prophetic Voices in Exile* (Philadelphia: Fortress Press, 1986).

98. "A Shape for Old Testament Theology, I: Structure Legitimation," CBQ 47 (1985): 28–46; and "A Shape for Old Testament Theology, II: Embrace of Pain," CBQ 47 (1985): 395–415.

99. "A Shape for Old Testament Theology," 1:30, emphasis added.

100. "A Shape for Old Testament Theology," 1:42.

101. "A Shape for Old Testament Theology," 2:398.

102. Walter Brueggemann, *Theology of the Old Testament: Testimony, Dispute, Advocacy* (Minneapolis: Fortress Press, 1997).

103. Among the more important examples of feminist biblical interpretation are Phyllis Trible, *God and the Rhetoric of Sexuality* (London: SCM Press, 1992); Phyllis Trible and Letty Russell, *Hagar, Sarah, and their Children: Jewish, Christian, and Muslim Perspectives* (Louisville: Westminster John Knox, 2006); Elisabeth Schüssler Fiorenza, *Bread Not Stone: The Challenge of Feminist Biblical Interpretation* (Boston: Beacon Press, 1984); idem, *In Memory of Her: A Feminist Reconstruction of Christian Origins* (2d ed.; London: SCM Press, 1995); and idem, *Sharing Her Word: Feminist Biblical Interpretation in Context* (Boston: Beacon Press, 1998). Feminist theologies from non-Western perspectives include Pui-lan Kwok, *Introducing Asian Feminist Theology* (Introductions in Feminist Theology 4; Sheffield: Sheffield Academic Press, 2000); Musa W. Dube, *Postcolonial Feminist Interpretation of the Bible* (St. Louis: Chalice Press, 2000); idem, "Fifty Years of Bleeding: A Storytelling Feminist Reading of Mark 5:24-43," 50–60; and idem, "Divining Ruth for International Relations," *Other Ways of Reading: African Women and the Bible*, ed. Musa W. Dube (Atlanta: Scholars Press, 2001), 179–95. See especially Gerda Lerna, *The Creation of Feminist Consciousness from the Middle Ages to 1870* (Women and History 2; New York: Oxford University Press, 1993); and M. J. Selvidge, *Notorious Voices: Feminist Biblical Interpretation* (1550–1920) (New York: Continuum, 1996).

104. Sallie McFague, *Metaphorical Theology: Models of God in Religious Language* (Minneapolis: Fortress Press, 1982).

105. Elizabeth Johnson, *She Who Is: The Mystery of God in Feminist Theological Discourse* (New York: Crossroad, 1992).

106. See her rejection of this dichotomy in *Sharing Her Word. Feminist Biblical Interpretation in Context* (Boston: Beacon Press, 1998), 9–12.

107. See my chapter on feminism in *Reconstructing Old Testament Theology. After the Collapse of History* (Overtures to Biblical Theology, Minneapolis: Fortress Press, 2005).

108. See my volume, *Reconstructing Old Testament Theology*, 102-82.

109. The summary of Schüssler Fiorenza's major insights that have impacted historical research follows. Then a brief section describes the historical and archaeological work of Carol Meyers. While there are biblical theologies that largely ignore the role and value of women in the Hebrew Bible/Old Testament, this leads to the hermeneutical failure of these texts.

110. Elisabeth Schüssler Fiorenza, *In Memory of Her: A Feminist Reconstruction of Christian Origins*, 2d ed. (London: SCM Press, 1995). Among her more substantial writings in addition to *In Memory of Her* are *Wisdom Ways: Introducing Feminist Biblical Interpretation* (Maryknoll, N.Y.: Orbis, 2001); *Jesus and the Politics of Interpretation* (New York: Continuum, 2000); *Rhetoric and Ethic: The Politic of Biblical Studies* (Minneapolis: Fortress Press, 1999); *Sharing Her Word*; ed. with Pui-lan Kwok, *Women's Sacred Scriptures* (Maryknoll, N.Y.: Orbis, 1998), *Jesus: Miriam's Child, Sophia's Prophet: Critical Issues in Feminist Christology* (New York: Continuum, 1994); *But She Said: Feminist Practices of Biblical Interpretations* (Boston: Beacon Press, 1992); and *Bread Not Stone* (Boston: Beacon Press, 1985, 1994).

111. Now see the sociohistorical assessments of Tal Ilan, including in particular her volume *Jewish Women in Greco-Roman Palestine: An Inquiry into Image and Status* (Texte und Studien zum antiken Judentum 44; Tübingen: Mohr, 1995).

112. See the development of this view in *Jesus: Miriam's Child, Sophia's Prophet.* Not all feminists agree with Schüssler Fiorenza's reuse of the Sophia imagery in the construc-

tion of the ministry of Jesus and the later identification of Jesus with Sophia. Luise Schottroff argues against this on the basis of noting that "Wisdom" in Israelite and Jewish religion belongs to patriarchal wisdom circles of sages who are teaching elitist men ("Wanderprophetinnen: Eine feministische Analyse der Logiaquelle," *Evangelische Theologie* 51 [1991]: 322–34. A.-J. Levine, a Jewish feminist New Testament scholar, also questions whether Q is actually so positive toward women ("Who's Catering the Q Affair? Feminist Observations on Q Paraenesis," ed. John G. Gammie and Leo G. Perdue; *Semeia* 50 [1990]: 145–62).

113. The book bearing this title speaks of Jesus as both the child of Miriam and the messenger of Woman Wisdom who continues to lead the church toward the realization of egalitarian vision.

114. A term she coins to describe the dominant male theological tradition that has developed throughout Christian history and male exegetical interpretations of scripture.

115. Schüssler, *Rhetoric and Ethic*, 191.

116. Ibid., 188.

117. See Carol Meyers, *Discovering Eve: Ancient Israelite Women in Context* (New London: Oxford University Press, 1988); with Ross S. Kraemer and Sharon Ringe, *Gender and the Biblical Tradition* (Louisville: Westminster John Knox, 1991); "The Family in Early Israel," in *The Family in Ancient Israel*, ed. Leo G. Perdue, et al. (Louisville: Westminster John Knox, 1997), 1-47; Charles E. Carter and Carol Meyers, eds., *Community, Identity, and Ideology: Social Science Approaches to the Hebrew Bible* (Winona Lake, Ind.: Eisenbrauns, 1996); Meyers, "Women and the Domestic Economy of Early Israel," in *Women in the Hebrew Bible*, ed. Alice Bach (London: Routledge, 1999), 33–43; and Meyers, Toni Craven, and Ross Kraemer, eds., *Women in Scripture: A Dictionary of Named and Unnamed Women in the Hebrew Bible, the Apocryphal/Deuterocanonical Books, and the New Testament* (Boston: Houghton Mifflin, 2000).

118. Ethnoarchaeology is a method "whereby ethnographic information is utilized for the interpretation of archaeologically retrieved data" ("The Family in Early Israel," 7). See especially the article of Charles E. Carter, "Ethnoarchaeology," *The Oxford Encyclopedia of Near Eastern Archaeology* (New York: Oxford University Press/American Schools of Oriental Research, 1997). Among the studies used by Meyers, see Michelle Zimbalist Rosaldo and Louise Lamphere, eds., *Women, Culture and Society* (Stanford: Stanford University Press, 1974); Ernestine Friedl, *Women and Men: An Anthropological View* (New York: Rinehart & Winston, 1975); Richard A. Gould and Patty Jo Watson, "A Dialogue on the Meaning and Use of Analogy in Ethnoarchaeological Reasoning," *Journal of Anthropological Archaeology* 1 (1982): 355–81; and Robert McC. Netting, *Smallholders, Householders: Farm Families and the Ecology of Intensive, Sustainable Agriculture* (Stanford: Stanford University Press, 1993).

119. See her essay, "Procreation, Production, and Protection: Male-Female Balance in Early Israel," first appearing in *JAAR* 51 (1983): 569–93, and later reprinted in *Community, Identity, and Ideology*, 489–514.

120. There are several examples of Feminist Jewish theology, including the works of Judith Plaskow (*Standing Again at Sinai: Judaism from a Feminist Perspective* [San Francisco: HarperCollins, 1990]); Tikva Fryma-Kensky (*Studies in the Bible and Feminist Criticism* [JPS Scholars of Distinction Series; Philadelphia: JPS, 2006]); idem, *In the Wake of the Goddesses: Women, Culture, and the Biblical Transformation of Pagan Myth* [New York: Free Press, 1992]); and Laura Levitt (*Jews and Feminism: The Ambivalent Search for Home* [New York: Routledge, 1997]).

121. For an introduction to rhetorical criticism, see James Muilenburg, "Form Criticism and Beyond," *JBL* 88 (1969): 1–18; Norman K. Gottwald, "Poetry, Hebrew," *IDB* 3 (1962): 829–38; Jared J. Jackson and Martin Kessler, eds., *Rhetorical Criticism: Essays in Honor of James Muilenburg* (Pittsburgh Theological Monograph Series 1; Pittsburgh: Pickwick, 1974); and Toni Craven, *Artistry and Faith in the Book of Judith*, 11–46. The classic statement is Trible's *Rhetorical Criticism: Context, Method, and the Book of Jonah* (Guides to Biblical Scholarship; Minneapolis: Fortress Press, 1994). Among the numerous New Testament approaches to new criticism, which impact the theology of the texts and their meaning for the contemporary church, see William Beardslee, *Literary Criticism of the New Testament*, Guides to Biblical Scholarship (Minneapolis: Fortress Press, 1970); Camille Focant, ed., *The Synoptic Gospels: Source, Criticism, and the New Literary Criticism* (Leuven: Leuven University Press, 1993); William S. Kurtz, *Reading Luke–Acts: Dynamics of Biblical Narrative* (Louisville: Westminster John Knox, 1993); Elizabeth Struthers Malbon and Edgar V. McKnight, eds., *The New Literary Criticism and the New Testament* JSNPTSUP 109 (Sheffield: Sheffield Academic Press, 1994); and Stephen D. Moore, *Literary Criticism and the Gospels* (New Haven: Yale University Press, 1989).

122. Phyllis Trible, *God and the Rhetoric of Sexuality* (London: SCM Press, 1992), 7. Her other powerful book is *Texts of Terror: Literary Feminist Readings of Biblical Narratives* (New Edition; London: SCM Press, 2002).

123. Trible, *God and the Rhetoric of Sexuality*, 7.

124. Phyllis Trible, "Five Loaves and Two Fishes: Feminist Hermeneutics and Biblical Theology," *Theological Studies* 50 (1989): 281.

125. Renita Weems, *Battered Love: Marriage, Sex, and Violence in the Hebrew Prophets* (OBT; Minneapolis: Fortress Press, 1995). Also see her book *Just a Sister Away: A Womanist Vision of Women's Relationships in the Bible* (San Diego: LuraMedia, 1988); her essay "Reading Her Way Through the Struggle: African American Women and the Bible," *Stony the Road We Trod: African American Biblical Interpretation*, ed. Cain Hope Felder (Minneapolis: Fortress Press, 1991), 57–77; and her commentary, the "Song of Songs," in *The New Interpreter's Bible*, vol. 5 (Nashville: Abingdon, 1997), 363–434. Other prominent womanist theologians include Karen Baker-Fletcher (*Sisters in the Wilderness: The Challenge of Womanist God-Talk* [Maryknoll, N.Y.: Orbis, 1993]); Katie Cannon (*Katie's Canon: Womanism and the Soul of the Black Community* [New York: Continuum, 1996]); Cheryl Sanders, *Living in the Intersection: Womanism and Afrocentrism in Theology* [Minneapolis: Fortress Press, 1995]); Jacquelyn Grant, *White Women's Christ and Black Women's Jesus: Feminist Christology and Womanist Response* (Atlanta: Scholars Press, 1989); and Emilie Townes, *In a Blaze of Glory: Womanist Spirituality as Social Witness* (Nashville: Abingdon, 1995).

126. See Delores Williams, *Sisters in the Wilderness: The Challenge of Womanist God-Talk* (Maryknoll, N.Y.: Orbis, 1993).

127. Weems, *Battered Love*.

128. Ada Maria Isasi-Díaz, with Yolanda Tarango, *Hispanic Women: Prophetic Voice in the Church—Toward a Hispanic Women's Liberation Theology* (San Francisco: HarperSanFrancisco, 1993); with Fernando F. Segovia, eds., *Hispanic/Latino Theology* (Minneapolis: Fortress Press, 1996); Ada María Isasi-Díaz, *Mujerista Theology: A Theology for the Twenty-First Century* (Maryknoll, N.Y.: Orbis, 1996); and *En la lucha = In the Struggle: Elaborating a Mujerista Theology* (Minneapolis: Fortress Press, 2004). Also see

her essay "'By the Rivers of Babylon': Exile as a Way of Life," *Reading from This Place*, 1:149–63.

129. Pui-lan Kwok, *Discovering the Bible in the Non-Biblical World* (Maryknoll, N.Y.: Orbis, 1995), 13.

130. R. J. Sugirtharajah, *The Bible and the Third World: Precolonial, Colonial and Postcolonial Encounters* (Cambridge, Mass.: Cambridge University Press, 2001), 117–19.

131. Kwok, *Discovering the Bible*, 31–38.

132. Wong Wai Ching, "Negotiating for a Postcolonial Identity: Theology of 'the Poor Woman' in Asia," *Journal of Feminist Studies in Religion* 16 (2000): 5–23. In addition, see her book *The Poor Woman: A Critical Analysis of Asian Theology and Contemporary Chinese Fiction by Women* (Asian Thought and Culture; New York: Peter Lang, 2002).

133. Mary John Mananzan et al., eds., *Women Resisting Violence: Spirituality for Life* (Maryknoll, N.Y.: Orbis, 1996). See Chung Hyun Kyung's essay in this collection, "Your Comfort vs. My Death," 129–40.

134. Kwok, *Discovering the Bible*, 38–42.

135. She refers especially to the work of Rey Chow, *Writing Diaspora: Tactics of Intervention in Contemporary Cultural Studies* (Bloomington: Indiana University Press, 1993), 55–72.

136. Kwok, *Discovering the Bible*, 77–99.

137. For this point, Kwok draws on the insights of Gale A. Yee, *Poor Banished Children of Eve: Women as Evil in the Hebrew Bible* (Minneapolis: Fortress Press, 2003). Yee demonstrates how "wicked" women function as "sexual metaphors" and "symbolic alibis" for political, economic, and social contests of male privilege and power. Texts including Ezek 23, which depicts two sexually insatiable sisters (Israel and Judah), are used to portray, not simply patriarchal violence, but more a "colonial ethnic conflict framed as a sexualized encounter" (p. 111).

138. See Musa W. Dube, "Savior of the World but Not of This World: A Postcolonial Reading of Spatial Construction in John," *The Postcolonial Bible*, ed. R. S. Sugirtharajah (Sheffield: Sheffield Academic Press, 1998), 118–35.

139. Just to mention one notable example is the introduction of Pui-lan Kwok, *Introducing Asian Feminist Theology* (Introductions in Feminist Theology 4; Sheffield: Sheffield Academic Press, 2000).

140. Musa W. Dube, "Postcoloniality, Feminist Spaces, and Religion," *Postcolonialism, Feminism, and Religious Discourse*, 100–120.

141. Musa W. Dube, "Towards a Postcolonial Feminist Interpretation of the Bible," *Reading the Bible as Women: Perspectives from Africa, Asia, and Latin America*, ed. Phyllis A. Bird; *Semeia* 78 (Atlanta: Scholars Press, 1997), 13.

142. Makhosanda N. Nzimande, "Towards a Postcolonial *Imbokodo* (African Women's) Hermeneutics in Post-Apartheid South Africa: A Case in Proverbs 1-9 (9:1-18)" (paper presented at the OTSSA, Sellenbosch, SA, September 2002).

143. See Musa W. Dube, "Savior of the World," 118–35.

144. Consult Musa W. Dube, *Postcolonial Feminist Interpretation of the Bible* (St Louis: Chalice Press, 2000), for a detailed discussion.

145. Ibid., 106. For additional insights on Dube's hermeneutics, see her essays: "*Batswakwa*: Which Traveller are You (John 1:1-18)?" and "To Pray the Lord's Prayer in the Global Economic Era (Matt. 6:9-13)," in Gerald O. West and Musa W. Dube, eds., *The Bible in Africa: Transactions, Trajectories and Trends* (Leiden, Brill: 2000), 150–62 and

611–30. In a recent publication, Dube uses African storytelling and divination methods to interpret biblical texts. See Dube's essays, "Fifty Years of Bleeding: A Storytelling Feminist Reading of Mark 5:24-43," 50–60, and "Divining Ruth for International Relations," in Musa W. Dube, ed., *Other Ways of Reading: African Women and the Bible* (Atlanta: Scholars Press, 2001), 179–95.

146. See Mercy Amba Oduyoye, *Introducing African Women's Theology* (Introductions in Feminist Theology 6; Sheffield: Sheffield Academic Press, 2001); and two of her essays: "Introduction: The Fire of the Smoke," in *Daughters of Anowa: African Women and Patriarchy*, ed. Mercy Amba Oduyoye (Maryknoll, N.Y.: Orbis, 1995); and "Biblical Interpretation and the Social Location of the Interpreter: African Women's Reading of the Bible," in *Reading from This Place*, ed. Fernando F. Segovia and Mary Ann Tolbert; vol. 2 (Minneapolis: Fortress Press, 1995), 33–51.

147. See Leonardo and Clodovis Boff, *Introducing Liberation Theology* (Tunbridge Wells, Kent: Burns & Oates), 49–63. Also see Boff, *Global Civilization: Challenges to Society and Christianity* (Tunbridge Wells, Kent: Burns & Oates, 2005); and idem, *Faith on the Edge: Religion and Marginalized Society* (San Francisco: Harper & Row, 1989).

148. José Míguez Bonino, *Doing Theology in a Revolutionary Situation* (Philadelphia: Fortress Press, 1975), 81. Also see, idem, *Christians and Marxists: The Mutual Challenge to Revolution* (Grand Rapids: Eerdmans, 1976).

149. Gutierrez, *Liberation Theology*.

150. Ferm, *Contemporary American Theologies*, 62.

151. Leonardo and Clodovis Boff, *Introducing Liberation Theology*, 50–51.

152. Fernando Segovia, "The Text as Other: Towards a Hispanic American Hermeneutic," in *Text and Experience*, ed., Daniel Smith-Christopher; Biblical Seminar 35 (Sheffield: Sheffield Academic Press, 1995), 276–98; ed. with Mary Ann Tolbert, *Reading from this Place* 1& 2 (Minneapolis: Fortress, 1995); ed. with Ada María Isasi-Díaz, *Hispanic/Latino Theologia* (Fortress Press, 1995); ed. with Mary Ann Tolbert, *Teaching the Bible: The Discourses and Politics of Biblical Pedagogy* (Maryknoll, N.Y.: Orbis, 1998); "Postcolonial and Diasporic Criticism in Biblical Studies: Focus, Parameters, Relevance," *Studies in World Christianity* 6 (1999): 177–95; ed. *Interpreting Beyond Borders* (The Bible and Postcolonialism 3; Sheffield: Academic Press, 2000); *Decolonizing Biblical Studies: A View from the Margins* (Maryknoll, N.Y.: Orbis, 2000); and *A Dream Unfinished: Theological Reflections on America from the Margins* (Maryknoll, N.Y.: Orbis, 2001).

153. Segovia, *Decolonizing Biblical Studies*, 34–52.

154. Segovia acknowledges the influence of William Safran, "Diasporas in Modern Societies: Myths of Homeland and Return," *Diaspora: A Journal of Transnational Studies* (1991): 1:83–99. Safran argues that the Jewish exilic experience has become the "ideal type" for all other diasporas, although Segovia takes issue with his model for identification of "diaspora."

155. Vincent L. Wimbush, ed., *The Bible and the American Myth: A Symposium on the Bible and Constructions of Meaning* (Macon, Ga.: Mercer University Press, 1999); idem, ed., *African Americans and the Bible: Sacred Texts and Social Structure* (New York: Continuum, 2000), and *The Bible and African Americans: A Brief History* (Facets; Minneapolis: Fortress Press, 2003).

156. Wimbush, *The Bible and African Americans*, 19.

AUTHORS

Benjamin D. Sommer is Professor in the Department of Bible and Ancient Semitic Languages at the Jewish Theological Seminary of America. He was previously the Director of the Crown Family Center for Jewish Studies at Northwestern University.

Robert Morgan is Emeritus Professor of New Testament, The Faculty of Theology, Oxford University.

Leo G. Perdue is Professor of Hebrew Bible, Brite Divinity School, Texas Christian University.

AUTHOR INDEX